INTERACTION IN
HUMAN DEVELOPMENT

CROSSCURRENTS IN CONTEMPORARY PSYCHOLOGY

A series of volumes edited by Marc H. Bornstein

PSYCHOLOGICAL DEVELOPMENT FROM INFANCY:
Image to Intention
BORNSTEIN AND KESSEN

COMPARATIVE METHODS IN PSYCHOLOGY
BORNSTEIN

PSYCHOLOGY AND ITS ALLIED DISCIPLINES
Volume 1: Psychology and the Humanities
Volume 2: Psychology and the Social Sciences
Volume 3: Psychology and the Natural Sciences
BORNSTEIN

SENSITIVE PERIODS IN DEVELOPMENT:
Interdisciplinary Perspectives
BORNSTEIN

INTERACTION IN HUMAN DEVELOPMENT
BORNSTEIN AND BRUNER

THE SEGMENTATION OF BEHAVIOR (*In preparation*)
BORNSTEIN

THE SIGNIFICANCE OF THE ATYPICAL IN PSYCHOLOGY (*In preparation*)
BORNSTEIN

INTERACTION IN HUMAN DEVELOPMENT

Edited by

MARC H. BORNSTEIN
*National Institute of Child Health
and Human Development
    and
New York University*

JEROME S. BRUNER
New York University

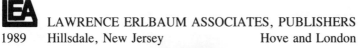 LAWRENCE ERLBAUM ASSOCIATES, PUBLISHERS
1989   Hillsdale, New Jersey   Hove and London

Lawrence Erlbaum Associates, Inc., Publishers
365 Broadway
Hillsdale, New Jersey 07642

Library of Congress Cataloging-in-Publication Data

Interaction in human development / edited by Marc H. Bornstein, Jerome
   S. Bruner.
       p.   cm. — (Crosscurrents in contemporary psychology)
      Includes bibliographies and index.
      ISBN 0-8058-0035-2
      1. Social interaction in children. 2. Child psychology.
   I. Bornstein, Marc H.   II. Bruner, Jerome S. (Jerome Seymour)
   III. Series.
      [DNLM: 1. Cognition.   2. Human Development.   3. Interpersonal
   Relations.   4. Language Development.   BF 713 I61]
   BF723.S62I58   1989
   155.4'18—dc19
   DNLM/DLC
   for Library of Congress   89-1603
                                                                                CIP

Printed in the United States of America
10   9   8   7   6   5   4   3   2   1

For
HANUŠ PAPOUŠEK
Friend and Colleague

Series Prologue

CROSSCURRENTS IN CONTEMPORARY PSYCHOLOGY

Contemporary psychology is increasingly diversified, pluralistic, and specialized, and most psychologists rarely venture beyond the confines of their substantive specialty. Yet psychologists with different specialties encounter similar problems, ask similar questions, and share similar concerns. Unfortunately, there are very few arenas available for the expression or exploration of what is common across psychological subdisciplines. The *Crosscurrents in Contemporary Psychology* series is intended to serve as such a forum.

The chief aim of this series is to provide integrated perspectives on supradisciplinary themes in psychology. The first volume in the series was devoted to a consideration of *Psychological Development from Infancy;* the second volume to *Comparative Methods in Psychology;* volumes three through five examined relations between *Psychology and Its Allied Disciplines* in the humanities, social sciences, and natural sciences; and the last volume concerned itself with *Sensitive Periods in Development.* The present volume focuses on interaction in psychological thinking and research. Future volumes in this series will attend to issues on the segmentation of behavior and role of the atypical in psychology. Thus, each volume in this series treats a different issue and is self-contained, yet the series as a whole endeavors to interrelate psychological subdisciplines by bringing shared perspectives to bear on a variety of concerns common to psychological theory and research. As a consequence of this structure, and the flexibility and scope it affords, volumes in the *Crosscurrents in Contemporary Psychology* series will appeal, individually or as a group, to psychologists with widely diverse interests. Reflecting the nature and intent of this series, contributing authors are drawn from a broad spectrum of humanities and sciences—anthropology to zoology—but representational emphasis is placed on active contributing authorities to the contemporary psychological literature.

Crosscurrents in Contemporary Psychology is a series whose explicit intent is to explore a broad range of crossdisciplinary concerns. In its focus on such issues, the series is devoted to promoting interest in the interconnectedness of research and theory in psychological study.

Marc H. Bornstein

Contributors to This Volume

Lauren B. Adamson, *Department of Psychology, Georgia State University, Atlanta, GA 30303*

Roger Bakeman, *Department of Psychology, Georgia State University, Atlanta, GA 30303*

Cindy S. Bergeman, *211 South Henderson Human Development Building, The Pennsylvania State University, University Park, PA 16802*

Marc H. Bornstein, *Child and Family Research, National Institute of Child Health and Human Development, Building 31, Room B2B15, 9000 Rockville Pike, Bethesda, MD 20892*

Magali C. Bovet, *Faculté de Psychologie et des Sciences de l'Education, Université de Genève, 24, rue Général-Dufour, 1211 Genève 4, SWITZERLAND*

Jerome S. Bruner, *200 Mercer Street (3B), New York City, NY 10003*

Susan Curtiss, *Department of Linguistics, University of California, 10833 Le Conte, Los Angeles, CA 90024*

Richard M. Lerner, *Division of Individual and Family Studies, S-110 Henderson Human Development Building, The Pennsylvania State University, University Park, PA 16802*

Charles J. Lumsden, *Clinical Science Division, Medical Sciences Building, Rm 7313, University of Toronto, Toronto M5S 1A8, CANADA*

Ellen Moss, *Laboratoire d'Ethologie Humaine, Département de Psychologie, Université du Québec à Montréal, Case postale 8888, Succursale "A", Montréal, Québec, H3C 3P8, CANADA*

Silvia A. Parrat-Dayan, *Faculté de Psychologie et des Sciences de l'Education, Université de Genève, 24, rue Général-Dufour, 1211 Genève 4, SWITZERLAND*

Robert Plomin, *211 South Henderson Human Development Building, The Pennsylvania State University, University Park, PA 16802*

Barbara Rogoff, *Department of Psychology, University of Utah, Salt Lake City, UT 84112*

Emanuel A. Schegloff, *Department of Sociology, University of California, 405 Hilgard Avenue, Los Angeles, CA 90024*

Catherine E. Snow, *Laboratory of Human Development, Graduate School of Education, Harvard University, Roy E. Larsen Hall, Rm 703, 15 Appian Way, Cambridge, MA 02138*

Floyd F. Strayer, *Laboratoire d'Ethologie Humaine, Département de Psychologie, Université du Québec à Montréal, Case postale 8888, Succursale "A", Montréal, Québec, H3C 3P8, CANADA*

Peter Strisik, *Department of Psychology, Georgia State University, Atlanta, GA 30303*

Jonathan Tudge, *Department of Psychology, University of Utah, Salt Lake City, UT 84112*

Jacques Vonèche, *Faculté de Psychologie et des Sciences de l'Education, Université de Genève, 24, rue Général-Dufour, 1211 Genève 4, SWITZERLAND*

David J. Wood, *Department of Psychology, The University of Nottingham, University Park, Nottingham NG7 2RD, England, UK*

Contents

INTRODUCTION

1 On Interaction

Jerome S. Bruner
New York University

Marc H. Bornstein
National Institute of Child Health and Human Development
and *New York University*

This is a book about the interactive side of human development. It is devoted to examining ways in which growth depends on human beings interacting with the resources in their environments—environments that are at once physical, biological, interpersonal, and cultural. We planned the book in such a way as to assure that a wide variety of interactive topics would be covered, in the hope that some theoretical coherence could be brought to this wide-ranging topic.

Our choice of this broad and disparate research domain was not fortuitous. It was our view that developmental psychology had been dominated for a decade or two by theories that sought primarily to formulate explanations of growth and development in terms of intra-individual factors: processes of accommodation and assimilation, of impulse control, of learning, of genetic predisposition, of cognitive representation, and so forth. When issues of interaction were treated in these theoretical accounts, it was usually in the spirit of taming them by showing how they were simply sources of variance that affected such processes as those just mentioned. We felt that developmental psychology seemed destined by habit or predilection to work with the model of a solo child coping, principally on his or her own, with a world that impinged on the individual sensorium, a world that needed to be sorted out, organized, represented, and so forth.

Wherever one looked, it seemed to us, there were forms of interaction that were important in their own right, forms of interaction whose nature was somehow not captured by being reduced to the role that they played as influences on intra-individual growth factors. Language acquisition is a case in point. It may well be that the prelinguistic child has an innate disposition to organize knowledge of language in terms of a highly limited range of ordering and transforming rules. But it has turned out to be the case, as shown by two decades of careful research, that the child's exposure to language is not a random one, as Chomsky originally proposed. There are crucial systematic features in the relation of a language-learning child and the adults with whom the child interacts. Indeed, there may be aspects of prelinguistic interaction that are not so much precursors of language as they are factors that actually predispose the child to language use. It may be (although the issue remains open) that once language mastery starts, it is genetically predisposed to run along certain rule-bound lines. But even if that is so, it now seems that language mastery depends on a web of interaction that is necessary for the appropriate *use* of language to develop. Not surprisingly, several chapters in this book deal with this problem in detail.

Our example emphasizes some of the complexities of the issues in interaction we must address. For one thing, there is a matter of interaction in the social sense: a learner and a tutor interacting with each other in some crucially patterned ways. For another, there is the question of interaction between genetic pre-dispositions on the one hand and experience with the environment on the other. But putting it that way is plainly too abstract to get hold of what we mean concretely by "experience with the world." What is this world that the child is experiencing, and how does the child integrate his or her knowledge of it? This brings us immediately to the issue of the interaction of the individual child and the culture. Forming friendships, for example, is not *just* an isolated activity of the individuals who befriend each other. It is also the expression of a cultural pattern that joins members of the culture in a manner characteristic of the culture as a whole.

So at very least, developmental interaction has several possible meanings: for example, interpersonal interaction, the interaction of genetic dispositions and experience, the interaction of the individual and the cultural, and so forth. And indeed, any version of interactionism adds its own methodological dimension. In conducting our studies and analyzing our data, for example, we blithely employ techniques that permit us to get estimates not only of which selected *individual* variables account for the variance of our measures of development, but how these variables operate in *interaction*. Multivariate analyses, indeed, may even invite us to skate out on thin ice that we might do better to avoid. Suppose, for example, that we are studying the richness of spontaneous play, and wish to correlate it (reasonably enough) with the strictness of parental discipline, on the one hand, and family religious affiliation, on the other. Then, because none of us likes to let opportunities go by, we compute an interaction for the two terms. And suppose we find that the interaction is significant for, say, Protestants and non-committed, but not for Jews or Catholics. Just what is the status of such an interaction? Does our independent measure of parental discipline have the same *meaning* in the interaction of Protestant parent-child pairs as it does in the other groups? Interaction in this technical statistical sense may breed more problems than it can possibly solve. Does the very model of the analysis of variance, for example, with its presuppositions about independence, fit the uses to which we put it? Would not the interpretive anthropologist's way of looking for culture patterns be better suited to our needs?

With issues like these in mind, we decided to solicit the wisdom of investigators who had been working on one or another aspect of interaction in their own research. Would each write something for us reflecting their experience? That was how this book was conceived. We knew that the range of topics would have to be great—not only because interaction is a complex idea, but because there were rich resources to be tapped. We drew up a list of authors and, of course, it was enormously long, much longer than any one book could hold. So, quite arbitrarily, we pared the list way down, and did so (we must admit) in a quite idiosyncratic way that will surely be apparent to anybody who knows the authors of this chapter.

What we received by way of manuscripts a year or so later outstripped our expectations. We had expected variety, to be sure, but our expectations were exceeded with virtually each new delivery of mail. And we had expected richness of insight, for we had chosen our contributors with due regard for their track records. We think the reader will agree that the intellectual feast set forth in the following chapters is indeed sumptuous.

But the richness and the variety have created a problem for us in this introductory chapter. We had hoped—and we admit that it was an optimistic vanity on our part—that we would, somehow, be able to manage a synthesis on interaction. We should have known better from the start. After all, we ourselves began with quite heterogeneous questions about interaction. Surely too, our distinguished roster of authors would have provided some syntheses if any were possible. A "grand" synthesis still seems out of reach; yet, there are some persistent problems, questions, and issues that appear and reappear in the various chapters, and we propose to comment on some of these here. We do not conceive of our role in doing so as either that of the summarizer or the critic—although we shall do some summarizing and commit some criticism as well. We should like to serve, rather, in the role of a Greek chorus, commenting on the action in the play as it proceeds.

The first of our topics is the interactional process whereby more experienced members of the culture—adults—transmit knowledge or skill or procedures to less experienced members of the culture—children. In shorthand, we refer to this as the issue of *transmission*.

Many of our authors touch on the transmission issue—some explicitly, some implicitly, and our comments in no sense cover all of their expositions. What does it mean for an adult to instruct a child, a matter discussed by several authors: Tudge and Rogoff; Wood; Curtiss; Snow; Schegloff; and Bovet, Parrat-Dayan, and Vonèche.

A long time ago, Edward Tolman (1949) addressed the issue of kinds of learning, and alleged that there were six. Interestingly, perhaps because his model learner was the laboratory rat, he had nothing to say about "learning from others," though Tolman touched on imitation. Now one thing we all seem to know is that transmission (in the "true" sense) appears to be an evolutionary prerogative of higher primate species. That true sense, however, turns out to be rather more specialized than may at first appear. Again, we all know that bird song is transmitted (e.g., Thorpe, 1951), in the sense that fledglings require exposure to adult bird song before they can produce a variant of the species song, and that there is some play in the range of songs that are learnable. And the oyster-catcher has a genetic repertory of three ways of breaking open a mussel, the one that develops depending on which is modeled by adult birds in its immediate environment (Tinbergen, 1951).

The evolutionary distance between *Avia* and *Homonides* is, of course, mind-bogglingly great. But the example underlines a point that seems central to Bovet, Parrat-Dayan, and Vonèche. It is impossible to teach anything to the young of a species that is not represented as a capability in their genome. It is a banal point. In their chapter, however, Bovet and her colleagues insist on a developmental extension of this principle that is not so banal: At any given stage of development, one cannot transmit anything to the child that does not mesh with the cognitive processes that are operative at that time, that are stage specific.

Tudge and Rogoff, however, make a somewhat different point. Following Vygotsky, they note that it is often the case that the growing child can take advantage of hints and other forms of aid offered by an adult—the set of phenomena that has now become celebrated as constituting the Zone of Proximal Development, or simply ZPD. They raise the interesting question (as does Wood in another chapter) as to what it is that an adult does or can do that would have the effect of helping a child beyond the point of understanding that the child can reach alone. In their chapter, Bovet, Parrat-Dyan, and Vonèche propose the generalized answer that all the adult can do is to provide knowledge that somehow fits the child's mode of reasoning. They even comment that a Geneva-inspired review of studies of "training" in the Piagetian conservation tasks shows mainly negative results. So, there seems to be some sort of contradiction between the views set forth by different contributors to this volume.

But a closer inspection, we believe, resolves this conflict in a fruitful way. In order to appreciate this resolution, there are two matters that need first to be taken into account. One has to do with the nature of the *presentation* of knowledge by the adult to the child; the other has to do with actual *processes* utilized by the adult and child in particular tasks. First, what difference does it make *how* a problem is presented to a child? As Bruner (1964), Donaldson (1978), Wood, Bruner, and Ross (1976), and most recently Edwards and Mercer (1987) have documented, there are many maneuvers by which a problem can be made recognizably manageable to a child. The most commonly successful approach is to enrich the context of the problem so that children can recognize exemplars of the problem that are within their range of competence. In Genevan terms, the adult teacher takes advantage of the phenomenon of *décalage,* presenting the problem in a manner connected to familiar problems that the child already knows how to solve. Or the tutor can reduce the complexity of the problem to the degrees of freedom that the child is able to deal with. Or, as Edwards and Mercer (1987) elegantly demonstrate, the child can be helped first to understand what the ground rules of the problem are: What are the givens in the problem that must be respected in formulating hypotheses toward a solution? Or, as Bruner (1963) noted a quarter century ago, constituent subfeatures of the problem required for its solution can be presented in advance of the more complex problem so that their incorporation in a later solution can be better assured. At its simplest, adult instruction can help the child concentrate attention on the features of the task involved in solution—as we know not only from the experiments of Wood and his colleagues, but from the still earlier work of Zeaman and House (1963).

In a word, then, there are strategies of teaching and presentation just as surely as their are strategies of problem solving. What literally creates the ZPD is the fact that better informed and "cognitively more sophisticated" adults are often able successfully to repair the difficulties inherent in a problem presentation so that although the child could *not* solve the problem before, he or she can do so after the repair has been introduced. Now, as Donaldson (1978) particularly noted, the Piagetian conservation tasks are of a kind that makes them strikingly impermeable to adult assistance. McGarrigle and Donaldson (1974), for example, showed that when a child appreciates the context of a problem, even Piagetian problems can be shown to be helped by hints that provoke the child beyond his or her measured stage of development.

All of this, in our view, only reinforces the general point made by Vonèche and his colleagues in their chapter. The task of "training" (or teaching, or whatever) is to devise means whereby one learns better how to fit problems to the present cognitive capabilities and logical operations of the child. If training procedures fail to take this truth into account, they fail. If theories of development fail to take it into account, they become static and unrepresentative of the kinds of happenings that transpire in the lives of all learners, young and old.

This, then, brings into question the claim that development proceeds via the succession of self-sufficient or autonomous stages. It is not that stages do not exist or that stage is not sometimes a useful concept. Rather, the *process* of growth seems not to be as strictly delimited by a series of autonomous stages. A child at one stage seems also to be engaged in constructing the bases for later stages. Hints from adults can help the child in this process of construction. And in this sense, the ZPD is as relevant to the Piagetian stages as it is to other forms of development. It is precisely this process of constructing later stages that is helped (or hindered) by the child's interaction with others—particularly with instructing adults.

In some respects, the quarrel is reminiscent of early debates in the field of language acquisition. It seems to us that the Genevan approach to training is somewhat like Chomsky's insistence on the sole relevance of competence in the study of language, looking only at the internal processes in play. It is this emphasis that led Chomskian theorists to make the needless and counter-to-evidence argument that the child only requires exposure to the language, even to degenerate instances of it, in order to grasp its rules of formation and transformation. And at the other extreme, those who argued that competence was irrelevant and performance was all, like B. F. Skinner (1957), fell into the equally impossible trap of assuming that experience was all that mattered—experience plus some spuriously stipulated process of imitation. As George Miller once put it, language acquisition theory was caught between two patently wrong views. The empiricist view was wrong because it was impossible: There was no way in which exposure alone could lead to learning linguistic rules, short of decades of reinforcement of a kind not found in the ordinary course of acquiring a language. The Chomskian view was wrong because it required a miracle: mastery of the language on the most minimal exposure and with no support from a language tutor.

Bruner (1983) attempted to resolve the issue by arguing that if there is a human predisposition to recognize only certain limited rules of grammar, the so-called Language Acquisition Device (and there is evidence to suggest that there is something like a LAD that operates, though not as sharp-focussed as Chomsky would have liked), then there is probably a human predisposition to aid the child's progress in this LAD direction by interacting linguistically with the child in a fashion to assist that progress (a Language Acquisition Support System, for which there is also suggestive evidence). That is to say, LAD and LASS between them assure the de facto astonishingly rapid acquisition of language by the young child—an acquisition that is more rapid than could be accounted for by either induction or by imitation.

The form of tutoring or training that helps the child across the ZPD is of the same conceptual order as the Language Acquisition Support System, in much the same way as the Language Acquisition Device is reminiscent of the stage rules or of "operatory intelligence" in the Genevan sense. The latter point can be made despite contemporary emphasis on the uniqueness of domain specific rules of reasoning. Even if it turned out to be the case that there were a half dozen more or less modular domains of intelligence, as Gardner (1983) suggested, one would quite properly assume that each had its own operatory rules and that each had its more or less restricted and unique orders of development.

This brings us to the chapters dealing with language and interaction. The principal lesson we learn from Snow's discussion, for example, is how syntactical acquisition, acquiring the rules of sentence formation and of sentence parts, scarcely begins to account for what is mastered in learning a language. Rather, the child is also mastering rules and maxims for dealing with discourse in interaction. We know from Snow's account, as from the work of Ninio and Bruner (1978) and others, that the acquisition of syntax occurs in the context of mastering cooperative turn-taking interaction with a language tutor. The mother and child establish action contexts between them into which language forms are gradually introduced as the mother senses that the child is ready for them. Or, as Stern (1985) taught us, for example, the child masters at least two forms of turn-taking in nonlinguistic vocal expression prior to mastery of exchange in conversation.

Curtiss's chapter raises the interesting additional question as to whether the more pragmatic, socially oriented language use of the child may not be mediated by different brain processes from those involved in mastering the formal syntax of the language. Her evidence suggests that they are separable, although they are not in fact usually separate during actual acquisition. But one can find instances of pathology—social pathology, as in isolation of the child, and neural lesions—that in fact may dissociate the two functions or processes. Indeed, one of us (J. B.) has had the opportunity of examining a young girl (a patient of Dr. Freda Newcomb's at the Churchill Hospital in Oxford) who showed marked social sensitivity in her strikingly agrammatical speech (turn taking, ingratiative gesturing, phonological patterns appropriate to such speech acts as demanding, requesting, etc.), although she could not construct a sentence.

Without forcing the matter, one might go so far as to suggest that syntax and phonology are, in the normal case, the machine language whose constituents are employed in constructing higher order, pragmatically relevant speech. But at the same time, the social interaction patterns can be partly mastered, so to speak, in a nonlinguistic medium—even agrammatic speech. And, as Curtiss shows us in her chapter, one can also find instances in which primitive grammatical speech develops with the child exhibiting no capacity to fit the language to social uses. In both instances, we find children who, by any standards, would be judged to have severe speech pathology. For obviously, the terminus of language acquisition is neither to utter parsable sentences that are unfit for interpersonal, interactive communication, nor to be able to be socially agreeable in interaction while not being able to communicate meaningfully in the medium of well-formed language.

This then brings us to the concluding remarks in Schegloff's chapter, where he challenges the developmentalist to account for the child's capacity so early to master the rules of conversational alternation, interruption, and the like. His challenge is a real one, and Snow would doubtless reply that the mastery of supersentential discourse includes the mastery of rules for juncturing sentences in conversation. But one wonders whether, again, the full panoply of rules of conversational sequencing is learned *in* conversation.

May we not be dealing here with something corresponding to Grice's (1975) discussion of the Cooperative Principle in human conversation. As Grice remarked, the maxim of relevance ("say only what is relevant") is learned in cooperative action first—whether in the phylogenetic or the ontogenetic sense of first—and then transferred more or less appropriately to the linguistic domain. In Bruner's (1983) work on the transition from prelinguistic to linguistic communication, it is plain that the child learns through games and play generally how to fit in an appropriate turn in a manner respecting the overall rules of the game in force. Once the principle of juncturing is mastered (and our species capacity for such early mastery is well-documented in Garvey, 1976), its transfer to other domains (including language) should pose no great theoretical problem. Yet, Schegloff is right in reminding us of the paucity of work relating to the ubiquitous phenomenon to which he brings our attention.

To sum up our discussion of *transmission,* it would be fair to say that we are dealing with an underdeveloped area of research and theory. It is also fair to say, as Edwards and Mercer (1987) alleged, that our tendency as developmentalists is to look too fixedly and exclusively at human development as if it were all "inside the skin," accomplished by a solo child operating vis-à-vis nature on his or her own. As anthropologists concerned with socialization are fond of reminding us, much of development has to do with entering a culture in which symbolic encounters and symbolic representations thereof are at least as important as encounters with the facts of nature encountered confrontationally. Our interpretation of the world of nature, indeed, is a highly encultured one. A great deal of early transmission undoubtedly consists of getting the child ready to play a part in the symbolic exchanges that, in their patterned entirety, constitute a culture.

The only excuse that we have to offer for not including a still broader representation of points of view about the nature of interaction—particularly the anthropological one—is that one book is necessarily a small sampling. At that, there are several chapters that touch on the subject: Schegloff's, Snow's, and particularly Lumsden's.

Asking developmentalists to write on interaction produced one particularly clear outcome: all our collaborators insisted on the many-faceted nature of interaction. As one of our authors began, "*Interaction* has many meanings" . . . almost as many, we found, as contributors to this anthology. But however widely our authors' interpretations of interaction varied, in one way or another most had something directly or indirectly to say about the prickly issue of "nature and nurture." So, we must say a brief word—the second main theme of this introduction— about the *interaction of genetic and experiential factors* that regulate the course of development.

Common protestations to the contrary notwithstanding, the nature-nurture question seems hardly defunct. The issue still lies not-quite-dormant in much developmental thought. Certainly, none of our authors fell into the classical trap of thinking about a once-for-all interaction of nature and nurture, each independently definable. Variant conjoint models proliferated chapter by chapter: Construals of reciprocal interaction were instantiated on the one hand by statistical model building driven by data, and on the other by abstract conceptualizations that reached well beyond operationalization and measurement. Nonetheless, the traditional "analysis of variance" of the interaction of a nature variable and a nurture variable still seems to be implicit in much contemporary work in development. Many researchers who deal with interactions appear to be weighed down by a traditional model of nature and nurture as separate terms (see Anastasi, 1958), however widespread the need to question these older conceptions.

Two chapters exemplify newer and more sophisticated approaches to the interaction issue especially well: the ones by Bergeman and Plomin and by Lumsden. The latter is a highly abstract effort to derive a developmental viewpoint from the historically informed sociobiological work of Lumsden and Wilson (1981); the former looks at the issues as they arise from a particularly elegant longitudinal study of development.

These chapters demonstrate two of the principal ways in which developmentalists have moved beyond once-for-all "main-effects" accounts of nature and nurture. One is by recognizing that the *conditional interaction* of these two kinds of effects itself constitutes a separate and significant force in development. The second way is through a reconceptualization of the issue that takes *temporal factors* in development into account. Both these approaches elevate the interaction term between nature and nurture to the status of a new kind of independent variable within the analysis of variance model.

Earlier approaches to the interaction of nature and nurture treated the two terms as more or less autonomous and static. As Lerner notes in his chapter, this main-effects approach treated organism and context as parallel vectors in a world of additive, linear combinations (see Reese & Overton, 1970; Sameroff & Chandler, 1975). Not surprisingly, this course led in the end to "logical traps" and "theoretical dead-ends." Most developmentalists today are reaching for a considerably more sophisticated interpretation of interaction by infusing the traditional analysis of variance model with an appropriately dynamic perspective. Lerner particularly points to the role of time in the unfolding of interaction. And Lumsden argues that all levels of analysis, from genes through culture, must be seen to interact through time rather than once-for-all. In a similar spirit, though in a more circumscribed way, Bakeman, Adamson, and Strisik focus on the importance of sequential analysis among behavior units that unfold over time in the dynamics of interpersonal interactions.

Lerner recounts the development of the contemporary notion of a "probabilistic epigenesis" (see Gottlieb, 1983) in life-span development. Life-span analysis encompasses evolution and ontogeny in attempting to understand both constancy and change in individual growth. Probabilistic epigenesis highlights the *bi*directional nature of individual and context: "The organism as much shapes the context as the context shapes the organism." Neither organism nor context constitutes the unit of analysis, but rather their interaction does, which is an important implication of this orientation to interaction. Different organismic attributes must be seen to have different implications for different developmental outcomes under different contextual conditions because the organism and the context are always embedded in one another. Attributes of the individual only have meaning for development with reference to the context and the time at which they are expressed. And context changes through time. So individual attributes can never be considered once-for-all, but only in a context whose temporal changes must be taken into account.

Lumsden's coevolutionary perspective springs from the allied axiom that "human beings are biological organisms exploiting a larger cultural environment." Lumsden and Wilson called this view "gene-culture transmission," the system whereby genetic and cultural factors mutually interact with each other. According to this view, biology sets likely developmental pathways for the individual who responds only to certain ranges of cultural input according to set biological rules. Neither social nor cognitive development proceeds solely on the basis of cultural transmission or genetic determinism. Lumsden stresses not only ontogenesis, but the larger role of evolutionary interactions (two readings of temporal) in this multilevel, reciprocating view of interaction in individual development. Recognizing the inherently probabilistic nature of human action, given the uncertainties of both natural environment and social structure, he attempts to give a picture that is both historical and at the same time not over-determined. Each individual develops in the context of an environment that has in turn been shaped by other individuals to construct the culture.

From Lumsden's formalization one may deduce that epigenetic rules of cultural evolution can evolve rather quickly in biocultural systems. This is an interesting step in the direction of closing the gap between slow evolutionary changes and very swift (but reversible) cultural ones. At the heart of his "formal sketch" of central properties of the coevolutionary system is the conceptual notion that there are three major interactive steps across levels of organization: from genes to the regularities of individual development and from there to culture . . . and then back to genes.

It is all well and good, of course, to preach new and more complex scientific philosophies about the nature of interaction. But any new philosophy should also demonstrate ways toward its implementation. The practical consequence of probabilistic epigenesis is the elevation of the *relation* between organism and context to a status that is greater in importance than either of its two constituents. In so doing, however, it adds significant difficulty to the empirical study of interaction. The relation between two highly variable constituents—like organism and context—is neither easily or reliably determined, nor is its conceptual status readily grasped.

Lerner favors his readers by going the additional mile to show how this new relational unit can be successfully transformed into a subject of research, even if a solution to comprehending parent-child interaction (his example) successively alternates focus between the effects of parent-to-child and the effects of child-to-parent interactions. He reviews the literature on such bidirectional effects, but of necessity leaves open the question whether it is even possible to study such effects "at any one moment." We may, indeed, be forced to think again about how much (or how little) information we can ever get about interaction in development with "one-shot" studies that lack a temporal dimension.

With the newer, more historically informed studies, it is no longer necessary for the nature-nurture issue to be so fraught with ideological overtones—as if an interest in genetic factors opened one to the suspicion of racist biases, whereas an interest in environmental ones left one open to the charge of shallow and optimistic environmentalism. We firmly believe (and it will already have become evident to the reader that we do) that it is impossible to characterize human development without a model that comes to grips with the *interaction* between these two forces. There are signs that such models are emerging—as witness the recent work of Scarr (1987), Plomin et al. (1988), and others. Behavioral geneticists warn us that classical genetic models dealing with such distinctions as genotypes and phenotypes, dominants and recessives, are not sufficient for our needs. Single genetic sites are not likely ever to be found to account for the kinds of complex developmental processes that we study in the interest of understanding interactive human behavior. We would do well not to assume that there are biological simplicities underlying the behavioral complexities of social development. Even the refined methods of modern recombinant genetics are likely to deepen our perplexities before they simplify our task. And the simplifications are not likely to be forthcoming until we do a far more comprehensive job of describing the regularities of interaction—whether in the social and emotional, or in the cognitive and verbal spheres of development.

Another way to bypass the static, once-for-all view of nature and nurture is through the ingenious selection and comparison of *study populations*. Bergeman and Plomin, for example, focus on contingent interactions between genotype and environment, by selecting individuals with certain genetic propensities in order to examine how they are differentially affected by different environmental factors. They use the method of study known as "Genotype-Environment Interactions" taken as a population concept. It is worth considering their logic by looking at their work in a little detail. Basically, they argue that interactions reflect nonlinear combinations of genetic and environmental effects and that genotype-environment interactions can be explained only after the main effects of each are removed.

Raising various genetically pure, distinctive strains of rats in distinctive environments permits just such a test—as in the well-known "maze-bright—maze-dull" study by Cooper and Zubek (1958). Maze-dull animals, for example, benefit from an enriched environment. Maze-bright ones don't need it. Adoption studies are analogous on the human level (Plomin, 1986). The genotypes of adoptive children are estimated from assessing their biological relatives. The effect of environments on these adoptive children can then be measured. The specific effects of genotype-environment interactions are afterward evaluated, and these interaction effects are meaningful whether or not genetic or environmental main effects emerge.

There is a fourth point about the chapters in this volume that, we think, is worth a special note. However abstract our authors' ideas about interaction-as-process may be, there is an increased sense of specificity in virtually every account. The child does not get something simply from interacting with peers or with parents. The nature of the interaction, its timing, and its reciprocity must all be taken into account. The same for adoption studies and for studies of language acquisition. How, what, when, and where must be specified if one is to understand the role of individual and contextual variables. Gone are the days (we hope) when bland statements can be made about attributing 60% of the variance to nurture, 40% to nature.

Again and again, we found, research and theory point to specific interaction experiences at specific times in development affecting specific facets of growth in specific ways. For example, in his chapter Bornstein distinguishes among several categories of interaction in caretaking, and then explores conditional relations among them in terms of how together they influence consequents in development. As Bornstein shows, straightforward longitudinal outcomes of "early effects" may be observed from time to time, but potentially significant influences are often conditional, meaning that categories of interaction exert effects in concert with one another and, of course, with the developmental status of the child. Moreover, his studies, as many others, demonstrate that specific early-life interactions more often project to particular, not general, developmental outcomes, whether in social or in cognitive spheres of competence in the child.

This means, we think, that developmental studies, by virtue of taking account of the specificities of interaction, will have to be much more mindful of the relation between data and theory. For it is plain that our choice of empirical methods (whatever our proclaimed theory may be) locks us into implicit theoretical straitjackets. And grand accounts of such processes as assimilation and accommodation, or of the processes of learning in development, will need to be implemented by methods of research and of statistical analysis that are appropriate to their theoretical claims. For just as a particular form of data analysis may force one into an implicit theoretical position, so a form of data analysis may negate the explicit theoretical position to which one gives allegiance.

It is naive to assume that "before-and-after" studies are guided by the simple logic of antecedent and consequent. If it is true (and it is hard to deny) that children have strong effects on their parents' behavior, then we cannot blandly suppose that one can sensibly design a study to evaluate the effects of, say, stern and permissive parents on stubborn and pliant children. The very parent variables we would study might be the outcome of the child variables we have chosen to use. And suppose the dependent variable in our four-fold analysis were school performance. How indeed might it be affected by this jumbling of variables? One surely needs a theoretical formulation more specific, less linear, and more searching than provided by an analysis-of-variance model that yields a vague interaction term between parent and child variables.

The consequences of this new emphasis on specificity are manifold. For empirical research, each term of an interaction needs to be delimited and interpreted in terms of its specifics. Generalizability must perforce be limited; in order to generalize about the effects of interaction, one must investigate its limits rather than taking them for granted. One kind of child-parent interaction may operate in one particular range of situations, not in another. The interaction of adoptive and biological genotype works under one circumstance, not another. The age of global claims appears to be at an end.

An interaction is not static, but it is specific. Certainly, then, a book about interaction in human development cannot be static, and it must be specific. Interactions themselves, as our authors firmly attest, modulate through time. Perhaps it is fitting, therefore, to close this introduction by raising some generic questions that we (editors and authors) pose implicitly or explicitly for our readers.

Which aspects of development are influenced by interaction? What are the mechanisms by which interactions affect the development of competencies? What courses do different interactions follow? Are interactions with different agents equally influential? What are the common features, and what are the notable differences, in interactions with different agents? How does interaction vary with the age/stage of the child vis-à-vis different outcomes? What are the common contexts in which different interactions take place? Why do some contexts facilitate, and others inhibit the function or efficacy of interactions? What methods are commonly in use to study questions regarding interaction? What are their advantages and disadvantages, and what other methods could be used? And of course, we could go on.

Development is intrinsically bound up with interaction. But only recently has interaction per se achieved the status of a primary target of developmental research and theory. With this volume we greet it. However demanding interaction may be to contemplate, and however exacting to operationalize, we believe that the study of interaction is decisive to the next step in comprehending human development.

REFERENCES

Anastasi, A. Heredity, environment, and the question "how?" *Psychological Review,* 1958, *65,* 197–208.

Bruner, J. S. *The process of education.* Cambridge: Harvard University Press, 1963.

Bruner, J. S. The course of cognitive growth. *American Psychologist,* 1964, *19,* 1–16.

Bruner, J. S. *Child's talk.* New York: Norton, 1983.

Cooper, R. M., & Zubek, J. P. Effects of enriched and restricted early environments on the learning ability of bright and dull rats. *Canadian Journal of Psychology,* 1958, *12,* 159–164.

Donaldson, M. *Children's minds.* London: Fontana, 1978.

Edwards, C., & Mercer, N. *Common knowledge.* London and New York: Methuen, 1987.

Gardner, H. *Frames of mind.* New York: Basic Books, 1983.

Garvey, C. Some properties of social play. In J. S. Bruner, A. Jolly, & K. Silva (Eds.), *Play: Its role in development and evolution.* Harmondsworth: Penguin, 1976.

Gottlieb, G. The psychobiological approach to developmental issues. In M. M. Haith & J. J. Campos (Eds.), *Handbook of child psychology: Infancy and biological bases* (4th ed., Vol. 2). New York: Wiley, 1983.

Grice, H. P. Logic and conversation. In P. Cole & J. Morgan (Eds.), *Syntax and semantics (Vol. 3): Speech acts.* New York: Academic Press, 1975.

Lumsden, C. J., & Wilson, E. O. *Genes, mind and culture: The coevolutionary process.* Cambridge: Harvard University Press, 1981.

McGarrigle, J., & Donaldson, M. Conversation accidents. *Cognition,* 1974, *3,* 341–350.

Ninio, A., & Bruner, J. S. The achievement and antecedents of learning. *Journal of Child Language,* 1978, *5,* 1–15.

Plomin, R. *Development, genetics, and psychology.* Hillsdale, NJ: Lawrence Erlbaum Associates, 1986.

Plomin, R., DeFries, J. C., & Fulker, D. W. *Nature and nurture during infancy and early childhood.* New York: Cambridge University Press, 1988.

Reese, H. W., & Overton, W. F. Models of development and theories of development. In L. R. Goulet & P. B. Baltes (Eds.), *Life-span developmental psychology: Research and theory.* New York: Academic Press, 1970.

Sameroff, A. J., & Chandler, M. J. Reproductive risk and the continuum of caretaking casualty. In F. D. Horowitz (Ed.), *Review of child development research.* Chicago: University of Chicago Press, 1975.

Scarr, S. *A model of interaction between genetic and environmental factors.* Paper presented at the biennial meeting of the Society of Research on Child Development, Baltimore, 1987.

Skinner, B. F. *Verbal behavior.* New York: Appleton-Century-Crofts, 1957.

Stern, D. N. *The interpersonal world of the infant: A view from psychoanalysis and developmental psychology.* New York: Basic Books, 1985.

Thorpe, W. H. The learning abilities of birds. *The Ibis,* 1951, *93,* 1–52, 252–296.

Tinbergen, N. *The study of instinct.* Oxford: Oxford University Press, 1951.

Tolman, E. C. There is more than one kind of learning. *Psychological Review,* 1949, *56,* 144–145.

Wood, D., Bruner, J. S., & Ross, G. The role of tutoring in problem solving. *Journal of Child Psychology and Child Psychiatry,* 1976, *17,* 89–100.

Zeaman, D., & House, B. J. The role of attention in retardate discrimination learning. In N. R. Ellis (Ed.), *Handbook of mental deficiency.* New York: McGraw-Hill, 1963.

INTERACTION IN
COGNITIVE DEVELOPMENT

2 Peer Influences on Cognitive Development: Piagetian and Vygotskian Perspectives

Jonathan Tudge
Barbara Rogoff
Department of Psychology
University of Utah

INTRODUCTION

Psychologists have become increasingly interested in the effects of the social context on individuals' cognitive development, influenced by the work of Piaget and Vygotsky. Although Piaget was primarily concerned with individual development, he believed that discussion between children has a role to play in cognitive development. Vygotsky's theory places a central focus on social interaction as a medium in which children develop, with people who are more skilled in the intellectual technologies of a culture assisting children in learning.

Following a discussion of similarities and differences in these theories, we examine research on the effects of social interaction between peers. Our goal is to suggest the circumstances under which peer interaction can foster children's cognitive development, and to place these suggestions in the context of the theories of Piaget and Vygotsky.

We suggest that shared thinking involving coordination of joint activity is central to the benefits of social interaction. We consider that social interaction does not carry blanket benefits, as is often assumed, but that social interaction facilitates development under certain circumstances that need more specification. One of the most important of these appears to be the possibility for the participants to understand another perspective or participate in a more advanced skill, either through active observation or through joint involvement in problem solving.

THEORETICAL PERSPECTIVES ON THE ROLE
OF SOCIAL INTERACTION:
PIAGET AND VYGOTSKY

In some ways Piaget and Vygotsky have striking similarities of approach. This is perhaps not surprising; the intellectual world in which they moved was similar. Both cited the work of the same major figures in the field, such as Baldwin, Buhler, Janet, and Stern. Piaget did not know of Vygotsky's work before the latter's death in 1934, and was only able to read it 25 years later (Piaget, 1962). But Vygotsky was very familiar with Piaget's work, and wrote an introduction (which eventually became a chapter in *Thinking and Speech,* 1987) to the Russian translation of *Language and Thought of the Child.*

Piaget and Vygotsky both argued for the importance of the genetic approach, studying psychological processes as they develop, either in microgenesis or ontogenesis. They also believed that development involves qualitative transformations rather than gradual growth increments. Piaget argued that children progress through a series of qualitatively distinct stages, applicable across all cognitive problems, in invariant order. Vygotsky's view of development did not involve such a general stagelike unidirectional progression, but his approach resembled Piaget's in seeing change as a "revolutionary" rather than an evolutionary process (Vygotsky, 1981b, p. 171).

Both theories have a dialectical basis in their conception of the developmental process and of the relation between the individual and society (Butterworth, 1982; Davydov & Radzikhovskii, 1985; Wozniak, 1975; Youniss, 1978). Moreover, both regarded the roles of the individual and the environment as inseparable. Piaget (1936/1952) described the interrelation of organism and environment in his discussion of assimilation and accommodation; Vygotsky's approach to the mutuality of individual and environment involves analysis of the embedded levels of phylogenetic development, sociohistorical development, ontogenetic development, and microgenetic development (Wertsch, 1985). Piaget and Vygotsky also shared the belief that children are active in their own development, that they arrive at knowledge of the world through activity.

Although both Piaget and Vygotsky acknowledged the role that the social world plays in cognitive development, they differed in emphasis on the integration of the social world and individual development, the theorized causal mechanisms relating social interaction to cognitive development, the timing in ontogenesis of the effectiveness of such interaction, the ideal role relations and type of social partner presumed optimal, and the possibility of regression as well as progression resulting from social interaction.

The Role of Social Interaction

Piaget's theory incorporates the view that the social world in which children develop has an important role to play in the developmental process. For example, in 1927, he argued that the development of the child is an adaptation as much to the social as to the physical milieu. "Social life is a necessary condition for the development of logic. We thus believe that social life transforms the individual's very nature." (Piaget, 1928/1977, p. 239). Toward the end of his life he declared that "the most remarkable aspect of the way in which human knowledge is built up . . . is that it has a collective as well as an individual nature" (1967/1971, p. 359).

However, despite these statements, social influences on development are not central to Piaget's theory, which focuses on the interaction of the child and the physical environment. The bulk of his genetic epistemology concerned the ways in which children come to understand physical and logical properties of the world while acting on it *as individuals*. His theory only touched occasionally on social factors, and he did not direct the work of his laboratory to investigate social influences (Forman & Kraker, 1985). Moreover, when Piaget summed up his thinking and his life's work (Piaget & Inhelder, 1966/1969; Piaget, 1970/1983), he emphasized the role played by equilibration; maturation, experience, and social interaction were accorded less significance. Here he downplayed the formative role of social interaction by stating that the importance of the social environment is restricted to accelerating or retarding the age at which children pass through the stages of development (Piaget, 1970/1983, p. 119). Nevertheless, Piaget's speculations have inspired a number of scholars working in the Piagetian tradition to cultivate the seeds of Piagetian social interactionism (e.g., Ames & Murray, 1982; Bearison, in press; Doise & Mugny, 1984; Murray, 1982; Perret-Clermont, 1980).

In contrast with Piaget's theory, Vygotsky's theory was built on the premise that individual development cannot be understood without reference to the social milieu, both institutional and interpersonal, in which the child is embedded. Vygotsky's theory stresses the channeling of individual thinking by social institutions and technologies developed over social history (such as schooling, literacy, mathematical systems, and mnemonic strategies). These enveloping social solutions for cognitive processing are made available to children through interaction with people who are more skilled than they, according to Vygotsky's "general genetic law of cultural development," "Any function in the child's cultural development appears twice, or on two planes. First it appears on the social plane, and then on the psychological plane" (Vygotsky, 1981b, p. 163). Vygotsky did not believe that every aspect of a child's psychological functioning was purely social. He distinguished between elementary (or natural) processes (such as involuntary attention and recognition memory) that are shared with animals, and higher mental processes. Higher mental processes distinguish humans from animals; they are inherently social, mediated by the cultural context in which humans live. For example, the difference between natural memory (e.g., recognition) and mediated memory (e.g., strategic recall) is that only the latter is influenced by sociocultural factors. The mediators, whether they are words, notches on sticks, numerical systems, and so on, are considered psychological "tools," which "are social, not organic or individual . . . . They are the product of historical development and are a form of behavior unique to humans" (Vygotsky, 1981a, p. 137).

Thus Vygotsky argued that rather than deriving explanations of psychological activity from the individual's characteristics plus secondary social influences, the unit of analysis should be social activity, from which individual functioning advances to a higher plane. Piaget's approach is the reverse—a focus on the individual as the unit of analysis, with social influence overlaid upon the individual's activity. Vygotsky noted this difference in approaches, stating that "Piaget thinks of the biological as primal, initial, and self-contained within the child. He views the biological as forming the child's substance. In contrast, the social acts through compulsion or constraint as an external force which is foreign to the child himself" (Vygotsky, 1987, p. 82), and, "In contrast to Piaget, we hypothesize that development does not proceed toward socialization, but toward the conversion of social relations into mental functions" (Vygotsky, 1981b, p. 165).

Mechanisms of Social Influence

The two theories also differ in their expectations of the means by which social influence impacts cognitive development. In Piaget's theory equilibration is the primary factor in cognitive development (Piaget, 1970/1983, pp. 122–123). Children are seen as striving to deal with discrepancies between their own ways of viewing the world (their schemes) and new information that comes their way, and reform their ways of thinking to provide a better fit with reality. When the scheme is altered so that the new experience fits more easily, equilibrium is reestablished at a higher level.

For the most part Piaget focused on the "cognitive conflict" brought about by the disequilibrium that occurs as an individual acts on the physical and logical environment. However, in early work, Piaget (1932, 1928–1945/1977) argued that cognitive conflict could arise in the course of social interaction, in discussions between children who hold different views on an intellectual or moral issue. Such logical discussion allows children to see that there is a different perspective that may not easily fit into their own preexisting perspectives.

Piaget believed that the same logical relations that children become able to understand regarding the physical world (the laws of "groupement") are practiced in social relations: "The social relations equilibrated in cooperation thus constitute 'groupements' of operations, exactly like all the logical operations exercised by the individual on the external world" (Piaget, 1945/1977, p. 159). Hence Piaget emphasized cooperation as the ideal form of social interaction promoting development. He conceived of cooperation as a parallel form of logic in which children would discuss propositions provoking cognitive conflict. Such discussion would lead to disequilibrium in the individual and attempts by the individual child to reach logical resolution of their internal cognitive conflict, leading to cognitive advances.

In Vygotsky's efforts to explicate the mechanisms that transform what is social (external to the child) into individual development, he argued that properties of social processes are not simply transferred into the individual. He held instead that the individual's appropriation of what had been practiced in social interaction involves active transformation. What had been social and what had been internal both undergo a process of dialectical transformation to become something qualitatively new. The child's understanding is not the accretion of thoughts or behaviors practiced socially, but rather involves qualitative transformations of social activities to fit the child's growing comprehension.

How does this occur? A central concept of Vygotsky's theory is mediation— that what is social is not directly converted into what is individual but passes through a link, a "psychological tool." One such mediating link is the "sign," of which words are the prime example in Vygotsky's theory. Words that already have meaning for the mature members of a community come to have the same meaning for the young in the process of social interaction.

Much of Vygotsky's (1987) discussion of egocentric speech is an explanation of the ways in which social processes are gradually internalized by children, eventually existing in purely internal form as inner speech. Even the actual process of interaction used initially to direct a child's attention may be later utilized as an aid to self-direction, when the child may engage in dialogue with her- or himself either aloud (in egocentric speech) or silently (in inner speech) (Vygotsky, 1987).

Higher mental processes, such as meaning or voluntary attention, are thus created and sustained by social interaction. Vygotsky believed that social interaction is important not only at the initial stages of development of an idea; arriving at a shared meaning of a gesture or word occurs in the process of actual interaction, but the social nature of the gesture or word always remains. In this way culturally available meanings are made known to children, are taken over by them, in time to be passed on to others.

A concept that Vygotsky (1978, 1987) proposed for understanding the social interactional nature of children's development is the "zone of proximal development," where children perform beyond the limits of their individual skill, supported by a more experienced person. In social interaction in the zone of proximal development, children are able to participate in more advanced problem solving than they are capable of independently, and in so doing they practice skills that they internalize to advance what they can do independently.

Piaget and Vygotsky shared an emphasis on the importance of partners' understanding of each other. For Piaget, the partners must have a common language and system of ideas, and grant reciprocity in attempting to examine and adjust for differences in their opinions. Piaget's emphasis on such reciprocity and intellectual exchange calls into question some interpretations of Piaget's view of cognitive conflict that focus more on the fact of disagreement (as an indicator of cognitive conflict) or even on contentiousness, than on the process of resolving those disagreements (e.g., Azmitia, 1988; Bearison, Magzamen & Filardo, 1986; Damon & Killen, 1982; Damon & Phelps, 1987). Piaget (1928/1977) emphasized the cooperative working out of differences of opinion through coming to understand the different perspectives and logically comparing their value. For Vygotsky, the child is assumed to be interested in gaining from the more expert partner and the expert is seen as responsible for adjusting the dialogue to fit within the child's zone of proximal development, where understanding is achieved with a stretch leading to growth. Both of these perspectives are similar in stressing the importance of a match between partners involving shared thinking.

The idea of cooperation in sharing thought processes, which appears in both Piaget's and Vygotsky's theories, is related to the linguistic concept of intersubjectivity (Rommetveit, 1976, 1985; Trevarthen, 1980). Intersubjectivity focuses on the joint understanding of a topic achieved by people working together and taking each other's perspective into account. The concept of intersubjectivity has appeared in discussions of both neo-Vygotskian and neo-Piagetian scholars (Gauvain & Rogoff, in press; Perret-Clermont & Schubauer-Leoni, 1981; Wertsch, 1984; Youniss, 1987).

Age Trends in the Effects of Social Interaction

In Piaget's view, the effects of social interaction derive from the possibility of logical argument between children with varying points of view. In his early writings, Piaget regarded this process as difficult for the preoperational child. "In order to argue, demonstrations and logical relations etc. have to be made explicit, all of which runs counter to the ego-centrism of the child under 7" (Piaget, 1923/1959, p. 71).

Piaget (1945/1977) specified that at the stage of concrete operations (from 7 to 11–12 years) children become able to cooperate and to coordinate points of view. Piaget claimed that there is an intimate correspondence between the development of logical operations and cooperation. He laid out three conditions under which equilibrium is achieved in intellectual exchange (Piaget, 1945/1977, pp. 160–162). First, the partners should have a common scale of intellectual values allowing them to understand terms in the same sense. This involves a language and a system of ideas on which they converge, providing a key that permits them to translate the differing conceptions of one partner to those of the other. Second, the partners should recognize a conservation of their propositions in which one does not contradict oneself, and in which partners search for agreement on propositions or find facts justifying their differences in points of view. Third, there should be a reciprocity between partners such that the propositions of each are treated interchangeably.

These three conditions are not fulfilled when egocentrism is operating. In the first edition of *The Language and Thought of the Child* (written in 1923) Piaget equated egocentrism with preoperational thinking, but in the chapter added to the third edition (1948/1959), Piaget presented evidence to show that during the years from three to six children are capable of engaging in discussion with peers. During this period the child "fluctuates between two poles, the monologue—individual or collective—and discussion or genuine exchange of ideas" (Piaget, 1948/1959, p. 258). Indeed, it may be considered essential for Piaget to take the position that egocentrism declines gradually during the preoperational period. Otherwise, one is left with the uncomfortable logical impasse that children cannot achieve concrete operational thought until they can coordinate two different perspectives simultaneously, but cannot achieve that feat until after having reached the concrete operational stage.

Piaget (1945/1977, 1964/1968) answered the question of whether children become capable of rational operations because their social development makes them able to cooperate, or whether an individual's logical acquisitions permit comprehension of others and allow cooperation, as follows: "Since the two types of progress proceed together, the question cannot be answered, except to say that they constitute two indissociable aspects of one single and same reality, simultaneously social and individual" (Piaget, 1945/1977, p. 158).

Vygotsky's greater emphasis on the social milieu of development led to a different view regarding the timing of the effects of social interaction, in which children are born as social beings who participate with others in beginning to perform higher mental functions. In the early years, adult assistance aids children in communicating effectively and planning and remembering deliberately. Vygotsky's view is exemplified in his discussion of the development of pointing. Vygotsky believed that young children use signs (such as a word or gesture) before they recognize their full significance, and those signs are imbued with meaning by adults. For example, the gesture of an infant stretching his or her hand in the general direction of an object is interpreted by an adult as pointing. It is *as* pointing that the gesture is responded to, and gradually the gesture takes on that significance for the child (Vygotsky, 1981a).

Thus, in Vygotsky's theory, the social world influences development from the beginning of life; independent activity occurs as children internalize culturally mediated higher mental processes they have previously been able to do only with help. This contrasts with Piaget's view in which the cognitive benefits of social interaction become evident only with the decline of egocentrism.

Ideal Role Relations of Partners

Piaget believed that discussion between peers is more valuable than discussion between an adult and a child. Interaction with an adult, Piaget stated in his early work, is essentially unequal; it is an asymmetrical interaction in which the adult has the power, and this disrupts the condition of reciprocity for achieving equilibrium in thinking (Piaget, 1945/1977, p. 165). Adults may be useful for providing answers to questions, but agreeing with an adult because that adult has more power will not lead to cognitive restructuring (Piaget, 1948/1959, p. 258). On the other hand, when a peer has a different perspective, no asymmetry of power exists. "Criticism is born of discussion, and discussion is only possible among equals: cooperation alone will therefore accomplish what intellectual constraint [caused by unquestioning belief in the adult's omniscience] failed to bring about" (1932, p. 409).

According to Piaget, lessons from adults often cause young children to abandon their own ideas for those presented, because their ideas are poorly formulated and only exist as an "orientation of the spirit" that cannot enter into competition with those of adults. But in such cases, children agree without examining the idea, and they do not learn to verify for themselves. It is only in adolescence that children learn to discuss as equals with their teachers, when they have "conquered their internal liberty" (Piaget, 1928/1977, p. 230).

In his early criticisms of adult-child interaction, Piaget focused primarily on the use of adult authority. However, he also allowed for the possibility that adults may be able to interact with children in a cooperative fashion that permits the sort of reciprocity required for children to advance to a new level of equilibrium: "It is despite adult authority, and not because of it, that the child learns. And also it is to the extent that the intelligent teacher has known to efface him or herself, to become an equal and not a superior, to discuss and to examine, rather than to agree and constrain morally, that the traditional school has been able to render service" (Piaget, 1928/1977, p. 231).

In his later writings Piaget acknowledged that adults act as "the source of educational and verbal transmissions of cultural elements in the cognitive sense" (Piaget & Inhelder, 1966/1969, p. 116). However, insofar as he believed that social interaction has a role in cognitive development, Piaget emphasized the importance of peer interaction.

By way of contrast, Vygotsky emphasized the impact of interaction with a more skilled partner; his notion of the zone of proximal development focuses on "problem solving under adult guidance or in collaboration with more capable peers" (Vygotsky, 1978, p. 86). Vygotsky's emphasis on interaction with more skilled partners is necessary to his theory, as such interaction is conceived as the means by which children become enculturated in the intellectual tools of their society. The agent of socialization must thus be someone who knows more than the child about those tools.

The theory is more complicated than this formulation suggests, however. The concept of the "zone of proximal development" requires not only a difference in level of expertise but an understanding on the part of the more advanced partner of the requirements of the less advanced child, for information presented at a level too far in advance of the child would not be helpful. Vygotsky's theory thus requires that the relation between the two partners be one of intersubjectivity, in which some measure of joint understanding of the task is obtained (Wertsch, 1984). Thus for Vygotsky, ideal partners are not equal, although their inequality should reside in understanding rather than power. For this reason, both adults and peers can bring about cognitive growth, but for growth to occur during peer interaction, the partner should be more advanced.

Direction of Development

In Piaget's theory, development proceeds in the direction of improvement. Children's notions of the world adapt to fit reality, leading to progress in development. Piaget characterized cognitive development as unidirectional progress through stages. True, Piaget accepted perturbations in the unidirectional flow (decalage), but the reasons for the delays in development were not incorporated into his theoretical stance.

Vygotsky's theory allows for the possibility of change in more than one direction. The direction of development in Vygotsky's theory is not unidirectional, as development is organized by social interaction leading children toward the skills of those around them. Children learn to use the tools and skills they practice with their social partners—and these differ both within and across societies. The fact that children learn currently accepted knowledge and skills from more competent partners implies a unidirectional slant to the theory, and as a Marxist psychology aimed in part at producing the "new Soviet man" some element of teleology is unavoidable. Nevertheless, Vygotsky's theory also encompasses the notion that children's interactions with others could lead to delays in development, abnormal development, or even regression according to the standards of the culture, under conditions in which partners seen as having greater skill are in fact incorrect or when adults doubt that children are capable of further development (Tudge, in press; Vygotsky, in press, pp. 153, 368; Zinchenko, 1987, personal communication). Such variations in development contrast with the unidirectional forward course of development postulated by Piaget.

Underpinnings of the Differences
Between the Two Theories

It is clear that Piaget's and Vygotsky's positions share some similarities while at the same time differing in important respects. The differences are likely to reflect contrasts in the aspects of development that the two theorists were trying to explain. As an epistemologist, Piaget focused his attention on the development of logic, and was particularly interested in the ways in which children make qualitative shifts in perspective in their understanding of the world. He was concerned with demonstrating that there is a logic with internal consistency at each stage of a child's development, a logic that differs qualitatively from that of an adult. Vygotsky, on the other hand, was concerned with the development of knowledge and skills for using culturally developed tools to mediate mental functioning. His focus was therefore on the ways in which more advanced members of a culture pass on to less mature members culturally acceptable practices and tools of which language is most important. Vygotsky's model of social interaction, therefore, was one in which the emphasis is on the development of shared understanding and meaning. Differences between the two theories may derive from the fact that Piaget studied replacements of one understanding with another that is qualitatively different, whereas Vygotsky studied the internalization of new information and skills that may not have conflicted with the child's existing beliefs.

RESEARCH ON PEERS AND THE EFFECTS
OF SOCIAL INTERACTION

This section focuses on studies of peer collaboration that examine what is learned through interaction and how the interaction takes place. The majority of the work that has been conducted in this area has been based on the Piagetian paradigm, although some neo-Piagetian scholars cite Vygotsky (e.g., Bearison, in press; Doise & Mackie, 1981; Doise & Mugny, 1984; Perret-Clermont, Brun, Saada, & Schubauer-Leoni, 1984). In addition, there is a growing literature based on Vygotskian foundations.

Although peer interaction has also been studied in schools in the context of peer tutoring (Ehly & Larsen, 1980; Harrison & Guymon, 1980) or peer cooperation (Damon, 1984; Damon & Phelps, 1987; Johnson & Johnson, 1975; Pepitone, 1980; Slavin, 1983), we do not focus on the bulk of this literature, because with few exceptions (e.g., Damon & Phelps, 1987) it is not set in the theoretical tradition of either Piaget or Vygotsky (Slavin, 1987). The research in these traditions demonstrates that children can learn from other children, but it tends not to examine the processes by which peers may foster each others' learning or development (Kerwin & Day, 1985).

Our discussion of peer interaction follows the same organization as the discussion of Piaget's and Vygotsky's theories, proceeding from mechanisms of social influence, to age trends in the effects of social interaction, the ideal role relations of partners, and the direction of development.

Mechanisms of Social Influence

Cognitive Conflict.   Scholars working in the Piagetian tradition have taken seriously what Piaget had to say about the effectiveness of "cognitive conflict" or "socio-cognitive conflict" induced by peer social interaction, and have argued that this conflict is effective in bringing about cognitive growth (Ames & Murray, 1982; Bearison, in press; Doise, Mugny & Perret-Clermont, 1975,

1976; Doise & Mugny, 1979, 1984; Perret-Clermont, 1980; Perret-Clermont & Schubauer-Leoni, 1981).

The task most commonly used to illustrate the effectiveness of this type of conflict is conservation, administered in the following way. Children are pre-tested individually to establish their status as conservers or nonconservers. In the experimental phase, pairs of children work on the same task. Generally the pairing brings together one child who is a conserver and one who is not to ensure that cognitive conflict (stemming from a difference in perspectives) is induced. The children are then asked to reach a joint decision about the task—for exam-ple, whether there are equal numbers of candies in two rows after those in one have been spread further apart. Finally, one or two posttests follow, in which the children are retested individually in order to assess development; that is, whether the nonconserver has learned to conserve.

Impressively consistent results have been reported. Based on a review of the research in this field, Murray (1982) pointed out that in approximately 80% of cases nonconservers attained conservation after having been paired with a con-serving peer. This may be contrasted with the fact that when teachers or psychol-ogists attempt to train conservation they are successful in only about 50% of cases (Murray, 1982). Thus, it would seem that peers may be more effective teachers than adults, although these studies do not directly compare the effective-ness of peers and adults as partners.

Imitation of a Model.   Some scholars have argued that the effective mecha-nism promoting development has nothing to do with cognitive conflict, but relates to imitation of a model who has provided the correct answer (Rosenthal & Zimmerman, 1972, 1978; Zimmerman & Lanaro, 1974). As a test of this hy-pothesis, Zimmerman and his colleagues paired conservers with adults who provided nonconservation (incorrect) responses. If imitation of a model is the crucial factor, they argued, the conservers should regress; this is precisely what happened. However, regression by conservers occurred only in the presence of adult modelers and was a temporary phenomenon; children who regressed re-verted to conservation soon after (Kuhn, 1972; J. Murray, 1974; Robert & Charbonneau, 1977, 1978). Robert and Charbonneau echoed Piaget, arguing that this regression is most likely the result of asymmetrical power relations between child and adult.

Further support for the view that the effects of interaction are not simply a result of imitation is that the justifications provided by new conservers often differ from those provided by their partners (Perret-Clermont, 1980), and that the new ability generalizes to other types of conservation problems (Ames & Mur-ray, 1982; Mugny & Doise, 1978).

Intersubjectivity.   As suggested earlier, Piaget emphasized cooperative un-derstanding. Discussion and sharing of perspectives may be one of the crucial factors in aiding development (Bearison, in press; Damon & Phelps, 1987;

Mugny, De Paolis, & Carugati, 1984; Mugny & Doise, 1978). Children who gained most from peer interaction on math, spatial, and balance beam tasks were those who more frequently shared ideas about the logic of the tasks with each other, focusing on solutions and strategies for handling the problem rather than on each other's role or behavior (Damon & Phelps, 1987). Peers engaging in either no arguments or a large number of arguments in Piagetian tasks were less likely to benefit from interaction than those whose relation was more balanced (Bearison, Magzamen & Filardo, 1986). Similarly, when one partner dominated the other partner in the course of trying to solve "Tower of Hanoi" problems or the partners were not constrained to come to a joint decision, the cognitive benefits of peer interaction were less than when the partners jointly worked on solving the problems (Glachan & Light, 1982; Light, Foot, Colbourn, & Mc-Clelland, 1987). Children working together on a logic game made significant advances in skill from pre- to posttest if they engaged in discussions of difference of opinion, but not otherwise (Light & Glachan, 1985). Berkowitz and Gibbs (1985) and Kruger and Tomasello (1986) also stressed the importance of *transactive* discussion, which they define as reasoning about one's partner's reasoning.

Researchers working within a Vygotskian framework have focused on the notion of co-construction of solutions. For example, Forman and her colleagues (Forman, 1987; Forman & Cazden, 1985; Forman, Gilman, Kaur, & McPhail, 1987; Forman & Kraker, 1985) examined the ways in which 9- to 14-year-olds arrived at greater understanding (of Piaget's chemicals task and a projection of shadows problem) in the course of "social coordination." A difference in perspectives between partners is seen as being valuable but of less benefit than the attempt to coordinate the perspectives and co-construct hypotheses to arrive at a joint answer. Forman (1987) argued that her data indicate that the most important aspect of this coordination is the ability on the part of the collaborating partners to employ "interpsychological regulation." Similarly, Gauvain and Rogoff (in press) found that though children who worked together on an errand-planning task performed no better than children who worked alone when later carrying out the task independently, the subgroup of children who shared in decision making performed better than children working in pairs that did not truly collaborate and children who worked alone.

Scholars in the Soviet Union have suggested that collaboration in peer interaction is beneficial for learning concepts from history (Kol'tsova, 1978) and understanding mathematical concepts (Semenov, 1978). Children's understanding of classification and complex trajectory construction sometimes improved in the process of solving joint tasks with age mates, and these advances persisted after the interaction (Rubtsov, 1981; Rubtsov & Guzman, 1984). "Under conditions of cooperation, an activity that is initially shared by those participating in it emerges as an original and fundamental foundation for the development of *individual* activity" (Rubtsov, 1981, p. 41). Rubtsov agreed with Piaget in focusing on parallels between the organization of joint activity and the organization of thought, but emphasized the influences of the social arrangements: "The relations determining the logic of an intellectual structure consist of compact condensed forms of mutual relationships among the participants in cooperation" (Rubtsov, 1981, p. 59). Martin (1985; Kol'tsova & Martin, 1985) similarly argued that cognitive benefits in a balance-scale task were most likely to occur in situations in which children in a team coordinated their activity.

Forman (1987) noted theoretical differences in the cognitive and social processes underlying collaborative problem solving in Piaget's and Vygotsky's theories. In Piaget's theory the parallels between cognitive and social processes are explained by the fact that both derive from the same central intrapsychological process, whereas in Vygotsky's theory the correspondence is due to the derivation of individual higher cognitive processes from joint social processes. These differing interpretations are accompanied by differences in the mechanisms: intersubjectivity and perspective-taking. Forman suggested that intersubjectivity (from the Vygotskian perspective) is a process that takes place across people, whereas perspective-taking and decentering (from the Piagetian perspective) are individual processes working on socially provided information.

Thus, within peer interaction research deriving from both Piagetian and Vygotskian theory, evidence is mounting that a crucial factor is the extent to which partners enter into each other's frame of reference and attempt to arrive jointly at solutions to problems. Thus conflict may most reasonably be considered an opportunity to discuss a problem and coordinate joint activity to solve it. However, as we point out in the next section, the age of the interacting partners must be taken into consideration.

Age Trends in the Effects of Social Interaction

The issue here is the extent to which young children can benefit from social interaction. Nonconservers, who have not reached the stage of concrete operational thought, benefit from interaction with conservers (Ames & Murray, 1982; Botvin & Murray, 1975; Murray, 1972; Perret-Clermont & Schubauer-Leoni, 1981; Silverman & Geiringer, 1973; Silverman & Stone, 1972). Children between the ages of 4 and 5 years have been found more likely to advance in cognitive skills after having been paired with another child than when working on the same task individually (Azmitia, 1987, 1988; Cooper, 1980; Koester & Bueche, 1980; Tudge, 1985).

On the other hand, some researchers have found limited benefit from interaction between preschoolers (Azmitia & Perlmutter, in press; Gauvain & Rogoff, in press). One reason may be that preschoolers provide fewer verbal explanations than older children. For example, Koester and Bueche (1980) found that although 4-year-olds were able to teach a block design task to children a year younger than them, they provided very little explanation and contented themselves primarily with demonstrations. Azmitia (1988) also found very little evidence that 5-year-olds learned a model copying task through discussion, but relied either on observational learning or guidance by a peer who was expert at the task. Cooper (1980) found that 3-year-olds were much less likely to engage in discussion and collaboration than 5-year-olds while trying to solve balance-scale tasks jointly. As Azmitia and Perlmutter (in press) argued, more attention needs to be paid to examining the role played by the age of participants when considering the effects of social interaction.

Thus, as Piaget argued, it may be the case that the benefits of peer social interaction, stemming specifically from discussion and coordination of perspectives, are found less often until children are able to hold their own point of view and that of another person simultaneously. However, this does not mean that prior to that time children are unable to benefit from social interaction, but rather, as Vygotsky would allow, that the benefits derive from learning skills or information in interaction with someone more capable at the task to be solved. A number of studies find benefits of social interaction for infants and preschoolers receiving guidance from adults, though here too the results with preschoolers are more equivocal than those with older children. (Rogoff, in preparation, reviews this literature.)

Ideal Role Relations of Partners

As we have discussed, Piaget held that interaction with peers, rather than adult-child interaction, was more likely to lead to cognitive development. In contrast, Vygotsky believed that interaction with a more capable partner was most likely to be conducive to development. Much of the work in the West that has been derived from Vygotsky has focused on adult-child interaction (e.g., Griffin & Cole, 1984; Rogoff, in press; Rogoff, Malkin, & Gilbride, 1984; Saxe, Gearhart, & Guberman, 1984; Wertsch, 1979, 1980; Wertsch, Minick, & Arns, 1984); but Vygotsky also believed that a "more capable peer" could be an effective partner.

The Relative Benefits of Adult-Child and Peer Relationships.   Although we focus on peer interaction, it is instructive to examine studies that compare the benefits of collaboration with an adult, as they address the question of relative expertise of partners. The benefits appear to vary according to the nature of the task, with peers being more useful than adults when the task primarily involves discussion of issues. Peers may provide each other with opportunities to discuss issues and to manage conversation that is less available in interaction with adults. French (1987) suggested that mother-child conversation is both more controlled by and supported by the mother, whereas conversations between preschool peers provide more opportunity or even necessity for reciprocal involvement and for children to institute and sustain discourse. While discussing moral issues, 7- and

11-year-old children expressed logical arguments more with their peers than with their mothers (Kruger & Tomasello, 1986). Though mothers requested idea clarifications more than did peers, children produced more self-generated clarifications of logic when interacting with peers, and were more likely to make comments related to their partner's logic with peers.

Most tasks used for adult-peer comparison have involved the learning of skills; development involving shifts in perspective in Piagetian tasks may follow a different pattern, though child-child and adult-child differences in these two domains have not been directly examined. An ongoing study by Radziszewska and Rogoff is attempting to compare the effectiveness of adults and peers as partners on tasks of skill learning versus shifts in perspective.

A problem with the existing studies is that the tasks examined are of interest to children but the children are less skilled than are adults. This means that the results of such comparisons of adults versus peers as partners may not generalize to the performance of peers as partners in tasks in which they are especially skilled or which they regard as in the domain of peer (rather than adult-child) activities. Hence the fact that adults generally prove more effective as partners than peers at teaching skills should be qualified as limited to adult-world tasks in which adults are more skilled.

Six-year-old children who worked on memory and classification tasks with adults learned more than those who worked with slightly older children (Ellis & Rogoff, 1982, 1986). The adult teachers used more verbal instruction in the course of teaching classification, were more likely to provide information on the category rationales, and elicited greater participation from the child partners. The child teachers appeared to focus on completing the immediate task of sorting items, to the detriment of the larger goal of teaching their partner how to do the task. "The child teachers appeared relatively unskilled at guiding instruction within the learner's region of sensitivity to instruction" (Ellis & Rogoff, 1986, p. 323). Similar differences between instructional styles of adult and 5-year-old teachers appeared in a study of puzzle completion by 3-year-olds (McLane, 1981).

Nine-year-old children gained more skill in errand planning from collaborating with parents than with peers (Radziszewska & Rogoff, in press). During collaboration, children working with adults planned more in advance than children who worked with peers. Those who worked with adults actually participated in the more sophisticated planning strategies promoted by the adults, and continued to use those strategies in subsequent independent posttests. Children working with peers employed the same sort of short-term planning that is used by children planning alone. It appears from these studies that planning with a skilled partner enhances children's later independent planning.

The difference between the adult and peer partners appears to be due to a combination of the variation in the skill in errand planning and their skill in communication and guidance. Peers who had received training in the errand-planning task, bringing their efficiency even with that of adults, proved to be more beneficial as partners than peers who were not trained in errand planning, but still not as beneficial as adult partners (Radziszewska & Rogoff, in preparation).

Children are interested (but not inherently skilled) in these tasks, which may not feature the type of information that peers might teach each other when away from adult influence. The tasks are thus useful for examining the skills of adults, but may not represent the natural skills of children in collaboration. It would be of interest to study naturalistic interaction between peers in tasks they do well and/or choose for themselves. As an approximation to this situation, we are currently investigating peer and adult interaction as partners who vary in expertise collaborate on learning computer software programs.

Differences in Expertise Between Peers.   For Piaget, peer interaction was viewed as interaction between equals. For benefits to occur there should be a difference of perspectives on a task, but the relation should be one of equality. In support of this view, neo-Piagetian scholars have demonstrated the development attained by pairing a nonconserver with a conserver. However, although the interaction is between peers in the sense of age-mates, their relation might be better thought of as a relation between an expert and a novice than between two equals. Tudge (1986b, 1986c) argued that nonconservers attain conservation in this context primarily because they have been paired with an expert.

Expertise is not necessary to achieve development, however. Some investigators have paired a nonconserver with another nonconserver or with a transitional conserver and found some evidence of development, although less than when nonconservers have been paired with conservers (Mackie, 1983; Mugny & Doise, 1978; Perret-Clermont & Schubauer-Leoni, 1981). Other researchers, working outside the Piagetian framework, have also provided evidence that pairing children at the same level has led to development (Forman & Kraker, 1985; Glachan & Light, 1982; Light & Glachan, 1985; Lomov, 1978; Rubtsov, 1981). However, other studies have found that collaboration between children at the same level led to no progress (Azmitia, 1988; Heber, 1981; Russell, (1982).

How can we make sense of these contradictory findings? Perhaps the contradictions would lessen if attention were paid to the cooperation between partners, rather than simply the presence of a partner. When both participants work at achieving an intersubjective understanding of the problem and collaborate to arrive at a solution, development appears more likely (Damon & Phelps, 1987; Forman, 1987; Gauvain & Rogoff, in press; Rubtsov, 1981). Conversely, when one partner dominates the proceedings (Glachan & Light, 1982), when the participants engage in argument and nothing more (Bearison, Magzamen & Filardo, 1986), or when they are not engaged in the task (Russell, 1982), interaction is likely to be less successful. Differences in the degree of intersubjectivity achieved by the partners may explain some of the differences in results obtained.

In addition, when the pair members have different skill levels, the degree of difference may be important. When the cognitive differences between pairs of peers are too great, development is not a likely consequence (Kuhn, 1972; Mugny & Doise, 1978). In Kuhn's (1972) research, for example, almost twice as many children who had observed a model one stage above them improved as did those who had observed a model two stages above them.

Damon (1984) suggested that different types of learning may be differentially facilitated by equal versus more expert partners. Focusing on the relative advantages of interaction with more expert peers (in tutoring) and equal peers (in collaboration), Damon suggested that peer tutoring may be most successful when one child knows more in some domain than another and when the information or skills are within a domain that children basically understand but need to extend. Damon (1984) felt that peer collaboration, on the other hand

> is an ideal technique for encouraging children to wrestle with intellectual challenges in difficult new principles. Learning to communicate accurately through written and spoken language, grasping the logic behind scientific formulas, and realizing the political rationale underlying a societal governance system can all be fostered in a collaborative peer interaction context. Such intellectual accomplishments stretch the boundaries of children's mental abilities. Consequently, they flourish best under conditions of highly motivated discovery, the free exchange of ideas, and reciprocal feedback between mutually respected equals. These are precisely the characteristics of collaborative interchanges between children. (p. 340)

Damon's suggestions may be an appropriate reconciliation of Vygotsky's and Piaget's views regarding the ideal role relations between partners in academic endeavors. Further research is needed to disentangle the circumstances in which social interaction benefits learning of academic material as the research to date is sparse, and results vary according to the age of children observed, the problem to be solved, and the relative skills of the partners. It is also important to study situations where children meet naturalistically and problem solving occurs under their management, to examine how peers serve as important cognitive facilitators.

The Direction of Development

Piaget and Vygotsky disagreed regarding whether peer interaction is associated with unidirectional development. In Piaget's view, because cognitive conflict provides an impetus for children to seek equilibrium at a higher level, the expectation would be for children to change their thinking only when faced with a perspective that fits reality better than their own. Vygotsky's theory allows for multiple directions in development, depending on the nature of the interactions, the information being provided, and so on. Thus, from the perspective of learning a particular skill, unidirectional development is not a necessary result of interaction (Vygotsky, in press).

In the literature dealing with the effects of social interaction very few examples of regression appear, with the exception of the work of Zimmerman and his colleagues (Rosenthal & Zimmerman, 1972; 1978; Zimmerman & Lanaro, 1974), in which there was no evidence of stability. The lack of evidence of regression may stem from the fact that most of the research in this area has been conducted with conserver-nonconserver pairs. Conservers know all that is to be known within the domain of conservation and, at least for Piagetians, one mark of conservation is an understanding of the "logical necessity" of that belief (Murray, 1987). Even if children do not have this feeling of logical necessity, there is evidence that conservers are more confident of their beliefs than nonconservers (Miller, 1986; Miller & Brownell, 1975; Miller, Brownell, & Zukier, 1977).

The degree of confidence appears to be an important variable. In a mathematical balance beam task in which pairs of children differed in terms of their level of thinking but neither partner could be considered an expert, many of the partners with greater skill regressed (Tudge, 1986b, 1986c). Regression in this case was a stable phenomenon. Development or regression appeared to be partly related to the confidence with which partners could predict the movement of the balance beam (Tudge, 1986a). Tudge speculated that in Piagetian conservation tasks, regression would seldom appear, because nonconservers would be unlikely to shake the beliefs of their conserving expert partners.

Dominance, as well as confidence, would appear to be a factor shaping the direction of development, at least in the short term. Zimmerman and his colleagues (Rosenthal & Zimmerman, 1972; 1978; Zimmerman & Lanaro, 1974) showed that conservers could be induced to adopt nonconservation responses (albeit temporarily) when paired with adults who provided erroneous nonconservation responses. Russell (1982) reported that compliance with a more dominant partner was the most likely cause of a changed viewpoint when pairs of nonconservers interacted. In more general terms, Goodnow (1987) argued that social power (in the sense of who in society determines what is to count as knowledge) is influential in shaping the direction of development.

CONCLUSIONS

Peers can have a profound impact on children's cognitive development. There is support both for Piaget's notion that peer interaction may benefit an individual's cognitive development, and for the Vygotskian position, which stresses the benefits of interaction with more advanced partners providing assistance within the zone of proximal development.

The question of whether social interaction increases in its impact as children become more logical, as Piaget proposed, receives some support in the findings of several studies with preschoolers that did not show benefits of social interaction with peers. The studies carried out with older children generally show benefits from collaboration. However, we would find it difficult to conclude that social interaction is not effective with young children because so many of their skills have clear links to social practice. Consider the necessity of social interaction for learning the culturally appropriate use of language—a skill associated with interaction with adults.

We suggest that it may be useful to differentiate between learning of skills and adopting new perspectives. The evidence suggests that adults may be better able than peers to help children learn skills and knowledge in the course of interaction. On the other hand, the type of free verbal interchange that seems influential in bringing about a change in perspectives may be more likely in peer interaction. Further research is clearly necessary to elucidate these differences.

Though both Piaget and Vygotsky mentioned play as providing cognitive opportunities, we have not delved into that topic in this chapter. However, it would be a fruitful topic to follow to understand the roles of peers in cognitive development, especially on tasks that are not under the control of adults (Bruner, Jolly, & Sylva, 1976). Outside (and perhaps within) academic topics, peers may fill important roles seldom taken by adults. They may be likely to foster exploration without immediate goals that in the long run lead to insightful solutions to unforeseen problems. They may encourage motivation and channel the choice of activities. And compared with the busy adults in children's environments, other children certainly offer their availability and time.

A further question raised but not yet resolved by the research is the extent to which children can benefit from interaction with others whose skills are not more advanced than their own. The literature suggests that the partner's confidence in the task (whether misplaced or not) and social dominance may be important variables affecting the benefits of social interaction.

The variable that appears essential for social interaction to be effective, stressed by Vygotskians and Piagetians and receiving recognition in research, is that of establishing intersubjectivity between partners. It is unlikely that merely sitting next to another person will enhance a child's skills. Neither cognitive conflict nor joint problem solving could function to enhance a child's skills or change a perspective unless the partners establish some degree of intersubjectivity, allowing opportunities for exchange of ideas or for active observation or joint involvement in a task. The notion of intersubjectivity deserves careful attention in the further progress of the literature on social interaction.

ACKNOWLEDGMENTS

We are very grateful for the comments of Margarita Azmitia, David Bearison, Ellice Forman, Artin Goncu, Evgenii Subbotsky, Jim Wertsch, Marc Bornstein, and Jerome Bruner, as well as for the financial support of Grant # HD16973 awarded to the second author from the National Institute of Child Health and Human Development.

REFERENCES

Ames, G. J., & Murray, F. B. When two wrongs make a right: Promoting cognitive change by social conflict. *Developmental Psychology, 1982, 18,* 894–987.

Azmitia, M. Expertise as a moderator of social influence on children's cognition. In M. Perlmutter (Chair), *Moderators of social influence on childrens' cognition.* Symposium at SRCD, Baltimore, MD, 1987.

Azmitia, M. Peer interaction and problem solving: When are two heads better than one? *Child Development,* 1988, *59,* 87–96.

Azmitia, M., & Perlmutter, M. Social influences on children's cognition: State of the art and future directions. In H. Reese (Ed.), *Advances in child development and behavior.* New York: Academic Press, in press.

Bearison, D. J. Interactional contexts of cognitive development: Piagetian approaches to sociogenesis. In L. Tolchinsky (Ed.), *Culture, cognition, and schooling.* Norwood, NJ: Ablex, in press.

Bearison, D. J., Magzamen, S., & Filardo, E. K. Socio-cognitive conflict and cognitive growth in young children. *Merrill-Palmer Quarterly, 1986, 32,* 51–72.

Berkowitz, M. W., & Gibbs, J. C. The process of moral conflict resolution and moral development. In M. W. Berkowitz (Ed.), *Peer conflict and psychological growth* (pp. 71–84). San Francisco: Jossey-Bass, 1985.

Botvin, G. J., & Murray, F. B. The efficacy of peer modeling and social conflict in the acquisition of conservation. *Child Development,* 1975, *46,* 796–799.

Butterworth, G. A brief account of the conflict between the individual and the social in models of cognitive growth. In G. Butterworth & P. Light (Eds.), *Social cognition: Studies of the development of understanding* (pp. 3–16). Brighton: Harvester Press, 1982.

Bruner, J. S., Jolly, A., & Sylva, K. (Eds.), *Play: Its role in development and evolution.* New York: Basic Books, 1976.

Cooper, C. R. Development of collaborative problem solving among preschool children. *Developmental Psychology,* 1980, *16,* 433–440.

Damon, W. Peer education: The untapped potential. *Journal of Applied Developmental Psychology,* 1984, *5,* 331–343.

Damon, W., & Killen M. Peer interaction and the process of change in children's moral reasoning. *Merrill-Palmer Quarterly, 1982, 28,* 347–378.

Damon, W., & Phelps, E. *Peer collaboration as a context for cognitive growth.* Paper presented at Tel Aviv University School of Education, June 1987.

Davydov, V. V., & Radzikhovskii, L. A. Vygotsky and activity-oriented psychology. In J. V. Wertsch (Ed.), *Culture, communication, and cognition: Vygotskian perspectives* (pp. 66–93). Cambridge: Cambridge University Press, 1985.

Doise, W., & Mackie, D. On the social nature of cognition. In J. P. Forgas (Ed.), *Social cognition: Perspectives on everyday understanding* (pp. 53–83). London: Academic Press, 1981.

Doise, W., & Mugny, G. *The social development of the intellect.* Oxford: Pergamon Press, 1984.

Doise, W., Mugny, G., & Perret-Clermont, A.-N. Social interaction and the development of cognitive operations. *European Journal of Social Psychology,* 1975, *5* (3), 367–383.

Doise, W., Mugny, G., & Perret-Clermont, A.-N. Social interaction and cognitive development: Further evidence. *European Journal of Social Psychology,* 1976, *6,* 245–247.

Ehly, S. W., & Larsen, S. C. *Peer tutoring for individualized instruction.* Boston: Allyn & Bacon, 1980.

Ellis, S., & Rogoff, B. The strategies and efficacy of child versus adult teachers. *Child Development,* 1982, *43,* 730–735.

Ellis, S., & Rogoff, B. Problem solving in children's management of instruction. In E. Mueller & C. Cooper (Eds.), *Process and outcome in peer relationships* (pp. 301–325). New York: Academic Press, 1986.

Forman, E. A, Learning through peer interaction: A Vygotskian perspective. *The Genetic Epistemologist,* 1987, *15,* 6–15.

Forman, E. A., & Cazden, C. B. Exploring Vygotskian perspectives in education: The cognitive value of peer interaction. In J. V. Wertsch (Ed.), *Culture, communication and cognition: Vygotskian perspectives* (pp. 323–347). Cambridge: Cambridge University Press, 1985.

Forman, E. A., Gilman, R., Kaur, B., & McPhail, J. *The negotiation of task goals & strategies in a collaborative problem-solving activity.* Paper presented at the meetings of the American Educational Research Association, Washington, DC, April 1987.

Forman, E. A., & Kraker, M. J. The social origins of logic: The contributions of Piaget and Vygotsky. In M. W. Berkowitz (Ed.), *Peer conflict and cognitive growth* (pp. 23–39). San Francisco: Jossey-Bass, 1985.

French, L. *Effects of partner and setting on young children's discourse: A case study.* Unpublished manuscript, University of Rochester, 1987.

Gauvain, M., & Rogoff, B. Collaborative problem solving and the development of children's planning skills. *Developmental Psychology,* in press.

Glachan, M., & Light, P. Peer interaction and learning: Can two ways make a right. In G. Butterworth & P. Light (Eds.), *Social cognition: Studies of the development of understanding* (pp. 238–262). Brighton: Harvester Press, 1982.

Goodnow, J. *The socialization of cognition: What's involved?* Paper presented at conference on Culture and Human Development, Chicago, November 1987.

Griffin, P., & Cole, N. Current activity for the future: The 20-ped. In B. Rogoff & J. V. Wertsch (Eds.), *Children's learning in the "zone of proximal development"* (pp. 45–64). San Francisco: Jossey-Bass, 1984.

Harrison, G. V., & Guymon, R. E. *Structured tutoring.* Englewood Cliffs, NJ: Educational Technology Publications, 1980.

Heber, M. Instruction *versus* conversation as opportunities for learning. In W. P. Robinson (Ed.), *Communications in development* (pp. 183–202). London: Academic Press, 1981.

Johnson, D. W., & Johnson, R. T. *Learning together and more: Cooperation, competition, and individualization.* Englewood Cliffs, NJ: Prentice-Hall, 1975.

Kerwin, M. L. E., & Day, J. D. Peer influences on cognitive development. In J. B. Pryor & J. D. Day (Eds.), *The development of social cognition* (pp. 211–228). New York: Springer-Verlag, 1985.

Koester, L. S., & Bueche, N. A. Preschoolers as teachers: Where children are seen but not heard. *Child Study Journal,* 1980, *10,* 107–118.

Kol'tsova, V. A. Experimental study of cognitive activity in communication (with specific reference to concept formation). *Soviet Psychology,* 1978, *17*(1), 23–38.

Kol'tsova, V. A., & Martin, L. M. W. Lichnostnie determinanti obshcheniya v usloviyakh sovmestnoi poznavatel'noi deyatel'nosti [Individual determinants of communication in the context of joint cognitive activity]. In B. F. Lomov, A. V. Belyaeva & V. N. Nosulenko (Eds.), *Psikhologicheskie issledovaniya obshcheniya* [Psychological studies of communication] (pp. 207–219). Moscow: Nauka, 1985.

Kruger, A. C., & Tomasello, M. Transactive discussions with peers and adults. *Developmental Psychology,* 1986, *22,* 681–685.

Kuhn, D. Mechanisms of change in the development of cognitive structures. *Child Development,* 1972, *43,* 833–842.

Light, P. H., & Glachan, M. Facilitation of individual problem solving through peer interaction. *Educational Psychology*, 1985, *5*, 217–225.

Lomov, B. F. Psychological processes and communication. *Soviet Psychology*, 1978, *17*(1), 3–22.

Mackie, D. The effect of social interaction on conservation of spatial relations. *Journal of Cross-Cultural Psychology*, 1983, *14*, 131–151.

Martin, L. The role of social interaction in children's problem solving. *The Quarterly Newsletter of the Laboratory for comparative Human Cognition*, 1985, *7*, 40–45.

McLane, J. B. *Dyadic problem solving: A comparison of child-child and mother-child interaction.* Unpublished doctoral dissertation, Northwestern University, 1981.

Miller, S. Certainty and necessity in the understanding of Piagetian concepts. *Developmental Psychology*, 1986, *26*, 3–18.

Miller, S., & Brownell, C. Peers, persuasion, and Piaget: Dyadic interaction between conservers and nonconservers. *Child Development*, 1975, *46*, 972–997.

Miller, S., Brownell, C., & Zukier, H. Cognitive certainty in children: Effects of concept, developmental level, and method of assessment. *Developmental Psychology*, 1977, *13*, 236–243.

Mugny, G., De Paolis, P., & Carugati, F. Social regulations in cognitive development. In W. Doise & A. Palmonari (Eds.), *Social interaction in individual development* (pp. 127–146). New York: Cambridge University Press, 1984.

Mugny, G., & Doise, W. Socio-cognitive conflict and structure of individual and collective performance. *European Journal of Social Psychology*, 1978, *8*, 181–192.

Murray, F. B. Acquisition of conservation through social interaction. *Developmental Psychology*, 1972, *6*, 1–6.

Murray, F. B. Teaching through social conflict. *Contemporary Educational Psychology*, 1982, *7*, 257–271.

Murray, F. B. Necessity: The developmental component in school mathematics. In L. S. Liber (Ed.), *Development and learning: Conflict or congruence* (pp. 51–69). Hillsdale, NJ: Erlbaum, 1987.

Murray, J. P. Social learning and cognitive development: Modeling effects on children: Understanding of conservation. *British Journal of Psychology*, 1974, *65*(1), 151–160.

Pepitone, G. A. *Children in cooperation and competition.* Lexington, MA: D. C. Heath, 1980.

Perret-Clermont, A-N. *Social interaction and cognitive development in children.* London: Academic Press, 1980.

Perret-Clermont, A.-N., & Schubauer-Leoni, M.-L. Conflict and cooperation as opportunities for learning. In P. Robinson (Ed.), *Communication in development* (pp. 203–233). London: Academic Press, 1981.

Perret-Clermont, A.-N., Brun, J., Saada, E. H., & Schubauer-Leoni, M.-L. Psychological processes, operatory level and the acquisition of knowledge. *Interactions Didactiques* (No. 2 bis). Universities of Geneva and of Neuchatel, 1984.

Piaget, J. *The moral judgement of the child.* New York: Harcourt Brace, 1932.

Piaget, J. *The origins of intelligence in children.* New York: Norton, 1952. (Original work published in 1936)

Piaget, J. *The language and thought of the child* (3rd Ed.). London: Routledge & Keagan Paul, 1959. (Original work published in 1923 and 1948)

Piaget, J. *Comments.* Cambridge: MIT Press, 1962.

Piaget, J. *Six psychological studies.* New York: Vintage Press, 1968. (Original work published in 1964)

Piaget, J. *Biology and Knowledge.* Chicago: Chicago University Press, 1971. (Original work published in 1967)

Piaget, J. Logique genetique et sociologie. In *Etudes Sociologiques* (pp. 203–239). Geneva, Switzerland: Librairie Droz, 1977. (Original work published in 1928)

Piaget, J. Les operations logiques et la vie sociale. In *Etudes Sociologiques* (pp. 143–171). Geneva, Switzerland: Librairie Droz, 1977. (Original work published in 1945)

Piaget, J. Piaget's theory. In W. Kessen (Ed.), *History, theory, and methods,* In P. H. Mussen (Ed.), *Handbook of Child Psychology* (Vol. I, pp. 294–356). New York: Wiley, 1983. (Original work published in 1970)

Piaget, J., & Inhelder, B. *The psychology of the child.* New York: Basic Books, 1969. (Original work published in 1966)

Radziszewska, B., & Rogoff, B. The influence of collaboration with parents versus peers in learning to plan. *Developmental Psychology, 1988, 24,* 840–848.

Radziszewska, B., & Rogoff, B. *The role of expertise in learning to plan with peers versus parents,* in preparation.

Robert, M., & Charbonneau, C. Extinction of liquid conservation by observation: effects of model's age and presence. *Child Development, 1977. 48,* 648–652.

Robert, M., & Charbonneau, C. Extinction of liquid conservation by modeling: Three indicators of its artificiality. *Child Development, 1978, 49,* 194–200.

Rogoff, B. The joint socialization of development by young children and adults. In M. Lewis and S. Feinman (Eds.), *Social influences and behavior.* New York: Plenum, in press.

Rogoff, B. in preparation. *Children as apprentices in thinking.* New York: Oxford University Press.

Rogoff, B., Malkin, C., & Gilbride, K. Interaction with babies as guidance in development. In B. Rogoff & J. Wertsch (Eds.), *Children's learning in the "zone of proximal development"* (pp. 31–44). San Francisco: Jossey-Bass, 1984.

Rommetveit, R. On Piagetian cognitive operations, semantic competence and message structure in adult-child communication. In I. Markova (Ed.), *The social context of language* (pp. 113–150). London: Wiley, 1976.

Rommetveit, R. Language acquisition as increasing linguistic structuring of experience and symbolic behavior control. In J. V. Wertsch (Ed.), *Culture, communication, and cognition: Vygotskian perspectives* (pp. 183–204). Cambridge: Cambridge University Press, 1985.

Rosenthal, T., & Zimmerman, B. J. Modeling by exemplification and interaction in training conservation. *Developmental Psychology, 1972, 6,* 392–401.

Rosenthal, T., & Zimmerman, B. J. *Social learning and cognition.* New York: Academic Press, 1978.

Rubtsov, V. V. The role of cooperation in the development of intelligence. *Soviet Psychology, 1981, 19*(4), 41–62.

Rubtsov, V. V., & Guzman, R. Ya. Psychological characteristics of the methods pupils use to organize joint activity in dealing with a school task. *Soviet Psychology, 1984–1985, 23*(2), 65–84.

Russell, J. Cognitive conflict, transmission, and justification: Conservation attainment through dyadic interaction. *Journal of Genetic Psychology, 1982, 140,* 287–297.

Saxe, G. B., Gearhart, M., & Guberman, S. B. The social organization of early number development. In B. Rogoff & J. V. Wertsch (Eds.), *Children's learning in the "zone of proximal development"* (pp. 19–30). San Francisco: Jossey-Bass, 1984.

Semenov, I. N. An empirical psychological study of thought processes in creative problem solving from the perspective of the theory of activity. *Soviet Psychology, 1978, 16*(4), 3–46.

Silverman, I. W., & Stone, J. M. Modifying cognitive functioning through participation in a problem-solving group. *Journal of Educational Psychology, 1972, 63,* 603–608.

Silverman, I. W., & Geiringer, E. Dyadic interaction and conservation induction: A test of Piaget's equilibration model. *Child Development, 1973, 44,* 815–820.

Slavin, R. E. *Cooperative learning.* New York: Longman, 1983.

Slavin, R. E. Developmental and motivational perspectives on cooperative learning: A reconciliation. *Child Development, 1987, 58,* 1161–1167.

Trevarthen, C. The foundations of intersubjectivity: development of interpersonal and cooperative understanding in infants. In D. R. Olson (Ed.), *Social foundations of language & thought* (pp. 316–342). New York: Norton, 1980.

Tudge, J. R. H. The effect of social interaction on cognitive development: How creative is conflict? *The Quarterly Newsletter of the Laboratory of Comparative Human Cognition,* 1988, *7,* 33–40.

Tudge, J. R. H. *Beyond conflict: The role of reasoning in collaborative problem solving.* Paper presented at the Jean Piaget Society, Philadelphia, May 1986a. (Reprinted in *Resources in Education* (ERIC), May 1987).

Tudge, J. R. H. *Collaboration and cognitive development in the USA and USSR.* Paper presented at the annual meetings of the American Psychological Association. Washington, DC, August 1986b.

Tudge, J. R. H. *Collaboration, conflict, and cognitive development: The efficacy of joint problem solving.* Paper presented at the Eastern Psychological Conference, New York, April 1986c. (Reprinted in *Resources in Education* (ERIC), February 1987)

Tudge, J. R. H. Vygotsky, the zone of proximal development, and peer collaboration: Implications for classroom practice. In L. Moll (Ed.), *Vygotsky and education.* Cambridge: Cambridge University Press, in press.

Vygotsky, L. S. *Mind in society: The development of higher psychological processes.* Cambridge, MA: Harvard University Press, 1978.

Vygotsky, L. S. The instrumental method in psychology. In J. V. Wertsch (Ed.), *The concept of activity in Soviet psychology* (pp. 134–143). Armonk, NY: Sharpe, 1981a.

Vygotsky, L. S. The genesis of higher mental functions. In J. V. Wertsch (Ed.), *The concept of activity in Soviet psychology* (pp. 144–188). Armonk, NY: Sharpe, 1981b.

Vygotsky, L. S. *The collected works of L.S. Vygotsky: Vol. 1. Problems of general psychology* (N. Minick, Trans.). New York: Plenum, 1987.

Vygotsky, L. S. *The collected works of L.S. Vygotsky: Vol. 2. Problems of abnormal psychology and learning disabilities.* (J. Knox & K. Stevens, Trans.). New York: Plenum, in press.

Wertsch, J. V. From social interaction to higher psychological processes. *Human Development,* 1979, *22,* 1–22.

Wertsch, J. V. The significance of dialogue in Vygotsky: Account of social, egocentric, and inner speech. *Contemporary Educational Psychology,* 1980, *5,* 150–162.

Wertsch, J. V. The zone of proximal development: Some conceptual issues. In B. Rogoff & J. V. Wertsch (Eds.), *Children's learning in the "zone of proximal development"* (pp. 7–18). San Francisco: Jossey-Bass, 1984.

Wertsch, J. V. *Vygotsky and the social formation of mind.* Cambridge, MA: Harvard University Press, 1985.

Wertsch, J. V., Minick, M., & Arns, F. J. The creation of context in joint problem solving action: A cross-cultural study. In B. Rogoff & J. Lave (Eds.), *Everyday cognition: In development in social context* (pp. 151–171). Cambridge: Harvard University Press, 1984.

Wozniak, R. H. Dialecticalism and structualism: The philosophical foundations of Soviet Psychology and Piagetian cognitive developmental theory. In K. F. Riegel & G. C. Rosenwald (Eds.), *Structure & transformation: Developmental & historical aspects* (pp. 25–45). New York: Wiley, 1975.

Youniss, J. Dialectical theory and Piaget on social knowledge. *Human Development,* 1978, *21,* 234–247.

Youniss, J. Social construction and moral development: Update and expansion of an idea. In W. M. Kurtines & J. L. Gewirtz (Eds.), *Moral development through social interaction* (pp. 131–148). New York: Wiley, 1987.

Zimmerman, B. J., & Lanaro, P. Acquiring and retaining conservation of length through modelling and reversibility cues. *Merrill-Palmer Quarterly,* 1974, *20*(3), 145–161.

3 Cognitive Development and Interaction

Magali Bovet
Silvia Parrat-Dayan
Jacques Vonèche
University of Geneva, Switzerland

INTRODUCTION

In this chapter, interaction and cognitive development are understood in the Piagetian perspective. As we attempt to show, this perspective is no frozen landscape forgotten somewhere on the slopes of the Alps or at the bottom of Lake Geneva after a previous glaciation.

No issue touches the thinking person more deeply than the relation of the individual to the world. Discussion takes many forms and gives rise to a number of questions, the answers to which never quite seem to stay put. The roles of the individual in history, the individual's place in the family, and the relative contribution of heredity and environment in determining intelligence raise questions that bear on one's general conception of the relation between organism and environment.

INTERACTION, CONSTRUCTION, AND LOGICAL DETERMINISM

Piaget's approach to the general issue of the relationship between the organism and the environment has been open to some misunderstanding. His insistence on slow development in the genesis of fundamental concepts and operations has sometimes been interpreted as meaning that the child learns these things primarily through commerce with the environment: Stimulus evokes response, and, depending on the outcome, future response tendencies are altered, habits built up gradually. Piaget labeled this form of interacting with the environment *empiri-*

cism. Piaget is far from agreeing with it, in spite of the efforts of some, especially Berlyne (1960), to turn Piaget into a sort of neo-behaviorist.

Piaget's reasons for rejecting empiricism are, in a way, similar to Chomsky's. Chomsky showed that children make syntactic mistakes that do not come, by any means, from their linguistic environment such as: "I falled from the wall." In a similar vein, Piaget demonstrated that children acquire conservation of the quantity of matter in spite of the fact that it is never taught in school or at home. Moreover, no one talks about it, nobody tells them that there is such a thing, and children do not ask about it. Children are not rewarded for attaining conservation either. If it were a matter of learning the right answer, how would we explain where children have gotten the wrong answer and reasons, only a few months before? As Piaget pointed out repeatedly, this observation agrees with what the history of science tells us about resistance to evidence because it does not fit into previously constructed ways of thought. Thus, there is no reason to credit the child with a facile empiricism, readily fitting thought to experience.

Does this mean that Piaget is a nativist like Chomsky? There would be many reasons to think so. First, Piaget's claim to be a structuralist would lead one to presume that he espoused all the tenets of structuralism, although he always specified that he was a genetic structuralist and, as such, not a nativist. Second, he claimed that "cognitive processes seem, thus, to be at one and the same time the outcome of organic autoregulation . . . and the most highly differentiated organs of this regulation at the core of interactions with the environment so much so that, in the case of man, these processes are being extended to the universe itself" (Piaget, 1971, p. 34). There is a teleological note in the concept of autoregulation, although Piaget, aware of this, preferred to use the word *teleonomic.* There is also a ring of idealism in the conception of cognitive processes as organs, because it seems to give a material reality status to ideas (although Soviet psychologists, for instance, would consider this as utmost dialectical materialism).[1] A more accurate reading of this phrase would be that cognition does not occur in any one of the conventionally defined organs, but draws on them and reorganizes them in a new set of functional relations.

Third, the claim of universality and completeness of cognitive processes seems another sign in favor of nativism. If children, who grow up in such varied environments, all develop in the same way, they must somehow be impervious to environmental factors, and they must be preformed in some fashion. If children grow up in the same way everywhere, then development is a mere unfolding of inherent structures that are incipiently present in the germ plasm.

Piaget has been vulnerable to this interpretation of his work because of his

---

[1]For instance, see S. L. Rubinstejn: *Osnovy obscej psixologii* (The Fundamentals of General Psychology) 1940, trad. AN SSR M. (2 ve/zd. 1976) and; *Principi i puti razvitija psixologii* (Principles and Patterns of Development of Psychology), 1959/zd. AN SSR M. demonstrating, once again, that materialism is topsy-turvy idealism.

insistence on the universality of stages. It would be incumbent on the interactionist to produce evidence that commerce with the environment does affect the course of development. For this reason, in the 1950s, studies on the learning of Piagetian concepts and operations came to occupy an important place in the theoretical discussion.[2] To say the least, they demonstrated that it is not easy to invent a way of accelerating the child's movement through states of cognitive growth, that existing structures resist changes, and that the child's mind is no direct copy of the external reality presented by experimenter or teacher.

Insofar as this result supported Piaget's antiempiricism, it seemed quite satisfactory. But it did leave the way open to the unfolding interpretation. In the 1970s, there was a concerted effort in many quarters to show that Piagetian concepts and operations are indeed amenable to change through learning experiments. So long as the experiment is planned in ways that respect the child's existing structures and elicit the child's own activity, some acceleration of growth can be achieved. No one actually believes that it is possible to transform a young child overnight into an adult, thus modest effects are theoretically satisfactory. It should be added, however, that acceptance of this point implies a tacit acceptance of much of the structuralist approach.

To contrast his own position with empiricism and apriorism, Piaget sometimes labelled it *interactionism*. But this term has often been used in a sense that does not quite fit Piaget. Hardly anyone who considers the subject goes to either extreme: It is widely accepted that the child's mentality is neither entirely inherited nor entirely determined by environmental forces. A compromise seems in order and the question is then transformed: What are the proportionate contributions of heredity and environment in the determination of intelligence? More precisely, what are the proportionate contributions of *variants* in heredity and in environment to variations in intelligence? People formulating the issue in this way may well call themselves interactionists.

This formulation has at least two aspects that are unacceptable to Piaget: first, the idea that intelligence is an amount that can be measured, rather than a structure that must be described and whose functioning must be understood and; second, the idea that heredity and environment are, for each individual, fixed components that determine intellectual outcome without affecting each other, rather than vectors whose developmental significance changes incessantly, depending on the structures already achieved. There are two features of Piaget's approach to the environment that, although not unique in Piaget, are characteristic of his thinking and worth pointing out. The environment is not conceived as something that happens to the child, not as a stimulus that elicits a response. Rather, children seek out those features of the environment to which they can

---

[2]See the chapter: "Is child stimulation effective?" by Bovet and Vonèche in *Genetics, environment and intelligence,* edited by A. Oliverio (1977), for complete references and evolution of those researches.

meaningfully respond, both by assimilating them to existing structures and by accommodating those structures to make continued assimilation possible. The initiative belongs to the child. The ordinary conception of the environment as determining behavior, rather than behavior determining the environment, is an extreme expression of a commonplace adult achievement, that highly cultivated paralysis summed up in the phrase: "I only followed orders." We must admit that this is a state that can be attained, but it is not typical of childhood.

In Piaget, moreover, the environment is nonspecific. One does not need clay balls or jars of water to learn about conservation. The materials are everywhere and unavoidable; clenching and unclenching the fist is just as good as flattening out a ball of clay. But even such simple events are so rich, so open to various logical structurings, that it is the child who sees in each experience that which he or she can draw on to grow, as it must be at that moment.

Piaget sometimes labelled his position *constructivism* to capture the sense in which the child must make and remake the basic concepts and logical thought-forms that constitute intelligence. Piaget prefered to say that the child is inventing, rather than discovering ideas. This distinction separates him both from empiricism and from apriorism. The ideas in question do not preexist out there in the world only awaiting their discovery by the child; each child must invent them. By the same token, because ideas have no a priori external existence, they cannot be discovered by simple exposure.

But we do not think the term *constructivism* goes far enough in characterizing Piaget's position. It is possible to believe that children construct their own mentality through their own activity without any preoccupation whatsoever with the development of logical structures underlying intellectual life. Indeed, this describes the romantic ideal of many progressive educators. There is something more austere in Piaget's constructivism. It goes beyond mere logicism, or the attempt to characterize each stage of development by a logical model. Piaget proposed that the functioning of the logic of each stage determines the structure of the stage that follows.

We suggest that the phrase *logical determinism* captures this essential aspect of Piaget's thinking. Interactionism, constructivism, logical determinism summarize the entirety of the position Piaget came to call *genetic epistemology*.

If learning were very fast and our resulting image of the world a very accurate copy of an unambiguous reality, we would all be empiricists. If there were no learning at all, whatever intelligence we possessed could be due only to pre-formed structures, and we would all be apriorists. The conception of learning therefore occupies a strategic role in discussions of the relation between organism and environment, and it is important to understand what Piaget has done with it. First, he defined learning as having only a limited role within a larger process of the functioning and growth of structures. Second, he insisted that learning of specific behaviors or contents can only take place within existing structures: The individual's action on the world is itself the operation of a structure, and in the process the individual assimilates new information to that structure, which sometimes requires changing the structure. Third, structures grow according to laws that are not given in the behavioristic associationism of stimulus-response psychology, or in the Gestalt laws describing the direct perception of an organized world. The function of cognitive growth is not to produce schemes that are more and more veridical copies of reality, but to produce more and more powerful logical structures that permit the individual to act on the world in more flexible and complete ways.

Having said this much, let us reexamine a problem that has suffused and troubled this whole discussion: Is it really necessary to demonstrate empirically that Piaget's stages are affected by variations in the environment, in order to offer a good alternative to preformism?

Piaget's answer to this question was evident. He did not get involved in the so-called Genevan learning experiments conducted by Inhelder, Sinclair, and Bovet (1974). Why so? Certainly not because of a division of labor among Genevans. Most probably because, as a good old biologist, he knew better. Biologists do not need to raise children in an oxygen-deficient environment to demonstrate that the blood carries oxygen all over the body and that the complex mechanisms for the formation of blood and assimilation of oxygen are indispensable for normal development. Similarly, it is possible that there are some aspects of intellectual growth that are both indispensable for normal functioning and dependent for their development on properties of the environment that are to be found everywhere on earth. It is hard to imagine, for instance, a high level of intelligence functioning without the idea of a permanent object as an invariant. At least for us, human beings.

As a scientist interested in studying the growth of ideas, Piaget attempted to study fundamental ideas rather than trivial ones. A fundamental idea is an indispensable one. To the extent that he was successful in his choices, it would be difficult to demonstrate that the variables of growth he had chosen are accessible to environmental manipulation.

This is not to say that, as an interactionist, Piaget does not face the task of specifying the way in which the environment influences development. But two quite different strategies can be imagined for attacking this problem. One would be to imagine a method that produced some very easily detectable effects without disturbing normal functioning, such as the psychological equivalent of physical isotopic tracers. Another, which has been more popular among researchers in the last 30 years, is to choose as objects of study things that obviously vary, even if they are not so fundamental.

As usual Piaget favored a third strategy. Instead of a frontal attack on this problem, he prefered to show the example of collaborative work. Characteristically, his books were written with many collaborators (6 for his first book *Language and Thought* and 40 at the highest period of the International Center for Genetic Epistemology). In addition, there was public controversy with other prominent scientists: Vigotsky, Wallon, Michotte, and Bruner—a Russian, a Frenchman, a Belgian, and an American. Moreover, he mentioned the existence of a whipping-boy quite often to visitors: logical empiricism, attacked at every yearly symposium of the Centre.

This complex, multilayered process of socialized reflection and explanation that gives the work we call Piaget's its full complexity and its extraordinary variety, was the starting point of the present study of cognitive development and interaction. At this point, we would like to make certain theoretical considerations about the results of training studies.

EVALUATION OF THE EFFECTIVENESS
OF SPECIFIC TRAINING STRATEGIES

Bovet and Vonèche (1977) reviewed and evaluated training studies on Piagetian concepts. The most striking result of these short-term training experiments was their partial lack of effectiveness. When progress between pre- and posttest was reported, it was never clear whether it was due to learning only or to a combination of factors, including learning; indeed, because the subjects who seemed to have benefited the most from training were also variously described as older, more mature, more articulate, and more advanced. This meant that they were more developed in the natural process of mastering conservation. Indeed the bulk of the subjects belonged to the transitional substage of conservation acquisition. In addition, oscillations are characteristic of this period. Consequently, these subjects might have been erroneously categorized in a substage inferior to their competence.

If the main results of training had been the clear possibility to speed up cognitive development, it would have meant that such development was under direct social control, with the sorry recognition of the meaninglessness of the stage concept. If cognitive development depended solely on social transmission and/or properties of the stimuli, there would be no reason for an invariant sequence of development. Knowledge would come either *in toto* or in a different order for every individual experience. If, on the other hand, there had been no possibility whatsoever to alter the stepwise process of cognitive development, then the hypothesis of a mere unfolding of genetic competences would have gained some validity, at least to the extent that reasoning on the null hypothesis is logically tenable.

What was observed was a natural order of acquisition with the possibility of activating the natural, spontaneous process of equilibration by proper stimulation at the proper moment and in the proper way. It led some psychologists to hold the view that development proceded by crises or critical periods during which the organism, normally sealed-off from the environment, opens up to it.

This form of geneticism is unplausible for three main reasons. First, an individual does not sit listlessly waiting for something to happen, but is actively engaged in the world. In addition, any form of behavior always occurs in interaction with others. Moreover, this model of an alternation of sensitivity and insensitivity to the environment relies on a nativistic argument concerning a hierarchy of dispositions according to which putative later forms cannot be manifested in the absence or suppression of earlier ones.

The only acceptable position seems to be a logical one. It would show that the passage from one form of cognitive behavior to another is regulated by a double process of internal regulation and external argumentation. The role of external argumentation would be one of separating time development from mere chronological unfolding or mechanical descent. It would elicit the general architecture of schemata by opposition to the accumulation model for the acquisition of knowledge. More than a logical structure, what is important in learning is the dynamic role played by differences in developmental rates (Piaget called them *décalages*) among the various schemata constructed by the child so far. In this perspective, there would be a radical change in our concept of cognitive development. The hallmark of a stage would no longer be its logical structure but its internal architecture. The necessity, from a logical viewpoint, of any such architecture would then be an ex post facto explanation aimed at separating past experience from genesis considered as an ideal ordering of systems of thought in the developing organism.

Cultural regulation would no longer be the motor of change but its regulator. Its main function would be the incessant reorganization of the different levels of cognitive development within a given subject. The aim of such an activity is obvious: to maintain the functional invariance or homeostasis of the individual by integrating novelty to old schemata and by differentiating schemata among themselves.

There are two main conclusions that can be drawn from this perspective. The first one is the centrality of the concept of interaction in developmental theory. The second one is the fading away of structuralism and logicism.

Let us deal with the second point first, because it seems to constitute a departure from Piaget's own position emphasizing the structural aspects of development more than the functional ones. The reasons for such a departure are rather obvious by now. First, a certain number of data have been gathered that seem to demonstrate that development does not proceed by inclusion of less general and encompassing structures into larger and more abstract ones (Boden, 1979). Second, the logico-mathematical structures envisioned by Piaget were more or less dated (and are thus outdated now) historically, because they corresponded to the state of affairs in mathematical logic at the time of Piaget's training and early career. Third, the adequacy of Bourbaki mother- structures to psychological data has been questioned both by psychologists and mathematical logicians (Vonèche & Vidal, 1985).

The inadequacy of the logico-mathematical model has led some, including

Piaget's early collaborators at the beginnings of the Center for Genetic Epistemology,[3] to embrace cybernetics. The probabilistic model advocated by Piaget in the 1950s represented a first aborted attempt at cybernetics within his own perspective. Later on, other cybernetical approaches were proposed by Sloman (1982) and Boden (1979) among others. Unfortunately, these models presented weaknesses similar to those of the mathematical models, namely the straight-jacketing into structures not made to receive the body of developmental data.

Thus, the structural approach left something to be desired. So some people, such as Garcia[4] began to speak of systems instead of structures. Others, such as Inhelder[5] and her group, went for procedures instead of structures. Essentially, these moves were dictated by caution about psychologists' use of models external to their own science.

The position taken here does not go so far as strategies and individual procedures, but tries to look for something different from strong and heavy structures: the notion of an internal architecture of interactions. From the structural approach, it retains the notion of a formal causality instead of a mechanical one. This sort of spatialization (involved in terms such as structure and architecture) of the locus of explanation is conceptually structuralistic. But the space considered here is merely functional as in architecture, that is to say an interactive and dynamic organization and not a sort of Boolean algebra. In other words, what is abandoned here is a certain number of assumptions implicit in structuralism as applied to social sciences: (1) all social/cultural phenomena constitute systems of signs; (2) language is the paradigmatic example of a sign system, and therefore the techniques of linguistic analysis are applicable to all social/cultural phenomena; and (3) the structure of language and other sign systems provides the clue to the structure of the human mind.

What is advocated here is a model of development that includes the subject, the object, the instruments of knowledge, and the milieu to the extent that it lends the instruments of knowledge to the subject. So far, psychologists have privileged one of these aspects: the subject in the posterity of Kant, Hegel, and Marx, the object for the descent of British empiricism, the instruments among those fond of logical positivism, and the milieu for those sociologically inclined to advocate revolutionary changes. Structuralists have thought that they could es-

---

[3]For a good treatment of this question, see the introduction to *Epistémologie génétique et équilibration* by Inhelder, Garcia, and Vonèche. Neuchâtel, Paris, Montréal: Delachaux et Niestlé, 1977.

[4]See *Vers une logique des significations* by Jean Piaget and Rolando Garcia. Geneva: Murionde, 1987.

[5]See "Procedures and structures" by B. Inhelder edited by D. R. Olson, *The social foundations of language and thought,* New York: Norton, 1980 and "On generating procedures and structures in knowledge" edited by R. Groner and W. F. Bischoff, *Methods in Heuristics,* Hillsdale, NJ: Lawrence Erlbaum Associates, 1983.

cape making a choice by crossing over to the empire of signs. But their semiotic metaphor was a ghost in the machine as fallacious as the present all-pervading gene, our new animistic metaphor for power, modern version of Molière's *Virtus dormitiva* "by virtue of which opium puts your daughter to sleep."

Here we attempt to show that we cannot separate thought from its objects and the world from the way we construct it. In the children's explanations of physical causality illustrating this chapter, there is a plurality of metaphors that both simplify and "complexify" the "phenomena to be rescued," in Aristotle's apt phrase. This plurality of metaphors, which is also to be found in the thinking of great thinkers, as Gruber (1981) showed, indicates a complex and lively interaction across different levels of experience in the child. We have tried to show, in the following pages, how such an interaction builds up into an "architecture" both qualitatively and quantitatively identifiable by the experimenter. It becomes evident that children favor a logical approach to eliminating the specificities of the object, or alternatively, emphasize only the physical specificities and overlook general properties. Gradually, they will integrate these two approaches either in an elasticity model of the transmission of movement or in a shock one before synthetizing them into one more complex model equilibrating shock and elasticity. In such a view the concept of interaction in cognitive development is considerably enriched.

SOME THEORETICAL CONSIDERATIONS
ON INTERACTIONS IN COGNITIVE DEVELOPMENT

It has been argued by some epistemologists (Hamlyn, 1978; Haroutunian, 1983; Toulmin, 1971) that Piaget's notion of interaction could not meet the criterion of functionality. The argument could be summarized as follows: For Piaget, there is, first, an innate process of assimilation and accommodation and, second, a feed-back from the environment resulting (third) in a series of trials aimed at resolving the disequilibria between the organism and the environment. For these epistemologists, such a position is untenable. They see three main difficulties. First, the response of the environment to the activity of the organism is never direct. In fact, they claim, the environment does not act directly on the subject, but on the subject's view of the environment's action. Therefore, the subject cannot distinguish between real conflicts and pseudoconflicts taking place in the course of cognitive development, unless the subject is preprogrammed for it.

Second, difficulty arises because, in such a system of interaction, conventional categories, such as conservation, classification, or seriation, seem to be acquired more biologically than socially. Indeed, they raise the question of the biological origin of social conventions. The dilemma for them is the following: either one holds, as Lorenz does, that social behavior is biologically predetermined, or one has to recognize a specificity to the social environment. Clearly, an interactionist, in their opinion, at least, cannot adhere to the first horn of the dilemma and must resort to the second.

Their third difficulty has to do with the unspecified nature of the acquisition of cultural values. This difficulty is a variation on the second one. They do not accept the reduction of cultural factors to biological ones. This has been a long-standing misunderstanding between Piaget and philosophers. Whereas Piaget underlines a continuity from organic to social structures, they hold a dualistic position according to which there is a fundamental difference between the two structures. In general, values, intentions, and social conventions are not physio-logical, even though they might have neurological correlates.

As we have seen earlier, there is indeed a ring of idealism in Piaget's notion of cognition as an extension of organic functioning. But Piaget's model of cognition is by no means physiological but logical. The real difficulty lies in the passage from physiological to logical structures, as in the passage from action (sen-sorimotoric intelligence) to thought (operational intelligence). How does an ac-tion get some truth-value attached to itself? How does a practical goal-orientated behavior get transformed into a reversible operation?

Saussure and the French structuralists after him got around the problem by making a sharp distinction between *language* and *parole* or competence and performance. Performance, for them, was mere execution, a simple by-product of competence without real interest.

Piaget's solution is biological to the extent that truth and values in general have a biological value: survival and adaptation. At this point, one could raise the question of the survival value of truth. At first glance, people incapable of mastering the famous INRC group seem to survive as well as those who attain this last level of development. Obviously, Piaget did not think of this simple-minded version of survival. By survival and adaptation he meant an increasing capacity on the part of the subject to master the environment. This is evident because, at the earlier stages of development, an external perturbation upsets the system entirely. This is the case of instinctive and reflex behaviors that go on regardless of the destruction of the environment as in the case of the wasps that continue to drive a hole in a destroyed substratum. Later on, the subject, higher on the developmental scale, takes into account the perturbation as it happens. It interacts with it. Finally, it anticipates the perturbation as one of the potentialities of the system, as in the case of the scientist for whom reality is just one among a set of possible occurrences.

To a certain extent, Piaget's solution is too simple to be true. It leads too easily to infinite progress. There should be more to interaction than this op-timistic view about the externally constructive role of meeting the environment in any new experience. After all, living and growing up is not simply a success-story.

In fact, growing is the result of an equilibrium between the homeostatic regulatory forces of the organism, on the one hand, and the imbalances of external solicitations, on the other. This is indeed a difficult conquest. Let us think, for instance, of the baby learning to interact visually or vocally with the mother. We know that mothers stop looking at their blind babies very early. Why? Essentially because of a lack of feed-back. The mother looks at the newborn when she picks it up. Instinctively, the newborn baby turns his or her head in the direction of the mother who smiles at the baby. However, after the end of the reflex period, blind babies stop "looking" at their mothers. As a result, their mothers do not pick them up as often, which hurts feelings on both sides.[6]

The same is true for vocal interactions with deaf-mute children. This does not mean that mothers of handicapped children are bad mothers. Usually, they find rather quickly the channels of communication open to their child and operate on them. But it shows that, in the usual situation, when a baby coos and the mother responds to it by cooing back, the baby has to learn rather quickly the correct answer of cooing in turn within less than a few minutes in order to keep the interaction going to the end of infancy. This is a real feat even though it is a daily one.

At the opposite end of the developmental spectrum, another example is given by the genesis of formal operations in adolescents. Gruber and Vonèche (1976) showed that, for some creative adolescents (the subjects were Marx, James, Freud, Piaget, Bohr, and Darwin) entering the stage of formal operations takes different forms depending on the sociocultural and individual historical conditions under which the subjects were operating. Moreover, they have shown that for psychologists to be able to perceive these phenomena, a similar detachment from the social forces tending to reserve the notion of mental development exclusively for children is necessary. Fighting the inertia of normal science is not easy. It requires revolutionary thinking as well as favorable interactions with the environment. This is the reason why such thinking has to come at the right time in the right place to become the right idea.

AN EXPERIMENTAL INSTANCE OF COGNITIVE INTERACTION: CAUSALITY TRAINING

In order to illustrate what we have already written about cognitive interaction, we are going to consider the empirical study of training for causal explanations in 10- to 11-year-old children. This topic has some special relevance to cognitive interaction because it deals with several forms of interaction at once.

First, causality being a scientific category (at least at one moment in the

---

[6]Freedman, D. "Smiling in blind infants and the issue of innate versus acquired." *Journal of Child Psychology and Psychiatry,* 1964, *5,* 171–184.

historical development of scientific concepts) it is the result of a social transmission. The question is whether or not this transmission is Lamarckian. In other words, do we impose causality on the child from the outside by mere exercise and repetition? It is worthwhile to investigate the nature of this transmission by applying a training routine that will or will not demonstrate its effects on children's ways of thinking.

In addition, causality deals with objects. So in addition to the social transmission by interaction with the adult trainer, there will be an interaction with objects qua objects with specific physical properties and behavior.

Furthermore, working with children means dealing with developing minds. Hence further questions about the reception, perception, and understanding of the nature of the questions posed by the trainer, the nature of the objects presented, the dialogue with the adult, the status of argumentation for children and adults, the readiness to read an experimental evidence in the same or in a different way from the adult, the necessity or not to go beyond mere lawfulness into causality, and so forth.

The causality training situation thus presents a rich opportunity to analyze experimentally the role of cognitive interaction in cognitive development.

Among all the possible instances of physical causality that were interesting to study, we had to find one that would be both interesting for our own purpose and simple enough for children of the ages under scrutiny. We selected a situation where explanation would be rather straightforward and, at the same time, complex enough to lend itself to the sorts of variations necessary to an experimental design involving pre- and posttests as well as various training sessions.

> The general procedure was as follows: In the pretest: a billiard ball was launched against a concrete wall. In four training sessions during which not only was there a launching of a billiard ball, but also a foam ball, and a clay ball were launched against, respectively, a concrete wall, a foam wall, and a clay wall. The two posttest sessions were identical to pretest. The first posttest was given one week after the last training session, and the second posttest after four weeks, in order to check the durability of the training effects.

Prior to any experimentation with the material, 25 children were requested to anticipate the results of each of the launching conditions and to give an explanation for each of the expected outcomes. Additional explanations were requested after experimentation. In the course of asking these explanations, the experimenter either suggested some possible explanations—this is called by us the *didactic-dialectical method*—or simply observed the cognitive conflict provoked in the subjects' minds by the various experimental situations—this is the standard Piagetian approach to training called *cognitive conflict method*.

The information given to the child by the experimenter is not similar to that dispensed in a physics class situation. There is not a passive child and an active experimenter. On the contrary, there is a co-construction of knowledge by the child and the experimenter through a dialogue in which notorious Piagetian positive counter-suggestions are maximized. The experimenter's tasks consisted, on the one hand, in drawing children's attention to the deformations of the wall and of the ball, and on the rebound or lack thereof. On the other hand, the experimenter suggested a possible causal explanation based on elasticity.

The general experimental design used control-groups, and the general instructions were as follows: "We are going to launch balls against walls, and you will forsee whether the balls come back or not. After that, you will look at the balls and explain why they come back if they do, and why they didn't, if they don't. O.K.?"

Children's explanations were of two sorts: Either they concentrated on the elasticity model, or they elaborated a shock and transmission system of explanation.

In the shock model, three successive levels could be distinguished: (1) a conception of the wall as a passive obstacle to the passage of the ball; (2) an idea that the wall's main property is one of sending back and away any object hitting it; and, (3) an elaborate explanation involving both the transmission of a force to the wall and a retransmission of part of the same force, at least, by the wall to the ball, this force being proportionate to the force of launching the ball.

There are three successive levels as well in the elasticity model. At the first level, children simply observed the phenomenon of elasticity in the foam ball, which explains the rebound of the ball. Accordingly, they did not anticipate any rebound from the billiard ball because it was not perceptually elastic. After witnessing the rebound, children at this level did not accept the elasticity model suggested to them. This is in sharp contrast with the attitude of children at the second level who transformed the proposed explanation and imagined a sort of elastic material within the billiard ball in order to explain the rebound. At the third level, children accepted the explanation by elasticity of the concrete wall as the reason the billiard ball came back as well. In addition to these two different lines of analysis, shock versus elasticity, in a fourth superordinate level of explanation children join the two lines of explanations either by juxtaposing elasticity with shock or by combining them.

Together with this qualitative analysis, a quantitative analysis was made. The main results were as follows: with the didactic-dialectical method, 10 children out of 15 progressed from pretest to posttest I and a few continued to progress from posttest I to posttest II; no regression was observed. With the cognitive conflict method, no progress was observed. Children remained at the same low level of explanation.

This apparently striking difference could be attributed to the tutoring aspect of the first method. But this is not the case, because the experimenter gave only elasticity explanations, whereas children produced shock explanations as well.

The difference in outcome between the two methods of training could be explained in terms of differential interaction. The qualitative analysis of responses in the cognitive conflict group showed that children carefully avoided any real conflict. Subjects adopted therefore two opposite strategies that, when used in combination, are characteristic of any scientific explanation. Either they gave a purely local and specific explanation for each and every situation presented to them by a sort of ad hoc procedure. Or, they looked for a global and general explanation that could apply to all situations. But the elements of the situation that they considered stable and permanent across all the situations were nonpertinent and rather sketchy. For instance, the cause of the rebound against the wall was the roundness of the balls. In this example, rolling was not differentiated from rebounding, nor action from reaction.

More profoundly, what is at stake here is the status attributed by the children to the object or their interaction with it. These children perceived clearly that objects could be considered either as stable, permanent, and identical, or as changing, different, and transient. They thought that these two perspectives were mutually exclusive. Either they adopted the logical position—*la physique de l'objet quelconque* in Piaget's apt phrase—and rid the object of all its transient properties. Or, they adopted an empirical stand and looked for what William James called the varieties of experience.

In the first case and under the influence of the recent impressive conquest of operatory conservation, children selected such aspects of the balls as their roundness, their weight, their force, the fact that they were all launched from the same point in the same way, and so forth. They made gallant efforts at universalizing the properties of objects, and they were right: A good scientific explanation is universal indeed.

In the second case, they were overwhelmed by the singularity of every experimental situation. Sometimes the balls were hard, sometimes they were soft, sometimes rough, sometimes smooth, sometimes light, sometimes heavy, and so on. So much so that there was no possible unifying principle behind the varieties of experiences. So one must find an explanation specific to every single situation.

Thus, when the interaction is limited to the object, children this age tend to adopt a conservative strategy that avoids confronting the cognitive conflict. They pay attention alternatively to complementary aspects of the total situation. Consequently, they repeat, in the domain of causality, what they were doing, at the logical level, when they were preconservers and could not mentally hold together two dimensions varying symetrically. In such a situation, the interactions with objects tend to slow down the course of cognitive growth.

In the didactic-dialectical method the explanations proposed by the experimenter confront the children with all the facets of the objects. The experimenter provides the child with alternative readings of the objects. In turn, the child is lead to novel readings that are not in line with the experimenter's suggestions. For instance, when the experimenter proposed elasticity explanation, the child gave shock ones. In this way, our subjects understood that there was a way out of mutually exclusive explanations and that arguments along one line of explanation should be put into perspective with arguments along the other line of explanation, and they should be confronted and analyzed in such a way as to bring deeper cogency to their initial explanations. This is the reason why we call this sort of explanation dialectical: Children have to take into consideration the total situation as a synthesis between one line of possible explanation and the antithetic one to give a correct answer to the question posed. Such a synthesis proceeds necessarily also from a form of abstraction witnessed by the appeal to *virtual* forces in the explanation (here, the invisible elasticity of the billiard ball). The main result of this research is probably the impossibility for children, left to themselves, to go from actuality to virtuality, whereas when an experimenter trains them to manage their cognitive problems through a dialectical interaction they accomplish this passage without great trouble.

One could attribute this progress to social factors such as modelling, imitating, or emulating an adult figure or to pedagogical conditioning. There is, however, one strong argument against such explanations as we have already pointed out: the fact that children generated shock explanations by themselves although they were presented only with elasticity ones. This result seems to rule out any modelling or conditioning effects. The very creativity of children during the training sessions and the tests suffices to reject any form of direct social transmission. There was no passing down of instructions. Rather, our children enjoyed being taken seriously in a lively exchange of ideas instead of simply being observed by the adult. This is what we call the co-construction of knowledge. If this three-way form of interaction (subject-object-experimenter) is called social, then we did some social training. But we would like to emphasize the cognitive dimension of the process as well as the solidarity of its three interactive components. It is not merely adding a social dimension, as so many social psychologists claim, that stimulates progress. But it is the new system of interelations created by this addition that transforms the training situation by forcing a decentration in the way children think about causality. At the cognitive level at which they were taken, they already had many of the necessary ingredients to give correct causal explanations: logic, mathematical conservation, as well as empirical observation grids. But they could not put them together into a coherent whole. Alternative readings of objects provided by the experimenter forced them to reorganize the apparently antithetic elements at hand into a superordinate synthesis of their cognitive system.

It should also be pointed out that such a reorganization at a high level of cognitive functioning should not be attributed to maturation or to the passage at a higher stage of mental development. Internal biological factor explanations should be ruled out here as were, before, merely environmental ones. The point here again is merely architectural.

Progress in cognitive development is brought about by interaction only, contrary to current trends of thinking in the field that tend to view development either as entirely dependent on genetic factors or due to social pressures exclusively. In addition, it should be noted that this experimentation refutes the criticism levelled in the past against earlier Genevan training studies that the rather limited progress obtained in these studies demonstrated that Piaget's interactionism was in fact a special form of nativism. Finally, this research shows that dialogue is an effective mover. In a time of terrorism, holocausts, and all sorts of warfare, this conclusion could be worth some afterthought.[7]

CONCLUSIONS

There are three types of conclusions that can be drawn from this chapter: one about learning, one about cognitive development, and one about interaction.

As far as learning is concerned, we have four simple principles. First, it is the learner who does the learning; second, the learner does it in her or his present; third, what matters most in learning is to go on with learning, and fourth, all learning is learning something. These simple principles demonstrate that some questions that are much debated now are either unreal or falsely posed. For instance, once the learning individual is placed at the centre of the learning process, what counts is what is learned, not how it is taught (teachers, books, or machines). If all learning is learning something, then reliance on one method or another becomes impossible. If learning has to meet the present of the learner, then some forms of learning are dead for Dewey's reasons: They do not meet the living present of the learner (his/her "cognitive capacity," as developmental psychologists call it). If what is important in learning is going on learning, then learning should not be limited to certain age groups and institutional settings.

Cognitive development bridges the gap between learning and interaction, because it provides the facts for understanding mechanisms that assure the transition from one level of knowledge to the next. In this respect, the most important conclusion that appears to follow from the findings reported here involves the different subsystems. At first these develop in relatively independent but partially parallel ways and interact in a complex manner, thus resulting in further elaboration of the subsystems in question.

So interaction appears at different levels in this chapter: interactions among the mental structures of the growing child, interactions with the features of the object, interactions among those features at the sensory, motoric, perceptual, representational, and conceptual levels, but also interactions with the experimenter.

Consequently, both interaction and interactionism require further analysis.

---

[7]For a detailed analysis of the experiment, see Bovet, M., Parrat-Dayan, S., Vonèche, J. Comment engendrer une explication causale par apprentissage? 1. Le rôle du dialogue, 2. Le rôle de l'objet, *Enfance*, 4, 297–323, 1987.

Interactionism does not arise from nothing. It is prepared by some aspects of Piaget's genetic epistemology and of system theories, discoveries in molecular and developmental biology, cognitive psychology, and ethology. It reframes some intractable problems in these fields and offers an alternative way of conceptualizing form and causation, change and variability, normality and necessity. Most of the time however, interactionism is only cosmetic in the sense that it simply rephrases the classical idea that there are two kinds of development: one to manifest the inherited form (the gene) and another for everything else. This is the standard nature-nurture opposition. This sort of interactionism is completely vacuous and obnoxious. Another sense of interaction emphasizes the necessity of viewing transactions between organisms altering their environments and being, in turn, altered by this intercourse. In this sense, what is argued for is a view of causality that gives weight to the idea that what a cause causes is contingent and thus is itself caused by a reciprocal selectivity of influences. What is central here is the idea of a mutual dependence of causes by opposition to the Cartesian reductionist confusion of perturbation with cause and to the Lockean mechanical division of causality into a concatenation of antecedents and consequents.

In such a view, the old opposition between nature and nurture becomes a false problem as unreal as a meaningless question, because there are no ghosts in the machine, only persons in the world, thinking, feeling, intuiting, sensing, deciding, acting, and creating without a need for programs in the machine, preprogramed wirings in the brain, and all the rest of metaphors for genes as ghost-in-the-machine of Man. Conversely, there is no place either in interactionism for a mere social historical reductionism to the environment à la Vygotsky, Leontiev, and Luria.

As unpopular as they are nowadays, we felt the need to restate these basic tenets of interactionism at the end of this chapter.

REFERENCES

Berlyne, D., *Théorie du comportement et opérations*. Paris: Presses Universitaires de France, 1960.

Boden, M. A. *Piaget*. Brighton: Harvester Press, 1979.

Boden, M. A. Chalk and cheese in cognitive science. *Cahiers de la Fondation Archives Jean Piaget*, 1982, *2*, 2–3, 29–50.

Bovet, M., & Vonèche, J. Is child stimulation effective? In A. Oliverio (Ed.), *Genetics, environment and intelligence*. Amsterdam: Elsevier North-Holland Biomedical Press, 1977.

Gruber, H. E. *Darwin on man*. Chicago: Chicago University Press, 1981.

Gruber, H. E., & Vonèche, J. Réflexions sur les opérations formelles de la pensée. *Archives de Psychologie*, 1976, *44*, 171, 45–55.

Hamlyn, D. W. *Experience and the growth of understanding*. London: Routledge & Kegan Paul, 1978.

Haroutunian, S. *Equilibrium in the balance*. New York: Springer-Verlag, 1983.

Inhelder, B., Sinclair, H., & Bovet, M. *Learning and the development of cognition*. London: Routledge & Kegan Paul, 1974.

Piaget, J. *Biology and knowledge*. Chicago: Chicago University Press, 1971.

Inhelder, B., Sinclair, H., & Bovet, M. *Learning and the development of cognition.* London: Routledge & Kegan Paul, 1974.

Piaget, J. *Biology and knowledge.* Chicago: Chicago University Press, 1971.

Saussure, F. de, *Cours de linguistique générale,* Paris: Payot 1922.

Sloman, A. Computational epistemology. *Cahiers de la Fondation Archives Jean Piaget,* 1982, *2,* 2–3, 51–97.

Toulmin, S. The concept of "stages" in psychological development. In T. Mischel (Ed.), *Cognitive development and epistemology.* New York: Academic Press, 1971.

Vonèche, J. J., & Vidal, F. Jean Piaget and the child psychologist. *Synthese,* 1985, *65,* 121–138.

4 Social Interaction as Tutoring

David Wood
Department of Psychology
University of Nottingham

INTRODUCTION

How much should we claim for the role of instruction in ontogenesis? Clearly, it would be easy to demand too much: to fall prey to what Piaget termed "magical thinking," whereby we attribute to the effects of instruction what is properly an achievement of the child. In this chapter, I attempt to etch out four dimensions or aspects of intellectual and social development in which formal and informal instruction play a major role. I argue that interactions between the developing child and more knowledgeable others lead to the creation of what I term *socio-sensory-motor structures* and to the formation (for the child) of new means-ends procedures. Such interactions are also implicated in the development of children's abilities for "self-regulation" and help to form the child's emerging concept of "self-as-learner."

Whilst stressing the importance of tutoring, I begin by acknowledging the genuine *interactive* or bidirectional nature of the developmental processes involved. Nor do I challenge the view that developing children are constructive architects of their own understanding. Indeed, I examine aspects of self-correction and self-instruction that, I argue, provide clear evidence of self-perfection and self-organization in cognitive and linguistic development. However, the epistemic activity of the child is often enveloped within the more overarching competence of others. It is social interactions that have this tutorial flavor that concern me here.

Issues concerning the nature and role of social interaction in ontogenesis divide contemporary theories of development. Debates about the process of imitation, for example, and about the role of modelling in development are symptomatic of more general disagreements about the nature of knowledge and the processes involved in coming to know. The stance adopted and explored here shares some common ground with Piagetian theory but also departs from it in some important ways. Although Piaget (1968) did afford an important role for social interaction in his theory, that role is limited, judged in relation to the position adopted here. Believing that inter-psychic and intra-psychic functioning develop toward the same operations of mind, Piaget's (1959) theory leads to an emphasis on *cognitive conflict* as the cornerstone of social constraints on ontogenesis. Thus, for example, two children at a similar stage of development may facilitate each other's cognitive development when they find themselves in disagreement. This motivates disequilibration and, eventually, the construction of more overarching intellectual schemes. Some evidence favoring this hypothesis exists (e.g., Doise & Mugny, 1984, Glachan & Light, 1982), and I do not wish to gainsay it. However, I suggest that an exclusive emphasis on cognitive conflict ignores processes of learning that have to do with the perfection of new schemes of action, recognition of patterns, regularities, practices, and rules. Recognition of regularities in nature, I argue, and the perfection of the ability to participate in and exert control over the processes that yield them, often (though not always) come about in the course of social encounters between the immature and more knowledgeable others.

Some time ago, in company with J. S. Bruner and G. Ross (Wood, Bruner, & Ross, 1976), I presented an analysis of tutorial interactions between adults and 3- to 5-year-old children in which, amongst other things, we argued that tutorial interactions of the kind we were studying were made possible by the fact that children are able to recognize but not yet produce states of the world that we were attempting to help them to bring about. Such recognition/production gaps, or precocious aspects of perception, as Piaget might have termed them, provide space for instruction. By means of a number of what we termed "scaffolding functions," one more knowledgeable than the learner may help to bridge such gaps, essentially by activating problem solving in the child. By helping children to attain goals that they can recognize but not initially achieve, instruction enables novices to reach higher levels of competence than they can achieve alone. Vygotsky (1978, p. 86) of course, had earlier theorized in similar (though broader) terms. He coined the now familiar expression "zone of proximal development" to draw attention to the gap that exists between a person's competence in some task or activity when they receive help from a more knowledgeable other and what they are able to achieve alone. I talk more about this concept and its theoretical justification later.

In evaluating the general significance of these ideas, we confront the issue raised at the start; how much should we rightly claim for a theory of instruction? Although instruction by another may serve to reduce gaps between perceptual and procedural understanding, I think we have to acknowledge that children sometimes, perhaps even generally, achieve such closure for themselves. Studies of language acquisition offer the clearest and most compelling empirical support for this contention (see Wood, 1988, for a fuller treatment). Observational, experimental, and intervention studies have each identified clear instances of self-correction by children. Investigations of the development of skill in narration in children aged between 4 and 10 years of age reported by Hickman (1985), for instance, provide many examples of children's spontaneous efforts at paraphrase and self-correction in storytelling. Such attempts are particularly evident in the narratives of 7-year-olds. Hickman reported that although not all attempts at self-correction result in less ambiguous more mature-sounding verbalizations, many do. These are achieved without any direct intervention or correction by others. Similarly, in a detailed study of children's developing command of the use and understanding of the determiner systems in English and French, Karmiloff-Smith (1979) cited cases where, during the course of experimental trials, children modified their own acts of communication to reduce the level of ambiguity in what they had to say. Thus, although children as young as 5 years of age were able to perform the experimental tasks set, they did so in less economical, more verbose and ambiguous ways than older children. Their success, however, showed that they could meet the needs of their listener in such contexts. But mere success did not, in the longer term, satisfy them, because they went on to develop more economical means of reference and classification. Such evidence, I suggest, implies that children must have some sense of what sounds right or what sounds more mature before they themselves are able to generate speech that fully satisfies their sense of correctness. Knowing what more mature speech sounds like, they are able to create, comprehend, and work on their own linguistic problem spaces.

Is the process of self-instruction implicated in such phenomena itself influenced by previous experiences as a learner-under-tuition? Put another way, what does the child internalize during the course of social interactions? I have already indicated that Vygotsky's concept of the zone of proximal development carries more theoretical weight than the notion of scaffolding. His concept is part of a general theory of cultural transmission, which holds that intra-psychic mental functions have their origins in, and take their form from, inter-personal activities in the external, social world. For Vygotsky, it seems, a child not only internalizes means-ends procedures towards the achievement of recognizable goals but also practices of self-regulation that are mental derivatives of the instructional process itself.

TUTORING AND DEAFNESS

Whereas the theme of this chapter is the study of aspects of social interaction viewed as tutoring, its topic is a developmental study of children who are born with a profound hearing loss or who become deaf before they learn to speak. By studying the impact of this sensory disability on processes of informal tutoring and more formal teaching, I believe we can cast into relief and explore the consequences of these social practices on human development generally. The main thesis I put forward and articulate emphasizes that the impact of deafness on personal and intellectual development cannot be understood nor explained if we consider only the relation between the child and the physical world, or the impact of the disability on the development of speech per se. Rather, I argue that the deaf child is likely to encounter a range of secondary handicapping conditions. These are a consequence of the impact of the child's disability on processes of social interaction that normally serve implicit tutoring functions and that facilitate the transmission of culture and competence. The two main topics that provide the context for this endeavor are the study of the transition from preverbal to symbolic communication and the role of modelling and imitation in the social construction of knowledge.

Until recently, very little was known about the early development of deaf children. Diagnosis of hearing-impairment usually occurs in the second or third year of life. Late diagnosis, coupled with the relative rarity of such children (most estimates put the incidence at around 1 per 1,000 births in developed countries) explains why so few deaf babies have been studied during the period when, normally, the foundations of communication are being constructed. However, taken in company with the study of somewhat older deaf children, the few studies that have been undertaken of deaf infants permit us to draw some tentative conclusions about the nature of their early development.

Deafness, by its nature, not only inhibits or prevents access to sound and speech, it is also likely to disrupt, in developmentally important ways, the formation of relationships between children and those around them. These disruptions, I argue, have an impact not only on the development of communication but also on aspects of cognition and on the nature of self-concepts. According to the thesis, put boldly tutorial functions that are often an unrecognized, implicit feature of everyday interactions between infants and adults are typically distorted in interactions between deaf babies and their hearing parents.

Observations of interactions between young deaf children and their parents (usually the mother, who, in most studies, is a hearing person) converge on a number of generalizations. Mothers of young deaf children, compared to those involved with hearing children of the same age, are described as "less permissive, more intrusive, more didactic, less creative, less flexible, and as showing less approval of their children" (Meadow, 1980, p. 80). When children begin to talk, mothers are less likely to respond contingently to their efforts at communication (Gregory & Mogford, 1981; Meadow, 1980). They tend to direct the verbal interaction through questions and make frequent attempts to repair what the child has tried to say.

At one level of description, such results are compatible with the self-evident conclusion that communication and mutual understanding are difficult to achieve with the deaf baby. The behavior of the parent is obviously a result of the baby's problems. But the adult's behavior, in turn, is the source of other personal, social, communicative, and cognitive difficulties for the baby. There is, so to speak, a bidirectional spiral of causation rather than a simple linear, cause-effect sequence involved.

The deaf infant, possessing little or no awareness of sound, has to discover the process of communication in early social encounters in ways that are not demanded of the hearing infant (Wood, Wood, Griffiths, & Howarth, 1986). To articulate and explain the nature and origins of this hypothesis, it is necessary for me to outline some of the findings that have come from studies of preverbal interactions between hearing infants and their caretakers in the first 18 months or so of life.

During the first 4 months or so of life, the hearing infant finds the human face, particularly when it is animated and making sounds, amongst the most compelling sources of attention. At about 4 months, around the time that reaching appears on the scene, infants begin to pay more attention to objects, events, and happenings in their immediate physical context. A caretaker, during this phase, when interacting with the infant, is likely to follow their flow of attention and say something, often with rather exaggerated vocal inflexions, about what it is the baby is looking at. At around age 10 months, the infant begins to coordinate people and objects (e.g., Brazelton, 1982, Bruner, 1983). Such coordinations occur in various ways. Games like giving and receiving objects, and the use of gesture and vocalization to attract attention or to demand service, for instance, emerge at around this time.

By 13 months, the baby is usually showing signs of more elaborate and sophisticated involvement in communication. For example, and this observation will prove of importance later, the infant at this age begins to draw out triangles of reference, looking, sequentially, from his or her partner in interaction to the object of communication; a phenomenon that Masur (1983) referred to as ''dual-directional signaling.'' At the same time, the coordination of gesture and vocalization emerges (Zinober & Martlew, 1985). Although infant pointing is observed at around 9 months of age, it is not coordinated with vocalization nor does it involve attention to the partner in interaction. Once dual-directional signaling appears it is increasingly likely, for a time, that when the child points and looks at his partner in interaction he or she will also vocalize. Zinober and Martlew suggested that the concurrent emergence of these various features of communication provide sufficient empirical grounds for the attribution of intentional communication to the infant. Soon after, of course, speech per se emerges.

Contrast this state of affairs with the findings of a longitudinal study of the development of communication in severely and profoundly deaf children (Wood et al., 1986, Tait & Wood, 1987). These children were filmed at three monthly intervals in face-to-face interactions with their teacher. At the beginning of the study, the children were aged between 3 and 5 years of age. Although at different stages of preverbal communicative development, none was yet able to converse. In order to assess their development during the 18-month period of study, close transcriptions were made of their vocalizations and gestures and of their patterns of visual attention.

What we sought from our observations were the answers to a number of questions. First, where did the child look while the teacher was talking to him? Did he look at her, or at the thing being talked about (in the early stages, all talk concerned things and events in the here and now), or was he looking elsewhere? Children varied in this respect. One, on the first recordings, almost never looked at the teacher nor at the object of communication. Other children did pay some attention to the teacher, though most of their time was spent looking at the thing being talked about. There were more subtle variations from child to child in the timing of attention and attention shifts relative to the teacher's speech. The patterns of attention of most of the children, on the early recordings, did not coincide with what the teacher was saying and doing. They were, for instance, just as likely to look away from the teacher while she was still speaking as they were to wait until she had finished. Given the severity of these children's hearing losses and their short acquaintance with hearing aids (their average age of diagnosis was 2 years, 3 months), it is certain that they could not understand what was being said to them when they were not looking at the interlocutor. Indeed, at this stage there was little evidence of comprehension when they did look at the teacher while she talked to them. They rarely, for example, responded to what she had said either by gesture or vocalization.

When (as most did) the children discovered how to integrate their attention with the temporal organization of teacher talk, some began immediately to vocalize in the turns left to them. There was a strong statistical relation throughout the period of study between the temporal patterning of their looking (i.e., the proportion of teacher speech-time the child spent looking at the teacher) and the probability that the child would respond vocally when the teacher ceased speaking. It was some months, however, before some of the children, having achieved dual-directional signaling, began to vocalize predictably within the turn-taking structure of the discourse. Finally, again after varying lengths of time, children began to play an increasingly autonomous and active role in discourse. They began to tell lies, interrupt the teacher, elaborate on answers to questions, open up topics of conversation, and tease.

Not all children achieved this state of affairs, and there are serious educational questions that should be (and since, have been) asked about the value of an oral approach to their education (as opposed to an approach implicating sign language). However, this is not the place to address what is a complex, emotive, and highly controversial topic. The main point for present purposes is to underline the fact that evidence of vocal communication in these children was closely predated by the emergence of dual-directional signaling, as has been found with much younger, hearing children. The establishment of reciprocity and structured interaction was a precursor to the development of symbolic communication.

Why should these deaf children take so long to master what seem to be visually mediated, nonverbal foundations of communication? The answer to this question, I suggest, holds out some important implications for our understanding of the implicit, tutorial functions involved in everyday social encounters with young hearing infants.

TUTORING AND THE FORMATION
OF SOCIO-SENSORY-MOTOR STRUCTURES

The hearing infant's experience of sound in the first 10 months of life plays an important role in the development of not only verbal but also so-called nonverbal communication. I suggest that when, as several studies show, adults talk over the young infant's experiences of the world, they coordinate the sounds of their voice with his or her visuo-motor activities. What emerges from such experiences are not sensory-motor but sensory-sensory-motor or socio-sensory-motor structures. With both major distance receptors intact, the infant's visual experiences are suffused with sounds. Classification and the development of concepts are not simply a product of coordinations achieved between an infant's actions and their direct sensory consequences on an inanimate world. Rather, such coordinations are often enveloped in speech sounds produced by others and contingent on the infant's stream of activity. Sounds are an implicit part of the infant's experience of the world. Speech creates the foundations for the beginnings of socially based segmentation or highlighting of actions and their consequences, leading to the classification and structuration of experience. Sounds thus possess meaning before the origins of speech in the child. That meaning may not be representational (rather, being presentational) but to the extent that sounds affect an infant's state of being in relation to objects, qualities and events, they are forming the foundations of interpretation and understanding.

Speech sounds made by others in his presence happen to a baby who can hear them. They are often speech sounds with distinctive acoustic attributes having special qualities of timing, amplitude, volume, and temporal organization (Bruner, 1983). Well before the emergence of the baby's first words, there is ample evidence of sensitivity and differential responses to such features of speech on the baby's part (Menyuk, 1971, chapter 3). The infant's state of being can be modulated by another's voice. Indeed, even the movements and emotional states of neonates can be modified through sound. For example, loud percussive sounds tend to startle or cause freezing, whereas low frequency sounds sooth and inhibit distress. Babies aged 8 months respond differentially and systematically to the intonation patterns of declaratives and interrogatives and their babbling shows evidence of contagion from their host langauge. Their vocalizations display supra-segmental contours similar to some of those found in adult speech (Nakazima, 1962).

On both receptive and expressive criteria, then, we have evidence that infants show a great deal of sensitivity and responsivity to speech sounds in the first year of life. The fact that hearing babies, but not deaf ones, begin to coordinate objects and people at 10 months also implies that the hearing infant's experience of sound during the stage at which he or she is attending to objects, events and some of the sensory consequences of his or her own activities plays an important role in the achievement of that coordination. When, for example, a young baby turns from an object or happening to his or her mother after she has uttered a distinctive or surprising sound (e.g., Bruner, 1983 p. 73) the foundations for dual-directional signaling are being laid. Sounds of caution, surprise, fear, approval, negation and the like become coordinated with things, places, people, and activities in ways that reflect their social significance and value.

When we talk over an infant's experiences, whatever our intentions in so doing, we are involved in natural tutoring. Babies who are robbed of such experiences lack the necessary basis for the development of communicative competence and all that this entails. It might be argued, however, that the slower development of preverbal communication in deaf infants arises as a consequence of some generalized, cognitive delay. If one subscribes to the view that the construction of the object, on Piagetian criteria, is a necessary, cognitive basis for the development of verbal symbolism, then any such delay would clearly be expected to result in arrested communication and language. Two lines of evidence militate against this hypothesis, however. Although few studies have been made of the cognitive development of deaf infants in the first year of life, for reasons already mentioned, one by Best and Roberts (1976) provides no evidence for any cognitive delay as indicated by performance on Piagetian tests of the substages of sensory-motor development. Studies of the development of sign language in deaf babies of deaf parents (who represent between 5% and 10% of the total population of preverbally deaf children) provide no evidence for linguistic delay. Although I know of no studies of such infants in the first year of life, the finding that first signs and aspects of early sign syntax develop in the second year of life and are not delayed (Quigley & Paul, 1984, pp. 95–97) is difficult to reconcile with the view that some general, cognitive delay in deaf infants is responsible for the findings already outlined.

Once the child's communication and language have been de-contextualized, so that the support of objects and happenings in the physical context of a speaker and listener ceases to be a sine qua non for the achievement of mutual understanding, then visual attention may remain locked on the current speaker and the demand for divided visual attention declines. However, whenever it is necessary to negotiate the meaning of a new symbol or a symbolic expression, be this made in reference to an object, quality, procedure, or whatever, the deaf child faces problems of divided attention, the need to employ the visual modality to monitor both acts and objects of communication.

This observation leads me to the core of the thesis I am attempting to articulate. The cognitive demands acting on the deaf child in working out what others are attempting to communicate, at whatever stage of development, in spontaneous or contrived, informal or formal instructional encounters, are more formidable than those facing the hearing child. Such demands on the children, I argue, are also likely to create problems for their interlocutor or tutor. Where such problems are not recognized or solved intuitively, communication, tutoring, and formal instruction will be disrupted. The processes involved may break down or, as becomes evident, lead to adverse consequences for the child. Thus, the transmission of knowledge and the facilitation of understanding are threatened not simply by impeded access to sound, but by distorted and sometimes destructive effects of deafness on processes of natural tutoring and more formal teaching. Let me explore and illustrate this argument with a couple of examples.

Attempts to introduce sign language into hearing homes of deaf babies demonstrate that more is at stake in helping to foster communication than the substitution of one language by another. Also important is the organization, timing, and content of parental communication. There are a few studies of the use of sign language by hearing adults with deaf infants and young children (e.g., Marmor & Petitto, 1979; Swisher & Thompson, 1985). To date, these agree in showing that hearing people are less skillful and successful in sign communication than are deaf, native signers. This is not simply because the hearing lack fluency in the production and concatenation of signs, but because they may not communicate in the same way as the deaf. Deaf parents are more likely than hearing signers to honor the temporal structure of the infant's activities to create a communicative system contingent on his or her activities and inferred mental states (Mogford, Gregory, & Hartley, 1980). Deaf parents are more likely to wait until the infant's attention comes naturally to focus on them before they attempt to communicate. Hearing parents tend to be more intrusive and overtly didactic, sometimes trying, literally and physically, to orchestrate the infant's role in the interaction to ensure his attention. They may, for instance, turn the child's head towards themselves, or try to insinuate their own face into the child's visual field. In so doing, they not only fail to solve their communication problems but also generate other sources of difficulty and frustration. In effect, they occasion a *reversal of contingency*. The infant whose head is tugged to one side or who finds a face obscuring his or her view, is likely to find the structure of his or her own activities dislocated and his or her own intentions frustrated. Even if the child recognizes the fact that the actions of the parent represent an intention to communicate, the child has to work out what lies behind their actions, diagnosing what is in their head as well as discovering what it is that they intend to refer to.

In formal learning situations, all children come, eventually, to face such problems. Indeed the direction of contingency in an interaction, who is contingent on the demands of whom, is one criterion that often marks off informal, spontaneous tutoring from intentional, formal teaching. It seems reasonable to suppose, however, that such demands lie beyond the competence of babies. Certainly, what we have discovered from studies of early communication between parents and infants indicate that it is usually the mature who strive to make their actions and efforts at communication contingent on the activities of the immature. Perhaps, then, the finding that interactions between hearing parents and deaf babies are often described as more negative in emotional tone and less mutually satisfying comes as no surprise.

What evidence we have about the way in which hearing parents and teachers use sign language implies that they tend to get the timing of communication wrong. Signing should begin when the infant's attention is fully trained on the interlocutor. This seemingly obvious requirement is far more difficult for a hearing person to achieve than one might suspect. Their natural, intuitive knowledge of communication, the very organization of their action in interaction, rests on the implicit assumption that others are in a position to receive and understand what they wish to communicate even when their eyes are not trained on the speaker. Such tacit expectations and the behavioral organization that embodies them are deeply at variance with the demands of skill in a visually based medium of communication; whether that system rests on movements of the hands or vocal apparatus.

TUTORING AS THE CONTINGENT CONTROL
OF LEARNING: FORMING MEANS-ENDS
PROCEDURES

Despite the fact that studies of nonverbal intelligence in the deaf population have revealed scoring distributions that are near normal, deaf children, on average, show much lower levels of academic achievement than their hearing peers (e.g., Quigley & Paul 1984, pp. 32–52). Even on nonverbal versions of Piagetian tests of concrete operational thinking, deaf children usually lag behind their hearing peers. Estimated delays in different concrete operational tasks range from 2 to 8 years (see Meadow, 1980, pp. 59ff). Attempts to demonstrate formal operational thinking in deaf people usually fail. Testing deaf children, particularly to explore their ability to reason abstractly, analogically, or hypothetically, creates many problems that I do not attempt to evaluate here. In general, however, the findings of experimental investigations of developmental stages in deaf children point to, at least, some delay, even in task domains which supposedly tap mental operations that children construct through their commerce with nature. Furth (1966) suggested that such experimental findings can be attributed to "experiential deficit." Here, I wish to explore the thesis, previously outlined, that the experiential factors involved rest on disrupted processes of tutoring and instruction.

A few years ago, I presented some of the findings that arose from a study of tutoring with deaf children between 3 and 5 years of age (Wood, 1980). The study was inspired by two main questions. Is it possible to teach preschool deaf children how to perform a task that, without instructional help, hearing children only master at around 7 to 8 years of age? Do the principles of instruction that dictate the way in which preschool hearing children learn also apply to the deaf? I rehearse some of the main findings here before drawing further implications from this study.

The task employed confronts children and their tutors with twenty-one blocks that can be assembled using a rather complicated arrangement of pegs and holes to form a pyramid. In order to complete the construction, children have to pay attention to the size and relative orientations of sets of four blocks and, having assembled these, pile them in an appropriate serial order to complete the pyramid. In previous studies with hearing children, we conceptualized and analyzed the instructional process in two related ways. An adult, intervening to help a child, might perform a number of scaffolding functions. For example, young children experience problems with this task when, having put two pieces together, they have to put the made-up pair to one side until they have assembled another (which can then be joined to the first to produce a four-piece level of the pyramid). By any number of devices, say by resting a restraining hand on the first-made pair, a tutor can help to organize the child's activities. Young children, having made a pair, usually attempt to add a third to it. The material resists their efforts. Basically, children encounter a detour problem in which they have to put aside a subsolution, work at another subsolution and then return to the main goal. By helping the child to avoid trying to add a third block to the initial pair the tutor ensures that the learner does not become frustrated nor lose sight of the goal by working at an insoluble subsolution. The tutor may also act, in so doing, as an external aid to memory. Should the child forget a previously constructed pair while concentrating on making another, the tutor may remind the child of its existence. They may also highlight critical features of the material, say size or the shape of a peg, which the child has overlooked or does not see as criterial. These and other scaffolding functions serve to augment and supplement children's limited expertise and information-handling capacities until they have gained sufficient local knowledge to free-up capacity. They are then able to appreciate the wider temporal and spatial context of their actions.

In a later series of studies, we looked in more detail at the moment-by-moment structure of tutorial interactions employing the concepts of "shared programs of action," "contingency," "control," and "region of sensitivity to instruction." Briefly, for these things have been described several times elsewhere, we conceptualize the instructional-learning process as one involving a shared program of activity in which the various decisions and operations that make up a plan for completing the task are distributed between tutor and tutee. Instructions and suggestions are classified in terms of one of five "levels of control." These range from demonstration, in which the instructor takes full responsibility for executing a particular part of the plan, to "general verbal prompts" such as "Now you make something," which leave the task of deciding on the next subgoal, the critical features that should guide selection of appropriate material, and the operations involved in construction to the child. Contingency is defined as instruction that is paced by moment-to-moment signs of success and failure by the child. So, where a child shows signs of success, any ensuing instruction should offer more scope for child control and greater degrees of freedom for potential failure. Following on failure, more help should be given immediately; control should be increased and degrees of freedom for error reduced.

Tutors who are maximally contingent (which is not nearly so easy as it may sound) effectively concentrate their instructions in the child's (ideally everchanging) region of sensitivity to instruction. Experiments have demonstrated that children taught in this way are more competent in doing the task alone, following instruction, than those taught less contingently (Wood, Wood, & Middleton, 1978).

Although we found that our sample of twelve deaf preschoolers did, in varying degrees, learn how to do this task, when we correlated our measure of tutorial contingency with their performance we found no significant relation. Later, we discovered the reason why. Briefly, two of our levels of control (general and specific verbal instructions such as "You make something" and "You need a piece with a hole in it") were defined in exclusively verbal terms. With the sound turned off on our video-recordings, however, we found that there were usually easily interpretable nonverbal sources of instruction that accompanied telling. When we analyzed the instruction in purely nonverbal terms, we found a significant correlation between our measure of instructional contingency and how well deaf children learned the task.

What is of importance here, however, was the finding that there was no positive correlation between the verbal and nonverbal contingency measures for the teachers of the deaf who acted as tutors in this study. Indeed, the correlation was negative: Teachers judged most contingent on the nonverbal measure came out very low on the verbal one. In contrast, the correlation between verbal and nonverbal activity for mothers tutoring their hearing children was extremely high. Put in other terms, although there was a close relation for the tutors of hearing children between nonverbal and verbal aspects of instruction, this was not the case for those attempting to teach the deaf.

A convincing explanation for this phenomenon would require many examples of the way in which the content, timing, and focus of nonverbal and verbal instruction varied from tutor to tutor. In general terms, however, the reason why some teachers were successful and others were not depended on the extent to which what they said and did conveyed similar information, and on the timing of instruction in relation to the deaf child's flow of attention. To illustrate: When a hearing child gets into difficulty, say he joins two pieces with a peg and hole but one piece is too large, a tutor might say to the child, "I think that one looks too big." At the same time, the tutor may touch the blocks, perhaps tracing their contour to illustrate a lack of symmetry. The tutee, meanwhile, should he or she wish, can not only listen to what the tutor says but also watch what the tutor does. The meaning or implication of what is being said is complemented and, potentially, established by what is being shown. This, we have argued, is an aspect of the process whereby the context-specific, procedural meanings of symbolic expressions are negotiated and made explicit.

Typically, what several teachers did when the child was in difficulty, perhaps as a response to the deaf child's need to divide attention, was to remove any offending block, bring it close to their face and say something like, "No, this one is too big." But this tactic serves to rob the child of state of task information that could be used to afford specific meaning to what is being said. Furthermore, contingency has been reversed. The child, poor in lip-reading and expressive speech at this stage, must work out what the adult intends to mean. Thus, any favorable conditions for the negotiation of meaning and for the provision of a contingent tutorial relationship are destroyed. Imagine this micro-world example magnified and played out in everyday life. The fact that deaf children experience some developmental delay and achieve less in schooling becomes, I suggest, understandable. The child does suffer "experiential deficit" but in the form of inhibited and even distorted access to those who would normally embody and share knowledge about the world, and skills in handling it.

TUTORING, IMITATION, AND MODELLING

In the introduction to this chapter, I commented on various perspectives on the role of instruction, both natural and contrived, in the development of the child. The studies I have just outlined were based on the assumption that concepts such as imitation and modelling are not sufficiently rich to provide adequate tools for understanding the ways in which children, through social interactions with and observations of the more mature, become competent and knowledgeable members of their culture. On first sight, the commonsense notion that children are only able to imitate the actions of others if they themselves already possess such actions as part of their repertoire seems logical and compelling. The only issue of substance left by such an account concerns the conditions under which children elect to attend to models or choose to imitate them. However, if we begin with the assumption that children not only attempt to impersonate others by imitating their actions but also try to emulate them by achieving similar ends or objectives, a different view of modelling becomes possible, one shared by Clementson-Mohr (1982). Let me begin with an illustration. Anyone watching the behavior of spectators at a tennis match, knowing nothing about spectator sports, might be misled into assuming that, because the head movements of most of the assembly are in temporal synchrony, some form of mass, behavioral contagion is at work. However, one familiar with the objectives of the crowd would appreciate that they are simply attending to the same events with similar aims in mind; to watch the progress of the match. The visible, surface similarity of their behavior stems from their exploitation of common morphology in the pursuit of the same interests, what Piaget (1962) referred to as ''behavioural convergence.'' Perhaps if our hypothetical, naive observer happened to notice a spectator whose view of the court was impeded by a tall person, he might see that spectator employing different behavioral means to maintain attention on the flow of the game. Generally, variation of means in the service of a maintained goal is evidence that any apparent convergence of behavior is a consequence of similar morphology, not imitation. Conversely, repeated effort towards the achievement of a specific form of action in relation to a model might strengthen the inference that the imitator's intention was truly to impersonate.

In our studies of children learning through direct tutoring and by self-instruction using film and photographs (Murphy & Wood, 1981), we have reported instances where children achieve common goals to those modelled, but do so by using idiosyncratic means that were never observed. Children may, then, profit from observing another's actions by discovering goals or end states to be achieved. Any ensuing, perceptual similarity in the behavior of the child and model may be a superficial phenomenon dictated by the fact that, sharing a common if somewhat differently sized form of life, they tend to employ the same parts of their body in similar ways to achieve common ends. The inferred intention of the learner, in this view, is not to achieve some match to sample mediated through an internal representation of the model's actions, but to achieve similar effects on the world. No doubt children do attempt to impersonate others and work hard at attempts to behave as like them as possible. The best may even go on to become professional impersonators. However, I think it is a mistake to assume that impersonation is the only or even the main intention driving so-called imitation.

In attempting to pursue recognizable or desired goals that they cannot yet achieve, children may, with expert guidance, discover that there are subgoals, detours, and obstacles en route to their achievement. The scaffolding functions we have identified go some way towards isolating the kinds of processes that, quite spontaneously, the more mature may enact in order to help children to discover and overcome such problems. In so doing, they help to transform the child's perception of the task and create new means to the achievement of goals. Of course, in one sense, some lower level of the behavioral hierarchy has to exist to provide the means for the creation of new, higher-order levels of behavioral organization. But the argument put forward here is that the construction, modularization, and automatization of new means-ends structures can be created in the context of social interaction.

The analysis of the growth of skilled action offered by Bruner (1973) is compatible with such a view as, at one level of analysis, is Vygotsky's account of the role of instruction in the formation of intra-psychic functions. But Vygotsky's theory affords a more general role for social interaction than I have considered in that he sees the origins of processes of reflection and intelligent self-regulation in social interaction. There are now a number of investigations reported in the literature that have explored the value of this thesis (e.g., Brown & Ferrara, 1985). Here, I want to continue the analysis of tutoring and the growth of competence in relation to the issue of self-regulation with reference to the development of deaf children.

TUTORING AND SELF-REGULATION

Luria and Yudovich, in 1971, argued that ''the time has long since passed when the deaf-mute child was regarded as differing from his normal counterpart only by the absence of hearing and speech'' (p. 32). The motivation behind this assertion stems from the Soviet view that speech forms the primary developmental base for self-regulation, planning, and other ''higher mental functions.'' ''Inner speech'' provides a language for thought, whereas ''inner dialogue'' represents the internalization of the other to form processes of dialectical reasoning. Lacking both receptive and expressive speech, deaf mutes, limited to gestures, fail to develop such higher mental functions. In consequence, their thinking remains context dependent, rigid, and impulsive. In the light of recent discoveries about the nature of sign languages, one could take issue with the implications implicit in Luria's views of the limited communicative and intellectual potential of gesture. However, notwithstanding this caveat, a wealth of research over the past two decades has proved largely consistent with Luria's hypothesis. Deaf people are often characterized as rigid, impulsive, concrete, and literal in their thinking and as being socially egocentric (e.g., Meadow, 1980). There are, however, marked individual differences in each of these characteristics that militate against the view that they are either a general, domain independent (Wood, Wood, & Howarth, 1983), or universal (Norden, 1975) consequence of deafness. Such evidence implies that features of cognition and personality, such as egocentrism and impulsivity, are not inevitable concomitants of deafness. Are they mediated by social interaction and attributable to inhibited access to the competence of others?

Any effort to help or to teach a child presents him or her with more than moment-to-moment guidance and examples of specific scaffolding functions. Observed over time, such activities are embedded in a deeper organization that, potentially, provides living examples of planning, control, and evaluation. These include heuristic aids to learning and problem solving such as rehearsal, means-ends analysis, subgoal analysis and backwards planning. It may well be that as children become familiar and competent partners in tutorial interactions they come to appreciate the larger structure implicit in such enterprises. Several observers of adult-child interaction have identified systematic individual differences in the character of parental tutorial styles and related these to aspects of the child's unassisted problem solving and to the way in which they act as tutees in interaction with unfamiliar adults (e.g., Haavind & Hartman, 1977). Brown and her colleagues (1982, 1985; Campione, Brown, & Ferrara, 1982) went even further. They argued that some children who find learning difficult lack specific skills in self-regulation. For example, studies of retarded children have identified problems of learning that stem from their inability to use strategies to aid memorization such as rehearsal and the imposition of some meaningful organization on material to be remembered. In a series of studies, Brown and her co-workers have demonstrated that such strategies can be taught to such children. The teaching strategies employed involve the externalization of self-regulatory activities by a teacher who models their use in a learner's presence. Later, the learner is encouraged to take over the role of teacher and helped to practice and perfect the strategies that have been modelled. Then, children are tested in different task contexts to see if they generalize the self-regulatory activities to new situations. Following Vygotsky, Brown argued that the successful outcomes from such research support the view that higher mental processes have their origins in social interaction.

As stated earlier, there is ample evidence favoring the view that children often correct and perfect their own competencies. Where systems of knowledge have an implicit, rule-governed structure, being, perhaps, modular in Fodor's (1983) sense, children are likely to discover regularities, draw inferences, and construct their own understanding. However, it seems plausible to suppose that strategies of self-regulation and heuristic planning, at least some features of which are culture-specific, are acquired in interactions with those who already embody and practice them. The study of deafness offers a further avenue for the study of such aspects of mind; another path towards an understanding of what gets internalized in the course of social interaction.

In the first place, as I have already tried to demonstrate, deaf children face problems in tutorial encounters because they are often subjected to what I termed a reversal of contingency. They are also likely to experience chronic over-control or ''over-scaffolding.'' By over-scaffolding I mean attempts to teach or help children that leave too little developmental space for the child to grow into. In the construction task experiment previously described, for instance, over-scaffolding is in evidence if a teacher readily increases help when a child shows signs of incomprehension or difficulty, but fails to relinquish initiative when the child succeeds. This phenomenon, perhaps a species of halo effect, in which past difficulties infect the adult's future expectations of a child, is commonplace in interactions between deaf children and hearing adults. For example, observations of classroom discourse (e.g., Wood et al., 1986, chapter 4) reveal a continuation of noncontingent over-control, which parallels that already discussed in relation to nonverbal communication. Briefly, conversations with deaf children are typically adult-dominated. The adult tends to take short verbal turns, uses simple registers of speech and dictates the course of any thematic coherence through frequent questions. As a result, discourse is seldom contingent upon any line of thought or communication initiated by the child. Children show few signs of curiosity, asking questions rarely. They often reply to questions monosyllabically and show little verbal initiative. Such verbal over-control inhibits children's epistemic activity and their readiness to communicate (Wood, 1986). However, we have also found that such features of discourse are neither universal nor inevitable and, using classroom intervention techniques (Wood & Wood, 1984), we have shown both that teachers can modify their styles and registers of discourse and that, when they do so, children become more verbal, show greater initiative and ask more questions. There is, then, a plausible and defensible case for the hypothesis that aspects of deaf psychology such as rigidity, literal, and concrete attitudes, a failure to entertain the hypothetical, and to sustain imagination, have their origins in social interactions, which typically display such characteristics. Thus, I suggest, deaf children internalize social practices that are common in their experience to display similar features in their own, intra-psychic functioning.

TUTORING AND THE GENESIS OF SELF-CONCEPTS

There is much to be done before the hypotheses I have just outlined can be sustained. The further we move away from immediate, short-term effects of tutoring towards proposed effects on more general features of cognition, the longer our conceptual and empirical supply-lines become and the more hesitant we must be. I conclude this chapter with an even more speculative line of thought.

Investigations by Dweck and her colleagues (1978) showed that teachers of mathematics usually behave differently towards boys and girls in math lessons. Dweck argued that the reactions of teachers towards signs of pupil success and failure vary according to the sex of the child involved. Girls, Dweck suggested, are more likely to receive the implicit message that any difficulty they encounter is to be expected (i.e., is attributable to a lack of competence), whereas boys are more likely to receive the disguised message that any difficulty they meet is a sign, not of any lack of competence, but of too little care or effort. Such differences are reflected not only in the attitudes and tutorial reactions of teachers; they are also found in the attitudes and performance of children, which become more pronounced with age (Department of Education and Science,

1981, p. 84). Dweck and her colleagues undertook classroom intervention studies that involved changing teacher behavior away from such gender-related differential activity. These demonstrated that it is possible to attenuate traditional patterns of sex differences in mathematics learning. Such findings also imply that learners internalize more than operations and procedures in the course of instruction; self-concepts and social representations of domains of knowledge are also being formed.

In a recent series of studies, we have tried to explore the relation between different methods of instruction and the 'micro-genesis' of tutor-tutee relations. In one study cited earlier in this chapter, where we evaluated the effects of different instructional styles on children's learning we made a number of informal observations. One instructional strategy, employed with 3-year-olds, involved attempts to teach by telling. Children were given verbal instructions, but the procedural implications that these were designed to solicit were never exemplified by showing or demonstration. Children in this group not only learned almost nothing about how to perform the task, they were often heard to complain that the task was "too hard" and it was difficult to persuade them to have another go at it after instruction. We also noted a certain coolness on the part of the children towards the experimenter-cum-tutor, which contrasted with positive social reactions received from children taught contingently (i.e., children taught according to the contingency rules described earlier).

In an attempt to test out the accuracy of these impressions, we undertook the following experiment. We trained an assistant in the rules of contingent and verbal teaching styles. She went on to teach two groups of children, one contingently the other verbally. Her performance was videotaped and later analyzed to show that she had followed the rules. After each instructional session, she was asked to take the child, with his or her mother, into another room. Her instructions were, having offered drinks and a snack, to ignore the child and to begin to read a book. Although she knew that this part of the proceedings was also being videotaped, she had not been told about our expectations regarding what might happen. When she attempted to read the book with a contingently taught child in attendance she never managed to get through the two minutes without interruption. All eight children in this group asked her questions, made a comment or established contact in one way or another. Of the verbally taught group, not one child addressed her and only one even looked at her during the same period.

The erstwhile tutor had been instructed, if children addressed her, to respond to them. If, after the 2 minutes reading time had ended, children had not already established contact, she was to try to establish conversation with them. Here, another series of predictions came into play. A second assistant had been trained in various coding systems that we have designed to study and analyze the structure of pedagogical discourse between teachers and children (e.g., Wood & Wood, 1984). This assistant was kept in ignorance as to the purpose of these observations until she had completed transcription and analysis of the recordings.

I need to say a little by way of background before outlining our predictions.

In our previous studies, which involved a wide age range of both hearing and deaf children from several different cultures, we found very tight, systematic relations between the manner in which a teacher controls and manages classroom discourse and various aspects of children's responses. For example, teachers who ask most questions and indulge in frequent attempts to repair what children have tried to communicate create a context in which children say relatively little, offer few ideas or contributions, ask almost no questions, and seldom elaborate on their answers to the teacher's questions. The more a teacher tells, informs, speculates and/or simply acknowledges what children have to say, the more initiative, questions, and elaborations children display.

We have also found that communication problems on a child's part increase the tendency of teachers both to control the discourse through questions and to try to repair children's offerings. Questions, particularly ones with specific, closed answers (such as responses to requests for color names, labels for familiar objects, personal names, ages, and the like) usually provoke some response from children, but seldom any elaboration or spontaneous comment. Following an answer, silence usually ensues, which tends to be filled by another adult question. A spiral of increasing teacher control is thus initiated that progressively inhibits response from the child. Eventually comes a question to which children give an inappropriate response or that they will not or cannot answer. Typically, the adult then repeats his or her question or in some way attempts to repair any ambiguity or lack of clarity in what the child has tried to say. The spiral of control becomes one of control and repair that further inhibits the child from taking part in interaction.

Back to the experiment: If, as we had expected, the verbally taught children would not relish the prospect of further involvement with the tutor (with whom they had failed to show signs of competence) then we would further predict that the child's reticence would result in control and repair on the tutor's part. This is what happened. Whereas discourse with the contingently taught children was rich in child questions, comments and observations, those with the verbal children were characterized by short, often monosyllabic responses to tutor questions. Discourse, with these children, never got off the ground as the tutor's natural response to the child's reticence, to provoke contact through questions, proved counterproductive.

I am suggesting that the character of tutorial activity, whether it is contingent and productive or noncontingent and overly didactic, affects more than the learning of new means-ends procedures and skill in self-regulation. What children internalize and generalize, I suggest, includes a social relationship that subsumes concepts of self-as-learner and other-as-tutor. Ineffective instruction produces a sense of incompetence in the young learner and shapes his or her attitudes towards what is being taught. The study I have just outlined thus represents an initial attempt to explore the micro-genesis of children's conceptualizations of their own competencies and an effort to probe more deeply into the complex issue of what gets internalized during the course of tutorial encounters.

CONCLUSIONS

I have explored the hypothesis that tutorial activity leads to the formation of what I have termed *socio-sensory-motor structures*. Such structures provide foundations for the social classification of experience and symbolic communication. Tutoring also involves the joint construction of means-ends procedures. I have discussed evidence that suggests that, in the course of tutorial encounters, tutees may also discover and internalize self-regulatory activities and heuristic aids to problem solving and thinking. A sense of self-competence, or a lack of it, may also be determined by the child's experiences as a learner-under-instruction. Tutorial interactions constitute the experiences out of which generalized notions of self-as-tutee and self-as-learner emerge. Thus, I suggest, the process of internalization involves the formation of hierarchical, internal structures with socio-sensory-motor structures at their periphery and concepts of self-competence at their core.

These hypotheses have been explored in relation to a developmental analysis of deafness. Deaf children are often subjected to abnormally high degrees of adult control and repair. I have referred to this process as over-scaffolding. This phenomenon arises, I believe, out of a desire on the part of the mature to help the deaf tutee to overcome problems of communication and learning. It represents an attempt to orchestrate the child's hoped-for role in tutorial interactions explicitly and carefully. In the short term, such exercises in control may yield predictable responses from the tutee. In the long term, they prove counter-productive and destructive. Tutees, over-controlled by external agencies in this way, are robbed of opportunities to exercise control for themselves and, hence, inhibited from learning how to practice and perfect their own competencies. Perhaps this observation is compatible with Vygotsky's criticism of approaches to teaching children with developmental disabilities which prevailed during his time (cited in Brown & Ferrara, 1985). He argued that the tendency with such children is to teach at the "lower boundary" of the zone of proximal development and, in consequence, to underestimate what they might achieve. Similarly, over-scaffolding fails in that it does not locate or work at the upper boundary of the child's region of sensitivity for instruction. Such tutoring, I suggest, also provides tutees with continual confirmation of their incompetence. Aspects of "deaf psychology" such as egocentrism, rigidity, and impulsivity, I have argued, are not inevitable, biological consequences of the disability but products of such distorted experiences in social interaction.

REFERENCES

Best, B., & Roberts, G. Early cognitive development in hearing impaired children. *American Annals of the Deaf*, 1976, *121*, 560–564.

Brazelton, T. B. Joint regulation of neonate-parent behavior. In E. Z. Tronick (Ed.), *Social interchange in infancy: Affect, cognition and communication*. Baltimore: University Park Press, 1982.

Brown, A. L., & Ferrara, R. A. Diagnosing zones of proximal development. In J. V. Wertsch (Ed.), *Culture, communication and cognition: Vygotskian perspectives*. Cambridge: Cambridge University Press, 1985.

Bruner, J. S. The organisation of early skilled action. *Child Development*, 1973, *44*, 1–11.

Bruner, J. S. *Child's talk: Learning to use language*. Oxford: Oxford University Press, 1983.

Campione, J. C., Brown, A. L., & Ferrara, R. A. Mental retardation and intelligence. In Sternberg, R. J. (Ed.), *Handbook of human intelligence* Cambridge: Cambridge University Press, 1982.

Clementson-Mohr, D. Towards a social-cognitive explanation of imitation development. In G. Butterworth & P. Light (Eds.). *Social cognition: Studies of the development of understanding*. Brighton: Harvester Press, 1982.

Department of Education and Science. *Mathematical development: Secondary survey report no. 2*. London: Her Majesty's Stationary Office, 1981.

Doise, W., & Mugny, G. *The social development of the intellect*. Oxford: Pergamon Press, 1984.

Dweck, C. S., Davidson, W., Nelson, S., & Enna, B. Sex differences in learned helplessness: The contingencies of evaluative feedback in the classroom, and III. An experimental analysis. *Developmental Psychology*, 1978, *14*, 268–276.

Fodor, J. A. *The modularity of mind*. Cambridge, MA: MIT Press, 1983.

Furth, H. G. *Thinking without language: Psychological implications of deafness*. New York: Free Press, 1966.

Glachan, M., & Light, P. Peer interaction and learning: Can two wrongs make a right? In G. Butterworth & P. Light (Eds.), *Social cognition: Studies in the development of understanding*. Brighton: Harvester Press, 1982.

Gregory, S., & Mogford, K. Early language development in deaf children. In B. Woll, J. Kyle & M. Deuchar (Eds.), *Perspectives in British Sign Language and deafness*. London: Croom Helm, 1981.

Haavind, H., & Hartman, E. *Mothers and teachers and their children as learners*. Report No. 1, Institute of Psychology, University of Bergen, Norway, 1977.

Hickman, M. E. The implications of discourse skills in Vygotsky's developmental theory. In J. V. Wertsch (Ed.), *Culture, communication and cognition: Vygotksian perspectives*. Cambridge: Cambridge University Press, 1985.

Karmiloff-Smith, A. *A functional approach to child language*. Cambridge: Cambridge University Press, 1979.

Luria, A. R., & Yudovich, F. *Speech and the development of mental processes in the child*. Harmondsworth: Penguin, 1971.

Marmor, G. S., & Petitto, L. Simultaneous communication in the classroom: How well is English grammar represented? *Sign Language Studies*, 1979, *23*, 99–136.

Masur, E. F. Gestural development, dual-directional signalling, and the transition to words. *Journal of Psycholinguistic Research*, 1983, *12*, 93–109.

Meadow, K. P. *Deafness and child development*. London: Edward Arnold, 1980.

Menyuk, P. *The acquisition and development of language*. Englewood Cliffs, NJ: Prentice-Hall, 1971.

Mogford, K., Gregory, S., & Hartley, G. *Deaf children with deaf parents and deaf children with hearing parents: A study of adult-child interaction*. Paper presented at the XXIInd International Congress of Psychology, Leipzig, East Germany, 1980.

Murphy, C. M., & Wood, D. J. Learning through media: A comparison of 4- to 8-year-old children's responses to filmed and pictorial instruction. *International Journal of Behavioral Development*, 1982, *5* (2), 195–216.

Nakazima, S. A Comparative study of the speech developments of Japanese and American English in childhood. *Studia Phonologica*, 1962, *2*, 27–39.

Norden, K. *Psychological studies of deaf adolescents*, Lund: Gleerup, Studia Psychologica et Pedagogica, Seria Altera, 39, 1975.

Piaget, J. *The language and thought of the child*. London: Routledge & Kegan Paul, 1959.

Piaget, J. *Play, dreams and imitation in childhood*. New York: Norton, 1962.

Piaget, J. *Six psychological studies*. London: University of London Press, 1968.

Quigley, S. P., & Paul, P. V. *Language and deafness*. San Diego, CA: College-Hill Press, 1984.

Swisher, M. V., & Thompson, M. Mothers learning simultaneous communication: The dimensions of the task. *American Annals of the Deaf*, 1985, 212–217.

Tait, D. M., & Wood, D. J. From communication to language in deaf children. *Child language teaching and therapy*, 1987, *3*, 1, 1–17.

Vygotsky, L. S. *Thought and language*. Cambridge, MA: MIT Press, 1962.

Vygotsky, L. S. *Mind in Society: The development of higher psychological processes*. Eds. M. Cole, V. John-Steiner, S. Scribner, & E. Souberman. Cambridge: Harvard University Press, 1978.

Wood, D. J. Teaching the young child: some relationships between social interaction, language and thought. In D. Olson (Ed.), *Social foundations of language and cognition: Essays in honor of J. S. Bruner*. New York: Norton, 1980.

Wood, D. J. Aspects of teaching and learning. In M. Richards & P. Light (Eds.), *Children of social worlds*. Cambridge: Polity Press, 1986.

Wood, D. J. *How children think and learn*. Oxford: Basil Blackwell, 1988.

Wood, D. J., Bruner, J. S., & Ross, G. The role of tutoring in problem solving. *Journal of Child Psychology and Psychiatry*, 1976, *17*, 89–100.

Wood, D. J., Wood, H. A., Griffiths, A. J., & Howarth, C. I. *Teaching and talking with deaf children*. Chichester: Wiley, 1986.

Wood, D. J., Wood, H. A., & Howarth, S. P. Mathematical abilities in deaf school-leavers. *British Journal of Developmental Psychology*, 1983, *1* (1), 67–74.

Wood, D. J., Wood, H. A., & Middleton, D. J. An experimental evaluation of four face-to-face teaching strategies. *International Journal of Behavioral Development*, 1978, *1*, 131–147.

Wood, H. A., & Wood, D. J. An experimental evaluation of the effects of five styles of teacher conversation on the language of hearing-impaired children. *Journal of Child Psychology and Psychiatry*, 1984, *25*, (1), 45–62.

Zinober, B., & Martlew, M. The development of communicative gestures. In M. D. Barrett (Ed.), *Children's single-word speech*. Chichester: Wiley, 1985.

II INTERACTION IN LANGUAGE ACQUISITION

5 Understanding Social Interaction and Language Acquisition; Sentences are not Enough

Catherine E. Snow
Harvard Graduate School of Education

INTRODUCTION

What can the study of social interaction tell us about language acquisition? Obviously, one's answer to this question depends heavily on one's position on some of the hoariest issues in language: the degree to which prelinguistic communicative development is continuous with or irrelevant to language development; the degree to which language development is embedded in or independent of communicative, pragmatic development; the degree to which language development is biologically prepared, and the nature of that biological preparation.

Even for those convinced of the crucial role played by special features of the child's social interactive environment in language development, there is considerable controversy about which special features are important, and exactly how they operate to facilitate language development.[1] A few claims are uncontroversial. No one denies that social interaction is a prerequisite to normal development, in language as in other domains. The question arises about special features of social interaction—whether there are aspects of the ways in which adults or

---

[1]There is even controversy over use of the term *facilitate* in talking about the relation between special features of the child's social interactive environment and language development. Facilitation implies a positive but not a necessary effect of social interaction; many researchers feel that some features of the social interaction are prerequisite to language development, not simply facilitative of it. As I hope to make clear later in this chapter, I use the term *facilitative* in reference to any particular feature because I believe individual features of social interaction are facilitative, not prerequisite, to normal language development. However, I also believe that *some* access to facilitative special features is prerequisite to language development, even though no single feature may be necessary for all children.

83

older children interact with infants and young children that are crucial or helpful to language development, and if so, what those features are and how they help. Needless to say, answering these questions requires going beyond the demonstration that babies and young children are interacted with in special ways, though careful description of the nature of the interactions they are engaged in is a first step in the research.

One goal of this chapter is to review a few of the specific hypotheses about the facilitative/prerequisite role of social interaction in language development, in an attempt to determine the current status of those hypotheses. These hypotheses represent one interpretation of the subtitle of this chapter: Concentrating on the sentences children produce is not enough if we are to understand how language acquisition occurs. We must consider those sentences in the socially managed linguistic and nonlinguistic context in which they occur. The specifics of social events that precede and that follow children's sentences may provide children with information about how their own utterances relate to the conventional language system they are in the process of acquiring. The nature of the social events that embed any particular child's sentences in contexts that make them meaningful (see Snow, Perlmann, & Nathan, 1987) is, of course, culturally specific. In going beyond an exclusive focus on the child's sentences as a route to understanding language acquisition, we are obliged to consider cultural differences in social interaction, and therefore in the social sources of language facilitation.

A second goal of this paper relates to another interpretation of the claim that sentences are not enough. I consider current limitations on thinking about the role of social interaction in language development that derive from simplistic views of what 'knowing a language' means and how to assess it. I argue that using sentential measures of language development—measures that reflect increasing sophistication only *within* utterance boundaries—blinds us to nonsentential domains of language proficiency that rely very heavily on the facilitation available from certain forms of social interaction.

SPECIFIC HYPOTHESES

As has been amply demonstrated, adult interaction with language-learning children differs in many ways from adult-adult interaction. Such differences are found in every culture that has been looked at, although the nature of the special features of adult-child interaction (and the nature of adult-adult interaction, for that matter) is quite culturally specific. Some of the special characteristics of adult-child interaction seem, prima facie, likely to be good candidates for features that facilitate language acquisition; one can see that they simplify or clarify information about the language in ways that might make it easier to process. Others seem to offer no particular help to the language learner, although they may serve other needs of the developing child; for example, use of diminutives and affectionate terms of address, which have more obvious emotional than linguistic functions.[2]

Much attention has been directed to potentially facilitative aspects of interactions with prelinguistic children for teaching about the basic structure of conversation (e.g., Snow, 1977), about the function of verbal expressions in organizing human attention and action (e.g., Bruner & Sherwood, 1976), and about the construction of integrated, extended sequences of events (Bruner, 1983a). Much of the value attributed to the early interactions described derives from their structure, which Bruner (1983a, 1983b) referred to as *formats*, and Snow et al. (1987) as *routines*. The structure not only constrains attention, reduces possible interpretations of actions, and sets up expectations within which the communicative value of specific expressions can be learned, but also places the child's actions and vocalizations in a context within which they are interpretable and pragmatically effective.

Many special features with potential facilitative effects have been proposed, both in the prelinguistic period and in the period of early language acquisition. I can deal here with only a few of these, and I have chosen four, for which the case seems to be particularly strong that they should help, and for which the findings are sufficiently complex that some review and reflection might be illuminating: joint attention, fine-tuning, negative feedback, and recasting. These four features are characteristic of mainstream middle-class, Anglo-American parents; because this is the group most often studied in seeking relations between social interaction and language development, features characteristic of this group are also the ones about which the most data are available. I do not mean to suggest that these are the four most important, most crucial, or most facilitative features in parent-child interaction, but they are worthy of examination as examples of how social interaction can contribute to language development.

It is, of course, commonplace to point out that the patterns of social interaction with infants and young children are a product of culture. In general, however, the culture argument has entered into thinking about the relation between social interaction and language development in only one way: Demonstrations that special features of social interaction hypothesized to facilitate language are absent in one culture or another have been taken to mean that they are also unnecessary in the cultures where they have been observed. I have discussed the speciousness of this reasoning elsewhere (Snow et al., 1987), in light of the

---

[2]Hugh Olmsted (in press) argued that in the Slavic languages the widespread use of diminutives serves to simplify the very complicated system of case and gender marking on nouns, so that the child is offered a salient, consistent system to start working on. He speculated that a similar function might be served by the diminutive in Dutch and German, because it is one of the few reliable correlates of gender in these languages, and thus provides predictability regarding case marking in German and adjective inflections in Dutch. It is very possible that other such procedures for linguistic simplification exist but that their value to the child-learner has not been noted.

remarkable robustness of the language development process and the associated necessity of assuming that several different mechanisms, each with its own social facilitator, are available to play a role in it. It is not necessary that each of the language-acquisition mechanisms be exploited by all children or by children in every culture—only that each culture provide a social context adequate for the operation of a few of the mechanisms. Thus, the nonuniversality of specific facilitative features constitutes no argument against the absolute necessity of some social facilitative features if language acquisition is to be successful.

It is also crucial to recognize that, from the point of view of the participants, the social interaction engaged in with a child is a product of a whole array of decisions, very few of which typically have anything to do with promoting language development. Rather, specific decisions about what to say to a child, how to respond to a child, and what caretaking or play activity to engage in with a child, can be seen in ethnographic analyses to form a pattern that in its totality generates as its primary product a new member of the culture. It is, thus, somewhat naive to discuss four special facilitative features of speech to children in mainstream middle-class Anglo-American homes as if they are independent of one another. In fact, the four features to be discussed can be seen to be of a piece in their reflection of the nature of the parent-child relation in the culture they characterize. All derive from a conversational model for parent-child interaction, in which children are treated as full-fledged conversational partners long before they can participate on an equal basis in exchanging information. All reflect the presumption that it is the adult's responsibility to keep the interaction and the conversation going, that children's conversational inadequacies must be compensated for. All relate to the adult desire to communicate with the child (not necessarily to teach the child anything about language). All reflect as well the adult attitude that minimal child accomplishments must be acknowledged and constituted as important achievements by virtue of the response they receive. The embedding of the identifiably facilitative features of parental speech to children in the cultural web of social-interactive meaning must be acknowledged—especially if we are planning to manipulate those special features for purposes of experimentation, remediation, or therapy.

Fine-Tuning and Joint Attention

Fine-tuning refers to the adjustment of the level of complexity in child-directed speech (CDS) in relation to the level of complexity of the child's own output and/or comprehension level. I have discussed elsewhere (Snow et al., 1987) the many methodological obstacles to demonstrating the existence of fine-tuning, and to finding effects of it on language development. The facilitative effect of fine-tuning is generally assumed to derive from its generation of an optimal discrepancy between the child's level and the level of the input. This optimal discrepancy presumably is small enough that the child understands, to some extent at least, the meaning of the utterance, but large enough that novel structures and structures not yet mastered by the child are modelled.

A problem that arises in assessing fine-tuning is that one must know a lot about the child's system in order even to guess what the optimal level in the CDS might be. Furthermore, the implicit presumptions have been that the optimal discrepancy is the same for all children and all stages of development—needless to say, these are totally unfounded assumptions. Perhaps these problems explain why clear effects of fine-tuning have been found only when the children observed were all at roughly the same stage of development, and furthermore that stage was early enough that it was possible to describe the children's systems fairly accurately. Furrow, Nelson, and Benedict (1979) found for children in the one-word stage that simpler CDS predicted faster growth over the succeeding 6-month period. Thus, in this study the optimal discrepancy seemed to be the smallest one; however, the mothers in the Furrow, Nelson, and Benedict sample spoke in utterances that had a mean length of about four words, still well above the mean length of their children's utterances.

Perhaps the major issue in reflecting on why positive effects of fine-tuning have not been more widely reported is the question of how fine-tuning might work to support language acquisition. There are a number of possibilities. One is captured by Krashen's (1985) comprehensible input principle (offered in his case for the facilitation of second language acquisition, but clearly derived from prior work and speculation about first language learning; e.g., Macnamara, 1972). The comprehensible input principle rests on the claim that language learning is impossible unless the input to the learner is comprehended; unless the meaning of the utterance is accessible, the task of analyzing correlations between meaning and form cannot be undertaken. Fine-tuning might facilitate language development only by virtue of the fact that, and to the extent that, it ensures comprehensible input.

The principle of comprehensible input is actually misnamed, however. Input that is fully comprehensible as language would not be expected to facilitate language development, simply because it does not display anything about language the child doesn't already know. The child's language system needs to be challenged by utterances that demonstrate where it is wrong and where it is insufficient. The challenging utterances must, however, be at least partially comprehensible, or the child will be unable to utilize the novel information they display. This combination of challenge and comprehensibility could be a product of optimal fine-tuning. One way to provide challenging input that is also comprehensible is, of course, to ensure comprehension via nonlinguistic routes. Topic, situation, and the child's history of interaction with the adult thus become extremely important factors in determining the optimal discrepancy the fine-tuning is meant to achieve.

If we accept this view, then it is clear that attempting to find fine-tuning across widely different situations in the child's life is likely to fail. The perfect mother will fine-tune the complexity of her speech in accordance with her expectations about comprehension, which are based in part on her knowledge of the child's access to nonlinguistic information about the topic. Thus, not only would the optimal difficulty level of adult speech increase as children got older (see George & Tomasello, 1984/85, for evidence that this occurs), but in addition the ideal mother's "situated talk" in novel situations would be simpler than in familiar situations; comments on absent or abstract topics would be simpler than comments on present, visible, concrete topics, and talk on novel topics would be simpler than talk on familiar topics. Anything, in fact, that decreased the likelihood that the child would understand should cause mothers to simplify their speech. Indeed, explicit signals from children of noncomprehension have been shown to decrease the complexity of successive adult utterances (Bohannon & Marquis, 1977), suggesting one mechanism by which fine-tuning occurs. Adult attempts to communicate with children, in a culture that assumes that the success of such communication requires the adult rather than the child to adapt (see Ochs & Schieffelin, 1984, for a discussion of child-raising vs. adult-lowering cultures), ensure some degree of fine-tuning of the complexity of the adult speech to the child's level.

Cultures such as the Anglo-American one, in which carrying on conversations with very young, linguistically inadequate children is considered appropriate, provide various procedures to the adult who must carry the burden of conversation. One is allowing children's nonverbal behaviors to count as ways of taking turns and of nominating topics. Perhaps the clearest example of fine-tuning is offered by the mother who responds to the pointing, showing, or giving action of her 1-year-old by naming the object involved. The label is fine-tuned in complexity (typically it includes only the name of the object, perhaps a determiner as well), constitutes a challenge to the child's system (because the child evidently did not know the name of the object), but ensures comprehensibility because the child has been allowed to select the topic.

Such effective fine-tuning relies on adult monitoring of the child's focus of attention and ability to predict what level of information about that focus of attention would best meet the child's needs. Tomasello hypothesized that occasions of joint attention between parents and very young children constitute unique opportunities for word-learning. He showed through correlational studies that frequency of joint attention predicts vocabulary growth (Tomasello & Todd, 1983), and in an experimental study that the words presented during periods of joint attention were learned better than those presented outside them (Tomasello & Farrar, 1986). Achieving joint attention with the very young children in the Tomasello studies is very much the responsibility of the adult; adults who monitor the child's visual attention and activity, and who follow-in have relatively frequent periods of joint attention, whereas adults who direct the child's attention achieve joint attention much less frequently. Dyadic differences in the frequency of joint attention are not (during this age period, at least) dependent on differences in children's ability or tendency to follow adult direction of attention. Later on, such differences may very well be a function of the effectiveness with which parents have established joint attentional formats, for example, naming routines in the context of book-reading (see Bruner, 1983a; Ninio & Bruner, 1978).

Although it makes perfect sense that children learn little from speech about objects they themselves are not attending to, it is important to realize that Tomasello's interpretation of his results implies much more than that child attention to objects is important. Joint attention is not defined as maternal attention to the child's object of attention, but as the mutual recognition that mother and child are attending to the same object or scene. Thus, the establishment of communication as well as joint focus of attention is hypothesized to be the special feature that facilitates language development. It is perhaps illuminating to contrast the joint attention hypothesis with the temporal contiguity hypothesis (Roth, 1987), which holds that children learn object labels presented within a brief temporal interval after the child's attention shifts to the relevant object. Correlational analyses (Roth, 1987) and an ongoing experimental study suggest that the crucial temporal interval is about 1 second. Roth's interpretation of these results rests heavily on a cognitive account, that young children do not recognize the relevance to their own focus of attention of the word offered by the adult unless the word arrives within the crucial temporal interval. Her interpretation does not require joint attention, however; mothers who monitor their children very carefully can provide the kind of input she hypothesizes is crucial without achieving the recognition by the child of the maternal attentiveness that is a criterion for joint attention as scored by Tomasello.

Both the joint attention hypothesis and the temporal contiguity hypothesis can be related to findings emerging from the studies of fine-tuning, and to the comprehensible input principle. At a time when children's own utterances are mostly nonverbal, and their entire vocabulary is under 50 words, optimally tuned input may, indeed, consist (at least in part) of single words. If those single words are to be comprehensible, they must be offered during periods of child attentiveness to the object labelled or within a brief interval after the child's attention shifts to that object. It is not so much that input is only comprehensible under these circumstances, as that under these circumstances anything the adult says will be presumed to be relevant to the topic established by attention to the object. Clearly, then, children are likely to make more progress in language acquisition if the input they get matches those expectations.

Feedback and Recasts

Most views of language development, however innatist, recognize the value to the language learner of feedback, especially negative feedback to ill-formed utterances. The controversy regarding feedback centers, not around whether it might help, but around whether children have access to it. One's conclusions about the degree to which children have access to negative feedback depend, of course, on what one is willing to count as negative feedback. Clearly, explicit corrections of children's morphological and syntactic errors are infrequent, and cannot be hypothesized to provide significant amounts of negative feedback. However, if one accepts the fairly uncontroversial view that children's utterances are intentionally communicative, adult clarification requests might constitute powerful sources of negative feedback precisely because they postpone the child's intended effect; they make clear to the child that the original formulation of the utterance was somehow inadequate. The question then becomes whether children's ill-formed utterances are more likely to elicit clarification requests than their well-formed utterances. Recent evidence (Bohannon & Stanowicz, in press; Demetras, Post, & Snow, 1986; Hirsh-Pasek, Treiman, & Schneiderman, 1984; Penner, 1987) suggests that they are, and that the distributional differences in responses to well- versus ill-formed utterances are sufficiently great that children could be using such information as a clue about where to correct their grammars. The information available from adult clarification requests is not perfectly reliable (i.e., well-formed utterances occasionally receive clarification requests, and ill-formed utterances often do not), indicating that the system that uses the information derived from such feedback must be fairly conservative. However, the usefulness of the information from feedback might be enhanced by parental tendencies to give negative feedback to child utterances with a single error, rather than to those with multiple errors (Bohannon & Stanowicz, in press). This fine-tuning of the feedback system may help children to focus on and learn from the information available in the adult response.

An alternative source of negative feedback is the availability of correct forms juxtaposed with incorrect child forms, such as happens when expansions and certain kinds of recasts are provided. Some clarification questions provide such corrected forms, for example:

CHILD: Me want a cookies.
MOTHER: What? You want a cookie?

In addition to this type of clarification question, however, many adult responses in fact signal understanding of the child utterance, and perhaps even affirm its correctness as a proposition, while still providing corrective feedback about its form, for example:

CHILD: Dat a big doggie.
MOTHER: That *is* a big doggie, isn't it?

Bohannon and Stanowicz (in press) found that adult repetitions with changes were much more likely to follow ill-formed than well-formed child utterances, and replicated the Demetras, Post, and Snow (1986) finding that exact repetitions almost exclusively followed well-formed child utterances, thus perhaps functioning as reliable indicators of well-formedness.

Using repetitions with changes as a source of negative feedback requires that children understand that the repetitions are meant to express the same meaning as their own previous utterances, and that they are in a position to compare the two versions. Evidence consistent with the second of these assumptions has been provided in two studies. Bohannon and Symons (1988) found that children tended to repeat recasts of their own ill-formed utterances, but not exact repetitions of their own well-formed utterances; Tomasello, Farrar, and Anselmi (1985) found that children were more likely to include gestures in their responses to clarification requests if their original utterances had contained pronouns rather than nouns. Both these findings indicate that children keep track of the form of their own utterances, at least for a turn or two into the conversation. One wonders, though, what the cues might be to the first of these conditions, that the child knows when the adult repetition is a paraphrase of the preceding child utterance. Consider the following dialogue:

CHILD: bird sing
MOTHER: the bird is singing
CHILD: bird singing pretty song
MOTHER: he's singing a pretty song
CHILD: eating bread
MOTHER: I don't think that's bread he's eating
CHILD: bread eating

The first and second maternal utterances in this fictitious dialogue are true expansions; that is, they are utterances that have no illocutionary force outside of expanding the child's utterance in order to confirm its content while correcting its form. The second child utterance, based on the expansion, is both more sophisticated and more correct than the previous child utterance. But the third maternal utterance is not *meant* as an expansion. It is meant as a denial of the child's proposition about the nature of the substance being eaten. Misinterpreting such responses as expansions would lead children to incorporate new, and incorrect, information into their language systems, of the sort that would generate the last child utterance. Why does this not happen more often? How do children know which adult utterances are reliable sources of information if compared with their own utterances, and which are not? Perhaps there are cues from adults, or reliable formal cues, that distinguish true expansions from other replies—we don't know because no one has looked.

It has been suggested (Baker & Nelson, 1984; Nelson, 1977, 1980; Nelson, Denninger, Bonvillian, Kaplan, & Baker, 1984) that recasts (defined to include expansions as well as adult responses to child utterances that incorporate content words from the child's utterance but also change the utterance in some way) are a special facilitative feature of social interaction with language-learning children. Nelson's research with recasts (reviewed in Nelson et al., 1984) experimentally demonstrates that targeted recasts work to speed the acquisition of specified structures. Recently, Baker, Pemberton, and Nelson (1985) also demonstrated that, under some conditions at least, recasts by the adult of her own utterances support the acquisition of the structure displayed in the recast, thus narrowing hypotheses about the mechanism of action that enables recasts to facilitate acquisition. Nelson's interpretation of this mechanism of action is highly cognitive; children compare the different versions of an utterance and, if they are at the right stage of development to use the information, analyze it to come to an understanding of the novel structure. As previously argued, regarding expansions, however, really understanding how children use this information requires knowing how they categorize the various sorts of recasts they hear. Some recasts constitute paraphrases of the original utterance (e.g., passives or topical left-dislocations). Others do not. Clearly, children cannot be learning language effectively if they operate exactly the same way on the following two sets of recasts:

(1) CHILD: the bird's eating all the crumbs.
     RECAST: all the crumbs are being eaten by the bird.
(2) CHILD: the bird's eating all the crumbs.
     RECAST: the bird has already eaten all the crumbs.

Whereas both these utterance pairs provide useful contrasts and comparisons of the type that might be used in a foreign language drill after the nature of the relation between the sentences had been explained to the students, the second would be disastrous for a learner who assumed that it provided information about how to make a stylistic contrast, as the first one does. Perhaps recasting is a special feature of social interaction with young children that is effective only for teaching a rather limited set of structures (though Nelson, 1987, summarizes its effectiveness for tag questions, passives, relative clauses, gerunds, reflexive pronouns, future tense and conditional verbs, auxiliaries, and complex noun phrases); if not, children must have some external-to-the-recast mechanism for determining the semantic relation between the recast and the original utterance.

Sentences in Social Contexts

We have considered four related special features hypothesized to facilitate language acquisition. There is good evidence from both correlational and experimental studies that two of them—joint attentional episodes and recasting—do facilitate acquisition; there is accumulating evidence that negative feedback occurs, and every reason to believe that it can and should facilitate language acquisition, but as yet no correlational or experimental demonstration that such is the case; finally, although there is not general agreement that grammatical fine-tuning occurs, and only very circumscribed evidence that it helps, it is implicated as a process that contributes to establishing joint attention and appropriate feedback.

It is crucial to note that any facilitative effects of these features of the social environment on language development are, in general, not independent of their effects on many other aspects of development, in particular their effects on enculturation (as the term is used by LeVine, in press). As LeVine pointed out, one derives contrasting conclusions about the long-term effects of early experience on development from studies that exploit individual differences within cultures and studies that compare development across cultures. So far, research on social facilitation of language acquisition has been conducted exclusively by looking at individual differences within cultures. This exclusivity has kept unavailable potentially illuminating data about group differences, and has often blinded researchers as well to the inherently cultural nature of the social behaviors they were using as predictors.

If we assume, from the universal success of language acquisition across cultures, that each culture selects some subset from the range of potentially facilitative special features and embeds these in its patterns of social interaction with children, then we should be equally prepared to expect some (perhap transient) diversity in the exact nature of the language outcome. Sufficient data are now available within the samples of English-speaking American children whose language development has been studied to affirm that alternative routes to language proficiency are possible (see, for example, Goldfield & Snow, 1989; Nelson, 1981, for reviews). An even wider variety of routes and of rates may constitute normal acquisition that will culminate in native speaker abilities across the world's societies. Just as culture defines what constitutes normal social interaction, it also defines what constitutes normal language ability. It is naive to expect uniformity, either in facilitative features or in definition of optimal outcome, given the deep, serious effect of culture on these matters.

ASSESSING A VARIETY OF OUTCOMES

Judging the effect of social interactive features on language development presupposes we know how to assess language development. Although some standard procedures for assessing language proficiency are widespread, I would argue they are not equally appropriate to all children, are decreasingly appropriate as children get older, and are too limited in the range of linguistic accomplishments they reflect. Since our language-outcome measures are so limited, the possibility for finding relations with features of the social interaction is also curtailed.

The standard measures of language development are familiar ones: vocabulary size, as reflected in diaries or maternal interviews during the first several months of language development, and in standardized vocabulary tests thereafter; and mean length of utterance (MLU), which tracks development quite well up to about age 4 years, at least for children who are developing normally and who are relatively analytic rather than holistic in their approach to language development. Many other measures of syntactic and morphological development have been used, of course, in various studies, although none has become standard as have vocabulary and MLU. Like MLU, however, these other measures concentrate on development in length or complexity within relatively small production units—utterances, phrases, words. Little attention is paid to indicators of development of conversational skill (using backchannels, acknowledging responses, responding reliably to utterances that oblige the listener to respond, such as greetings, questions, and compliments), of pragmatic skill (appropriateness, manipulation of indirectness), of discourse skill (topic maintenance, topic elaboration, cohesion across utterances in narratives), of skill in dealing with the demands of various interactive situations (adjusting to an absent audience by using more explicit reference, adjusting to an audience with whom one does not share background knowledge by filling in more information), or of genre differentiation (using genre appropriate strategies for various sorts of narratives, expositions, and arguments). The unavailability of measures in these and other areas of language means that the hypothesis of social facilitation for language development has been tested for only a few language outcomes, and may have been tested most assiduously for those language outcomes where we can least expect to see large effects.

Individual Differences in Outcome

MLU was first proposed as a developmental index by Brown (1973), who demonstrated its value in reflecting the development of his subjects Adam, Eve, and Sarah. MLU is calculated, according to Brown's rules, on a sample of child utterances that excludes both imitations of preceding adult utterances and memorized material (rhymes, songs, expressions like "happy birthday," and so forth). Whereas these exclusions make perfect sense if MLU is meant to reflect the child's ability independently to manipulate morphological markers and to produce novel word combinations, they make less sense if MLU is used as the single developmental index of language ability. Many children rely on imitations of adult utterances (often somewhat restructured and expanded) and on memorized material ("deferred imitations") as a resource in communicating and as an object of analysis in expanding their language systems. Individual differences in reliance on imitation are quite large (Snow, 1989), and it is clear that, for highly imitative children at least, ignoring the material within imitative utterances underrepresents their language abilities (see Clark, 1977; Peters, 1983; Snow, 1981, 1983 for case studies of such children).

It is not at all clear what the sources of individual differences in imitativeness are, though considerable evidence suggests that highly imitative children have highly imitative mothers (Folger & Chapman, 1978; Masur, 1984; Snow, 1989). These findings have been interpreted as a direct effect of parent on child, although they could equally cogently be interpreted as showing a transactional effect. In terms of questions about the social facilitation of language development, it seems very likely that the child who (for whatever reason) is inclined to imitate would benefit from a rather different set of special features than the nonimitative child. Recasting, for example, would be of much less use to the imitator, who is evidently analyzing output in preference to input, than to the analytic child. Phonetic clarity of the type documented by Bernstein-Ratner (1987) in the input language might be much more important to the analytic child, who is scanning the input for units, than to the imitator, who is willing to process large chunks without worrying too much about phonetic detail or segmentation within the chunks. Imitative children might benefit much more in terms of their language development from exposure to rhymes, songs, and games with predictable verbal markers, because these activities provide the kind of input they are naturally inclined to use. Analytic children might discount the large and often incomprehensible chunks of speech provided in these contexts as useful for language acquisition.

No one has looked for differential patterns of relations between features of the social/linguistic environment and language outcomes for highly imitative and nonimitative children. In order to find such differences, one would like to have measures of language level that are sensitive to the development reflected in the imitative children's expanded and deferred imitations, to complement measures like MLU that reflect analytic skills. Most children, of course, show a combination of analytic and holistic strategies in learning language, and a complete picture of their language level would require having both sorts of measures available.

Pragmatics, Discourse, and Conversation

The existence of individual differences in learning styles dictates that we must seek indices of development that reflect the intermediate stages passed through by the full range of children. In addition, we must recognize that the typical contexts for collecting child language restrict variation in the kinds of language skills one can see. Conversations with familiar adults who provide much scaffolding of structure, who support the child's participation in the conversation, and who allow the child to exploit shared knowledge cannot reveal the child's skill in conversational initiation, in topic control, in explicit and clear presentation of information, and in many other areas.

It seems clear that the special features proposed to facilitate such alternative language outcomes might be quite different from those that have been found to facilitate vocabulary and MLU. Joint attention, for example, seems very power-ful as a vocabulary facilitator, and recasting and feedback have obvious potential in helping the child learn about morphological marking. But what social facili-tators might be expected to promote the child's skill at, for example, pragmatic appropriateness? In American homes, at least, specific politeness markers are evidently taught by direct instruction ("Say please?", "What do you say?", etc.; see, for example, Gleason, 1980; Gleason & Weintraub, 1976; Greif & Gleason, 1980). The appropriately polite use of indirect rather than direct forms has not been reported to be fostered in this way, however, and we can only speculate that it is promoted in American children by modelling, and by the transmittal of information about social relationships that enable the child to infer when such forms are appropriate. In contrast, Japanese mothers directly teach their children about how to interpret and produce indirect speech (Clancy, 1986), no doubt because the ubiquity of indirect forms in Japanese requires that children master them relatively early.

The issue of what social facilitators work to promote the acquisition of skill in monologue tasks deserves more attention. The term *monologue task* is being used here to refer to those language performances that are increasingly required of American children as they pass through toddlerhood and enter nursery school and kindergarten classrooms. It includes such performances as are elicited in many homes at the dinner table ("Tell daddy what we did today") or for the amusement of visitors ("Granny wants to know about your trip to the circus"), as well as those expected by teachers during sharing time, or in response to higher-level comprehension questions about reading material. The special de-mands placed on the child by the need to perform in these ways are quite different from the demands of conversational interaction with a familiar partner. Whereas special features that derive from conversational interactions seem to facilitate the development of language skills displayed during conversation, it is likely that different social facilitators might operate to support monologue skills. A higher MLU is not irrelevant to performance in monologues, but it clearly is not the only or the major indicator of such skill. The search for the social facilitators of monologue skills becomes particularly important when we realize that it is monologue, much more than conversational, language skills, that pre-dict literacy and school achievement (Snow, Cancino, Gonzalez, & Shriberg, 1989; Sulzby, 1985).

Full-scale analyses of the skills required to perform well on monologue tasks are unavailable; consequently we do not have good developmental indices for these tasks. However, it seems likely that relevant language skills include control over such features as the following: use of intra- and intersentential connectors such as *because, whereas, moreover, however;* control of tense sequencing; use of relative clauses, for the explicitation of reference; knowledge of low frequen-cy lexical items, to make lexical rather than deictic reference possible; control of techniques for maintaining cohesion, such as anaphora and paraphrase; control of devices for topic reinstatement; and control of various devices used to hold the floor.

What social experiences might produce the skills required to do well at relatively autonomous performances of narratives and explanations? Two very different hypotheses present themselves, in the absence of any relevant data. One hypothesis holds that such monologue skills derive from experience participating in dialogues that display many of the specific characteristics desired in the monologue. Thus, hearing a topic discussed over several conversational turns might help a child learn how to sustain a topic over many utterances in a monologue. Participating in highly adult-structured retellings of familiar events may help the child to develop skill in autonomous narrative. Experience in answering questions about pictures while book-reading might show the child what kinds of questions need to be answered in a picture description, and help the child to answer those questions even if they are not posed by a conversational partner. This *co-construction hypothesis* holds, then, that collaborative participation in the construction of long, multiparty texts facilitates children's abilities to produce long texts by themselves.

A very different hypothesis, which might be termed the *autonomy hypothesis,* holds that withdrawal of collaborative support provides the child with the chance to learn how to produce monologues. Demanding that the child provide more and more information about jointly experienced events, upping the ante (Ninio & Bruner, 1978) for child contribution to picture discussions, and reduced willingness to negotiate the child's meaning in favor of forcing the child to be clear about her own intentions would all constitute opportunities for the child to practice producing monologuelike forms, and to discover the actual demands on the monologue-speaker.

Both the co-construction hypothesis and the autonomy hypothesis would imply that practice with extended texts contributes to the child's ability to produce such texts. Both hypotheses would suggest that the child who never hears or participates in extended discussions of a topic would show deficiencies in producing monologues. But the precise social mechanism that is presumed to facilitate the child's skill, beyond mere exposure, is quite different under the two hypotheses.

The view offered here, that the social antecedents of monologue skills might be quite different from the features that facilitate sentence-level language skills, is fairly novel, thus little research is available to guide us in assessing either the co-construction or the autonomy hypothesis. Studies of the development of narrative—one of the monologue forms children come to control fairly early— provide some hints about developmental antecedents. Wells (1981), Cox and Sulzby (1982), Schieffelin and Eisenberg (1984), and Engel (1986), documented how parents elicit from their children personal report narratives, collaborate in producing them, and provide opportunities for practice and for display. For recurrent events, children develop a generalized script that constrains the narrative (Nelson & Gruendel, 1981), in part as a result of the information gained from mother-child conversations. The ability to produce such narratives and script-reports may well emerge out of children's earlier demonstrated abilities to maintain cross-utterance cohesion (Foster, 1979) and cross-speaker cohesion (Bloom, Lightbown, & Hood, 1975; Pellegrini, 1982), and out of their experience with conversations in which adults struggle to incorporate the child utterances into a coherent dialogic text (Ochs, Schieffelin, & Platt, 1979; Sachs, 1979; Snow, 1977; Snow, Dubber, & deBlauw, 1982; Wells, 1978).

Experience with nonpersonal narratives may be most richly available to children from book reading, especially recurrent reading of particular books. Snow and Goldfield (1982) demonstrated that experience discussing a series of narrative pictures enabled one child to move toward independent narrative production. Maternal speech is more complex during book reading than during play (Snow, Arlman-Rupp, Hassing, Jobse, Joosten, & Vorster, 1976), and book reading is a context in which long cohesive texts can be produced with relatively young children (Ninio & Bruner, 1978; Snow & Goldfield, 1983). Experience with book reading during the preschool years is differentiated by social class (e.g., Heath, 1986; Ninio, 1980; Teale, 1986), and is of course also strongly related to later school success (see Goldfield & Snow, 1984, for a review). This relation has most often been interpreted as having to do with the opportunity to learn about print or about the features of literacy. In fact, though, it may be an effect that is mediated by the social facilitation of children's monologue skills.

Searching for the social antecedents of monologue skills becomes a particularly important task when we realize that skills at monologue tasks seem to show far greater individual and group differences than do skills at the sentence-level tasks reflected in MLU and other syntactic outcome measures. Although sentence-level syntactic skills do not show social class differences, and social class differences in language skill during face-to-face conversational tasks are minimal, monologue tasks (retelling a story, answering open-ended questions, giving explanations, defining words, and participating in discussion) typically reveal rather large social class differences (Bernstein, 1971; Blank, 1975; Blank, Rose & Berlin, 1978; Dickinson & Snow, 1987; Farran, 1982; Feagans, 1982; Rackstraw & Robinson, 1967; Tough, 1977).

CONCLUSION

Research on language acquisition and on social/environmental facilitation of language development has concentrated on sentence-level skills; that is, on those indices of development that reflect changes in length, complexity, and completeness of phrases and single utterances. There is now considerable evidence that experience with certain kinds of social interactive and conversational events during the first few years of life facilitates development as measured by these indices. Four special features of social interaction with children were discussed here, and the status of the evidence regarding their contribution to language development was assessed. Other studies have shown facilitative effects on sentence-level language skills of such additional special features as semantic contingency, and negative effects of maternal directiveness (see Cross, 1978; Snow, 1984 for reviews).

In addition to the sentence-level language skills whose social antecedents have been so extensively researched, children need to develop text-level or monologue skills, which require control over the devices needed to relate a series of utterances to one another. Control of these monologue skills shows more individual and group variability than does control of the sentence-level skills. The forms that monologue genres take, the frequency with which they are employed in everyday life, and their social and communicative functions vary not just across families, but also across ethnic and social class groups (e.g., Heath, 1983). Thus, one might expect that a child's early social interactions with caregivers contribute even more crucially to the development of these monologue skills than to the development of sentence-level skills, which show greater uniformity in pace of development and in ultimate level attained. Nonetheless there is very little evidence available about the social interactive experiences that contribute to the development of monologue skills, and much of the available evidence relates to school-aged children, although the individual, social class, and cultural differences in control of these skills are well-established in children entering kindergarten (Dickinson & Snow 1987; Heath, 1983; Scollon & Scollon, 1982; Sulzby, 1981). Assessment of the relation between early interactive experiences and monologue language skills seems very likely to reveal that a different pattern of facilitation exists than for sentence-level language skills.

ACKNOWLEDGMENTS

I would like to express my appreciation to Michael Tomasello, who read an early version of this chapter and made extremely helpful comments upon it, to the Ford Foundation, which is funding my research on social interaction and monologue skills. Preparation of this chapter was also supported by the National Institute of Child Health and Human Development (HD23388).

REFERENCES

Baker, N., & Nelson, K. E. Recasting and related conversational techniques for triggering syntactic advances by young children. *First Language*, 1984, 5, 3–22.

Baker, N., Pemberton, E., & Nelson, K. E. *Facilitating young children's language development through stories: Reading and Recasting.* Paper presented at the Boston University Conference on Language Development, Boston, MA, October 1985.

Bernstein, B. *Class, codes and control (Vol. 1)*. London: Routledge & Kegan Paul, 1971.

Bernstein-Ratner, N. The phonology of parent-child speech. In K. E. Nelson & A. van Kleek (Eds.), *Children's language* (Vol. 6). Hillsdale, NJ: Lawrence Erlbaum Associates, 1987.

Blank, M. Mastering the intangible through language. In I. Aaronson & R. Rieber (Eds.), *Developmental psycholinquistics and communication disorders*. New York: NY Academy of Sciences, 1975.

Blank, M., Rose, S., & Berlin, L. *The language of learning: The preschool years*. New York: Grune & Stratton, 1978.

Bloom, L., Lightbown, P., & Hood, L. Structure and variation in child language. *S.R.C.D. Monographs* 40, 1975.

Bohannon, J. N., & Marquis, A. L. Children's control of adult speeach. *Child Development*, 1977, *48*, 1002–1008.

Bohannon, J. N., & Stanowicz, L. The issue of negative evidence: Adult responses to children's language errors. *Developmental Psychology*, in press.

Bohannon, J. N., & Symons, V. *Conversational conditions of children's imitation*. Paper presented at the Biennial Conference on Human Development, Charleston, SC, April, 1988.

Brown, R. *A first language: The early stages*. Cambridge, MA: Harvard University Press, 1973.

Bruner, J. *Child's talk: Learning to use language*. New York: Norton, 1983a.

Bruner, J. The acquisition of pragmatic committments. In R. Golinkoff (Ed.), *The transition from prelinguistic to linguistic communication*. Hillsdale, NJ: Lawrence Erlbaum Associates, 1983b.

Bruner, J., & Sherwood, V. Peekaboo and the learning of rule structures. In J. Bruner, A. Jolly, & K. Sylva (Eds.), *Play: Its role in development and evolution*. Harmondsworth: Penguin, 1976.

Clancy, P. The acquisition of communicative style in Japanese. In B. Schieffelin & E. Ochs (Eds.), *Language socialization across cultures*. New York: Cambridge University Press, 1986.

Clark, R. What's the use of imitation? *Journal of Child Language*, 1977, *4*, 341–359.

Cox, B., & Sulzby, E. *Evidence of planning in dialogue and monologue by five-year-old emergent readers*. Unpublished paper, Northwestern University, 1982.

Cross, T. G. Mothers' speech and its association with rate of linguistic development in young children. In N. Waterson & C. Snow (Eds.), *The development of communication*. New York: Wiley, 1978.

Demetras, M., Post, K., & Snow, C. E. Negative feedback to first language learners. *Journal of Child Language*, 1986, *13*, 275–292.

Dickinson, D. K., & Snow, C. E. Interrelationships among prereading and oral language skills in kindergartners from two social classes. *Research on Childhood Education Quarterly*, 1987, *2*, 1–25.

Engel, S. *Learning to reminisce: A developmental study of how young children talk about the past*. Doctoral thesis, C.U.N.Y., New York, 1986.

Farran, D. Mother-child interaction, language development and the school performance of poverty children. In L. Feagans & D. Farran (Eds.), *The language of children reared in poverty*. New York: Academic Press, 1982.

Feagans, L. The development and importance of narratives for school adaptation. In L. Feagans & D. Farran (Eds.), *The language of children reared in poverty*. New York: Academic Press, 1982.

Folger, J. P., & Chapman, R. A pragmatic analysis of spontaneous imitation. *Journal of Child Language*, 1978, *5*, 25–38.

Foster, S. *From nonverbal to verbal communication: A study of the development of topic initiation strategies during the first 2½ years of life*. Doctoral dissertation, University of Lancaster, 1979.

Furrow, D., Nelson, K., & Benedict, H. Mothers' speech to children and syntactic development: Some simple relationships. *Journal of Child Language*, 1979, *6*, 423–442.

George, B., & Tomasello, M. The effect of variation in sentence length on young children's attention and comprehension. *First Language*, 1984/85, *5*, 115–128.

Gleason, J. B., & Weintraub, S. The acquisition of routines in child language. *Language in Society,* 1976, *5,* 129–136.

Gleason, J. B. The acquisition of social speech: Routines and politeness formulated. In H. Giles (Ed.), *Language: Social psychological perspectives.* London: Pergamom Press, 1980.

Goldfield, B., & Snow, C. E. Reading books with children: The mechanics of parental influence on children's reading achievement. In J. Flood (Ed.), *Understanding reading comprehension.* Newark, DE: International Reading Association, 1984.

Goldfield, B., & Snow, C. E. Individual differences in language acquisition. In J. B. Gleason (Ed.), *Language Development,* 2nd Edition. Columbus, OH: Merrill, 1989.

Greif, E., & Gleason, J. B. Hi, thanks, and good-bye: More routine information. *Language in Society,* 1980, *9,* 159–166.

Heath, S. B. *Ways with Words.* New York: Cambridge University Press, 1983.

Heath, S. B. What no bedtime story means: Narrative skills at home and at school. In B. Schieffelin & E. Ochs (Eds.), *Language socialization across cultures.* New York: Cambridge University Press, 1986.

Hirsh-Pasek, K., Treiman, R., & Schneiderman, M. Brown and Hanlon revisited: Mothers' sensitivity to ungrammatical forms. *Journal of Child Language,* 1984, *11,* 81–88.

Krashen, S. *The input hypothesis: Issues and implications.* London: Longman, 1985.

LeVine, R. Enculturation: A biosocial perspective on the development of self. In D. Cicchetti & M. Beeghly (Eds.), *The self in transition: Infancy to childhood.* Chicago: University of Chicago Press, in press.

Macnamara, J. Cognitive basis of language learning in infants. *Psychological Review,* 1972, *79,* 1–13.

Masur, E. *Imitation in a social context: Mother-infant interactions at the beginning of the second year.* Unpublished manuscript, Northwestern University, 1984.

Nelson, K. Individual differences in language development. *Developmental Psychology,* 1981, *17,* 170–187.

Nelson, K., & Gruendel, J. Generalized event representations: Basic building blocks of cognitive development. In M. Lamb & A. Brown (Eds.), *Advances in developmental psychology* (Vol. 1). Hillsdale, NJ: Lawrence Erlbaum Associates, 1981.

Nelson, K. E. Facilitating children's syntax acquisition. *Developmental Psychology,* 1977, *13,* 101–107.

Nelson, K. E. Theories of the child's acquisition of syntax: A look at rare events and at necessary, catalytic, and irrelevant components of mother-child conversation. *Annals of the New York Academy of Sciences,* 1980, *345,* 45–67.

Nelson, K. E. Some observations from the perspective of the rare event cognitive comparison theory of language acquisition. In K. E. Nelson & A. van Kleek (Eds.), *Children's language* (Vol. 6). Hillsdale, NJ: Lawrence Erlbaum Associates, 1987.

Nelson, K. E., Denninger, M. M., Bonvillian, J. D., Kaplan, B. J., & Baker, N. D. Maternal input adjustments and non-adjustments as related to children's linguistic advances and to language acquisition theories. In A. D. Pellegrini & T. D. Yawkey (Eds.), *The development of oral and written languages: Readings in developmental and applied linguistics.* Norwood, NJ: Ablex, 1984.

Ninio, A. Picturebook reading in mother-infant dyads belonging to two subgroups in Israel. *Child Development,* 1980, *51,* 587–590.

Ninio, A., & Bruner, J. The achievements and antecedents of labelling. *Journal of Child Language,* 1978, *5,* 1–15.

Ochs, E., & Schieffelin, B. Language acquisition and socialization: Three developmental stories and their implications. In R. Schweder & R. LeVine (Eds.), *Culture theory.* New York: Cambridge University Press, 1984.

Ochs, E., Schieffelin, B., & Platt, M. Propositions across utterances and speakers. In E. Ochs & B. Schieffelin (Eds.), *Developmental pragmatics*. New York: Academic Press, 1979.

Olmsted, H. Dimunitive morphology of Russian children: Simplified subset of nominal declension in language acquisition. In *Memorial volume for Alexander Lipson*. Columbus, OH: Slavia Publishers, in press.

Pellegrini, A. The construction of cohesive text by preschoolers in two play contexts. *Discourse Processes*, 1982, *5*, 101–108.

Penner, S. Parental responses to grammatical and ungrammatical child utterances. *Child Development*, 1987, *58*, 376–384.

Peters, A. The units of language acquisition. Cambridge, England: Cambridge University Press, 1983.

Rackstraw, S. J., & Robinson, W. P. Social and psychological factors related to variability of answering behavior in 5-year-old children. *Language and Speech*, 1967, *10*, 88–106.

Robinson, W. P. The elaborated code in working class speech. *Language and Speech*, 1965, *8*, 243–251.

Roth, P. Temporal characteristics of maternal verbal styles. In: K. E. Nelson & A. van Kleek (Eds.), *Children's language* (Vol. 6). Hillsdale, NJ: Lawrence Erlbaum Associates, 1987.

Sachs, J. Topic selection in parent-child discourse. *Discourse Processes*, 1979, *2*, 145–153.

Schieffelin, B., & Eisenberg, A. Cultural variation in children's conversations. In R. Schiefelbusch & J. Pickar (Eds.), *Communicative competence: Acquisition and intervention*. Baltimore: University Park Press, 1984.

Scollon, R., & Scollon, S. *Narrative, Literacy and Face in Interethnic Communications*. Norwood, NJ: Ablex, 1982.

Snow, C. E. Development of conversation between mothers and babies. *Journal of Child Language*, 1977, *4*, 1–22.

Snow, C. E. The uses of imitation. *Journal of Child Language*, 1981, *8*, 205–212.

Snow, C. E. Saying it again: The role of expanded and deferred imitations in language acquisition. In K. E. Nelson (Ed.), *Children's language* (Vol. 4). New York: Gardner Press, 1983.

Snow, C. E. Parent-child interaction and the development of communicative ability. In R. L. Schiefelbusch & J. Pickar (Eds.), *The acquisition of communicative competence*. Baltimore, MD: University Park Press, 1984.

Snow, C. E. Imitativeness: A trait or a skill? In G. Speidel & K. Nelson (Eds.), *The many faces of imitation in language learning*. Springer-Verlag, 1989.

Snow, C. E., Arlmann-Rupp, A., Hassing, Y., Jobse, J., Joosten, J., & Vorster, J. Mothers' speech in three social classes. *Journal of Psycholinguistic Research*, 1976, *31*, 424–444.

Snow, C. E., Cancino, H., Gonzalez, P., & Shriberg, E. Giving formal definitions: An oral language correlate of school literacy. In D. Bloome (Ed.), *Literacy in functional settings*. Norwood, NJ: Ablex, 1989.

Snow, C. E., Dubber, C., & de Blauw, A. Routines in parent-child interaction. In L. Feagans & Dr. Farran (Eds.), *The language of children reared in poverty: Implications for evaluation and intervention*. New York: Academic Press, 1982.

Snow, C. E., & Goldfield, B. Building stories: The emergence of information structures from conversation and narrative. In D. Tannen (Ed.) Georgetown University Roundtable on Language and Linguistics 1981, Analyzing discourse: Text and talk. Washington, DC: Georgetown University Press, 1982.

Snow, C. E., & Goldfield, B. Turn the page please: Situation-specific language learning. *Journal of Child Language*, 1983, *10*, 551–570.

Snow, C. E., Perlmann, R., & Nathan, D. Why routines are different: Toward a multiple-factors model of the relation between input and language acquisition. In K. Nelson & A. van Kleeck (Eds.), *Children's language* (Vol. 6). Hillsdale, NJ: Lawrence Erlbaum Associates, 1987.

Sulzby, E. *Kindergartners begin to read their own compositions: Beginning readers' developing knowledge about written language.* Final report to NCTE. Evanston, IL: Northwestern University Press, 1981.

Sulzby, E. Children's emergent reading of favorite storybooks: A developmental study. *Reading Research Quarterly,* 1985, *20,* 458–481.

Teale, W. H. Home background and young children's literacy development. In W. H. Teale & E. Sulzby (Eds.), *Emergent literacy: writing and reading.* Norwood, NJ: Ablex.

Tomasello, M., Anselmi, D., & Farrar, J. 1985. Young children's coordination of gestural and linguistic reference. *First Language,* 1985, *5,* 199–210.

Tomasello, M., & Farrar, J. Joint attention and early language. *Child Development,* 1986, *57,* 1454–1463.

Tomasello, M., & Todd, J. Joint attention and lexical acquisition style. *First Language,* 1983, *4,* 197–212.

Tough, J. Children and programmes: How shall we educate the young child? In A. Davies (Ed.), *Language and learning in early childhood.* London: Heinemann, 1977.

Wells, G. Variation in child language. In P. Fletcher & M. Garman (Eds.), *Language acquisition.* London: Cambridge University Press, 1979.

Wells, G. Some antecedents of early educational achievement. *British Journal of Sociology of Education,* 1981, *2,* 181–200.

6 The Independence and Task-Specificity of Language

Susan Curtiss
Department of Linguistics
University of California, Los Angeles

> *Scholarship is the process by which butterflies are transmuted into caterpillars.*
>
> —(Fodor, 1983)

INTRODUCTION

In the normal developing child the concurrent development of motor, social, cognitive, and linguistic ability is a striking fact. This multiplistic character of normal development has greatly influenced theoretical models of all aspects of child development, such that most models stress the interconnections between areas of development and posit general learning mechanisms underlying the changes that occur with increasing age across domains.

Theoretical models of language development currently reflect this state of affairs, but this was not always the case. As a result of the Chomskyan revolution in linguistics, during the 1960s child language researchers concentrated on studying structural aspects of language acquisition apart from context. However, researchers soon began moving towards a focus on the larger language-learning context, identifying nonlinguistic knowledge as well as factors in the environment that are potentially important concomitants of language development. Today, most models of language acquisition stress the nonlinguistic context in which language growth occurs. The effects of this theoretical focus are two-fold: (1) to view the larger developmental context in which language acquisition is embedded as the base upon which language growth can be explained, and (2) to posit nonspecific learning strategies or discovery procedures that extract the general and homologous principles underlying knowledge in several interconnected domains, including language.

In this chapter, I argue that, to adequately account for the acquisition of grammar, a different kind of language acquisition model is necessary—one that holds that the principles and constraints embodied in grammar may be unique to grammar and require task-specific learning mechanisms; that is, ones specifically designed for grammar acquisition. Nevertheless, development of a fully normal linguistic/communicative system involves development of several different components and an intimate coordination among them.

In the first part of this chapter, I discuss the major current models of language acquisition and their theoretical support. In the second part, I present empirical research findings from several populations that bear directly on the issues at hand. In the third part, I describe a model of language as a cognitive system that is an outgrowth of our own research, is consistent with the findings of others, and argues for a specific view of language and language acquisition. The last part presents summary discussion and conclusions.

MODELS OF LANGUAGE ACQUISITION

There does not appear to be a consensus in the field of child language research regarding what needs to be explained or what constitutes explanation for language acquisition. In fact, the task of trying to account for how children learn to speak (or sign) and understand the language of their community has proved to be such a difficult one that the bulk of research in the field has shifted away from explanation of child language acquisition to the description of child language—a change Pinker (1985) characterized as a shift in research emphasis from first order issues to second order concerns.

There have been legitimate attempts to construct theoretical models of language acquisition, but these attempts reflect the lack of consensus regarding explanation. Therefore, despite these models, the basic questions of language acquisition remain essentially unanswered: (1) what is learned, (2) how is input utilized, and (3) how does learning proceed?

Perhaps the fundamental question regarding language acquisition revolves around the central puzzle of how a child changes from being in a nonlinguistic or prelinguistic state to becoming a language knower. A theory of language acquisition must make explicit the mechanisms underlying this change. In so doing, it must make explicit how a child reaches each intermediate stage (knowledge state) along the way and moves from one stage to another, eventually attaining full adult linguistic competence. An explanatory theory must also account for how children do this on the basis of input they encounter and can process.

There may not be disagreement on this set of goals for a theory. But there appears to be substantial disagreement as to what set of facts and/or what knowledge the theory must account for, and therefore where to look for explanations. For some researchers the fact that language serves communication is primary. As a result, for them not only must acquisition of the rule system underlying the social-communicative uses of language be included in a language acquisition theory, but an understanding of all aspects of the growing system must incorporate an explanation in terms of their communicative base. To other researchers, the fact that language is a cognitive system (and only one of many) is central. To these scholars, a theory of language acquisition must reflect the principles and constraints that shape the growing cognitive abilities of the child, both linguistic and nonlinguistic. Explanations for the emergent linguistic system must be sought in terms of its larger cognitive base. For these two groups of researchers, then, there is a focus on nonlinguistic explanations for linguistic phenomena. For a third group, however, the linguistic knowledge of the language learner largely apart from other domains of knowledge is primary. For them explanations for language acquisition must be sought in terms of the character of knowledge eventually attained. The explanations this group seeks are largely linguistic explanations for linguistic phenomena.

The fact that nearly all children successfully acquire language and do so within a relatively short period of time supports the contention that a strong set of constraints is involved in acquisition, and most models of language acquisition propose constraints to accommodate this fact. They differ, however, in where their hypothesized constraints lie. As a result they also differ in where they place the burden of acquisition and the primary explanations they offer for the facts of acquisition.

There are three major theoretical approaches to language acquisition. Each is discussed in turn with comments on its current theoretical status.

The Social/Interaction Model

Language is a specialized and conventionalized extension of cooperative action. To be understood properly, its acquisition must be viewed as a transformation of modes of assuring cooperation that are prior to language . . .

—Bruner, 1975, p. 2.

The social/interaction model (Bruner, 1975; Nelson, 1977; Newson, 1978; Snow, 1972, 1977; Snow & Ferguson, 1977;) is the model formulated by those stressing that language has a communicative base and can be accounted for on the basis of its communicative substructure. The constraints that are considered by this model to be relevant to the acquisition process (at least those discussed in the pertinent literature) are external to the child. They are found in the environment in the structure of the interaction routines engaged in with the child, and in the restricted nature of the linguistic input the child receives. The major tenet of this model is, then, that there are factors and constraints in the linguistic/communicative environment that facilitate the acquisition process and help to explain it.

The first set of factors that are stressed includes the embedding of language in social contexts that are repetitive and familiar to the child and the accompaniment to language of nonlinguistic communicative cues. The use of language in the context of familiar and frequently repeated social interactions and routines is claimed to serve several ends: It presents language as an instrument for regulating joint action and joint attention, it sets up associations between specific words and phrases and specific activities and events that in turn focus attention on the communicative underpinnings of the code; it provides abundant opportunities for imitation and rehearsal, and it ties the use of the linguistic code to conversational settings from which to learn the basic principles of speech acts and discourse (Bruner, 1975; Keenan & Schieffelin, 1976; Snow, 1972). The use of accompanying nonlinguistic devices to signal meaning (e.g., gestures) serves as an interpretative base onto which linguistic structure can be mapped (Macnamara, 1972, 1977; Zukow, Reilly, & Greenfield, 1979).

There is considerable evidence that language is indeed embedded in the kind of social/communicative contexts described by this model. However, a central fact of language acquisition to be explained, stated from a communicative point of view, is how a child changes from being a solely nonlinguistic communicator into a linguistic communicator as well. The proposal that these first factors comprise crucial elements in the environment does not account for this fact. The mechanisms by which these elements are used for acquisition, that is, by which children apprehend the (correct) associations between linguistic events and social events, by which they extract the rules governing speech acts and discourse, or by which they map linguistic structures onto nonlinguistic ones, must be made explicit, and they have not yet been (see Shatz, 1982, for relevant discussion). Thus the explanatory value of having identified these purportedly crucial characteristics of early communicative interaction with the child remains to be demonstrated.

The second set of factors stressed by this model deals more directly with acquisition of the linguistic code itself. It concerns the nature of the linguistic input to the child. The model stresses that primary linguistic input to children (labeled ''motherese'' by Newport, Gleitman, & Gleitman, 1977) has a number of special properties. It is a greatly reduced, simplified, and repetitive version of the adult linguistic system, and it is modified to correspond to (perhaps be slightly in advance of) the linguistic level of the language-learner (Cross, 1977; Snow, 1972; Snow & Ferguson, 1977) so that it maximizes its usefulness to the child as a model of what is to be learned (e.g., ''intelligent text presentation'' as in Levelt, 1975). The basic claim involved asserts that this specialized input serves as an ideal language-teaching model and that its special character plays a causal role in language acquisition.

A large number of studies are descriptive of the fact that mothers and other caretakers do not talk to their young children as they would to their adult peers. Two of the key claims about the character of speech to children appear to have little support, however: (1) that "motherese" is simple along some definable dimension of structural complexity, and (2) that it is "fine-tuned" to the linguistic abilities of the child. (See Gleitman, Newport, & Gleitman, 1982; Hoff-Ginsburg & Shatz, 1982; Newport, Gleitman, & Gleitman, 1977; and Wexler & Culicover, 1980, for review and discussion of these points as well as other aspects of this model.) Moreover, the central claim that "motherese" plays a causal role in language acquisition has not been borne out (Gleitman et al., 1982; Schiff, 1979), a finding consistent with the considerable cross-cultural differences in the character of caretaker speech to children that have been reported (Ratner & Pye, 1984; Schiefflin & Ochs, 1983). As with the first set of factors, then, the mere identification of qualities of speech to children, which set it apart from other speech, does not explain how it affects language learning. The mechanism(s) by which these special properties of input are recognized and utilized by the child must be proposed. In the end, sound claims concerning the effect of specific properties of input cannot be made without knowing the nature of the language acquisition apparatus.

This is not to say that certain general and even specific claims of this model will not in the long run be found to be true, even apart from the obvious and undisputed assumption that the linguistic environment makes language learning possible and has a direct influence on what is learned (e.g., which language is acquired). It is of interest, however, that in those instances in which careful research demonstrates the character of the input to have a clear effect on language learning (e.g., Furrow, Nelson, and Benedict, 1979; Gleitman et al., 1982; Newport, Gleitman, & Gleitman, 1977) the findings would argue for a child-directed acquisition process rather than the environmentally directed acquisition process proposed by the social/interaction model. However, the theoretical viability of a communicatively based explanation of language acquisition is a separate issue from the validity of the specific claims of the social/interaction model in its current form, and there is considerable work on the adult system from which such a model might draw.

Cognitive Models of Language Acquisition

We are suggesting that there is a great borrowing going on, in which language is viewed as a parasitic system that builds its structures by raiding the software packages of prior or parallel cognitive capacities.
—Bates, 1979, p. 6.

The models falling into this category stress the fact that language is only one of many cognitive systems to develop in childhood, and thus focus on cognitive factors to explain and understand language growth. They all view language acquisition as a child-driven process. Therefore, according to a cognitivist view, the constraints implicated in language acquisition are internal to the child.

There are several different versions of cognitive models of language acquisition, each making somewhat different claims. The strongest form of those models stressing cognitive factors in language acquisition contends that language is rooted in and emerges out of nonlinguistic sensorimotor intelligence and is but one instantiation of its final stage—the attainment of symbolic-representational ability (Inhelder, Lezine, Sinclair, & Stambak, 1972; Piaget, 1962, 1980). It also contends that sensorimotor intelligence is prerequisite to language, because it is prerequisite to all forms of symbolic ability. Moreover, because language is only one manifestation of a general symbolic capacity, the same cognitive structures and operations thought to underlie other forms of symbolic thought (i.e., deferred imitation and symbolic play) are thought to underlie language. Language acquisition beyond the emergent stage is, according to this model, made possible and inevitable by the cognitive schemes and operations underlying all intellectual development beyond the sensorimotor period (Piaget, 1980). Language is thus tied to nonlinguistic cognitive function throughout its development.

Research testing this form of the model has not supported many of its strong claims. For example, that sensorimotor intelligence is a prerequisite to all aspects of language learning (see Corrigan, 1978, 1979 for reviews). As a result, and consistent with the growing rejections of a strict Piagetian account of mental development more generally, most scholars within this framework favor a modified version of this model, a version sometimes referred to as a *neo-Piagetian* or a *correlational* model (e.g., Bates, Benigni, Bretherton, Camaioni, & Volterra, 1977; Case, 1978; Ingram, 1978).

This modified model proposes that there are critical ties between language and nonlinguistic cognition based on common cognitive principles and structures, but these ties exist only between specific linguistic milestones and specific cognitive attainments. The development of these common structures yokes specific abilities to each other at specific moments in development (Corrigan, 1978, 1979). Some of the proposals of this model include critical ties between sensorimotor stage VI and the emergence of single words expressing notions of location and possessor (Bates et al., 1977; Ingram, 1978), the ability to follow several invisible displacements of an object and the ability to comment on the disappearance and reappearance of objects (Corrigan, 1978; Miller, Chapman, & Bedrosian, 1977), the ability to combine two or more gestural schemes and the transition into multiword speech (Nicholich, 1977; Thal & Bates, 1988), preoperational intelligence and metapragmatic comments (Bates, 1976), reversibility and productive nominalization and polite requests, (Bates, 1976; Ingram, 1975) conservation of continuous quantity as well as dencentrism, and comprehension and production of passives (Beilin, 1975; Ferreiro, 1971; Sinclair & Ferreiro, 1970).

One version of this model holds that the nonlinguistic attainments are actually prerequisite to the related linguistic developments (Ferreiro, 1971; Veneziano, 1981). A second version of the model posits only that both developments are tied, in each case by a common underlying structure (Bates, 1979). In both versions, however, nonlinguistic cognitive structures are the foundation of mental development, whether it be language acquisition or nonlinguistic cognitive growth.

The constraints governing linguistic (and nonlinguistic) development are not explained in detail by this model. Processing constraints such as short-term memory and attentional space limitations are referred to and suggested as candidate constraints impinging on language acquisition (e.g., Case, 1978; Shatz, 1977). But specific proposals regarding how these constraints actually interface with the learning apparatus of the child to predict the course of language acquisition have yet to be made. It must be recognized, however, that arguing for strong constraints on processing capacity in the child requires that the child bring to the language acquisition task powerful language-learning mechanisms in order for language acquisition to go forward and result in full linguistic competence in spite of these processing constraints.

Current versions of cognitive models suffer additionally from the fact that none of them explicates the mechanisms by which they might propose that learning takes place. All of the cognitive models propose that language and at least certain nonlinguistic developments are based on shared underlying structures. This proposal necessarily implies the existence of structural commonalities or at least structural parallels across related domains. Some attempts have been made to identify such structural similarities (Greenfield & Schneider, 1977; Greenfield, 1978; Greenfield, Nelson & Saltzman, 1972), with the accompanying contention that structural similarities between different domains make language acquisition less difficult and less of a mystery. The alleged structural parallels have been argued to hold only at a general and superficial level, however (Curtiss, Yamada, & Fromkin, 1979). In any case, without specifying (not just naming) the mechanisms by which children recognize (hardly transparent) analogous structural principles, it is not clear how any of the mysteries of language acquisition have been cleared up.

For a cognitive model to explain how cognitive factors can account for the fact of language acquisition, it will have to specify the nature of the internal, representational structures of children.

> The Cognitive Theory requires that children have available to them a system of representational structures similar enough in format to syntactic structures to promote language learning, and at the same time, flexible and general enough to be computable by children's cognitive and perceptual faculties on the basis of nonlinguistic information. Until we have a theory of the child's mental representations that meets these conditions, The Cognitive Theory will remain an unsupported hypothesis. (Pinker, 1979, p. 271)

The present inadequacies of cognitive models do not imply that some or all of their basic tenets will not in the long run be upheld. There is a growing concensus in the field of developmental psycholinguistics, based on close examination of early child language data in particular, that what occurs in the earliest stages of language development may be best characterized as conceptually constrained and conceptually driven (but see Hyams, 1986). The extent to which such models are explanatory for language acquisition, however, will depend on their explication of the child's mental apparatus that makes not only cognitive development but language acquisition possible and inevitable.

Linguistic Models

In the case of grammars a fixed, genetically determined system . . .
narrowly constrains the forms they can assume.
                              —Chomsky, 1980a, p. 35.

What I refer to here as linguistic models are the models of language acquisition proposed by those for whom the ultimate achievement of full linguistic competence is the most impressive and important fact of acquisition (e.g., Gleitman & Wanner, 1982; Klein, 1981; Pinker, 1984; Roeper, 1972, 1982; Roeper & Williams, 1987). Guided by theoretical models of adult grammar, linguistic models of language acquisition stress the abstract, highly complex nature of the structural principles to be acquired. Such models assume that the richer and the more abstract and complex the knowledge to be acquired, the more tightly constrained the process of acquisition will have to be. Thus, proponents of linguistic models assert that acquisition is only possible if children come to the language-learning situation equipped with knowledge about the form of possible grammars and possible linguistic rules (Notice the essential difference between this type of constraint, which aids the language learner and the type of constraint proposed by cognitive models, which limits the power of the language learner; but see Turkewitz & Kenny, 1982.) From this standpoint, the essential questions of language acquisition (termed "the logical problem of language acquisition," Baker, 1979) have been crystallized into three questions a theory of acquisition must eventually answer: How acquisition happens within the boundary conditions of (1) such a short time, (2) data that vastly underdetermine what is learned, and (3) no access to negative evidence to assist in learning.

Within the framework of linguistic models of language learning, there have been at least two different positions regarding the nature of the acquisition process. One might best be defined as the hypothesis-generating position (e.g., Wexler & Culicover, 1980); a second, the parameter-setting position (Chomsky, 1981; Hyams, 1986; Roeper & Williams, 1987).

In the first position, children (already armed with innate knowledge about language that highly constrains the hypothesis space upon which inductions are made formulate hypotheses about the structure of their particular language based on the data they receive. To this extent, the course of language acquisition is both child-driven and data-driven. Furthermore, because full linguistic competence is acquired in a relatively short time, this position holds that the learner must be exposed to complex grammatical structures early on. (Note the difference between this position and that of the ''motherese'' hypothesis, which contends that simplicity of input facilitates acquisition.)

In the second position, innate knowledge about language is assumed to be sufficiently rich so as to bias the language learner to consider only a small set of structural possibilities that differ solely in relation to particular settings of one of a predetermined set of possible instantiations or parameters of a principle of grammar. This second position places little significance on the quality or timing of the input data because the learner is hypothesized to rely very little on input.

In both positions, language acquisition is viewed as a maturationally constrained process. But in the first position, considerable learning is thought to occur, in the form of language-particular rule construction, whereas in the second position, learning per se does not take place (except with respect to a language's individual lexicon and some idiosyncratic properties as well). Rather, acquisition is seen as an innately specified series of choices in which options become fixed. Movement from one stage of grammar to another is triggered by the maturation of universal grammatical principles or peripheral (nonlinguistic) mechanisms that allow for the consideration or reanalysis of key input data.

Linguistic models may have progressed further towards explanation than other models. They are concerned with characterizing the linguistic mental apparatus of the child to which end they incorporate constructs from linguistic theory consistent with some currently advocated formal theory of grammar (e.g., with lexical functional grammar, as in Bresnan, 1978; Pinker, 1984, or with government-binding theory, as in Chomsky, 1980b, 1981; Hyams, 1986). Recent acquisition research within a linguistic framework has furthermore suggested candidate mechanisms by which input data are selectively processed and used by the child to extract key language particular information (e.g., Borer & Wexler, 1987; Gleitman and Wanner 1982). These models perhaps more than the others, then, have addressed themselves to all three acquisition questions: (1) what is learned, (2) how input is utilized, and (3) how language acquisition proceeds. However, they largely ignore the role that conceptual and social knowledge might play in the acquisition of a system which, after all, has two central functions: communication and representation/ideation.

The Task-Specificity of Language

In addition to its different focus, each of the models discussed makes different predictions regarding the relation language development should hold to other aspects of development. The social/interaction model, which contends that language is communicatively based and that the communicative environment directs the course of language acquisition, predicts that key differences in the communicative environment will result in different outcomes of language acquisition, and that we should not find children who show dissociations between linguistic competence and communicative competence. The strong cognitive model, which like the other cognitive models holds that nonlinguistic cognitive structures are the basis of language development, predicts that language will develop only after the attainment of prerequisite, nonlinguistic cognitive structures. All cognitive models predict that language should be impaired to the extent that (related) cognitive development is impaired. Linguistic models entertain the possibility that grammar is based on unique and domain-specific structural principles whose acquisition requires task-specific learning mechanisms. This premise allows for the relative independence of language acquisition from other areas of development.

Central to these different predictions on the relation between language and other aspects of mind is the issue of the task-specificity of language and language learning. There are basically two positions on this issue: (1) that language is based on structural and organizing principles that define other knowledge domains as well as language; (2) that language is based on structural and organizing principles that are unique to it or domain-specific. The first position implies that language is learned by a nonspecific-learning mechanism, perhaps a general inductive procedure. This position is neutral with regard to the claim that such a learning mechanism is highly constrained. It allows for the possibility that learning is essentially unconstrained as well as for the possibility that learning is a highly constrained process, perhaps even so constrained that the learning process itself shapes the character of what is learned (e.g., Newport, 1982; Turkewitz & Kenny, 1982; Newport, in press). The second position necessitates the existence of a language-specific learning mechanism, and dictates that the mechanism be highly constrained. Otherwise, the learner could formulate too many hypotheses about language (only some of which would be true) or tolerate too many missettings of linguistic parameters to be ensured of learning language within a human lifetime.

Important theoretical work has appeared recently that grapples extensively with issues of learnability, in particular, language learnability (Anderson, 1977; Clark, 1988; Gold, 1967; Pinker, 1984, 1985, 1987; Wexler, 1977, 1982; Wexler & Culicover, 1980; Wexler and Manzini, 1987). All of this work points to the requirement that language structure be highly constrained and its acquisition similarly constrained. But although some questions of language learnability may be resolved on logical-theoretic grounds, whether language itself is based on domain-specific principles and whether language acquisition is achieved by a task-specific learning device, are questions that require empirical resolution.

The second part of this chapter is devoted to empirical data from a variety of populations that bear on these last two questions. In so doing, they also have bearing on the models of language acquisition already outlined. In the last part, I return to a discussion of these issues.

RESEARCH ON THE TASK-SPECIFICITY
OF LANGUAGE

The research discussed later deals with populations who evidence the selective impairment or selective preservation of language learning abilities. These populations are our focus because they, more than normals or individuals who show across-the-board impairments, help to elucidate the true and necessary dependency relationships between language and other areas. To illustrate, take two abilities, A and B, hypothesized to be fundamentally related. The hypothesized relationship between A and B may be one of dependency, wherein B is prerequisite to A or otherwise essential for the emergence or expression of A, or one resulting from shared underlying bases or origins. On either hypothesis, it would be predicted that A could not develop or remain undisrupted independent of B. To the extent that A and B consistently appear tied, then, even in individuals with abnormal and uneven cognitive functioning, we have strong evidence in support of one of these hypotheses; that is, of a necessary and fundamental tie between them. To the extent that A and B can develop or be disrupted independently, however, we have evidence that the two abilities may not be so tied.

Individuals with Selective Impairments in Language Learning

Linguistic Isolates. Individuals who have been reared in social isolation enable us to test hypotheses about the necessary and sufficient conditions for linguistic and nonlinguistic growth. Only certain cases of such individuals provide revealing data for the issue of the task-specificity of language, however. These are cases where the language/nonlanguage profile is highly disparate. Cases such as these help to illuminate the separability and domain-specificity of different mental abilities. I discuss three cases that meet this description. The first is Kaspar Hauser; the second, Genie; and the third, Chelsea.

There is considerable disagreement as to the validity of the case of Kaspar Hauser as several writings assert that Kaspar Hauser was an imposter and not a socially isolated child at all. There are over 2,000 documents regarding this case, however; and the vast majority of them substantiates the validity of this case and provides interesting and detailed information about Kaspar Hauser's postisolation progress. The key sources of information on this case were highly regarded professionals in their time with undisputed credentials (Daumer, 1832; Pietler-Ley, 1927; Von Feuerbach, 1832). Additional careful research and examination of this case has also been conducted (e.g., Heyer, 1964; Pies, 1966), and the reader is referred to these sources for more information and detail.

Kaspar Hauser was apparently isolated from the age of 3 or 4 years until he was a teenager of about 15 or 16 years. He had been kept in a small room, totally isolated, supplied with food and otherwise cared for while he was asleep (or, perhaps, drugged). The size of the room prohibited him from standing erect or lying flat, and during his imprisonment he neither stood nor walked. During these years he never spoke or was spoken to.

Upon his release and subsequent discovery in 1828, Kaspar Hauser's remarkable capacity was revealed (and documented and described in numerous writings). He made strikingly rapid progress in almost every area. Within months of his discovery he displayed remarkable ability in drawing, memory, and reasoning capacity. He lived only 5 years after he was found, but during that time was noted for his astonishing intellect. He was consistently reputed to philosophize about all he was learning, about life in general, and about his own past. Within that short 5-year period after his discovery, he learned to read and write and became competent in mathematics and several other academic areas.

His linguistic progress, although rapid and impressive in certain respects, reportedly stood alone as the single area of mental function that remained problematic. Semantic aspects of language (German) were apparently readily mastered. Upon entering society he immediately began learning words, acquired a sizeable vocabulary within a very short period (a few months), and began combining words into short sentences also within a remarkably short time (again, a few months). The vocabulary he mastered and the logical wellformedness and complexity of the propositions he evidently comprehended and produced were sufficiently sophisticated to allow him to participate actively in philosophical and intellectual discussions as time went on. Yet, in contrast, he displayed consistent and persistent difficulties with the grammar of German.

> To the astonishment of all, . . . he . . . very soon learned to speak, sufficiently, at least, in some degree to express his thoughts. Yet, his attempts to speak remained for a long time a mere chopping of words, so miserably defective . . . that it was seldom possible to ascertain . . . what he meant to express by the fragments of speech which he jumbled together.

From a later description,

> His enunciation of words which he knew, was plain and determinate, without hesitating or stammering. But, in all that he said, the conjunctions, participles, and adverbs were still almost entirely wanting; his conjugation embraced little more than the infinitive and he was most of all deficient in respect to his syntax, which was in a state of miserable confusion. The pronoun *I* occurred very rarely; he . . . spoke of himself in the third person, calling himself Kaspar. (Von Feuerbach, 1832, translated by Simpkin & Marshall)

He reportedly never mastered German syntax or morphology, evidencing a selective grammatical deficit that stood in marked contrast with his impressive intellectual abilities in all other areas, including conceptual aspects of language (here being encapsulated as semantics). It is testimony to his remarkable cognitive gifts that he could communicate so effectively and at such a high level, given his linguistic deficiencies.

The second relevant case is Genie. There have been a number of published reports on the case (Curtiss, 1977; Curtiss, 1979; Curtiss, Fromkin, Krashen, Rigler, & Rigler, 1974; Curtiss, Fromkin, & Krashen, 1978; Fromkin, Krashen, Curtiss, Rigler, & Rigler, 1974) and the reader is referred to these for more information. Although certain details about Genie's early life remain unknown, there is a considerable information on both the case history and her life subsequent to her discovery.

Genie was isolated for a period of 12 years, from the age of 20 months to 13 years, 7 months. Her life prior to her isolation involved physical restraint and most probably malnutrion and neglect. She was born at the 50th percentile in height and weight but fell beneath 16th percentile by her first birthday. During her first year, she wore a physically restraining Frejka splint for 7 months to correct a congenital hip dislocation.

Beginning at the age of 20 months, however, Genie was both physically restrained and isolated. She was confined to a small bedroom in the back of the family home where she was tied to an infant potty seat by means of a harness. Left in this room for over 12 years, she was fed only infant food and received practically no visual, tactile, or auditory stimulation of any kind, including little linguistic input. There was no TV or radio in the home, and because of the father's extreme intolerance for noise, all speech in the home was kept at a nearly inaudible volume. Genie's brother and father were her primary caretakers, and by design, neither spoke to her. When Genie was 13-1/2 years old, her mother managed to escape, with Genie, from the home. Shortly afterward Genie was discovered. She could barely walk, couldn't chew or bite, and neither understood nor spoke language.

From the time of her discovery on, Genie avidly explored her surroundings and began to show clear conceptual and intellectual progress. She quickly began organizing and classifying her environment (evidenced by her play activities, and a little later, by her language), and followed a course of steady growth and development. Her mental age (MA) as measured by standard psychological measures of IQ, (for example, the Leiter International Performance Scale, the Wechsler Intelligence Scale for Children, and the Raven's Progressive Matrices) increased one year for each year post discovery. Within 4 years of her discovery, she had clearly attained most aspects of concrete operational intelligence, including both operational and figurative thought (e.g., reversibility, decentrism, spatial rotation).

In contrast to Kaspar Hauser, Genie's mental profile was far more uneven. She demonstrated fully developed, even superior abilities in the domain of visual-spatial function (e.g., Gestalt and part/whole abilities, spatial rotation, spatial location, conservation of spatial features, and knowledge about visual-spatial features, such as size, shape, and color); but demonstrated impaired verbal short-term memory and linguistic function. Like Kaspar Hauser, however, she showed a discrepancy between her acquisition of semantics on the one hand, and her acquisition of grammatical rules on the other.

Within a few months after her discovery in 1970, Genie began to produce single words and then acquired vocabulary rapidly. Within 3 to 4 months of her first words, she had acquired an expressive vocabulary of 100 to 200 words and began to combine two words at a time. Even her early vocabulary included words for color concepts, numbers, emotional states, and all levels of category membership (superordinate, basic, subordinate), including subtle distinctions (e.g., pen, marker; jumper, dress). Her acquisition of lexicon and the expression of meaning relations, including multipropositionality, steadily progressed and increased. (See Curtiss, 1977, 1981, 1982, for more details.)

In contrast, her utterances remained largely agrammatic and hierarchically flat. Her ability to produce sentences developed only in so far as she was able to produce increasingly longer strings and strings that increased in propositional complexity. Her speech, even after 8 years, remained essentially devoid of closed class morphology and of most syntactic devices and operations, as illustrated later. This dissociation between semantics and syntax seen in Kaspar Hauser's case, then, was a hallmark of Genie's language, too.

Examples of Genie's Utterances

Yellow poster.
Mike paint.
Applesauce buy store.
Small two cup.
Little white clear box.
I like elephant eat peanut.
Neal come happy; Neal not come sad.
Tomorrow R. coming tomorrow Thursday.

Dark blue, light blue, surprise square and rectangle.
Genie have Momma have baby grow up.

Genie's linguistic limitations extended to the use of language for effective interactive purposes. Her utterances were consistently well-formed with regard to their presuppositional and implicative structure and generally adhered to Grice's conversational postulates (Grice, 1975). That is, Genie was sensitive to the information needs of her listener, and she was generally truthful, relevant, (always) brief, and on topic. However, her means of initiating, participating in, and controlling or regulating verbal interaction were greatly restricted. She possessed an impoverished set of linguistic-pragmatic devices and relied heavily on simple statements of the proposition or on repetition (of her own or others' statements of the proposition) to perform a variety of pragmatic functions—introducing topics, continuing topics, acknowledging and responding to comments, requests and questions, making comments and requests, and asking questions. Moreover, she failed to use social rituals (e.g., "Hi, How are you?") or conversational operators (e.g., "well, O.K.")—the trappings that help to make a conversation sound normal. Thus, those aspects of effective communication depending on her appreciation of conversational content and the communicative intent and needs of her listener were least impaired, whereas those aspects of effective communicative interaction depending on socially conditioned skills of conversational participation were sorely deficient.

A third case involves a hearing-impaired adult, Chelsea, who is attempting first language acquisition in her thirties. Three weeks prior to Chelsea's delivery, Chelsea's mother was hospitalized for a hemorrhagic bladder infection, possibly as a result of cytomegalovirus, a common cause of congenital deafness; and within the first month of Chelsea's life, her mother suspected that Chelsea was deaf. Unfortunately, because Chelsea was born and raised in a remote, rural community without diagnostic, rehabilitative, or educational resources for the deaf, and because she was misdiagnosed, she received no instruction or training of any kind.

Chelsea was discovered when a neurological and audiological examination was requested by local social services. At that time, at age 32, she was fitted with hearing aids, and a program of language instruction and cognitive evaluation was begun. Testing to date shows a striking scatter in linguistic abilities, but a more even cognitive profile, with a consistent MA of approximately 10 years (N. Dronkers, 1987).

Chelsea's linguistic performance exhibits marked discrepancies between her lexical abilities and her ability to combine vocabulary into appropriate, semantically well-formed, and grammatical utterances. Her lexicon has steadily increased and appears to be organized along normal semantic lines, as evidenced by her above-12th-grade-level performance on the Producing Word Associations subtest of the Comprehensive Evaluation of Language Functions (CELF) (Semel & Wiig, 1980). In contrast, her multiword utterances are, almost without exception, unacceptable grammatically, and often propositionally unclear or illformed as well. Her lexical knowledge seems limited to (denotative) definitional cores and does not appear to encompass either subcategorization information or logical structure constraints (in contrast to Genie and probably Kaspar Hauser as well). Likewise, her expressive language appears at its best, limited to the production of combinations of semantically relevant substantives, unelaborated morphologically, and ungoverned by constraints on word order, as illustrated in the following examples:

Examples of Chelsea's Utterances

The small a the hat
Richard eat peppers hot.
Orange Tim car in.

Banana the eat.
I Wanda be drive come.
The boat sits water on.
Breakfast eating girl.
Combing hair the boy.
The woman is bus the going.
The girl is cone the ice cream shopping buying the man.

Chelsea's discourse skills appear at least superficially to be almost the flip side of Genie's. Chelsea's topic-related skills are limited; that is, her ability to contribute to a topic's progress is poor, and she does not consistently appear to remain on topic. These limitations may, however, reflect Chelsea's comprehension difficulties coupled with her difficulties in constructing coherent propositions. Her other discourse abilities seem remarkably well-developed. For example, the range of speech acts she displays, her use of social rituals, and her use of conventional conversational operators are rich and appropriate.

The cases of Kaspar Hauser, Genie, and Chelsea, then, suggest that there may be a critical difference between conceptual (semantic) aspects of language on the one hand, and rules of grammar (here syntax and morphology) on the other. This critical difference has three potential (related) bases: First, the learning capacity these individuals displayed and utilized for other intellectual domains was insufficient and/or inappropriate for learning grammar (in Kaspar Hauser's case, even extraordinary intellect wasn't sufficient). Second, the learning principles underlying grammar acquisition were selectively impaired from birth; or, third, by the time they were discovered, Chelsea, Genie, and Kaspar Hauser had passed the age at which such mechanisms were still functional. In Genie's case, she is reported to have begun talking before she was isolated, suggesting that, in her case at least, language learning was proceeding normally before it was interrupted. In any event, all of these explanations for the selective linguistic deficits these cases displayed point to a task-specific grammar acquisition ability. Their cases further suggest, however, that not all aspects of language may require task-specific abilities. In Genie's and Kaspar Hauser's cases, lexical and propositional semantics developed with apparent ease. This area of language at least appears to be accessible to other learning strategies or developmental principles. The rate and level of mastery of lexical and propositional semantics may furthermore reflect or be tied to nonlinguistic conceptual and intellectual ability. This possibility, however, leaves Chelsea's problems with propositional form unexplained, suggesting that lexical semantics and propositional semantics may be differentially vulnerable to age at acquisition, with lexical semantics the more resilient of the two.

The effective use of language for communicative purposes is a less clear matter. Genie's case suggests that those parameters of communication tied to the needs and intentions of the listener may depend on the cognitive abilities of the child for their development; whereas those parameters of verbal communication reflecting culture-specific phrases and routines (topic introducers, request forms, forms of acknowledgement, etc.) are tied to the social development of the individual. Because Chelsea grew up in a healthy, loving family environment, her ready acquisition of the culture-specific conventions of discourse would, then, be predicted. Her topic-related difficulties, however, remain unexplained.

Childhood Hemiplegics With and Without Hemidecortication.   The children discussed in this section include those who have suffered prenatal, perinatal, or childhood left-hemisphere lesions. One group of children had surgical removal of the diseased hemisphere; the other groups did not.

The first group of children acquired unilateral lesions of the left hemisphere before or at birth. Such children, who retain both hemispheres and who therefore develop with one diseased hemisphere, are commonly referred to as *hemiplegic.* A number of studies on hemiplegic children are well known in the literature (Annett, 1973; Basser, 1962; Bishop, 1967; Hood & Perlstein, 1955), but only one study presents detailed information on the language and nonlanguage abilities of their subject population (Rankin, Aram, & Horwitz, 1980). I therefore rely only on the data presented in the Rankin et al. study in discussing this population.

Rankin et al. reported on three children who sustained left-hemisphere lesions. Seven separate measures were used to assess language ability (two phonology, two lexical, and three syntax tests), and the Leiter International Performance Scale was used to measure nonverbal intelligence. At the time of testing, the children were 6 to 8 years old, with an average age of 7 years, 11 months.

All three children showed intact ability (or equivalent ability to the children with unilateral right-hemisphere damage) on the phoneme discrimination and expressive lexicon tests. On all of the other linguistic measures, however, the left-hemisphere damaged children were impaired, with their most severe decrements in comprehension of syntax. All three of the children also showed delayed onset of one and two-word speech. With one exception, all of the children in the study, both left- and right-damaged, had below-average Leiter scores; but the left-hemisphere lesioned children showed slightly greater deficits in MA.

The findings of this study indicate right-hemisphere deficiency in language acquisition and performance. The linguistic areas least impaired under right-hemisphere control were phonology and lexical semantics, although even these areas showed some decrements. Greatest impairments were displayed in receptive syntax.

A second population involves children who sustained unilateral lesions in childhood. Although several studies have been carried out on relevant populations (Dennis, 1980c; Woods, 1980; Woods and Carey, 1979; Woods & Teuber, 1978), one in particular has reported detailed findings (Aram, Ekelman, Rose, & Whitaker, 1985). Aram et al. studied both left- and right-hemisphere-lesioned cases and found that children with damage to either hemisphere had impaired lexical comprehension and production, but only children with left-hemisphere lesions had MLU's significantly shorter than nonimpaired controls and impaired comprehension and production of grammatical structures, as evidenced both by formal tests and spontaneous speech.

The third population included here is a group whose linguistic abilities have been studied in great detail (Dennis, 1980a, b; Dennis & Kohn, 1975; Dennis & Whitaker, 1976, 1977). They are ten hemidecortidate children. One group had Sturge-Weber syndrome and had one cortical hemisphere removed within the first year of life to control perinatal seizures; the second group also sustained cortical pathology within the first year of life, but had hemispherectomy later in childhood.

In a series of studies Dennis and her colleagues have systematically studied IQ, cognitive skills, and language abilities in all of these children. At each data collection point (during the 8-year period of study), IQ and almost all cognitive skills were equivalent in both left- and right-hemidecorticates. The exceptions to the impressive similarity in mental abilities are in the area of visual-spatial function, where the left-hemidecorticates outperform the right, and in language, where the right-hemidecorticates outstrip the left.

Both the semantic and syntactic abilities of this population have been studied in detail. No differences were found in the size or range of receptive or expressive lexicon in the two groups. In addition to equivalent levels of performance, no difference between the groups was found in the apparent processing strategies utilized for word access or retrieval. Thus both hemispheres appear equivalently able to acquire and access at least common words, except that the left-hemidecorticates, but not the right, evidenced problems using rhyming cues to access words (the only phonological operation tested). Thus the two hemispheres, though equivalent in their phoneme discrimination and production abilities, may be unequal in their ability to perform phonological computations.

Relational and propositional semantics also do not appear to be similarly developed in both hemispheres. The structure of interrelations between words, apprehended in part on the basis of the componential structure of word meaning, appears less tightly organized and less well-integrated with other aspects of linguistic structure. For example, the meaning of a word is partly defined by sentence context; yet extracting semantic information involving conceptual focus (information typically signalled by surface syntactic structure and sentence intonation patterns), determining functional relations in passive sentences, and using interpretative rules such as negation in conjunction with syntactic structure, are all inadequately and inefficiently performed by the right hemisphere. As a consequence, semantic processes, even when they hinge directly on word-meaning (as with entailment or implicature), are affected and impaired in the right hemisphere.

Syntactic deficits are equally apparent in the right hemisphere. The left-hemidecorticates take longer to discriminate all sentence types, are poorer at sentence repetition, and poorer at comprehension of complex syntactic structures. In addition, the two hemispheres appear to process sentence structure differently, even for structures they can both interpret correctly. In contrast, the isolated right hemisphere demonstrates more proficiency with the structuring of conversational discourse (Lovett, Dennis, & Newman, 1986).

These hemidecorticate cases suggest two conclusions. First, like the hemiplegic cases previously discussed, the hemidecorticate cases indicate that the right hemisphere is inferior to the left as a language learner. The right hemisphere shows deficits in phonology, in syntax, and in the integration of semantics with syntactic structure. In this population as with others discussed, though, lexical semantic abilities appear well-developed. Second, the findings Dennis reported suggest that the right hemisphere utilizes different processing strategies than the left hemisphere to encode and decode syntactic structures. These findings, if supported, indicate that the right hemisphere differs from the left in both capacity and strategy for linguistic function (but see Bishop, 1983). And this is true despite equal intellectual capacity in both hemispheres. These cases thus suggest that grammar acquisition requires task-specific ability, that this ability is tied to the left hemisphere (in most individuals), and that the right hemisphere utilizes distinct processing strategies for language, despite their inadequacies.

Individuals with Selectively Preserved Language Abilities.   If the acquisition of at least certain aspects of language is a domain-specific affair, then in principle it should be possible to find evidence for their selective preservation. That is, it should be possible to find children who demonstrate selectively preserved language acquisition despite other deficits. This section presents evidence that such children do exist.

The extent to which language acquisition may be based on task-specific mechanisms has been the focus of research in our laboratory for some time (e.g., Curtiss, 1988; Curtiss, Kempler, & Yamada, 1981; Curtiss, Yamada, & Fromkin, 1979). I now present data from several case studies we have conducted. These case studies involve children who are mentally retarded but who have surprisingly intact linguistic function despite their pervasive cognitive deficits. We have data from several such cases; three of them are discussed here. In two of the three cases, the etiology of the retardation is unknown.

Each of the children to be discussed was the subject of an in-depth study examining both language and nonlanguage abilities. Comprehension and production of morphology, syntax, and semantics were assessed in detail, as was conversational skill. Nonlinguistic assessment included testing and observation of short-term memory, logical reasoning, visuo-construction, play, drawing, classification, seriation, and number concepts (see Curtiss, Kempler, & Yamada, 1981, for a full description of the methodology involved).

The first child is Antony, a child of 6 to 7 years when we studied him (see

Curtiss & Yamada, 1981, for a detailed description of the case). Antony's IQ estimates ranged from 50–56. At chronological age (CA) 5 years, 6 months, his MA was 2 years, 9 months. Parental reports indicate speech onset at 1 year, and full sentences at 3 years, despite numerous professional reports of pervasive developmental delays in many areas.

We found Antony's language profile quite the opposite of Genie's. Antony's language is well-formed phonologically and structurally rich. It is fully elaborated with closed class morphology and includes syntactic structures involving movement, embedding, and complementation. Its strengths therefore, lie in phonology, syntax, and morphology. Antony's language is semantically quite deficient, however. His lexical specifications are incomplete; sometimes inaccurate. This results in incorrect word usage, one problem frequently leading to miscommunications with others. Propositional content, unless quite simple, is also often confusing and incompletely expressed. He frequently fails to grasp the presupposition and implicature of his own and others' utterances, causing consistent communication failures. Antony's language is therefore well-formed generally only out of context.

Antony's conversational abilities include a wide range of pragmatic functions and intentions (e.g., naming, turn-taking, commenting, requesting, protesting, responding to requests and questions, and acknowledging); and he has learned the conventional means for expressing them (rejoinders, words, and phrases of acknowledgement, request phrases, etc.). He is not, however, sensitive to the needs of his listener. His topic maintenance skills are poorly developed, and he rarely appears to be concerned with being relevant or informative. For example, in dyadic discourse he inappropriately introduced new topics 30% of the time, failed to ratify an old topic across speakers (in ways aside from new topic introduction) or did so at inappropriate points 11% of the time, and elaborated on his own old topic inappropriately 8% of the time.

(A=Antony; E=Examiner)
E: Does he look happy here?
A: Wagon.
E: What's happening here?
A: The dog.

Although some of these percentages may seem low, they are all considerably higher than we have found with normal 4-year-olds for whom the percentage of errors in these mentioned categories ranges from 4.5% (for establishing new topics inappropriately) to 0% (for inappropriate topic elaborations).

In general, although there were exceptions, Antony seemed to be limited to very short communicative exchanges. Although he would continue to take turns when conversationally appropriate, longer exchanges placed a burden on his limited communicative ability that he could meet only by introducing a new topic, or repeating a prior utterance either of his own or of his partner.

(A = Antony, M = Mother)

A: He's a man.
M: Yeah, but what did he used to do before?

A: Lucan's a man.
M: What's he asking him for?
A: Dunno. Don't you know?
M: I think it's money. Wants to borrow some money.
A: Borrow some money.

A: He's [Lucan's] talking. Fighting?
M: Yeah, they call it boxing.
A: Boxing, fighting.
M: Well, yeah, fighting, boxing.
A: Lucan fighting?

The contrast between Antony's extensive use of imitation in testing situations, and in second and third turns in discourse, compared to the near absence of imitation and the use of novel productive speech in other circumstances points to the separation of syntactic ability from communicative ability.

In summary, it appears that Antony has acquired the grammatical system separate from the semantic structures that are mapped onto sentences by means of the grammar, and separate from the rules guiding the use of grammar for effective communication. To the extent that this is true, he may be said to have acquired an autonomous syntax.

Antony's nonlinguistic profile reveals a further dissociation of grammar from other abilities. In structured and unstructured situations his attention span was markedly short. Many tasks we successfully administered to normal 2-year-old children proved too difficult for Antony to grasp. On those tasks for which he was able to give a measurable performance, he showed substantial deficiencies in almost every area. His drawings were prerepresentational; his play was at the 1- to 2-year level; he was unable to perform any of the classification tasks; his logical reasoning abilities were at the 2-year level. His nonlinguistic cognitive level appeared to be at or just below sensorimotor stage VI (normally attained at approximately 20–24 months), with nonlinguistic symbolic abilities (e.g., play, drawing, copying) below that. His one area of nonlinguistic strength was auditory-verbal short-term memory, in which he performed *above* age level.

The second case is Marta, a teenager studied from the age of 16 to 18 (Yamada, 1981, 1983). Marta's IQ estimates range from 41–44. All developmental milestones are reported to have been delayed, including speech onset and other linguistic developments. From the age of about 4–5 years, however, language clearly stood apart as Marta's area of greatest strength.

Marta's linguistic profile is much like Antony's. Her speech is well-formed phonologically, is fully elaborated morphologically, and embodies rich and complex syntactic structures. Like Antony, she produces errors demonstrating that her utterances are not merely (delayed) repetitions of someone else's speech, but her utterances are generally much longer and propositionally more complex and convoluted than Antony's, as illustrated in the following examples. In addition, her lexicon is much richer and contains many more quantifiers and adverbs than Antony's, as is also illustrated in the following examples.

Samples of Antony's Speech	Samples of Marta's Speech
Do you got a brother?	It's down the street in a house my second home'n my mother is really sworn.
I don't want Bonnie coming in here.	Last year at (name of School) when I first went there, three tickets were gave out by a police last year.
I don't know who he got	She, does paintings this really good friend of the kids who I went to school with last year and really loved.
I want to see who's in that class.	He won't even recognize until you see his bangs are cut.
I would not have an ice cream.	The police pulled my mother an' so I said he would never remember them as long as we live!
I don't got friends, I got my brother named David.	Well, we were taking a walk, my Mom, and there was this giant, like my mother threw a stick.
I doed this already.	I haven't shown you my garage yet, but dad would be really hard.
That's tying his shoe.	We should go out an', um go out, and do other things.

Although Marta has a larger vocabulary than Antony, their lexical semantic abilities are quite parallel. Much of Marta's lexicon is incompletely specified, not for grammatical features, but for semantic features involving sense reference. Thus, she, too, often misuses words, most frequently words referring to number, time, manner, and dimensionality. The propositional content of her utterances, though apparently rich and varied when only a small sample of her speech is considered, is largely repetitious of a small repertoire of themes and at its best is loosely structured.

Her conversational performance is strong in those areas incorporating conventionalized social routines and early developed pragmatic functions (Dore, 1978), weakest in the areas of topic maintenance, relevance, informativeness, and truthfulness. Consequently, Marta also appears to have an advanced level of grammatical knowledge alongside dramatically less-developed semantic and pragmatic ability.

Marta's nonlinguistic performance shows further dissociation between grammar and other knowledge domains. She lacks almost all number concepts, including basic counting principles; her drawing is repetitive and at a preschool level; her play behavior is limited—symbolic play noted on one occasion; her auditory verbal memory span appears to have an upper limit of three units, and logical reasoning and operational thought are at an early preschool level. Unlike Antony, she does not appear to have *any* area of strength or well-developed ability in her nonlinguistic profile. She does, however, appear to have some conscious cognitive appreciation of language as an object of contemplation in its own right (i.e., metalingusitic ability). On imitation tasks, she is able both to detect and correct surface syntactic and morphological errors and at times to detect semantic anomalies as well. In addition, she is sensitive to foreign accents and often makes comments about such accents or the use of a foreign language (e.g., ''they're speaking Spanish, can you hear it?'', ''the mother's accent spits right out the mouth.''). Thus, Marta has not only acquired remarkably developed grammatical knowledge in contrast to all other aspects of mental ability, that knowledge has developed beyond the stage of unconscious acquisition to a stage allowing for some conscious awareness and manipulation.

The third case is Rick, a mentally retarded 15-year-old who suffered anoxia at birth and evidenced pervasive developmental problems throughout his childhood. Rick was institutionalized most of his life in a state hospital for the severely retarded (Curtiss, 1988b for more details).

Rick's language profile is quite parallel to the other two cases—well-developed phonological, morphological, and syntactic ability alongside poorly developed lexical and propositional semantic ability. In addition, he makes frequent lexical errors and occasional morphological errors, both indicating that at least much of his speech is novel and productive. However, he also makes frequent use of a small set of phrases in combination with novel phrases giving his speech, over extended discourse periods, a somewhat repetitive quality. The following are some examples of his speech.

Samples of Rick's Speech
He's the one that plays around like a turkey.
You already got it working.
If they get in trouble, they'd have a pillow fight.
She's the one that walks back and forth to school.
She can get a ponytail from someone else.
It was hitten by a road; but one car stopped and the other came.
She must've got me up and thrown me out of bed.
I find pictures that are gone.
Would you please give me the trash can?

Rick is an extremely social child and has well-developed interactive linguistic skills. He makes appropriate use of social rituals and other conventionalized conversational forms. His semantic deficiencies impede his communicative effectiveness, however, because he often misinterprets or fails to understand the presuppositions or implicature of utterances directed to him and often makes lexical and propositional errors of his own, as evidenced in the following examples.

(S=Susie; R=Rick)

S: . . . tell us what she looks like.
R: She looks like she has blonde hair.
S: What color is blonde?
R: Black.

S: How does she wear her hair?
R: She wears it up in a pony tail.
S: How long is it?
R: It's big around her pony tail.
S: When she takes her pony tail out, how long is it?
R: It's, uh, shorter.
S: Shorter than what?

R: Like whiskers.
S: Is it as short as yours?
R: Yes.
S: How can she get it in a pony tail?
R: She can get a pony tail from someone else.

He thus shows the kind of linguistic/pragmatic profile that Antony and Marta have—a highly developed grammatical system coupled with impaired semantic knowledge and pragmatic skills reflecting sensitivity to the needs of the listener.

Rick's nonlanguage profile is most similar to Anthony's, although Rick is more readily testable. Rick's drawing and copying were prerepresentational. He could rote count to 20 and knew some of the basic counting principles, but could count correctly only set sizes up to five, and his number reasoning was primitive. His classification abilities were at the 2 to 3-year level, and his logical reasoning and operative thought performance were also at an early preschool level. In contrast, he performed at the 6- to 7-year level in auditory verbal short-term memory.

All three of these children performed very poorly on tests of language comprehension involving pictures. They had difficulty attending to more than one picture at a time and choosing between them. These attentional and cognitive limitations contributed to their severely impaired comprehension performance, which stood in marked contrast to their well-developed expressive grammatical ability.

Antony, Marta, and Rick nonetheless show striking dissociations between knowledge of grammar (rules of phonology, morphology, and syntax) and conceptual aspects of language (semantics), and between grammar and nonlinguistic cognitive abilities. Antony and Rick's auditory short-term memory abilities were higher than any other nongrammatical area, but Marta's auditory short-term memory performance was as deficient as the rest of her cognitive profile; thus good auditory short-term memory cannot be a requisite for acquiring expressive grammatical ability. These cases are consistent with the suggestion presented earlier, that there is a close tie between lexical and propositional semantic development and nonlinquistic cognitive level. These cases further complement Genie's and Chelsea's data on pragmatic abilities, providing additional evidence that communicative functions related to meeting the needs of one's communicative partner may be linked to cognitive level, whereas other communicative devices may be yoked to social development and social intelligence. Evidence that communicative ability, in any case, rests on different knowledge than grammar comes additionally from a case study by Blank, Gessner, and Esposito (1979) in which a child developed structural knowledge of language in the absence of almost all communicative skills. Acquisition of structural linguistic knowledge in the absence of communicative skills is also reported for many schizophrenic and autistic children (Elliot & Needleman, 1981; Goodman, 1972; Kanner, 1943). Our data demonstrate for the first time, however, the acquisition of considerable structural knowledge of language without the support of concomitant conceptual and cognitive growth.

A MODEL OF LANGUAGE

The research summarized here points to several conclusions:

(1) grammar (rules of phonology, morphology and syntax) is based on domain-specific cognitive principles;

(2) grammar acquisition may be functionally independent from the development of lexical and propositional semantics and from pragmatics;

(3) grammar acquisition may be independent of growth in nonlinguistic domains of intelligence;

(4) knowledge of grammar appears to be mediated principally by the left hemisphere, even in acquisition;

(5) lexical and propositional semantic abilities are tied to nonlinguistic conceptual and cognitive function; and,

(6) language comprehension may be linked to aspects of intellectual ability not required for language production.

This model builds upon the model explicated by Chomsky (1980c) and incorporates several of the same assumptions. In Chomsky's model language is divided into two primary components: (1) the computational component (the rules of grammar), and (2) the conceptual component (the rest). Like Chomsky's model, this model assumes that grammar is computational in character and assumes that each component is based on distinct principles. However, we divide the conceptual aspects of language from the communicative aspects, using the data from (abnormal) acquisition to support this division.

The social/interaction model asserts that language is communicatively based, that factors in the communicative environment guide and determine the course of language acquisition, and that the linguistic system is learned on the basis of the rules governing the social-interactive use of language. Cognitive models assert that language is a reflection of and bound to nonlinguistic cognitive development, and that language and at least some nonlinguistic abilities are based on common structural principles. Linguistic models assert that language acquisition is possible only if children are equipped with considerable innate knowledge about language; it thus is not tied to the nonlinguistic learning capacity of the child. They furthermore assert that what is learned may be characterized by autonomous or domain-specific structural principles.

The data already reviewed demonstrate the untenability of all three of these models in their pure forms. First, all of the data presented point to an apparent unshakable tie between the development of lexical and propositional semantics and conceptual/cognitive knowledge. This tie appears to hold regardless of the population, and regardless of the preservation or impairment of other aspects of linguistic function. The evidence for this tie is made stronger by the fact that it emerges in an attempt to elucidate the separability of language from other aspects of mind. Moreover, it is inconsistent with linguistic models of acquisition that do not specify or even recognize a special relation between at least this one major aspect of language and nonlinguistic knowledge.

In addition, the data from Genie, Antony, Marta, Rick, and other populations referred to (e.g., autistics and the case in Blank et al., 1979) indicate that the knowledge of linguistic pragmatics is separable from knowledge of grammar, but is yoked in different ways both to social-communicative knowledge and to nonlinguistic cognitive knowledge. The contrast between Chelsea and Genie, in particular, suggests that knowledge of the linguistic conventions for coding communicative intentions and socially contingent responses is acquired through social experience, and neither depends on nor is the source for other aspects of linguistic knowledge. Data from Genie, Antony, Marta, and Rick suggest a separation of this experientially tied aspect of pragmatic knowledge from "topic maintenance" aspects of pragmatic knowledge, which appear to be tied specifically to cognitive awareness of the needs of one's communicative partner. As our data reveal that both aspects of pragmatic ability are demonstrably independent of grammatical knowledge, the data fail to support the social/interaction model. Experience of the rules governing the social-interactive use of language appears to be the basis for learning just that, the rules governing the social-interactive use of language, not the rules of grammar.

Furthermore, all of the data presented point to a dissociation of syntax and morphology (i.e., grammar), from both semantics and pragmatics. In the data considered, this dissociation is shown to hold in the case of selective linguistic impairment as well as selective preservation of language. The principles that subserve grammar and the principles by which grammar is learned appear to be distinct from those underlying semantics, pragmatics, and other cognitive systems. This finding refutes basic tenets of the social/interaction model and of cognitive models of language acquisition, but supports current linguistic models of the adult system in which each module of grammar is considered an autonomous system and grammar in toto is considered an autonomous faculty of mind. Our findings, then, provide direct evidence for the independence of grammar as a cognitive system and for the task-specificity of grammar acquisition.

CONCLUSIONS

Language is such an integral part of the mind that it is difficult to conceive of how or in what sense language or any part of it could be considered an independent aspect of cognition. Two of the three major approaches to the study of language acquisition reflect this disposition. A child comes into the world an unlearned, per-(or pre-)locutionary being, and in the context of nurturing and interaction with others and with the environment becomes a knowing and intentionally communicative being. Language development reflects *that* this is happening and sometimes *what* seems to be happening as well. And in the final outcome, the intelligent behavior of a mature human being is complex, multidimensional, and reflective of a complex and interdependent network of knowledge. This fact has made it difficult and inherently unreasonable for many whose goal is ultimately to develop a unified theory of mind or behavior to consider language apart from the larger context in which it is embedded. To such scholars, a unified theory of mind will of necessity embody general principles—general learning principles, general organizing principles, and general principles governing behavior. To scientists holding such assumptions, the integrated nature of development and mature behavior is testimony to the correctness of this basic position. Consequently, development and behavior should be examined as they are—embedded in a multidimensional mold.

To others, however, the complexity of human behavior and intelligence would appear to defy their being based on only general principles. To these scientists, each area of intelligence and behavior must be examined individually, then the principles found to underlie them compared and if possible, conflated. In an attempt to do this, ways must be found to examine the domain in question on its own.

It seems to me that by attempting to isolate and then examine a particular domain, both basic positions are tested; for only by examining each domain deeply enough to discover the abstract principles underlying it can these principles then be compared across domains. To elucidate the potential separability of language, I have attempted to present data that would help illustrate whether and in what ways language is tied to other abilities and thus can perhaps be explained on the basis of these other abilities. I focused in particular on data relevant to the assertions of the three major approaches—that language is communicatively based, that language is tied to nonlinguistic cognitive abilities, that language is not tied to these other systems. First of all, it was found that language is not "all of a piece." Some aspects of language do not appear separable from other domains. Lexical and propositional semantics appear yoked to conceptual and intellectual ability. Pragmatic aspects of language appear linked in part to social knowledge and in part to intellectual function. In contrast, however, grammar was shown to be dissociable from other knowledge domains, neither explained nor acquired by reference to other systems of knowledge or by reference to the larger context in which it is embedded.

Importantly, however, *normal* language requires the intimate and complex integration of grammar *with* semantics and pragmatics. As much as they provide evidence for the independence of the principles underlying the distinct knowledge systems involved, the data we have considered display how essential their interaction is for normal language development and behavior. And although it is important to appreciate the distinction between them in order to properly characterize them, it is the beautiful interweaving of one with the other that results in the magnificient communicative and cognitive code that is human language.

REFERENCES

Aram, D., Ekelman, B., Rose, W., & Whitaker, H. Verbal and cognitive sequelae following unilateral lesions acquired in early childhood. *Journal of Clinical and Experimental Neuropsychologypy,* 1985, *7,* 55–78.

Anderson, J. Induction of augmented transition networks. *Cognitive Science,* 1977, *1,* 1125–157.

Annet, M. Laterality of childhood hemiplegia and the growth of speech and intelligence. *Cortex,* 1973, *9,* 4–33.

Baker, C. Syntactic theory and the projection problem. *Linguistic Inquiry,* 1979, *10,* 533–581.

Basser, L. S. Hemiplegia of early onset and the faculty of speech with special reference to the effects of hemispherectomy: Two case studies. *Brain,* 1962, *85,* 427–460.

Bates, E. *Language and context: The acquisition of pragmatics.* New York: Academic Press, 1976.

Bates, E. *The emergence of symbols.* New York: Academic Press, 1979.

Bates, E., Benigni, L., Bretherton, I., Camaioni, L., & Volterra, V. From gesture to the first word:

On cognitive and social prerequisites. In M. Lewis & L. Rosenblum (Eds.), *Interaction, conversation and the development of language.* New York: Wiley, 1977.

Beilin, H. *Studies in the cognitive basis of language development.* New York: Academic Press, 1975.

Bishop, D. V. M. Linguistic impairment after left hemidecortication for infantile hemiplegia? A reappraisal. *Quarterly Journal of Experimental Psychology,* 1983, *35A,* 199–207.

Bishop, N. Speech in the hemiplegic child. In *Proceedings of the 8th Medical and Educational Conference of the Australian Cerebral Palsy Association,* Melbourne: Tooranga Press, 141–153, 1967.

Blank, M., Gessner, M., & Esposito, A. Language without communication: A case study. *Journal of Child Language,* 1979, *6,* 329–352.

Borer, H., & Wexler, K. The maturation of syntax. In T. Roeper & E. Williams (Eds.), *Parameter setting.* Dordrecht, Holland: D. Reidel Publishing Co, 1987.

Bresnan, J. A realistic transformational grammar. In M. Halle, J. Bresnan, & G. Miller (Eds.), *Linguistic theory and psychological reality.* Cambridge, MA: MIT Press, 1978.

Bruner, J. The ontogenesis of speech acts. *Journal of Child Language,* 1975, *2,* 1–19.

Case, R. Intellectual development from birth to adulthood: A neo-Piagetian interpretation. In R. Siegler (Ed.), *Children's thinking: What develops?* Hillsdale, NJ: Lawrence Erlbaum Associates, 1978.

Chomsky, N. On cognitive structures and their development: A reply to Piaget. In M. Piattelli-Palmarini (Eds.), *Language and learning: The debate between Jean Piaget and Noam Chomsky.* Cambridge: Harvard University Press, 1980a.

Chomsky, N. On binding. *Linguistic Inquiry,* 1980b, *11,* 1–46.

Chomsky, N. *Rules and Representations.* New York: Columbia University Press, 1980c.

Chomsky, N. *Lectures on government and binding:* The Pisa lectures. Dordrecht: Foris Publications, 1981.

Clark, R. Parallel Processing and learnability. Unpublished ms, 1988.

Corrigan, R. Language development as related to stage 6 object permanence development. *Journal of Child Language,* 1978, *5,* 173–190.

Corrigan, R. Cognitive correlates of language: Differential criteria yield differential results. *Child development,* 1979, *50,* 617–631.

Cross, T. Mothers' speech adjustments: The contribution of selected child listener variables. In C. Snow & C. Ferguson (Eds.), *Talking to children.* London: Cambridge University Press, 1977.

Curtiss, S. *Genie: A psycholinguistic study of a modern-day "wild child".* New York: Academic Press, 1977.

Curtiss, S. Genie: Language and cognition. *UCLA Working Papers in Cognitive Linguistics,* 1979, *1,* 15–62.

Curtiss, S. Dissociations between language and cognition. *Journal of Autism and Developmental Disorders,* 1981, *11,* 15–30.

Curtiss, S. Developmental dissociations of language and cognition. In L. Obler and L. Menn (Eds.), *Exceptional Language and Linguistics.* New York: Academic Press, 1982, 285–312.

Curtiss, S. The special talent of grammar acquisition. In L. Obler and D. Fein (Eds.), *The Exceptional Brain.* New York: The Guilford Press, 1988a, 364–386.

Curtiss, S. Abnormal language acquisition and the modulatory of language. In F. Newmeyer (Ed.), *Linguistics: The Cambridge survey. Vol. II. Grammatical theory: Extensions and implications.* Cambridge: Cambridge University Press, 1988b.

Curtiss, S., Fromkin, V., & Krashen, S. Language development in the mature right hemisphere. *Journal of Applied Linguistics,* 1978, *39–44,* 23–27.

Curtiss, S., Fromkin, V., Krashen, S., Rigler, D., & Rigler, M. The linguistic development of Genie. *Language,* 1974, 50, 528–554.

Curtiss, S., Kempler, D., & Yamada, J. The relationship between language and cognition in development: Theoretical framework and research design. *UCLA Working Papers in Cognitive Linguistics,* 1981, *3,* 1–59.

Curtiss, S., & Yamada, J. Selectively intact grammatical development in retarded child. *UCLA Working Papers in Cognitive Linguistics,* 1981, *3,* 61–91.

Curtiss, S., Yamada, J., & Fromkin, V. How independent is language? On the question of formal parallels between grammar and action. *UCLA Working Papers in Cognitive Linguistics,* 1979, *1,* 131–157.

Daumer, G. *Mittheilungen Uber Kaspar Hauser.* Nurnberg, 1832.

Dennis, M. Language acquisition in a single hemisphere: Semantic Organization. In D. Caplan (Ed.), *Biological studies of mental processes.* Cambridge: MIT Press, 1980a.

Dennis, M. Capacity and strategy for syntactic comprehension after left or right hemidecortication. *Brain and Language,* 1980b, *10,* 287–317.

Dennis, M. Strokes in childhood I: Communicative intent, expression and comprehension after left hemisphere arteriopathy in a right-handed 9-year-old. In *Language development and aphasia in children.* New York: Academic Press, 1980c.

Dennis, M., & Kohn, B. Comprehension of syntax in infantile hemiplegics after cerebral hemidecortication: Left hemisphere superiority. *Brain and Language,* 1975, *2,* 475–486.

Dennis, M., & Whitaker, H. Language acquisition following hemidecortication: Linguistic superiority of the left over the right hemisphere. *Brain and Language,* 1976, *3,* 404–433.

Dennis, M., & Whitaker, H. Hemispheric equipotentility and language acquisition. In S. Segalowiitz & F. Gruber (Eds.), *Language development and neurological theory.* New York: Academic Press, 1977.

Dore, J. Variation in preschool children's conversational performances. In K. Nelson (Ed.), *Children's language,* (Vol. I). New York: Gardner Press, 1978.

Dronkers, N. *Chelsea's Cognitive and Neuropsychological Status.* Paper presented at the annual meeting of the Orton Dyslexia society. San Francisco, November 1987.

Elliot, D., & Needleman, R. Language, cognition and pragmatics: The view from developmental disorders of language. *UCLA Working papers in Cognitive Linguistics,* 1981, *3,* 199–207.

Ferreiro, E. *Les Relations Temporelles dans le langage de l'enfant.* Geneva: Droz, 1971.

Fodor, J. *The Modularity of Mind.* An essay on faculty psychology. Cambridge: MIT Press, 1983.

Fromkin, V., Krashen, S., Curtiss S., Rigler, D., & Rigler, M. The development of language in Genie: A case of language acquisition beyond the 'critical period' *Brain and Language,* 1974, *1,* 81–107.

Furrow, D., Nelson, K., & Benedict, H. Mothers' speech to children and syntactic development: Some simple relationships. *Journal of Child Language,* 1979, *6,* 423–442.

Gleitman, L., Newport, E., & Gleitman, H. *The current status of the motherese hypothesis.* Unpublished manuscript, 1982.

Gleitman, L., & Wanner, E. Language acquisition: The State of the state of the art. In E. Wanner and L. Gleitman (Eds.), *Language acquisition: The state of the art.* New York: Cambridge University Press, 1982.

Gold, E. Language identification in the limit. *Information and Control,* 1967, *10,* 447–474.

Goodman, J. A case study of an autistic savant: Mental function in the psychotic child with markedly discrepant abilities. *Journal of Child Psychology and Psychiatry,* 1972, *13,* 267–278.

Greenfield, P. Structural parallels between language and action in development. In A. Lock (Ed.), *Action, symbol and gesture: The emergence of language.* London: Academic Press, 1978.

Greenfield, P., & Schneider, L. Building a tree structure: The development of hierarchical complexity and interrupted strategies in children's constructive activity. *Developmental Psychology,* 1977, *13,* 299–313.

Greenfield, P., Nelson, K., & Saltzman, F. The development of rule bound strategies for manipulating seriated cups: A parallel between action and grammar. *Cognitive Psychology,* 1972, *3,* 291–310.

Grice, H. Logic and conversation. In I. D. Davidson & G. Harmon (Eds.), *The logic of grammar.* Encino, CA: Dickson Press, 1975.

Heyer, K. *Kaspar Hauser und das Schicksal Mitteleuropas un 19, Jahrudert.* Stuttgart: Verlag Freires Geistesleben, 1964.

Hoff-Ginsburg, E., & Shatz, M. Linguistic input and the child's acquisition of language. *Psychological Bulletin,* 1982, *92,* 3–26.

Hood, P., & Perlstein, M. Infantile spastic hemiplegia II. Laterality of involvement. *American Journal of Physical Medicine,* 1955, *34,* 457–466.

Hyams, N. *Language acquisition and the theory of parameters.* Dordrecht, Holland: R. Reidell Publishing Co, 1986.

Ingram, D. If and when transformations are acquired by children. In D. Dato (Ed.), *Developmental Psycholinguistics: Theory and applications.* Washington, DC: Georgetown University Press, 1975.

Ingram, D. Sensori-motor intelligence and language development. In A. Lock (Ed.), *Action, gesture and symbol: The emergence of language.* New York: Academic Press, 1978.

Inhelder, B., Lezine, I., Sinclair, H., & Stambak, M. Les debuts de la fonction symbolique. *Archives Psychologigue,* 1972, *41,* 187.

Kanner, L. Autistic disturbances of affective contact. *Nervous Child,* 1943, *2,* 217–250.

Keenan, E. O., & Schieffelin, B. Topic as a discourse notion: A study of topic in the conversations of children and adults. In. C. Li (Ed.), *Subject and topic.* New York: Academic Press, 1976.

Klein, S. *Syntactic theory and the developing grammar. Reestablishing the relationship between linguistic theory and data from language acquisition.* Unpublished Doctoral Dissertation, UCLA, 1981.

Levelt, W. What became of LAD? *Peter de Ridder Publications in cognition.* I. Lisse, Holland: Peter de Ridder Press, 1975.

Lovett, M., Dennis, M., and Newman, J. Making reference: The cohesive use of pronouns in the narrative discourse of hemidecorticate adolescents. *Brain and Language,* 1986, *29,* 224–251.

MacNamara, J. The cognitive basis of language learning in infants. *Psychological Review,* 1972, *79,* 1–/13.

MacNamara, J. From sign to language. In J. MacNamara (Ed.), *Language learning and thought.* New York: Academic Press, 1977.

Miller, J., Chapman, R., & Bedrosian, J. *Defining developmentally disabled subjects for research: The relationships between etiology cognitive development and language and communicative performance.* Paper presented at the Second Annual Boston University Conference on Language Development, October 1977.

Nelson, K. Facilitating Children's syntax acquisition. *Developmental Psychology,* 1977, *13,* 101–107.

Newport, E. Constraints on learning and their role in language acquisition: Studies of the acquisition of American Sign Language. *Language Sciences,* in press.

Newport, E. Task specificity in language learning? Evidence from speech perception and American Sign Language. In E. Wanner & L. Gleitman (Eds.), *Language acquisition: The state of the art.* New York: Cambridge University Press, 1982.

Newport, E., Gleitman, L., & Gleitman, H. Mother I'd rather do it myself: Some effects and non-effects of motherese. In C. Snow & C. Ferguson (Eds.), *Talking to children* London: Cambridge University Press, 1977.

Newson, J. Dialogue and development. In A. Lock (Ed.), *Action, gesture and symbol: The emergence of language.* New York: Academic Press, 1978.

Nicholich, L. Beyond sensorimotor intelligence: Assessment of symbolic maturity through analysis of pretend play. *Merrill-Palmer Quarterly,* 1977, *23,* 89–99.

Piaget, J. *Play, dreams, and imitation in childhood.* New York: Norton, 1962.

Piaget, J. Schemes of action and language learning. In M. Piattelli-Palmarini (Ed.), *Language and learning: The debate between Jean Piaget and Noam Chomsky.* Cambridge: Harvard University Press, 1980.

Pies, H. *Kaspar Hauser, eine Dokumentation.* Ansbach: Brueghel Verlag, 1966.

Pietler-Ley. *Kaspar Hauser Bibliographie.* Ansbach: Breughel Verlag, 1927.

Pinker, S. Formal models of language learning. *Cognition,* 1979, *7,* 217–283.

Pinker, S. *Language learnability and language development.* Cambridge, Mass: Harvard University Press, 1984.

Pinker, S. Language learnability and children's language: A mutidisciplinary approach. In K. Nelson (Ed.), *Children's language* (Vol. 6). New York: Gardner Press, 1985.

Pinker, S. Resolving a learnability paradox in the acquisition of the verb lexicon. Center for Cognitive Science, MIT, 1987.

Rankin, J., Abram, D., & Horwitz, S. *A comparison of right and left hemiplegic children's language ability.* Paper presented at the annual meeting of the International Neuropsychological Society, 1980.

Ratner, N. B., & Pye, C. Higher pitch in babytalk is not universal: Acoustic Evidence from Quiche Mayam. *Journal of Child Language,* 1984.

Roeper, T. *Approaches to a theory of language acquisition.* Unpublished Doctoral Dissertation. Harvard University, 1972.

Roeper, T. The role of universals in the acquisition of gerunds. In E. Wanner & L. Gleitman (Eds.), *Language acquisition: The state of the art.* New York: Cambridge University Press, 1982.

Roeper, T., & Williams, E. (Eds.), *Parameter setting,* Dordrecht & Holland: D. Reidel Publishing Co, 1982.

Schiefflin, B., & Ochs, E. A cultural perspective on the transition from prelinguistic to linguistic communication. In R. M. Golinkoff (Ed.), *The Transition from prelinguistic to linguistic communication* Hillsdale, NJ: Lawrence Erlbaum Associates, 1983. (pp. 115–131).

Schiff, N. The influence of deviant maternal input on the development of language during the preschool years. *Journal of Speech and Hearing Research,* 1979, *22,* 581–603.

Semel, E. and Wiig, E. Clinical Evaluation of Language Function (CELF). Columbus, OH: Charles E. Merrill Publishing, 1980.

Shatz, M. The relationship between cognitive processes and the development of communication skills. *Current Theory in Motivation Series,* 1977, *25,* 1–42.

Shatz, M. On mechanisms of language acquisition: Can features of the communicative environment account for development? In L. Gleitman & E. Wanner (Eds.). *Language acquisition: The state of the art.* New York: Cambridge University Press, 1982.

Sinclair, H., & Ferreiro, E. Comprehension, production, et repetition des phrases à mode passif. *Archives Psychologigues,* 1970, *40,* 1–42.

Snow, C. Mother's speech to children learning language. *Child Development,* 1972, *43,* 549–565.

Snow, C. Mother's speech research: From input to interaction. In C. Snow & C. Ferguson (Eds.), *Talking to children.* Cambridge: Cambridge University Press, 1977.

Snow, C. and Ferguson, C. *Talking to children: Language input and acquisition.* Cambridge: Cambridge University Press, 1977.

Turkewitz, G., & Kenny, P. Limitations on input as a basis for neural organization and perceptual development: A preliminary theoretical statement. *Developmental Psychobiology,* 1982, *15,* 357–368.

Veneziano, E. Early language and nonverbal representation: A reassessment. *Journal of Child Language,* 1981, *8,* 541–563.

Von, Fuerbach, A. Example of a crime on the intellectual life of man. Ansbach, 1832.

Wexler, K. Transformational grammars are learnable from data of degree 2. *Social Sciences Working Papers,* no. 129. School of Social Sciences, University of California, Irvine, 1977.

Wexler, K. A principle theory for language acquisition. In E. Wanner & L. Gleitman (Eds.), *Language acquisition: The state of the art.* New York: Cambridge University Press, 1982.

Wexler, K., & Culicover, P. *Formal principles of language acquisition.* Cambridge, MA: MIT Press, 1980.

Wexler, K. & Manzini, M. R. Parameters and learnability in binding theory. In T. Roeper & E. Williams (Eds.) *Parameter Setting.* D. Reidel Publishing Co., Dordrecht, the Netherlands, 1987.

Woods, B. Observations on the Neurological basis for initial language acquisition. In D. Caplan (Ed.), *Biological studies of mental processes.* Cambridge, MA: MIT Press, 1980.

Woods, B., & Teuber, H. L. Changing patterns of childhood aphasis. *Annals of Neurology,* 1978, *3,* 273–280.

Woods, B., & Carey, S. Language deficits after apparent clinical recovery from childhood aphasia. *Annals of Neurology,* 1979, *6,* 405–409.

Yamada, J. Evidence for the independence of language and cognition: Case study of a "Hyper-linguistic" adolescent. *UCLA Working Papers in Cognitive Linguistics,* 1981, *3,* 121–160.

Yamada, J. *The independence of language: A case study.* Unpublished Doctoral dissertation. University of California, Los Angeles, 1983.

Zukow, P., Reilly, J., & Greenfield, P. Making the absent present: Facilitating the transition from sensorimotor to linguistic communication. In K. Nelson (Ed.), *Children's language* (Vol. 3). New York: Gardner Press, 1979.

7

Reflections on Language, Development, and the Interactional Character of Talk-in-Interaction

Emanuel A. Schegloff
Department of Sociology
University of California, Los Angeles

INTRODUCTION

The main theme that I want to pursue concerns what I call the *double interactivity of talk-in-interaction*. After drawing out several implications of this double interactivity for our understanding of the character of the resources of a language, I try to balance the "theoretical" tenor of these reflections with an account of a brief dinner table exchange between a young boy and his mother, which may help to ground my theme empirically. In the course of the account, I call on analytic resources drawn from conversation analysis that have no prima facie relation to the larger themes of the chapter, in the hope of suggesting how such basic research into the practices of talk-in-interaction can be of relevance and use to more focused or thematic inquiry, and should therefore be in everyone's tool kit—or department. I end with some preemptive responses to potential doubts from those who worry about applying this form of analysis to neophyte interactants.

THE DOUBLE INTERACTIVITY OF TALK

In references to the double interactivity of talk-in-interaction, one level of interactivity refers to the collaborative character of what occurs in talk-in-interaction, even when to all appearances only a single speaker is in action. By now this theme should be very familiar, but in an intellectual milieu still self-absorbed by what is considered a "cognitive" revolution, it could perhaps do with some repeating.

One Order of Interactivity:
Joint Production of Talk

What occurs in interaction is not merely the serial externalization into some joint arena of batches of talk, hatched in private (or even socialized) intentions, and filled out with the docile artifacts of "language" (as in many versions of speech act theory, discourse analysis, and the like). This treats the mind/brain as the scene of all the action, and the space of interaction as a structureless medium, or at least a medium whose structure is beside the point with respect to what is transmitted through it, as the composition of telephone cable is beside the point for the conversations transmitted through it. But interaction is that for which the talk is conceived; its character is shaped by the structure of opportunities to deliver a message in the first place, and so forth. And what children have to learn to get on with their lives is not just a syntax, and a lexicon, and so forth, but some of the following as well, many of them by now quite familiar.

Children have to learn not to talk when another is talking. (Except when it is allowed, as in choral greetings or good wishes—the kids at the party do not say "Happy Birthday!" one after the other.) And when overlapping talk occurs anyway, they have to learn to listen while talking, or talk while listening, so that the simultaneous talk can be adjusted to that of the other.

Then, they have to learn to recognize when another is talking—for example, that another can "be talking" even though not at the moment producing sounds as, for example, when they are trying to remember a name in the course of an as-yet-unfinished sentence/utterance.

Then (these "thens" are used to mark increments on a list, not temporal or analytic stages; if we knew the latter, we would know a lot), they have to learn that they can still be thought to be interrupting even though the speaker has finished a sentence—for example, when a story is in progress.

Then, they have to learn that they can still be interrupting though no individual speaker has any recognizable unit like a story underway—for example, when a topic is said to be in progress (by which the adults will sometimes mean a sequence, such as arrangements making, in the course of which a number of discrete and different topics may be taken up; see Schegloff, forthcoming a).

In other words, children have to learn that talk-by-one-person is nonetheless an outcome, which it takes the whole assemblage to produce. Sometimes that involves others-than-the-speaker remaining quiet; at other times it involves them in talking as well, in brief increments, precisely placed in the continuing talk of the primary speaker, the absence of such talk (or cognate body behavior; see Goodwin, 1979, 1980, 1981) being able to induce considerable modification, even disruption, in the talk of "the speaker." The "talk of the speaker" is then an interactional product, in one sense of the term (Schegloff, 1981).

And children will have to learn how the relevant interactional and sequential organization(s) here—primarily the organization of turn-taking (see Sacks,

Schegloff, & Jefferson, 1974), but I have mentioned others as well—operate formally, as well as how the local company or cohort of participants is administering them on that occasion, and with respect to children, in particular with respect to *them*. (For a discussion of the bearing of these issues concerning turntaking, and this level of detail in data, on children's acquisition of language, and socialization more generally; see Ochs, 1979.)

Related and cognate sets of considerations are posed by other of the generically relevant sorts of organization in talk-in-interaction—sequences (Sacks, 1987; Schegloff, forthcoming a, b), repair (Jefferson, 1974; Schegloff, 1979; Schegloff, Jefferson, & Sacks, 1977), the overall organization of single episodes of conversation (Schegloff, 1986; Schegloff and Sacks, 1973), reference (Sacks, 1972a, 1972b; Sacks & Schegloff, 1979; Schegloff, 1972), and so forth.

And all of these organizations incorporate recipient-design considerations; that is, a selection from and deployment of the resources available for talking and conduct generally sensitive to, and oriented to, and displaying the sensitivity and orientation to, who the co-participants are, what the context is (in the varied senses of that term that can be relevant at any moment).

Let me give an anecdotal example.

Deb and her teen-aged daughter Naomi are visiting at the home of Deb's nephew Billy, age 4 years, 11 months. Deb and Naomi are planning a shopping trip. The following exchange occurs.

Deb: We'll pick up some sunglasses for you, Naomi.
((pause))
Deb: Do you have sunglasses, Billy?
Billy: Yeah, but they're much too small for Naomi.

Among the things we can see that Billy has seen are these:

(1) Although Deb's first turn here is addressed to Naomi, Billy has attended to it.

(2) He has analyzed out of it that Naomi does not now have sunglasses, and that there is a current interest in her having some.

(3) Out of Deb's second utterance, Billy has analyzed that it is addressed to him, that he owes a response, that he owes it in next turn, which should follow directly.

(4) He has seen also that a question has been asked, but that is not all; that through that question some other action or actions are being prosecuted. He responds both to the question and to what is being done through it, and, in keeping with the canonical ordering of such multiple responses, he deals with those facets in that order—first an answer, than a responsive action.

(5) He sees that Deb's question is asked on behalf of something else, some

subsequent action that may be undertaken or not, contingent on his response to this one (what we have elsewhere termed a "presequence"). Although almost certainly Deb's question was meant to be doing a preoffer (if the answer is "no," she will invite him along on the shopping trip and buy him some sunglasses as well), he responds to it as if it were a prerequest (if he allows that he has sunglasses when an intention has just been expressed to rectify Naomi's lack of them, he will be asked for his). So he first gives a truthful answer to the question, and then proceeds to block the progression that it implicates for a next part of the sequence—a request, by denying that the glasses he has could satisfy it.

Though he may have misanalyzed the type of "pre" Deb was doing, the grounds for it may well have been right; he uses the sequential context, the preceding utterance, and the source and relevance of what has been addressed to him, and that yields for him the reading that the glasses being asked about are for Naomi.

So, together with all the aspects of the organization of talk as an activity in its own right, which kids like Billy pick up, there is also the understanding that talk-in-interaction is an instrument for doing things, for doing practical actions, and one has to figure out what someone is doing by talking in the way that they do, if one is to respond to it properly.

All this, as I say, is what should no longer need saying. But there is another level of interactivity as well. And it goes to the lexicon, to the semantic and conceptual nets, as well. It has to do with the constitution of language, if there is such a thing and whatever it may be. What I have in mind is the following.

A Second Order of Interactivity: The Character of Language

The organization of conversation, of talk-in-interaction more generally, includes among its generic components (those apparently relevant and in play whenever talk is in progress or even incipient, the latter making it potentially relevant to interaction over-and-above talk) what we call the organization of repair (Schegloff, Jefferson, and Sacks, 1977). This is a set of practices, an organized set of practices, by which parties to talk-in-interaction can address troubles in speaking, hearing, and understanding the talk.

The presence of such an organization, its generic presence and relevance, allows language (and perhaps other domains of and resources of conduct, but not all of them—not gesture or facial expression) to be constructed differently than might otherwise have been imagined. It need not, for example, be unambiguous. It need not have invariant mappings of signs or symbols and their signifieds. It need not have a syntax that assigns but a single interpretation to a given expression. That is why what has been considered the sloppiness of natural as compared to formal languages is so deeply mistaken. It is because persons wanting to make certain uses of language for particular sorts of discourse do not avail themselves of the practices of repair—logicians and scientists, rather than rhetoricians—that natural language seems such a blunt and inelegant instrument. It is because that which converted its features into flexibility has been sacrificed to other needs. But, of course, we regularly find ways of sneaking it back in again.

Notice, then, that talk-in-interaction is interactive quite apart from (1) its contextuality, by reference to which it is virtually always responsive or prosponsive, and (2) its collaborativeness, in the sense that whatever gets done is a joint achievement. Those senses aside, the sorts of components from which it is fashioned—sounds, words, sentences—have the character they do, and are formed the way they are, in part because they are to inhabit an environment in which the apparatus of repair is available (although not always invocable easily and without interactional consequences, such as possibly prefiguring disagreement; see Sacks 1987), and in which flexible arrangements can be permitted, as compared to discourse domains like those of science and logic where it cannot, and whose building blocks must therefore be (so it is claimed, at least) of a different character.

And so our articulatory apparatus and our practices of articulation and hearing can have developed the way they did in part because repair is there to catch such troubles as may arise. And the lexicon. And so forth.[1]

If the capacity for deploying the practices of language is a fact of the biology of humans, as it is nowadays fashionable to underscore, certain suppositions would seem to be warranted about it, of a sort quite different from those ordinarily understood to follow. Here I mention only one.

If the conduct of language as a domain of behavior is biological in character, then we should expect it (like other biological entities) to be adapted to its natural environment. What is the primordial natural environment of language use, within which the shape of linguistic structures such as grammar, have been shaped? Transparently, the natural environment of language use is talk-in-interaction, and originally ordinary conversation. The natural home environment of clauses and sentences is turns-at-talk. Must we not understand the structures of grammar to be in important respects adaptations to the turn-at-talk in a conversational turn-

---

[1]There is increasing evidence that the practices of repair are available and employed from very early on. With respect to self-repair, see, for example, Clark, 1978; Clark & Andersen, 1979; Iwamura, 1980; McTear, 1985, which show self-repair to be in use at least as early as 1½ to 2 years of age. Garvey (1984) suggested that repair on other's talk (what she calls "contingent queries") are used by children as least as early as 32 months; they surely are understood and responded to earlier than that.

taking system with its interactional contingencies? Must we not understand the constitution of a lexicon, at least in part, by references to the organization of repair that operates in the natural environment in which the elements of the lexicon are in the first instance deployed?

A CASE IN POINT

With these themes in mind, consider the following brief episode from what must surely be one of the most recurrently central settings of talk-in-interaction across the variations within the human species—the evening meal.

> A small family is having dinner. The boy, Rob, about 6 years old, has a largish piece of meat speared on his fork. He leans over the table and holds a position above his plate with the fork to his mouth, gnawing on the piece of meat. A moment after he assumes this position, his mother looks over at him, and holds the look for a few seconds. Rob straightens up, is no longer gnawing at the fork. Mother turns away from him, and the following exchange occurs. (The doubled letters in M's second turn indicate clearly enunciated consonants.)

> M: Cut that (up)/(out), Rob
> (0.2)
> R: Hm?
> M: I saidd, "Cutt itt."
> R: ((Transfers fork from right to left hand))

Consider the following sets of observations:

1. In this exchange Mother looks over at Rob just after he starts doing something she is about to treat as improper, as something he should do differently. She holds that look at him and says nothing. When he stops that activity, she looks away. And *then* she speaks to the matter, "Cut that up, Rob," an utterance with which Rob exhibits himself to have some trouble.

Note then that while Rob is doing the deed, she does not comment on it, though she is looking at it, and indeed seems to be "doing looking at it," timing the arrival of her gaze on him and its departure from him by reference to his starting and stopping the gnawing. Post hoc propter hoc, here, is not so much a logical fallacy as a principle of interactional interpretation (and it is its source in the latter that very likely led to the need to formulate it as the former).

Thus, Rob sees that she looked at him gnawing without comment; did she approve then? But parents do use a fixed stare to show that they see something sanctionable going on, inviting the child to see that they see, and to adjust the behavior accordingly. But does he see that "she looked at [*him gnawing*]?"

Does he see that as what she was looking at? Does he see her "looking" as "noticing?" "Noticing" requires an object; it is a formulation of looking, a grasp of looking, that takes the looking to have had something—some event or feature—which prompted it. So for Rob to have seen her looking as "looking at" or "noticing" involves him in grasping something about himself that is/was its object.

Correlatively, if there is a way for adults to recognizably "do looking at" or "do noticing," then they can prompt a self-examination by the target to find what was being noticed, what was being looked at. Such a device by adults can turn on, can invoke, "guilty knowledge," it can invoke "examine thyself to see what blameworthy thing I am looking at." In looking without commenting, she gives him a chance to deal with whatever may be wrong first, before any overt sanction on her part. A sort of "preference for self-correction" is involved here, then, but not for trouble in speaking, hearing or understanding, but rather an aspect of table manners.

In not commenting until he stops, something else is done. She does not sanction him for this occasion, or at least not directly. She uses this occasion to provide the relevant opportunity for instructing him on how to deal with problems of this sort. How does she do that? She does it in part by waiting until the end of the current episode; saying/doing it *then* is a way of doing it "for next time."

This is a general resource in interaction. A bus rider will stand with a hand on the cord that makes the bell ring and informs the driver that someone wishes to get off. A passenger will place a hand on the cord and hold it there until the bus pulls away from one stop, lest the driver misinterpret what was meant as indicator for the next stop as a tardy indication about the prior one. (And there can be an orientation to this formal timing feature, even when no ready interpretation can be accorded its result, as when a person about to answer a ringing phone pauses with a hand on the receiver, one not lifting it until the current ring ends, another not lifting it until a next ring begins, each apparently oriented to some unequivocal orientation to nextness; see Schegloff, 1986).

Of course this issue of timing is a recurrent one for children. Are the parents' instructions meant to be carried out "now," or "when next relevant?" What is "now?" Directly after the end of the utterance in which the instruction is delivered? As the next activity after the child finishes whatever he or she is engaged in? The next time the sort of thing to which the instruction pertains comes up? When *is* the child to clean up the room?

And so mother may here hold off "cut that up, Rob" so as to bring off not that the current chewing be abandoned for the cutting, but that when a next bite is to be taken, it be gotten by cutting and not by gnawing, and one way to do this is to hold off the utterance until the current spate of activity has been brought to a close, which is what Rob's straightening up from the bent-over-plate position displays.

2. Consider mother's injunction to Rob, and what follows it. This kind of utterance makes one of a limited set of response types relevant next; it is what we call a "first pair part of an adjacency pair" (Heritage, 1984; Levinson, 1983; Schegloff & Sacks, 1973). Here the mandate is for some action, and the preferred response type is a compliant action, or some behavioral indication that such an action or course of action is being launched. In the episode being examined here, the transfer of the fork from right to left hand a bit later on is such an incipient act of compliance (preparatory to picking up the knife with the right hand?). Where the response is otherwise an embodied action, it may be marked in the talk by what we can term a "compliance marker," such as "O.K.," "right," and the like. (The absence of such a marker, as in the present data, may indicate a certain lack of enthusiasm, or even sullenness, but without detailed inspection of the relevant data such a line cannot be pursued here. Nonetheless, it may be noted that the insertion of some other conduct between a first and second pair part has generally been understood as projecting a dispreferred, or less-than-preferred, response to be "in the works" (see Pomerantz, 1978, 1984; Sacks, 1987). And here the compliant action is delayed by an inserted sequence, so that the absence of a compliance marker, with the resultant compliance-stances already suggested as possible inferences, is an orderly and not unfamiliar trajectory of events.)

As noted, between mothers's injunction and Rob's incipient compliance (he does not actually go on to comply at this point) there intervenes a sequence, of the sort we term *repair*. This repair is canonical in a number of respects. It is initiated by a/the recipient of the talk containing the trouble source, who leaves it for the speaker of the trouble-source to deal with the trouble. The repair is initiated in the turn after the trouble-source turn, which is where virtually all such "other-initiated" repairs are initiated (and, indeed, is initiated there after a brief gap of silence, which is also quite common; for this and other points in this paragraph; see Schegloff, Jefferson, & Sacks, 1977). It is responded to and completed in the next turn, which is also canonical, and is responded to there by the prior speaker, the speaker of the trouble-source.

The Sacks Substitution

There is one respect, however, in which this fragment differs from a practice frequently observed in such repair sequences (though by no means as common as the regularities previously referred to as canonical). The observation was first called to my attention by my late colleague Harvey Sacks, and I will refer to it as the "Sacks substitution." Sacks noted that in the environment of repair, pro-terms[2] regularly get replaced by the full-forms to which they referred, even when

---

[2]"Pro-terms" are "reduced" forms used to replace so-called "full forms" in certain contexts; pro-nouns are the most familiar type used in lieu of full noun phrases, but there are "pro-verbs" as well, for example, "do" or "did" as in the data fragment taken from US:33–41, where "did it" is being used in place of "broke the glass out" which then replaces it.

those pro-terms were not, or were not clearly, the source of the trouble. For our purposes, a very few instances (selected to include pro-term references to places, persons, and actions) will have to suffice to exemplify this practice.

So, upon repetition, pro-term references to *place* may be substituted for by a fuller form of reference.

US:32[3]

Vic:	My pail's there,
James:	Hoh?
Vic:	My pail is in yuh *hall*way.
	(simplified transcript)

CDHQ:41–42

D:	You very happy up there?
S:	Pardon?
D:	I say are you very happy where you are?

The replaced pro-term may be used for reference to *persons*:

CDHQ:2   The scene is a Civil Defense Headquarters in the aftermath of a hurricane.

A:	. . . They haven't seen anything a' the Salvation Army.
B:	Oh the Salavation *Army*,
B:	⌈ They- they already got there, ( ).[4]
C:	⌊ No they ( )
C:	They've left already.
→ C:	They ⌈ came in an' left.
→ A:	⌊ I beg yer pardon?
→ C:	Red Cross has been there an' *left*.
C:	The Salvation Army's the one that stayed *on*.
A:	I-I just gotta call from Chief Lorenzo, an' uh Superintendant Bassuto, an' they're on the scene,
C:	on ⌈ what scene.
A:	⌊ But a Red Cross unit is there.
C:	Must be speakina two different locations.

Haley (1959):329

Jones:	What do they want with us?
Smith:	Hm?
Jones:	What do they want with you and me?

---

[3]These labels identify the source of the following data citation.

[4]Empty parentheses are used to mark places where the transcriber can hear that the speaker is talking but cannot make out the talk well enough to transcribe. Their size is roughly proportional to the extent of such talk.

The pro-term may refer to an *action* (and in the following instance the repair is self-initiated, rather than being responsive to a request by interlocutor).

US:33–41   Someone has broken James' window and he repeatedly asks who it was in a very loud voice—"All I WANNA KNOW WHO IT WAS" (p. 34); later (p. 39), "AH *STILL* DON' KNOW WHO DUH HELL *DID* IT;" later (p. 40), "AH WOONA KNOW WHO *DID IT*. THEN I CN KNOW WUD DUH DO." Finally (p. 41),

James: I WANNA GET TUH WHO, DID EH BROKE THAT GLASS. *TH*AT'S ALL AH WANT,

Here the pro-term "did [it]" is replaced by a full form formulation of the action being referred to.

Or the replaced pro-term may refer to an "*object*," though different senses of "object" are involved in each of the following instances.

US: 23

Vic: He *plugs* it in, he *plugs* the TV in, 'n walks over duh TV en starts adjust it.
          (simplified transcript)

SB: 1:10–4

B: And that went wrong.
       (1.0)
A: Well, uh
B: That surgery, I mean.

SBL: 1:3–2

A: Well, if you will uh after you go by, uh then I think I could arrange for you to see it tomorrow, (0.2)
A: -to see the interior.

One practice that we find associated with repair, then, is that when repair is undertaken, pro-terms may be replaced by their full-form references, whether as the point of the repair or as its by-product.

The Sacks Substitution Applied to the Case in Point

With the practice of the Sacks substitution noted, we can observe that when mother responds to Rob's "Hm?", she does not employ it. She does not, for example, offer as her repair solution, "Cut up the meat" or "cut that piece up," or the like. She makes a point of marking that she is repeating, with the self-quotation format "I said," and then retains a pro-term reference, albeit a different one, into the repeat (while dropping the "up"), "Cut it," but enunciating the terminal consonants with underscored clarity, almost as if it were sloppy articulation of these that engendered Rob's "problem." Although the Sacks substitution has not yet been shown to have the robustness as a practice that other features of repair have, we can explore the question, "What might mother be doing in not employing it here?"

In responding to mother's utterance with the initiation of repair, Rob takes up the position that he has trouble with the utterance. The form of repair initiation he employs is among the weakest available; it displays virtually no grasp of the preceding utterance (as, for example, a full or partial repeat might do). It displays no grasp that he has been given an injunction or instruction, or has been sanctioned in some way. Thereby it displays no grasp that his preceding conduct was in any way subject to sanctioning. That does not mean, of course, that he has no such grasp; only that the interactional tack he has adopted takes that form.

Now one need not actually hear a fully articulated, acoustically pure signal conveying an unambiguous message in order to know what someone is saying, or what they are doing in saying whatever they are saying. Regularly, an orientation to a projectable next action or course of action, an orientation to a domain of mutual relevance, allows a recipient to hear and grasp what is being said and done from a partial uptake of a partially flawed "signal." What some utterance is, and is doing, is assembled from both its content and its context, its position and its composition, the acoustic and visual "signals" and the textures of relevance with which they interact.

So claiming to have not heard or not grasped is also potentially to take the stand that there was not such a domain of shared relevance, or a projected and/or projectable course of action, that would have allowed the claimant to figure out what the other was saying/doing. Where sanctions or accusations or injunctions are at issue, this can be tantamount to a denial of "guilty knowledge." Its classic form is in the parent's severe calling of the misbehaving child's name, only to have it treated innocently as a summons, which requires in return nothing more than a "what"? (Or, like the prompt to a player whose next turn it is, or a speaker whose turn is next, who respond to the prompt with the same "what?", revealing in such cases their inattentiveness to the proceedings through not recognizing that the use of their name was not a summons but a prompt to a prescheduled, and now due, next action.) In this case, of course, we might wonder whether, on the one hand, the mother's sustained gaze at Rob's gnawing at the meat would not have been understood as establishing a domain of reference that the ensuing utterance invokes, or whether, on the other hand, withholding her comment until after the behavior in question had been arrested did not make the reference of her utterance specifically veiled.

And we have to note that mother's utterance, even held off as it is, is not just an injunction or instruction, or request. In setting out an alternative way of eating, it can do a complaint about his prior behavior. It is the reference of the "that" to what he had just been gnawing on that makes this "future-oriented" injunction a comment on prior behavior as well. The timing by which it was held off until he broke off the gnawing was a way of positioning the target time for the relevance of the instruction, not for disengaging the utterance—qua both sanction and instruction—from the conduct that prompted it.

Now mother might well have incorporated full-form references into her initial utterance in this sequence: "Cut the meat up, Rob." In employing a pro-term, "Cut that up, Rob," she builds on her orientation to the gnawing on the meat that her just-concluded gazing will have made visible. Her use of "that" requires Rob to solve its reference; it shows that she takes him to have the necessary resources—to know, or to be able to figure out, what "that" is, what "cutting" might refer to here, and why cutting it might be in point. Rob's "hm?" denies that he can do these things, denies that he knows what is being referred to, what action is being pressed on him, what in his prior conduct requires reform.

Should mother respond to the "hm?" by replacing the pro-term with its full-form reference, she will have allowed Rob his plea of ignorance. She will have shown herself to treat his trouble in grasping her utterance as having its pro-term as its source, and that he might in fact be unaware that something he did, something related to the eating of the meat on his fork, was the target of her complaint and injunction.

Instead of redoing her utterance with transformations that might remove such a source of trouble in understanding, she treats it as a sort of hearing problem, to be solved by repeating and using clearer articulation. So she not only repeats; she does "doing repeating." (In fact, she does "doing repeating" without actually repeating. She did not actually say what she says she said. She did *not* say "Cut it;" she said "cut that up." Though, to be sure, the argument could be developed that she here invokes and displays a *members'* equivalence rule, which it would be mistaken to criticize in the terms that I have employed.) And in repeating, she heavily emphasizes the terminal consonants of her words, as if (as noted earlier) it were the failure to articulate those clearly which had been the source of Rob's trouble. What she pointedly does not do is relieve him of the need to solve the pro-term. Although she replaces the pro-term "that," she replaces it with another pro-term, "it," a shift reflecting a sequential step further removed from the target of the referent, but which also presumes, and even more deeply because it drops the proximity component of the term, that recipient will know what is being referred to. Mother thereby disallows Rob's disavowal of guilty knowledge. In insisting that he solve the utterance in the form in which she has presented it, and in insisting on this successfully (he *does* solve it), a small ceremony of innocence is played through and punctured.[5]

---

[5]Compare the following two exchanges from another dinner occasion involving a different family and their guest, Madeleine. In the first fragment, Stevie is being told to stop something he is doing, and the talk is organized along the lines discussed in the text of this paper. In the second fragment,

Note that the trajectory of this episode depends on the availability of the resources of repair doubly. On the one hand, it is partially constituted through the very deployment and working through of repair relevant utterances. On the other hand, the availability of ways of talking that allow speakers (here, the mother) to invoke recipients' (here, Rob's) knowledge in an implicit way itself turns on the generic presence and invocability of repair resources in interaction. Because such resources are generically available in talk-in-interaction to resolve troubles in hearing and understanding should they arise, the resources deployable in talk-in-interaction can be very different in their constitution and composition than they might otherwise be (they can be multi-referential, for example), and their deployment can be different than it might otherwise be (it can be designedly ambiguous, for example). In this respect, the episode between Rob and his mother turns on the *invocability* of repair rather than its *invocation*.

CONCLUDING REMARKS

But hasn't a silk purse been made of a sow's ear here? Hasn't too much been made of the slightest of events? Does this occurrence even merit the honor of status as an event? I was once asked by a well respected student of children's language acquisition about my analysis of a very brief excerpt from an ordinary interaction (subsequently published as Schegloff, 1987, 1988). She remarked that before the presentation began, the data looked uninviting—neither particularly orderly nor particularly substantial or consequential, surely nothing as textured as the analysis had made it out to be. Might this not be a creation of the analytic procedures? Could any bit of talk in interaction turn out to be random or disorderly? After all, students of language acquisition find lots of things they think of as mere mistakes, as the product not of doing something subtle, but of doing something badly, incompetently.

---

less than a minute later, Stevie is being offered more food and the themes discussed in the text are not in point. Here, the pro-term reference (''more'') is expanded on the repeat.

(1) Oolie: Chicken Dinner 13:41

Mad:	Don't (plet) that,
Stevie:	Huh?
Mad:	Don't ( ) that.
Dad:	C'mon = ←
Mad:	= Come on (•) ⌈ sit back up an' talk to us.
Dad:	⌊ Come on Stevie. Come si down.

(2) Oolie: Chicken Dinner 14:08

Mad:	D'you want some more Steven,
Stevie:	Huh,
	(1.0)
Dad:	Y'want some more chicken, ←
Stevie:	mm hm.

On the other hand, we wonder how children learn language and its felicitous use; how they learn to conduct themselves properly, and effectively; how they learn to deal with the moment to moment contingencies of life, and life in interaction, including (perhaps especially) the life in interaction through which they learn about life in general. Although the argument should be pressed that interaction at this level of detail (and "below") is demonstrably real and consequential for participants of any age and skill, for the not-yet-competent—the children, the strangers, and so forth—it is even more substantial. Time is slower, each aspect larger, recognizing and negotiating through the contingencies a more robust project, and all of it potentially being both done and learned at the same time. They learn to deal with the moment-to-moment contingencies of life in interaction, and the details of language use and conduct, *in* the moment-to-moment contingencies of life in interaction, with their deployments of language and other conduct. The language learned there has its character and structure informed by the structure and contingencies of interaction, just as the practices for using the language are so informed. Until our understanding incorporates that informing as well, we will remain ill-informed.

ACKNOWLEDGEMENTS

My thanks to Elinor Ochs and Gene Lerner for guidance with respect to clarity and bibliography. Responsibility for remaining deficits in either regard, or others, is mine, of course.

REFERENCES

Bruner, J. *Child's talk: Learning to use language.* New York: Norton, 1983.

Clark, E. V. Awareness of language: Some evidence from what children say and do. In A. Sinclair, R. J. Jarvella, & W. J. M. Levelt (Eds.), *The child's conception of language.* New York: Springer, 1978.

Clark, E. V., & Andersen, E. S. Spontaneous repairs: awareness in the process of acquiring language. In *Papers and reports on child language development*, No. 16, Stanford University, 1979.

Garvey, C. *Children's talk.* Cambridge: Harvard University Press, 1984.

Goodwin, C. The interactive construction of a sentence in natural conversation. In G. Psathas (Ed.), *Everyday language: Studies in ethnomethodology.* New York: Irvington, 1979.

Goodwin, C. Restarts, pauses and the achievement of a state of mutual gaze at turn beginning. *Sociological Inquiry,* 1980, *50,* 272–302.

Goodwin, C. *Conversational organization.* New York: Academic Press, 1981.

Haley, J. An interactional description of schizophrenia. *Psychiatry,* 1959, *22,* 321–332.

Heritage, J. *Garfinkel and ethnomethodology.* Cambridge: Polity Press, 1984.

Iwamura, S. G. *The verbal gains of pre-school children.* London: Croom Helm, 1980.

Levinson, S. C. *Pragmatics.* Cambridge: Cambridge University Press, 1983.

Jefferson, G. Error correction as an interactional resource. *Language in Society,* 1974, *2,* 181–199.

McTear, M. *Children's conversation*. Oxford: Blackwell, 1985.

Ochs, E. Transcription as theory. In E. Ochs & B. Schieffelin (Eds.), *Developmental pragmatics*, (pp. 43–72). New York: Academic Press, 1979.

Pomerantz, A. M. Compliment responses: notes on the cooperation of multiple constraints. In J. Schenkein (Ed.), *Studies in the organization of conversational interaction*. New York: Academic Press, 1978.

Pomerantz, A. M. Agreeing and disagreeing with assessments: some features of preferred/dispreferred turn shapes. In J. M. Atkinson & J. Heritage (Eds.), *Structures of social action*. Cambridge: Cambridge University Press, 1984.

Sacks, H. An initial investigation of the usability of conversational data for doing sociology. In D. N. Sudnow (Ed.), *Studies in social interaction*. New York: Free Press, 1972a.

Sacks, H. On the analyzability of stories by children. In J. J. Gumperz & D. Hymes (Eds.), *Directions in sociolinguistics*. New York: Holt, Rinehart & Winston, 1972b.

Sacks, H. On the preferences for agreement and contiguity in the organization of sequences in conversation. In G. Button & J. R. E. Lee (Eds.), *Talk and social organization*. Clevedon: Multilingual Matters, 1987.

Sacks, H., & Schegloff, E. A. Two preferences in the organization of reference to persons and their interaction. In G. Psathas (Ed.), *Everyday language: Studies in ethnomethodology*. New York: Irvington, 1979.

Sacks, H., Schegloff, E. A., & Jefferson, G. A simplest systematics for the organization of turntaking for conversation. *Language, 1974, 50*, 696–735.

Schegloff, E. A. Notes on a conversational practice: Formulating place. In D. N. Sudnow (Ed.), *Studies in social interaction*. New York; Free Press, 1972.

Schegloff, E. A. The relevance of repair to syntax-for-conversation. In T. Givon (Ed.), *Syntax and semantics 12: Discourse and syntax*. New York: Academic Press, 1979.

Schegloff, E. A. Discourse as an interactional achievement: Some uses of 'uh huh' and other things that come between sentences. In D. Tannen (Ed.), *Analyzing discourse: Text and talk*. Georgetown University Roundtable on Languages and Linguistics; Washington, DC: Georgetown University Press, 1981.

Schegloff, E. A. The routine as achievement. *Human Studies, 1986, 9*, 111–151.

Schegloff, E. A. Analyzing single episodes of interaction: An exercise in conversation analysis. *Social Psychology Quarterly, 1987, 50*, 101–114.

Schegloff, E. A. Discourse as an interactional achievement II: An exercise in conversation analysis. In D. Tannen (Ed.), *Linguistics in context: Connecting observation and understanding*. Norwood, NJ: Ablex, 1988.

Schegloff, E. A. On the organization of sequences as a source of 'coherence' in talk-in-interaction. In B. Dorval (Ed.), *Conversational coherence and its development*. Norwood, NJ: Ablex, forthcoming a.

Schegloff, E. A. Goffman and the analysis of conversation. In P. Drew & A. Wootton (Eds.), *Erving Goffman: Exploring the interaction order*. Cambridge: Polity Press, 1988.

Schegloff, E. A., & Sacks H. Opening up closings. *Semiotica, 1973, 7*, 289–327.

Schegloff, E. A., Jefferson, G., & Sacks, H. The preference for self-correction in the organization of repair in conversation. *Language, 1977, 53*, 361–382.

III CHILD-CARETAKER INTERACTION

8 Genotype-Environment Interaction

C. S. Bergeman
Robert Plomin
College of Health and Human Development
The Pennsylvania State University

INTRODUCTION

Interaction has many meanings. This chapter focuses on a specific category of statistical interaction, genotype-environment (GE) interaction. Although this is a very restricted view of interaction, it has the merit of leading directly to empirical research that attempts to identify statistical interactions between genetic and environmental effects, thus going beyond the traditional approach of behavioral genetics that stops with the estimation of genetic and environmental main effects. We are interested in identifying interactions in which individuals with certain genetic propensities are affected differently by environmental factors, one type of "organismic specificity" that emerged as the missing link in a review of early experience and human development.

> Both from basic and applied data it has become increasingly clear that the relationship of early experience to development will be mediated by the nature of the organism on which the experience impinges. Unfortunately, virtually nothing is known about the specific organismic characteristics which mediate differential reactivity to the early environment. (Wachs & Gruen, 1982, p. 247)

The purposes of this chapter are, first, to define the quantitative genetic concept of genotype-environment interaction, differentiating it from interactionism and genotype-environment correlation; second, to provide an overview of methods to estimate the effect of GE interaction on phenotypic variance; third, to describe three types of ordinal GE interactions; and, last, to provide examples of GE interactions in behavioral genetic research with animals and human beings.

GE INTERACTION VERSUS INTERACTIONISM

Discussions of genotype-environment interaction have often confused the population concept with that of individual development; the latter view has been called *interactionism* (Plomin, DeFries, & Loehlin, 1977). Usually interactionism refers to the truism that behavior cannot occur unless there is both an organism (nature) and an environment (nurture)—as indicated in the frequently cited quotation, "the organism is a product of its genes and its past environment" (Anastasi, 1958, p. 197). In this sense, interactionism is the view that environmental and genetic threads are so tightly interwoven that they are indistinguishable.

Behavioral genetic research, however, does not apply to a single individual; the focus is on variance, differences among individuals in a population. If we could directly measure genetic and environmental effects for individual human subjects, we could explicitly test models about genetic and environmental influences on traits of interest. Instead, behavioral genetic analyses proceed indirectly, estimating genetic and environmental components of variance from the phenotypic variances and covariances of identical twins and fraternal twins, natural and adoptive families, and other groups in which certain genetic and environmental relations are known or assumed to hold. For example, environmental differences can occur when genetic differences do not exist, such as individual differences observed within a pair of identical twins. Also, genetic differences can be expressed in the absence of environmental differences, exemplified by differences among animals of a genetically heterogenous population reared in the same controlled laboratory environment. Several texts detail behavioral genetic methods and assumptions (e.g., Ehrman & Parsons, 1981; Fuller & Thompson, 1978; Hay, 1985; Plomin, DeFries, & McClearn, 1980).

In addition to the main effect influences of heredity and environment, GE interaction can contribute to the total phenotypic variance. As mentioned earlier, in behavioral genetics, GE interaction refers to the possibility that individuals of different genotypes may respond differently to specific environments (Plomin, DeFries, & McClearn, 1980.) Alternatively, GE interaction can be described as the differential effects of environments on individuals with different genetic propensities.

GE INTERACTION VERSUS GE CORRELATION

It is also important at the outset to distinguish genotype-environment interaction from a related quantitative genetic concept called "genotype-environment correlation." GE correlation is what developmentalists frequently mean when they refer to GE interaction. GE correlation literally refers to a correlation between genetic deviations and environmental deviations as they affect a particular trait. In other words, GE correlation is a function of the frequency with which certain genotypes and certain environments occur together. For example, if musically talented children are reared in environments that enhance their talent, there is a positive correlation between genetic differences in talent and environmental differences. Three types of GE correlations have been described (Plomin, DeFries, & Loehlin, 1977)—passive, reactive, and active.

In passive GE correlation, parents give their children both genes and an environment that is favorable (or unfavorable) for the development of a trait. For example, one of the most heritable personality traits is shyness (Plomin & Daniels, 1986). If parents are shy, they transmit a tendency towards shyness genetically, and being shy themselves, they also provide an environment that might foster shyness in their children.

In reactive GE correlation, people react differently to individuals of different genotypes. Parents may recognize that their child is shy, and encourage outgoing behavior to try to help their child overcome the shyness. Teachers might also react to a trait, and provide an environment that fosters (positive) or discourages (negative) genetically influenced traits in their students.

An important concern underlying interactionism and organismic theories in general is an emphasis on the child's active role in selecting or even creating environments. In behavioral genetics this is known as active GE correlation: The child contributes to his own environment and may actively seek an environment related to his genetic propensities. For example, a shy child is likely to avoid social interactions with strangers.

Although GE correlation is an interesting and possibly important concept, identification of specific GE interactions is a more tractable problem, and the remainder of the chapter focuses on GE interaction.

GE INTERACTION

The concept of GE interaction represents an important perspective for understanding environmental influences on individual development. Rearing environment might differentially affect the expression of genetic propensities; similarly, the effect of the environment on development might depend on an individual's genotype. Rather than searching for environmental influences that equally affect

159

all individuals on average, GE interaction focuses on environmental influences that may powerfully affect only a small group of individuals with certain genetic dispositions.

As indicated earlier, GE interaction refers to statistical interactions in the analysis-of-variance sense—the sum of squares that remains after main effects and within-cell variation are removed. Statistical interaction is well-named: "Interaction variations are those attributable not to either of two influences acting alone but to joint effects of the two acting together" (Guilford & Fruchter, 1973, p. 249). GE interaction is due to the nonlinear combination of genetic and environmental effects; in other words, it represents conditional relation in which the relation between X and Y depends on another variable. GE interaction is the extent to which observed variance can be explained by genetic and environmental influences considered together after the main effects of heredity and environment are removed.

If genotypes can be replicated—as they can for inbred mice—and several individuals of each genotype can be reared in different environments, then an analysis of variance can be performed. The two-way classification of genotypes by environments yields estimates of the variance between genotypes, the variance between the environmental treatments and the variance attributable to the interaction of genotype with environment. If there is no interaction, then genotypes that differ in one environment will differ to the same degree in other environments.

Figure 8.1 illustrates some hypothetical examples of GE interaction, which

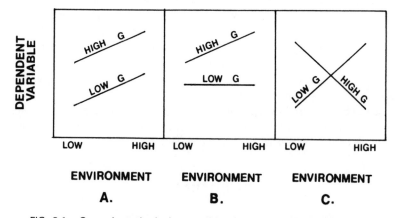

FIG. 8.1. Some hypothetical examples of genotype-environment interaction. The first example, shows main effects with no interactions, in this case, main effects and interactions are independent. In the last figure, the opposite is true—interactions occur without main effects. Such reversed effects are rare. The middle example is the most likely type of interaction—an environmental factor has an effect only for certain genotypes.

make the point that main effects and interactions are independent. For example, main effects can occur without interaction, as in Figure 8.1. Interactions can also occur without main effects as in Figure 8.1C; however, disordinal interactions of this sort are rare. The most likely type of interaction, an ordinal interaction, is illustrated in Figure 8.1B: An environmental factor has an effect only for certain individuals.

To illustrate analyses of ordinal GE interactions in humans, a 2 × 2 factorial design can be used: One independent variable is genotype, and other is an environmental variable, and the scores in the cells are the dependent variable. A 2 × 2 analysis of variance indicates the effect of environmental influences independent of genotype, the effect of genetic influences independent of environment and the GE interaction. To the extent that a trait is heritable—that is, to the extent that there is genetic influence on average in the population—the genetic propensity of an adopted individual can be estimated from the phenotype of a biological relative. This genotypic estimate can then be studied as it interacts with measured aspects of the environment to affect scores on the phenotype of interest. For brevity, we use the phrases ''high G'' and ''low G'' to denote extremes of genetic influence for a particular trait, and we intend them as population concepts referring to genotypic differences among individuals. ''High G'' refers to individuals with a genetic propensity to score high for a given trait, and ''low G'' refers to individuals with a heredity tendency to score low on the trait of interest.

THEORIES

The search for GE interactions is difficult in part because no theory exists to guide the selection of types of interaction analyses or the variables to be included in these analyses. Indeed, it is likely that the processes underlying GE interaction will differ for different combinations of behavioral and environmental measures. Nonetheless, given our focus on ordinal interactions, we suggest three possible types of GE interactions.

As illustrated in Figure 8.2A, a Type I GE interaction occurs when the environment has a greater impact on individuals with a genotype to score low for a given trait. That is, genotypes to score ''high'' (high G) on a certain trait express high phenotypic scores regardless of the characteristics of the rearing environment. For example, individuals genetically predisposed towards extraversion may be extraverted regardless of their family's social control, whereas individuals predisposed towards low extraversion may be affected by the family's level of control.

The second possible type of GE interaction occurs when the environment affects individuals with a genotype to score high for a given trait, but not ''low G'' individuals. Thus, the resulting interaction, a Type II interaction, depicted in

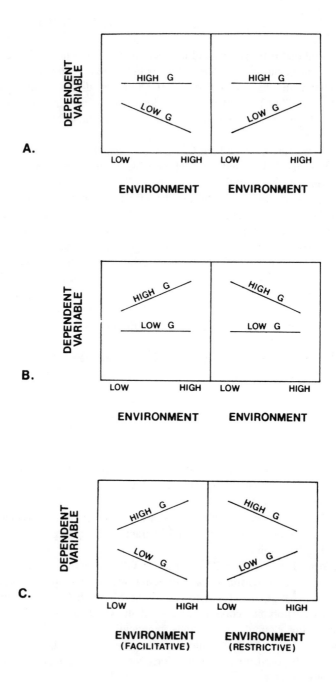

FIG. 8.2. Examples of three types of ordinal GE interactions: (a) Type I; (b) Type II; and, (c) Type III.

Figure 8.2B, will be a Type I interaction upside down. In our extraversion example, a genotype to score high on the extraversion trait ("high G") should be either exacerbated or diminished by families high in control, whereas individuals with a genetic tendency for low extraversion scores ("low G") might be little affected by control.

The difference between Type I and Type II GE interactions can be definitional. That is, our example could be phrased in terms of "high G" for introversion rather than "low G" for extraversion. We feel that it is important conceptually, however, to distinguish between the possibilities that, for a given trait, environmental factors might affect one end of the distribution more than the other.

A third type of GE interaction occurs when the environment influences both "high G" and "low G" individuals, but in opposite directions. Type III interactions have been suggested in the GE interaction research of Henderson (1968, 1970, 1972) in which different inbred strains of mice were reared in different environments. In his research, Type III GE interactions emerged in that genetic differences between strains were masked in high controlling environments and emerged in more permissive environments. That is, a restrictive environment reduces the overall magnitude of genetic effects and suppresses genetic variation, whereas a less restrictive environment allows genetic differences to emerge, as illustrated in Figure 8.2C. For example, in highly controlling families, genetic differences between individuals' extraversion might be muted in contrast to less controlling families.

ASSESSMENT OF GE INTERACTION:
ANIMAL RESEARCH

Studies of GE interactions have been facilitated by the availability of inbred strains of mice that differ genetically among strains but are nearly identical genetically within strains. Rearing various inbred strains of mice in several distinct environments permits a direct test of genetic main effects, environmental main effects, and GE interactions.

The best-known study of GE interaction (Cooper & Zubek, 1958) used selectively bred lines of rats rather than inbred strains. The rats had been selectively bred to run through a maze with few errors ("maze bright") or with many errors ("maze dull"). Rats from these two lines were reared under one of two conditions: An "enriched" condition with brightly colored cages and many moveable toys, or a "restricted" condition with gray cages and no moveable objects. Animals reared under these enriched and restricted conditions were compared to maze-bright and maze-dull animals reared in a normal laboratory environment, data from another study.

Figure 8.3 shows the maze-running errors for these rats. For selectively bred

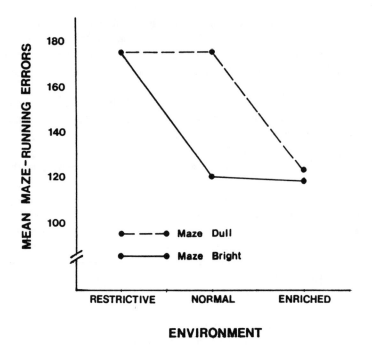

FIG. 8.3. GE Interaction: Maze running errors for maze-bright and maze-dull rats reared in restricted, normal and enriched environments. (Adapted from Cooper & Zubek, 1958)

rats reared in a normal laboratory environment (the condition in which they had been selectively bred), there was a large difference between the two lines. The enriched condition had no effect on the maze-bright animals, but it substantially improved the performance of the maze-dull rats (a Type I example). On the other hand, an impoverished environment was extremely detrimental to the maze-bright rats, but had little effect on the maze-dull rats (similar to Type II). The results suggest GE interaction because the effect of restricted and enriched environments depends on the genotype of the animal. It should be noted that "ceiling" and "floor" artifacts of measure could produce the same results (Henderson, 1979). This study, with its connotations for human cognitive development, stimulated interest in the concept of GE interaction.

As mentioned earlier, a series of studies involving thousands of mice of different inbred strains systematically explored GE interaction (Henderson, 1967, 1970, 1972). Characteristics of the environment—such as level of nutrition, environmental enrichment, or stress imposed on the mice prior to testing— affected subsequent performance on many behavioral measures. Inbred strains differed considerably in their response to rearing environments. For example, enriched environments enhanced the ability to locate food in a large test box for some strains but not others (Henderson, 1970). However, although significant GE interactions were detected in these studies, few were consistent within studies or across studies (see review by Fuller & Thompson, 1978). A review of earlier animal research also found little evidence for GE interactions (Erlenmeyer-Kimling, 1972).

ASSESSMENT OF GE INTERACTION: HUMAN RESEARCH

In research with human beings, it is not possible to select multiple copies of genotypes from pure inbred strains as in the case of mice, nor is it possible to subject them to environments as extreme as the deprived or enriched environments used in laboratory research on nonhuman animals, which may make it even more difficult to identify reliable GE interaction. Human behavioral genetic research is subject to the mixed blessing of working with naturally occurring genetic and environmental variation: The cost is a loss of experimental control and the benefit is the increased likelihood that the results of the research will generalize outside the laboratory.

One approach to GE interaction in human behavior was suggested by Jinks and Fulker (1970): A component of variance due to GE interaction is suggested by a significant correlation between the sums and differences of identical twins reared apart (MZA) for a particular measure. Pair sums for MZA reflect hereditary resemblance and differences within MZA can only be ascribable to environmental influences; for example, a positive correlation between pair sums and pair differences for MZA means that twins with higher scores for a particular characteristic experience greater environmental differences. It should be noted that the environment is not measured directly in this analysis that is directed at a components-of-variance approach. Using data from studies of MZA, some evidence for GE interaction of this type was found for extraversion and vocabulary, but not for neuroticism or a test of reasoning (Jinks & Fulker, 1970).

A method for isolating specific GE interactions using the adoption method has been proposed (Plomin, DeFries, & Loehlin, 1977). In this approach, the genotype of adopted children is estimated from the scores of their biological relatives on any behavior of interest—to the extent that heredity is important, scores of biological relatives predict the genotypic value of adopted-away children. The environment of the adopted children can be estimated using any measure of the adoptive home environment or characteristic of the adoptive parents. The absence of a relation between genotype and phenotype will be indicated in the analysis by the absence of a main effect for genotype. Similarly, the association between the environmental measure and the phenotype to test for the main effects of environment. GE interactions can emerge regardless of whether genetic or environmental main effects are observed.

The 2 × 2 paradigm is only illustrative. Full use of the data from this design entails analysis of the same variables in a continuous rather than dichotomous manner, using hierarchical multiple regression (HMR) analysis (Cohen & Cohen, 1975), which removes main effects of genotype and environment and then assesses the significance of their interaction. This approach has been systematically applied in two adoption studies.

Colorado Adoption Project

The Colorado Adoption Project (CAP) is a longitudinal prospective study of genetic and environmental influences in behavioral development. A full adoption design is employed that includes adopted children and their biological and adoptive parents as well as matched nonadoptive children and their parents (Plomin & DeFries, 1985; Plomin, DeFries, & Fulker, 1988). HMR analyses were applied to the CAP infancy data (12 and 24 months) as well as the early childhood (ages 3 and 4) measures (Plomin & DeFries, 1985).

Utilizing the CAP infancy data, 15 analyses of GE interaction for mental development using biological mothers' IQ as an estimate of genotype and several indices of environmental influence in the adoptive homes were conducted: Adoptive mothers' and fathers' IQ, the Home Observation for Measurement of the Environment (HOME; Caldwell & Bradley, 1978) general factor, and two second-order factors from the Family Environment Scale (FES; Moos & Moos, 1981). The dependent measures were the 12- and 24-month Bayley Mental Development Index (Bayley, 1969) scores and the average of the 12- and 24-month Bayley scores. None of the interactions were significant. Thus, systematic, nonlinear effects of genetic and environmental influences on infant mental development are not apparent from the CAP data.

The same conclusion was drawn from analyses of GE interaction in other domains of infant development. For behavioral problems, 30 GE interaction analyses produced only four significant interactions. In the domain of infant temperament, 80 GE interaction analyses were conducted and only two significant interactions were found, fewer than expected on the basis of chance alone ($p < .05$).

The data for 3- and 4-year-olds in CAP were analyzed in a similar manner in order to explore GE interactions in early childhood. In brief, the results of the GE interaction analyses in early childhood confirm the observation in infancy that few interactions can be found. In fact, of the 67 HMR analyses, not one was statistically significant ($p < .05$); finding fewer interactions than expected by chance suggests that HMR criteria for significance are too conservative and, for this reason, the few marginally significant interactions that emerged from these analyses might be meaningful.

Results indicate that, for the Sequenced Inventory of Communication Development (SICD; Hedrick, Prather, & Tobin, 1975) the HOME Encouraging Developmental Advance factor has a positive effect only for bright children (Type II interaction); in contrast, warmth of a home has an effect on the SICD only for children who are less bright (Type I interaction). Interactions with behavioral problems and temperament suggest Type I interactions: The environment has an effect on children without a strong genetic propensity—"low G." For example, when their biological mothers are high in neuroticism, adopted children have more behavioral problems regardless of the neuroticism of their adoptive mothers; however, adoptive mothers' neuroticism leads to increased behavioral problems for children whose biological mothers are low in neuroticism.

Despite these interesting and reasonable examples of GE interactions, it should be reiterated that the CAP parent-offspring adoption design has uncovered few examples of GE interaction (Plomin, 1986). Consider that the genotypic estimate relies on biological parents and their adopted-away offspring. Thus, the genotypic estimate is at best an estimate of half of the adoptees' genotype— and less if genetic effects in childhood and adulthood differ—which greatly limits the power to detect genotype-environment interactions using first-degree relatives.

Swedish Adoption/Twin Study of Aging

The exploration of GE interaction can be enriched by the study of identical twins reared apart. Monozygotic twins who are separated at birth, or soon there after, and reared apart (MZA) provide a unique natural experimental situation for comparing the performance of two identical genotypes within two separate environments. In terms of GE interaction, this adoption design provides much stronger estimates of G than adopted-apart first-degree relatives, although it is limited by the rarity of identical twins reared apart. Nonetheless, at the present time, there are two ongoing studies of MZA—the Minnesota Study of Twins Reared Apart (Tellegen, Lykken, Bouchard, Wilcox, Segal, & Rich, 1988) and The Swedish Adoption/Twin Study of Aging (SATSA; McClearn, Pedersen, Plomin, Nesselroade & Friberg, 1987).

The results presented here from the SATSA, which provides an unprecedented opportunity to study the genetic and environmental origins of individual differences in an elderly population (average age = 59 years). HMR GE interaction analyses were conducted using measures of extraversion and neuroticism (Floderus, 1974) for 99 pairs of identical twins reared apart. The early rearing environment was measured retrospectively by a modified version of the Family Environment Scale (FES; Moos & Moos, 1981) and an index of socioeconomic status (SES). In brief, the HMR predicts one twin's (twin A) score on a personality variable (for example, extraversion) from the other twin's (twin B) extraversion score (a measure of genotype), an FES measure of the environment (twin A), and the two-way product of these variables. Complete details of this study are provided elsewhere (Bergeman, Plomin, McClearn, Pedersen, & Friberg, 1988).

For a variety of personality measures in SATSA, 108 GE interaction analyses produced 12 significant GE interactions; 5.4 would be expected by chance when $p < .05$ (Bergeman, 1987). Some illustrative examples involving extraversion and neuroticism are provided here.

For extraversion, three significant GE interactions were found. All three were associated with control-related dimensions of the FES: Control ($F = 8.73$), Organization ($F = 7.50$), and System Maintenance (the second-order factor that is comprised of the Control and Organization scales; $F = 9.42$). The interactions (depicted in Figure 8.4 as 2×2 ANOVAs) reflect Type I GE interactions. In general, a genotype for high extraversion (depicted as "high G") is not affected by a controlling or restrictive environment. In contrast, the environment affects individuals with a genotype for low extraversion scores ("low G"). That is, "low G" individuals reared in a low controlling environment have significantly higher extraversion scores than "low G" individuals reared in environments perceived as highly controlling. These GE interactions accounted for approximately 6% of the variance.

Neuroticism showed significant GE interactions with socioeconomic status (SES), the FES Active scale, and the FES second-order factor of Personal Growth ($F = 4.13$, $F = 6.89$, $F = 3.51$, respectively), as shown in Figure 8.5. The GE interaction between neuroticism and SES appears to be Type I: "Low G" individuals are affected by environment but "high G" individuals are not. That is, individuals with a genotype for low neuroticism ("low G") score higher on the neuroticism scale when reared in a high SES environment than in a low SES environment. On the other hand, individuals with a genotype for high neuroticism scores ("high G") showed no differences across levels of SES.

The GE interactions between Neuroticism and the FES Active Scale, as well as FES Personal Growth, appear to be Type III interactions. Possibly these GE interactions mean that individuals with a "high G" for neuroticism score lower on neuroticism when the family environment is perceived as highly active or high in FES Personal Growth; in contrast, individuals with a "low G" show an

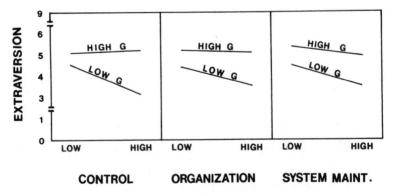

FIG. 8.4.   GE interactions with extraversion.

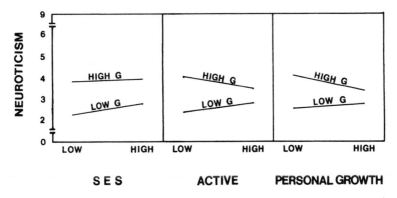

FIG. 8.5.   GE interaction with neuroticism.

increase in their neuroticism scores. Thus, both the "high G" group and the "low G" group are affected by rearing environment, but in opposite directions. This Type III interaction could be construed to be similar to the interactions seen in the mouse research—that is, that genetic effects are masked in high controlling environments—if familial push towards personal growth (which includes, along with Activity, a push towards Achievement and Independence) is viewed as control. Thus, genetic differences between "high G" and "low G" differ in the less controlling family environment but not in the more controlling families.

CONCLUSIONS

Although it is reasonable to assume that genotypic expression can be differentially influenced by early rearing environment, GE interaction is rarely considered in human research. One problem in the past has been that no theory exists to guide the selection of the variables to be included in these analyses. For this reason, we have proposed three possible types of ordinal GE interactions. (Disordinal GE interactions are unlikely to occur.)

One type suggests that environment has a greater impact on individuals with a genotype for low scores for a given trait. Several examples were cited in support of Type I interactions—for example, extraversion is affected by familial control only for individuals with a low genetic propensity towards extraversion.

A second type of GE interaction is essentially a Type I interaction "upside down." That is, the environment affects "high G" individuals but not "low G" individuals. Examples of Type II interactions were also found: The HOME Encouraging Developmental Advance factor affects SICD performance only for bright children.

The third type of GE interaction occurs when the environment influences both "high G" and "low G," but in opposite directions. Most of the evidence for this type has come from mouse research, and the support is for a particular variety of Type III interaction: Genetic effects are masked in high controlling environments and emerge in more permissive environments. That is, a restrictive environment may reduce the overall magnitude of genetic effects, whereas a less restrictive environment allows genetic differences to emerge. An example of Type III interactions was found in the interaction between neuroticism and familial activity and personal growth.

Although it is difficult, if not impossible, to compare the SATSA results with the CAP results, it is interesting to note that more significant GE interactions were detected in the SATSA sample than in the CAP data. These differences could be explained in a multitude of ways, but two possibilities particularly interest us.

First, the difference may be ascribable to increasing interactions with development. That is, given the results of few interactions in infancy and early childhood with an increase in adulthood, will we find increasing interactions as the CAP sample is followed into later childhood and adolescence?

A second and more likely explanation maintains that the MZA design of SATSA provides more powerful estimates of the genotype than the first-degree relatives design of the CAP. The MZA design might find more GE interactions for this reason. One way to test this hypothesis is to conduct GE interaction analyses using dizygotic twins reared apart, which are available in the SATSA sample; these analyses are in progress.

Although small, the percentage of variance explained by GE interaction is still of empirical relevance. These types of analyses have important implications for intervention research: By identifying interactions in which individuals with certain genetic propensities are affected differently by environmental factors, a new perspective for understanding environmental influences on individual development emerges. That is, if certain types of interactions can be attributed to specific behavioral and environmental measures, interventions can be directed at populations most likely to benefit.

REFERENCES

Anastasi, A. Heredity, environment, and the question "How?". *Psychological Review,* 1958, *65,* 197–208.

Bayley, N. *Manual for the Bayley scales of infant development.* New York: Psychological Corporation, 1969.

Bergeman, C. S. *Genotype-environment interaction in temperament development: Identical twins reared apart.* Unpublished Master's Thesis, Pennsylvania State University, 1987.

Bergeman, C. S., Plomin, R., McClearn, G. E., Pedersen, N. L., & Friberg, L. T. Genotype-environment interaction in personality development: Identical twins reared apart. *Psychology and Aging,* 1988, vol. 3, 399–406.

Caldwell, B. M., & Bradley, R. H. *Home observation for measurement of the environment.* Little Rock, University of Arkansas, 1978.

Cohen, J., & Cohen, P. *Applied multiple regression/correlation analysis for the behavioral sciences.* New York: Halsted Press, 1975.

Cooper, R. M., & Zubek, J. P. Effects of enriched and restricted early environments on the learning ability of bright and dull rats. *Canadian Journal of Psychology,* 1958, *12,* 159–164.

Ehrman, L., & Parson, P. A. *The genetics of behavior.* Sunderland, MA: Sinauer Associates, 1981.

Erlenmeyer-Kimling, L. Gene-environment interaction and the variability of behavior. In L. Ehrman, G. Omenn, & E. Caspari (Eds.), *Genetics, environment, and behavior: Implications for educational policy.* New York: Academic Press, 1972.

Floderus, B. Psycho-social factors in relation to coronary artery disease and associated risk factors. *Nordisk Hygienisk Tidskfift Summlementum,* Stockholm, Sweden, 1974, *6.*

Fuller, J. L., & Thompson, W. R. *Foundations of behavior genetics.* St. Louis: C. V. Mosby, 1978.

Guilford, J. P., & Fruchter, B. *Fundamental statistics in psychology and education.* New York: McGraw-Hill, 1973.

Hay, D. A. *Essentials of behaviour genetics.* Oxford: Blackwells, 1985.

Hedrick, D. L., Prather, E. M., & Tobin, A. R. *Sequenced Inventory of Communication Development.* Seattle: University of Washington Press, 1975.

Henderson, N. Prior treatment effects on open field behaviour of mice: A genetic analysis. *Animal Behaviour,* 1967, *15,* 364–376.

Henderson, N. The confounding effects of early rearing environment on discrimination learning in housemice. *Developmental Psychobiology,* 1968, *79,* 146–152.

Henderson, N. D. Genetic influences on the behavior of mice can be obscured by laboratory rearing. *Journal of Comparative and Physiological Psychology,* 1970, *73,* 505–511.

Henderson, N. D. Relative effects of early rearing environment on discrimination learning in housemice. *Journal of Comparative and Physiological Psychology,* 1972, *79,* 243–253.

Henderson, N. Adaptive significance of animal behavior: The role of gene-environment interaction. In J. R. Royce & L. P. Mos (Eds.), *Theoretical advances in behavioral genetics* (pp. 243–287). The Netherlands: Sijthoff & Noordhoff, 1979.

Jinks, J. L., & Fulker, D. W. Comparison of the biometrical genetical, MAVA, and classical approaches to the analysis of human behavior. *Psychological Bulletin,* 1970, *73,* 311–349.

McClearn, G. E., Pedersen, N. J., Plomin, R., Nesselroade, J. R. & Friberg, L. *SATSA: Effects of rearing environment on behavior later in life.* Manuscript report of the Institute for the Study of Human Development, The Pennsylvania State University, 1987.

Moos, R. H., & Moos, B. S. *Family environment scale manual.* Palo Alto, CA: Consulting Psychologists Press, 1981.

Plomin, R., DeFries, J. C., & Fulker, D. W. *Nature and nurture during infancy and early childhood.* New York: Cambridge University Press, 1988.

Plomin, R. *Development, genetics, and psychology.* Hillsdale, NJ: Lawrence Erlbaum Associates, 1986.

Plomin, R., & Daniels, D. Genetics and shyness. In W. H. Jones, J. M. Cheek, & S. R. Briggs (Eds.), *A sourcebook on shyness: Research and treatment* (pp. 63–80). New York: Plenum, 1986.

Plomin, R., & DeFries, J. C. *Origins of individual differences in infancy: The Colorado Adoption Project.* New York: Academic Press, 1985.

Plomin, R., DeFries, J. C., & Loehlin, J. C. Genotype-environment interaction and correlation in the analysis of human behavior. *Psychological Bulletin,* 1977, *84,* 309–322.

Plomin, R., DeFries, J. C., & McClearn, G. E. *Behavioral genetics: A primer.* San Francisco: W. H. Freeman, 1980.

Tellegen, A., Lykken, D. T., Bouchard, T. J., Wilcox, K., Segal, N., & Rich, S. Personality similarity in twins reared apart and together. *Journal of Social and Personality Psychology,* 1988, *54,* 1031–40.

Wachs, T. D., & Gruen, G. *Early experience and human development.* New York: Plenum, 1982.

9 The Co-construction of Representational Activity During Social Interaction

F. F. Strayer
Ellen Moss
Laboratoire d'Ethologie Humaine,
Département de Psychologie,
Université du Québec à Montréal

INTRODUCTION

Biological models of developmental plasticity posit two different, but complementary processes that regulate the impact of early experience on individual growth. *Experience-dependent adaptation* entails forms of developmental change induced by information available in the immediate environment. In contrast, *experience-expectant adaptation* involves genetically controlled processes that predispose individuals to actively seek specific patterns of external information (Greenough, Black, & Wallace, 1987). Individual differences in accessing forms of expected experience canalize subsequent development by attenuating responses to stimulation from the external world. Hominid evolution has undoubtedly involved both experience-expectant and experience-dependent adaptation. However, the ontogeny of primate perceptual-motor systems is often viewed as an extreme example of experience-dependent adaptation. At first glance, emphasis on such environmental determination seems only to reassert the commonsense view that during the course of evolution, the emergence of more sophisticated learning abilities was associated with increasing developmental plasticity and greater freedom from biological constraint. However, in the context of experience-expectant adaptation, differential impact of time-based, or maturationally expected events on the growing organism reflect prevailing biological constraints whose roots are to be found in the phylogenetic history of the species. In the case of most primates, such constraints entail a primary sensitivity

173

to information from the social entourage. Recent theories about the biological bases of primate intelligence suggest that mutual adaptation within stable social contexts favored transformations in representational capacities where thinking about social relationships within particular group settings contributed increasingly to individual fitness (Humphrey, 1976). At an ontogenetic level, such a biosocial approach to cognitive activity stresses differences in early social experience that canalize individual cognitive growth and produce individual variation in patterns of information processing.

From this perspective, cognitive growth depends on both the active role of the organism in seeking, or generating appropriate interactive experience with familiar social others, and on the social support, or scaffolding provided by these primary social partners during early phases of development. Social interaction requires mutual coordination of individual attention that leads increasingly to similar perceptions and to common representations of shared experience. Instead of stressing inherent differences in intellectual ability, a biosocial model of cognitive growth places primary emphasis on variations in social experience that orient individual growth and generate phenotypic variability in the nature of early representational activity. The exchange of information during social interaction requires representing ongoing joint activity in order to monitor and revise the course of the social episode. In contrast, more traditional models of cognitive development have focused primarily on children's interaction with the world of objects. Rather than examining children's strategic adjustments in daily encounters with natural social partners, researchers have been preoccupied with representational activity in relation to the physical world. Such object-centered approaches to early representation provide only a partial view of developmental changes in cognitive processes (Charlesworth, 1976).

Accepting social relations as a prime-mover of cognitive development has direct implications for how we approach the relation between experience with objects and the development of representational activity. In natural settings, physical objects generally serve as instruments that facilitate social interaction (Musatti, 1986). Both adults and children use objects to focus communication, and to actively modulate the nature of mutual participation (Nadel, 1986). The strategic shifting of attention between a social partner and a physical object permits maximizing both play and exploration while conserving the coordination of the social episode. At a cognitive level, dyadic communication entails processing information about the context of immediate interaction as well as information about the socioaffective state of the social partner. As the number of active agents in a social episode increases, there is a corresponding increase in the complexity of information processing demands for the young child. Early and repeated exposure to information exchange within familiar polyadic settings should be associated with more rapid emergence of complex forms of representational activity. In fact, studies of the potential effects of early daycare on cognitive functioning suggest a relation between time in group care and greater planfulness and problem-solving ability (Macrae & Herbert-Jackson, 1975; Strayer, Moss, & Blicharski, 1988).

SOCIAL RELATIONS AS CONTEXTS
FOR COGNITIVE GROWTH

Past research has demonstrated a number of direct links between children's cognitive functioning and the quality of early social relations (Hunt, 1986). Growth in representational ability has been associated with progressive internalization of the affective quality of the primary attachment relationship (Main, Kaplan, & Cassidy, 1985; Pipp & Harmon, 1987). Studies examining the influence of attachment on cognition in the first 3 years report that security of attachment is associated with more active exploration and greater representational abilities (Hazen & Durrett, 1982), greater skill in negotiating the physical environment (Cassidy, 1986; Slade, 1987), greater task-persistence (Frodi, Bridges, & Grolnick, 1985), and higher levels of exploratory play (Harmon, Suwalsky, & Klein, 1979). In contrast, insecure attachment has been linked to poorer mastery motivation in play with objects. Although insecure-avoidant toddlers manifest a high level of object play, they do so in a less goal-oriented fashion (Frodi et al., 1985; Harmon, Suwalsky & Klein, 1979). Insecure-resistant toddlers appear to show the least object engagement and to require the most parental management (Main, 1973). These initial findings on how primary attachment may relate to patterns of cognitive processing are consistant with the notion that behavioral and attentional mechanisms activated during the course of social interactions structure children's emerging representational activity in qualitatively different ways. However, an exclusive focus on the attachment figure as the primary agent of cognitive socialization neglects the potential contribution of other social partners to the child's growing representational competence. Within a modern biological framework, the central role of maternal responsiveness in psychological models of early development must be attenuated by a more general consideration of the diversity of other available social resources (Strayer, 1984). More in keeping with a biosocial model, parental investment theory would predict that the primary attachment system is synergistically associated with the establishment of multiple social bonds (Trivers, 1972).

Aside from general considerations about how information provided by primary caregivers may constrain children's intellectual growth, attention must also be given to child differences that contribute to the communication exchange where emerging cognitive skills are practiced. Empirically, one approach to this problem is to compare groups of same-aged children who differ in cognitive ability. For example, quasi-experimental contrasts of interaction in normal dyads and dyads where children were at risk for cognitive delays suggests that parental communication styles are adjusted in response to the child's observed competence (Cohen, Beckwith, & Parmelee, 1978; Mash & Johnson, 1982). Cunningham, Siegel, Spery, Clark, and Bow (1985) concluded that mothers maximize communication by modulating the complexity of verbal exchange to a level consistent with the child's current level of comprehension.

THE SOCIAL CONSTRUCTION
OF REPRESENTATIONAL TACTICS

Although the partner's responsiveness has been linked to the development of cognitive skills (Beckwith, Kopp, Parmelee, & Marcy, 1976; Wachs & Gruen, 1982; White & Watts, 1973), it remains unclear how specific actions by social partners lead to changes in children's representational activity. Researchers generally agree that early caregiver responsiveness is an important predictor of both social and cognitive development. Contingent responsiveness during the first year of life establishes an interpersonal context for turn-taking that later serves as a primary channel for the child's acquisition of more advanced social and cultural information. During the second year, the content of parental speech facilitates the elaboration of simple sign-symbol identification, as well as perceptual and functional associations (Trevarthen, 1987). From the third year on, social exchanges facilitate the child's emerging ability to represent abstracted information and activate the child's emerging metacognitive ability to operate on existing mental representations (Flavell, Speer, Green, & August, 1981). More advanced mental operations permit the child's application of available representational tactics in a wider range of situations.

A co-construction analysis of information exchange requires that social communication be conceptualized within a transactional framework. Such exchange presumably guides the young child in constructing plans and strategies for more optimal problem solution. In contrast to studies of early communication that employ micro-analyses of sequential patterns of dyadic exchange to document the constraining influences of social partners (Bakeman & Brown, 1980; Brazelton, Koslowski, & Main, 1974; Stern, 1977; Strayer, 1980; Trevarthen, 1979), studies of cognitive growth have usually examined global correlations between measures of parent and child performance. Even cognitive studies that examine relations between dyadic communication and early cognitive functioning often reduce the dynamics of information exchanged during interaction to measures of individual activity. For example, rate of mother encouraging play or rate of child asking questions (Cunningham et al., 1985) are familiar measures in the current cognitive developmental literature. Such indices of individual contributions to information exchange fail to capture the co-adaptive processes that characterize social interaction and influence cognitive growth (Rogoff, 1984; Strayer & Trudel, 1985).

One of the more accessible contexts for studying the co-construction of representational activity is joint problem solving during semistructured play. Previous research has identified a number of specific activities that can be used to describe the informational content of social exchange during play interactions (Belsky, Goode, & Most, 1980; Frankel & Rollins, 1983; Price, Hess, & Dickson, 1981; Sigel, 1982). For example, tactics for orienting the partner to task are prerequisite for coordinating joint attention. Adult task-related approval provides information about the social value of obtained results, knowledge about means-ends relations, and recognition of the child's efforts (Hess & Shipman, 1965; Sigel, 1982). Verbal and nonverbal modeling of particular actions (Case, 1978; Klahr, 1978) provides information about subgoal sequencing, which facilitates representation of potential transformations of the problem space. Elaborative tactics such as labeling (Ninio & Bruner, 1978) and perceptual or functional cueing (Case, 1978; Vliestra, 1978) focus the partner's attention to pertinent environmental features or isolated components of the problem space. In contrast, metacognitive tactics enable the manipulation of existing mental representations and distancing from particular actions and objects in order to restructure plans in the service of goal attainment (Flavell et al., 1981). Strategies such as predicting consequences, checking results, activity monitoring, and reality testing are critical to the child's ability to be self-regulating in a variety of problem-solving situations (Brown & DeLoache, 1978). All of these diverse tactics constitute potentially useful categories in a descriptive system designed to trace the flow of information between members of a dyad actively engaged in problem solving.

Adult demands induce the child to formulate alternatives, to coordinate plans, and to evaluate consequences of thought and action. Particularly during the toddler and early preschool period, adult interventions are critical to the planning, regulation, and coordination of ongoing problem-solving activity (Brown & DeLoache, 1978; Brown, Palincsar, & Armbruster, 1986; Flavell, 1976). As the child matures and becomes more capable of generating and monitoring plans, the sensitive caregiver should assume a more indirect role allowing maximal opportunities for the child to test and practice emerging skills. For example, a parent who allows a preschool child to combine functional and perceptual representations before proposing a restructuring or verifying tactic facilitates the child's mental separation from the observable field (Sigel, 1982). Generally, parental directives that indicate concrete solutions focus attention on objects, and indirectly restrict the child's elaboration of plans and strategies, thus limiting restructuring of current representations of the problem space.

An equally important question in the study of the co-construction of representational activity is the role of the child in advancing the collaborative process. The quality and diversity of both representational and interactive tactics in the child's repertoire can directly influence the course of joint play. Researchers working within a Vygotskian framework have emphasized the role of parental support in optimizing representational growth within the child's zone of proximal development (Sigel, 1982; Wertsch, McNamee, McLane, & Budwig, 1980). The capacity of parents to appropriately monitor their child's representational activity, and as a result, to regulate optimally the flow of information during interaction, influences cognitive growth by maximizing social support when the child is confronted with specific representational difficulties. The analysis of bidirectional constraints within social interaction accentuates different, yet complementary contributions of two social partners to the co-construction of representational activity. Of equal importance are mutual processes that lead to increasing similarity in the construction of shared representations. A primary form of social exchange that mediates much of the influence of social variables on children's representational activity entails spontaneous reciprocal imitation (Nadel, 1986). Dyadic matching of particular actions during social exchange can be seen as a basic socializing mechanism that permits the restructuring of affective, cognitive, and social skills learned in the course of interactions with different social partners. The occasion to benefit from imitation of multiple models in different social contexts could allow children to play a more active role in the co-construction of representational activity by providing a greater diversity of established representational tactics and a wider choice of activities more adapted to particular environmental demands.

The empirical examination of co-constructionist hypotheses about the growth of representational activity requires a more in-depth consideration of four interrelated issues: (1) the quality of information exchange during children's early communication with adults; (2) the sequential patterning of dyadic exchange during communication; (3) the influence of developmental levels on variations in the form and content of representational activity; and, finally, (4) the role of social partners as constraining influences on children's cognitive activity during joint problem solving. Given the developmental significance of the preschool period for the emergence of the ability to coordinate mental representations and the hypothesized importance of social experience in the development of such abilities, the study of young children with differing early social experience has both theoretical and practical significance.

A synthesis of biosocial views about the direct link between human intelligence and human sociability with psychological models of social scaffolding of representational activity raises intriguing questions about how patterns of primary attachment might interact with diversity of early social experience to differentially shape the development of problem-solving skills. The hypothesis that strategies learned in the course of social transactions with familiar partners are generalized to problems encountered during play with objects provides a set of novel predictions about the early development of representational activity. In accordance with traditional attachment theory, we might predict that a secure primary bond with mother would be associated with greater facilitation of the use of more mature representational tactics during problem solving. However, because the development of problem-solving activities has also been associated with opportunities to participate with both adults and peers, we might also expect that the larger social network of children with early day-care experience (Strayer, Jacques, & Gauthier, 1984; Strayer & Trudel, 1984; Strayer, Trudel, Noël, & Legault, 1988) would also stimulate the more rapid emergence of mature representational activity. Adaptation within a stable peer group provides frequent occasions for distancing from particular actions in order to analyze and plan appropriate social strategies. Such experiences should facilitate the more rapid development of metacognitive abilities. From this perspective, we could predict that both social intelligence and social competence depend as much on the complexity and diversity of early social relationships, as on the socio-affective equilibrium of the child's primary social bond. For securely attached infants who begin daycare in the fourth quarter of the first year, a time of consolidation of the attachment system (Ainsworth, Blehar, Waters, & Wall, 1978; Bretherton & Waters, 1985), we would expect that the use of imitation as a communicative mechanism underlying the growth of representational activity would be accelerated by social demands of multiple relationships within the day-care and home settings.

METHODS

The quality of the mother-child bond was evaluated using the Attachment Q-Sort Questionaire (Waters & Deane, 1982). The questionaire was completed by 93 middle-class, French-speaking mothers within a few weeks of their child's second birthday. Approximately half of these children had been enrolled in an infant day-care program during their first year of life, whereas the others had no regular day-care experience during the course of the research. The Attachment Q-Sort provided a profile of the quality of the mother-child social bond derived from the relative weighting of 100 descriptive items that characterized children's attachment behavior during the first 3 years. Indices of socio-affective security, interpersonal dependency, and general sociability were computed by comparing obtained individual profiles with theoretically optimal profiles for each of these developmental constructs (Waters & Deane, 1985). However, in this study, rather than simply selecting children on the basis of their construct scores, we decided to examine the extent to which the Q-Sort procedure provided homogenous categories of children who could be characterized by reported differences in the quality of the early attachment relationship. This empirical approach to classification of primary relations permitted deriving natural groupings of toddlers who were similar with respect to a variety of attachment-related behaviors.

Using complete linkage hierarchical clustering techniques with correlation matrices as indices of similarity between individual profiles on the 100 Q-Sort items, we identified three classes of children with similar Q-Sort scores. These initial findings were validated in split-half analyses that showed that the classification scheme was stable across randomly selected subsamples of subjects. In order to evaluate whether the three empirical clusters corresponded to qualitatively different patterns of primary attachment, groups of children were contrasted with respect to construct scores for security, dependency, and sociability. One-way analyses of variance indicated that attachment classes differed in a linear manner on each of the three theoretical constructs in the Q-Sort Questionaire. Class I children were the most secure, most sociable, and least dependent, whereas Class III children were the least secure, least sociable, and most dependent. The three clusters showed the strongest mean difference on the security dimension, so they were labeled the Secure, Average, and Insecure groups. In our subsequent analyses of problem-solving activity, a subsample of 32 children (16 from Class I and 16 from Class III) was selected to represent the two extreme clusters in our attachment classification. Children in each subgroup were evenly distributed with respect to gender and early socialization experience.

All subjects were videotaped with their mother during semistructured play sessions at home when the children were 18 and 30 months old. Three modalities of information exchange (nonverbal gestures, statements, and questions) were coded separately using a taxonomy of qualitatively distinct representational tactics. The descriptive categories were regrouped on an a priori basis into four classes of problem-solving behaviors (see Table 9.1), which reflected the mother's and child's attention to the partners conduct, references to objects, representations of problem-solving actions, and distancing activities (Moss & Blicharski, 1986).

The description of problem-solving activity required simultaneous coding by two highly trained observers. One observer focused on the mother, and the other followed the child. Observers noted all instances of the above tactics that were used by their respective focal subjects, as well as whether a recorded act was directed to a social partner or towards an object. Inter-observer reliability in coding this information was assessed regularly using Cohen's Kappa; all Kappa indices were greater than 0.85. Data were entered separately into two OS-3 event recorders that were connected to a common digital time signal written on one of the audio tracks of the VHS video recording system. This device permitted accuracy to a tenth of a second. The original data records included both the coded forms of individual activity and their exact time of appearance. It was thus possible to recompose a literal, temporally based transcript of all dyadic exchange during the entire problem-solving session. Computer software that merged the two data files also identified separate sequences of social problem solving. Whenever more than 5 seconds elapsed without any activity emitted by either the mother or child, a special code was automatically inserted to denote sequence transitions.

TABLE 9.1
Coding Taxonomy for Dyadic Exchange of Information

Classes of Activity	Problem-solving Tactics
A. Action Categories	1. Subgoal Reference & Rule Elaboration
B. Object Characteristics	2. Perceptual Cues 3. Functional Cues 4. Labeling
C. Conduct Management	5. Approval 6. Disapproval 7. Orientation to Task
D. Distancing Tactics	8. Reality Testing, Predict Consequences, & Verify Results

FINDINGS

Our first set of analyses focused on individual differences in the nature of representational activity during episodes of dyadic play. Repeated measures analyses of variance (day-care experience, attachment category with age as a repeated factor) were conducted with three types of dependent measures: (1) rate of problem-solving activity, (2) relative use of response modalities, and (3) differential use of specific problem-solving tactics. During each assessment period, day-care children had higher rates of representational activity. The overall rate of dyadic activity was associated with the number of observed interaction sequences; day-care children also had a greater number of separate sequences during a given play episode. Given these preliminary differences in quantity of problem-solving activity, subsequent analyses were conducted using relative frequency measures that controlled for individual hourly rates of representational tactics.

The relative use of nonverbal signaling activity declined as a function of age for all children. In contrast, the relative use of both statements and questions increased. However, the rate of change in the latter two measures differed as a function of early socialization experience. Day-care children used more statements, whereas home-reared children asked more questions. Analyses of children's relative use of specific tactics revealed a series of age effects for labeling, functional cues, subgoal identification, and distancing activity. These initial analyses revealed only a single significant effect for early social experience; day-care children used substantially more distancing activity. Although there were no direct effects for the attachment classification, there was a significant interaction between form of early care and security of attachment; day-care secure children used the greatest proportion of distancing tactics, whereas secure home-reared and insecure day-care children relatively both showed more distancing activity than the insecure home-reared group. Similar analysis of maternal use of different representational tactics showed only age effects. At 30 months, mothers used more labeling, perceptual cues, and distancing tactics. These latter analyses showed no systematic variation in maternal activity that could be attributed to either attachment classification or children's early day-care experience.

These preliminary findings trace broad zones of representational activity that are normative for the second and third year of life. The acquisition of object labels, extended exploration of the relation between objects and other forms of representation, as well as increased capacity to coordinate different elements of a problem space constitute major challenges in the toddler's zone of proximal development. As we hypothesized, day-care experience appeared to impact primarily on the emergence of children's distancing representations. Insecurity of attachment appeared to have a minor depressing effect on the developmental rate of these more abstract cognitive skills, an effect clearly attenuated if the insecure children were exposed to early day-care experience. The anticipated differences in the relative use of distancing tactics as a function of the diversity of early social relationships provided initial support for the biosocial hypothesis that the nature and quality of early social bonds shapes children's emerging representational activity. Somewhat unexpectedly, differences in problem solving appeared more related to age and early socialization than to security of attachment. However, the effects of the primary bond may be more evident in analyses of patterns of social exchange between the mother and child, rather than in analyses of individual rates of representational activity.

To better examine how interactive factors constrain patterns of information flow during joint problem solving, the coded sequences of mother and child activity were reanalyzed in terms of patterns of social interaction. These analyses entailed merging the separate behavioral records for each member of a dyad in order to isolate first order transitions between component acts of dyadic exchange. Figure 9.1 provides a graphic illustration of this analytic procedure. Twenty-six hypothetical behaviors are portrayed in sequential order by letters of the alphabet. Dyadic exchanges are indicated by diagonal lines connecting behavioral elements from the two streams of individual behavior. Elements separated by a sequence break (more than 5 seconds without coded activity) are not included as instances of dyadic exchange. In this example of three interaction sequences, there are five dyadic exchanges initiated by the mother and seven by the child. The set of exchanges initiated by the child (indicated by dark arrows) can be described as lag zero child behaviors leading to lag one maternal responses, whereas the set of mother-initiated exchanges are lag zero maternal acts followed by lag one child responses.

Analysis of the behavioral records for the 32 dyads revealed a total of 7,692

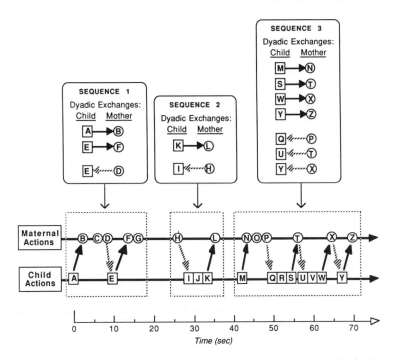

FIG. 9.1. Example of dyadic exchange coding in three hypothetical sequences.

child-initiated exchanges, and 7,707 mother-initiated exchanges. As is evident in the example from Figure 9.1, some behavioral acts were counted both as responses in a preceeding exchange initiated by one partner and as initial elements in the subsequent exchange initiated by the other. Developmental changes in the quality of dyadic problem solving can be traced by examining qualitative changes in the form of transitions between mother and child activity embedded within observed episodes of dyadic interaction. Separate transition matrices were calculated for mother- and child-initiated exchange at the two age levels, because our initial analyses showed strong differences in representational activity as a function of age. The patterns of dyadic exchange at 18 and 30 months are presented in Tables 9.2 and 9.3. The first column in each matrix shows the baseline probability for the use of specific representational tactics as an initial element during dyadic exchange. The last eight columns in each matrix reflect the probability of first-order transitions for each type of response given the initial action in the exchange. Finally, the column totals show the baseline probability for particular forms of partner response.

At 18 months (Table 9.2A), 53% of child-initiated exchanges began with a subgoal reference, and, in general, mothers responded to 31% of the time with information about subgoals. However, they responded to 37% of child subgoal

TABLE 9.2
Probability of Patterns of Information Exchange at 18 Months

A: Child-Initiated Exchanges: (Total Frequency = 3332)

Activity	Prob. of Initiation	Prob. of Maternal Response Given Initial Action							
		1	2	3	4	5	6	7	8
1. Subgoals	.53	.37[a]	.15[b]	.06	.15	.10	.02	.06	.09
2. Labeling	.12	.18[b]	.50[a]	.03	.13	.08	.01	.04	.03[b]
3. Perceptual	.03	.27	.14	.15[a]	.15	.08	.04	.09	.07
4. Functional	.15	.25[b]	.17	.04	.25[a]	.12	.04	.07	.06
5. Approval	.03	.14[b]	.12	.11	.18	.25[a]	.05	.04	.12
6. Disapproval	.02	.44	.11	.03	.17	.06	.04	.06	.10
7. Task Orient	.09	.32	.27	.03	.12	.05[b]	.03	.09	.10
8. Distancing	.03	.37	.15	.07	.07	.09	.03	.08	.14
Response Prob.	1.00	.31	.21	.05	.16	.10	.03	.06	.08

B: Mother-Initiated Exchanges: (Total Frequency = 3340)

Activity	Prob. of Initiation	Prob. of Child Response Given Initial Action							
		1	2	3	4	5	6	7	8
1. Subgoals	.31	.64[a]	.07[b]	.03	.10[b]	.03	.03	.07	.03
2. Labeling	.21	.36[b]	.31[a]	.03	.15	.02	.01	.09	.03
3. Perceptual	.05	.54	.04[b]	.12[a]	.11	.02	.03	.09	.05
4. Functional	.20	.52	.09	.02	.22[a]	.03	.02	.07	.03
5. Approval	.09	.51	.12	.01	.14	.12[a]	.02	.06	.02
6. Disapproval	.02	.45	.08	.08	.17	.00	.03	.14	.06
7. Task Orient	.05	.50	.11	.07	.12	.00	.05[a]	.14[a]	.01
8. Distancing	.08	.65[a]	.06[b]	.02	.10	.03	.02	.07	.06
Response Prob.	1.00	.53	.13	.03	.14	.03	.02	.08	.03

[a]Indicates significantly above expected value (chi-square > 6.64, p < .01).
[b]Indicates significantly below expected value (chi-square > 6.64, p < .01).

initiatives with information about task subgoals. In Table 9.2B, mothers initiated 31% of their dyadic exchanges with references to subgoals, and children responded to these initiations with subgoal information 64% of the time. This particular response rate exceeded the child's baseline probability for this form of representation by 11% (i.e., .64 less .53).

At 30 months (see Table 9.3), the baseline use of subgoal tactics decreased for both mothers and children, however, the matching of subgoal activity persisted as a characteristic form of information exchange. At both age levels, the greatest proportion of child-initiated dyadic exchanges involved subgoal representations, whereas functional cues constituted the second most frequent form of initiation, and labeling the third. At 30 months, there was a modest reduction in the probability of children starting exchanges with task orientation, and a slight increase in their use of distancing tactics as the initial act in social exchange. A similar pattern of baseline use was evident in mother-initiated exchanges, although at 18 months, mothers used slightly more labeling tactics.

Contingency analyses of particular patterns of dyadic exchange were conducted using data from raw frequency transition matrices (Colgan, 1978). These analyses, which adjust for differences in baseline use of specific behaviors, permit the identification of particular patterns of exchange that occur significantly more or less often than chance. In Tables 9.2 and 9.3, exchanges occur-

TABLE 9.3
Probability of Patterns of Information Exchange at 30 Months

A: Child-Initiated Exchanges: (Total Frequency = 4359)

Activity	Prob. of Initiation	Prob. of Maternal Response Given Initial Action							
		1	2	3	4	5	6	7	8
1. Subgoals	.41	.32[a]	.13[b]	.09	.16	.12	.04	.02	.13
2. Labeling	.16	.23	.32[a]	.07[b]	.13	.07[b]	.04	.01	.13
3. Perceptual	.07	.11[b]	.14	.30[a]	.11	.12	.10[a]	.03	.10
4. Functional	.22	.23	.14	.10	.25[a]	.12	.05	.02	.11
5. Approval	.04	.27	.11	.04	.16	.16	.04	.02	.19
6. Disapproval	.02	.31	.04[b]	.09	.19	.02	.09	.15[a]	.12
7. Task Orient	.03	.40[a]	.13	.07	.09	.04	.02	.12[a]	.12
8. Distancing	.05	.25	.07[b]	.08	.15	.11	.02	.05	.27[a]
Response Prob.	1.00	.26	.16	.10	.17	.11	.04	.03	.13

B: Mother-Initiated Exchanges: (Total Frequency = 4367)

Activity	Prob. of Initiation	Prob. of Child Response Given Initial Action							
		1	2	3	4	5	6	7	8
1. Subgoals	.27	.53[a]	.14	.04[b]	.17[b]	.04	.01	.03	.04
2. Labeling	.16	.33[b]	.33[a]	.05	.19	.03	.01	.02	.04
3. Perceptual	.11	.37	.09[b]	.19[a]	.22	.04	.02	.01	.04
4. Functional	.18	.43	.10[b]	.05	.31[a]	.03	.03	.01	.04
5. Approval	.09	.48	.15	.06	.21	.04	.00	.01	.05
6. Disapproval	.03	.35	.17	.09	.19	.01	.10[a]	.01	.09
7. Task Orient	.02	.27	.19	.07	.20	.05	.08[a]	.06[a]	.09
8. Distancing	.13	.44	.13	.04	.15[b]	.09[a]	.03	.03	.09[a]
Response Prob.	1.00	.43	.16	.06	.21	.04	.02	.02	.05

[a]Indicates significantly above expected value (chi-square > 6.64, p < .01).
[b]Indicates significantly below expected value (chi-square > 6.64, p < .01).

ring with a greater than chance frequency are indicated with a superscript a, whereas those occurring less often than expected are shown with a superscript b. In Table 9.2A, eleven forms of child-initiated exchange differed significantly from expected values given baseline scores. Five of these patterns involved greater than expected rates of direct matching by mothers during information exchange. There was evidence for immediate imitation of representational content in sub-goal references, labeling, perceptual cues, functional cues, and approval. In contrast, the six forms of dyadic exchange that occurred less often than expected involved dissimilar patterns of representational activity. In mother-initiated matrices, there were 13 patterns of significant dyadic exchange. Children matched maternal initiation for each of the aforementioned five categories, as well as for task orient. In addition, children were more likely to use subgoals following maternal distancing, and disapproval following maternal task orient. In the mother matrix, there were also seven patterns of dyadic exchange involving dissimilar patterns of representation that were significantly infrequent.

A more complex pattern of dyadic exchange was evident at 30 months. Table 9.3 shows that 15 forms of child-initiated and mother-initiated exchange differed significantly from baseline predictions. Once again, there was substantial evidence for greater than expected rates of direct imitation in both matrices: mutual matching was evident for subgoals, labeling, perceptual cues, functional cues, task orientation, and distancing tactics. In addition, maternal disapproval was followed more often than expected by child disapproval (Table 9.3B). Table 9.3A shows that at 30 months child perceptual cues also led significantly less often to maternal subgoals and more often to maternal disapproval, whereas child disapproval led more often to maternal task orient. Similarly, child task orient was more likely to be followed by maternal subgoals. For mother-initiated exchange (Table 9.3B), task orient was more likely to lead to child disapproval, whereas maternal distancing had a significant tendency to lead to child approval. Both transition matrices in Table 9.3 show six patterns of nonmatched dyadic exchanges that occurred significantly less often than expected given respective baseline scores.

These preliminary analyses of social interaction as a function of age illustrate the central role of dyadic matching as a primary form of information exchange during joint problem solving with toddlers. At 18 months, the only dyadic transitions occurring more often than expected involved matching of information between the two social partners. Although at 30 months, similar patterns of dyadic matching predominate in both child and mother-initiation matrices, a number of other transitions also occur with greater than chance frequency. In the child-initiation matrix, there is evidence that mothers begin to increase negative feedback as a reaction to the child's use of perceptual cues. Such a finding supports notions that mothers adjust interactive styles to accommodate the child's developing ability to represent different kinds of information. In addition, mothers now respond more often to child disapproval by redirecting attention to the task. Although such direct regulation of the child's attention may appear as an effective teaching tactic, closer inspection of Table 9.3B indicates that in some cases, maternal task orientation also leads to further expressions of disapproval by the child. The general increase in baseline rates of distancing at 30 months is associated with a significant increase in the probability of mutual matching; and finally, maternal use of distancing becomes increasingly associated with an increase in children's approval.

Although these particular forms of social exchange can be viewed as normative components of mother-child interaction at 18 and 30 months, the preceeding analyses do not address how the patterns of exchange vary in relation to the child's early social experience and attachment classification. This latter question involves recompiling the exchange data into separate transition matrices for dyads with similar attachment and social experience classifications. Following the suggestions of Bakeman, Adamson, and Strisik (this volume), the relative contribution of socialization variables to group differences in the pattern of social exchange was assessed by fitting log-linear models to the resulting multiple contingency table.

Our first modeling effort explored the similarity of the complete exchange matrix for each of our subgroups. In this analysis, eight by eight transition matrices similar to those in Tables 9.2 and 9.3 were constructed for the four attachment/socialization subgroups at each age level. These transition matrices were construed as a single dependent variable with 64 discrete levels in a logit analysis with age, attachment classification, and type of early social experience as predictor variables. Separate analyses were conducted for child- and mother-initiated exchanges.

A comparison of the relative strength of each predictor variable was obtained by calculating the partial chi-square associated with each component in the saturated logit model. Table 9.4 shows the obtained Likelihood Ratio Chi-Squares for child-initiated and mother-initiated exchanges. The inclusion of each successive term in a proposed model decreases the "No Effect" chi-square by the value indicated, and thus directly improves the "goodness of fit" index in the log-linear analysis. Visual inspection of the partial chi-square indices suggest that age was the most important predictor of the pattern of social exchange regardless of social group, and that many of the remaining components were significantly associated with variations in the dynamic of mother-child interaction. These initial analyses indicate that a multiple factor model is needed to adequately account for these empricial data. For both mother- and child-initiated exchange, the best fitting model included the three main effects (age, attachment, and experience) as well as two two-way interactions (age by attachment and attachment by experience) (Likelihood Ratio Chi Squares < 83.05, df $= 63$, $p > .05$). The complexity of the empirical models of dyadic information exchange indicates that both early social experience and quality of primary attachment influence the dynamics of interaction during joint problem solving.

TABLE 9.4
Indices of Association between Socialization Variables
and the Dynamic of Mother-Child Information Exchange

	Type of Dyadic Exchange					
	Child-Initiated			Mother-Initiated		
Effect	Chi-Square	DF	p <	Chi-Square	DF	p <
No Effects Model	1188.07	441	.001	1206.11	441	.001
Age	497.52	63	.001	493.16	63	.001
Attachment	119.21	63	.001	139.64	63	.001
Experience	100.67	63	.003	106.55	63	.001
Age by Att	116.30	63	.001	118.20	63	.001
Age by Exper	70.29	63	.250	60.34	63	.580
Att by Exper	108.57	63	.001	94.63	63	.010
Age by Att by Exper	87.15	63	.025	83.05	63	.050

Note: Indices are Likelihood Ratio Chi-Squares from a complete logit model without the indicated term. These indices reflect the decrease in "goodness of fit" if a term is excluded from the saturated log-linear model.

More direct evidence for the co-construction of representational activity was provided by examining the relative contribution of both partners to information exchange during social interaction. In a second set of analyses, we examined how the quality of mother and child responses varied in relation to initiated actions by the social partner. Multiple contingency tables were again constructed separately for mother and child transition matrices at each age level and again analyzed using the logit log-linear procedure. In these second analyses, the quality of dyadic response was treated as a dependent variable (with eight levels) that was to be predicted from the quality of the partner's initiations (also eight levels), primary attachment classification, and early care experience. As in the preceeding analyses, the relative contribution of the independent measures in predicting observed response patterns was again assessed by systematically excluding each single component from the completely saturated logit model and noting the resulting reduction in goodness of fit.

In each of the four analyses, the No Effects Model was clearly unable to predict the observed patterns of dyadic exchange. Thus, the baseline response tendencies of either mothers or children were unable to account for the observed patterns of social interaction. More interestingly, the partial chi-squares associated with the partner factor indicated that the immediately preceeding action in the dyadic exchange provided the best prediction of the quality of both mother and child response patterns. In these analyses of social constraint, there was a general lack of significant association for other components in the log-linear models. The only exception to this general trend was the significant partial chi-square associated with the interaction of attachment classification and quality of maternal initiations as a predictor of child responses at 30 months. This latter effect suggests that the maternal influence of children's representational activity at 30 months differed as a function of attachment classification. The nature of this difference is best illustrated by examining the patterns of dyadic transitions for the two attachment groups. Table 9.5 shows the two exchange matrices for mother-initiated activity at 30 months.

In both matrices, there is strong evidence for children's tendency to match the pattern of initiated maternal activity. However, only insecure children showed a significant tendency to match maternal disapproval, and to show disapproval

TABLE 9.5
Maternal Constraint on Child Representational Activity at 30 Months

A: Secure Attachment Relations: (Total Frequency = 2175)

Activity	Prob. of Initiation	Prob. of Child Response Given Maternal Action							
		1	2	3	4	5	6	7	8
1. Subgoals	.26	.52[a]	.14	.03[b]	.16	.05	.02	.03	.05
2. Labeling	.15	.35[b]	.39[a]	.03	.13	.03	.01	.02	.05
3. Perceptual	.10	.39	.08[b]	.22[a]	.18	.04	.01	.01	.06
4. Functional	.18	.44	.09[b]	.07	.30[a]	.02	.03	.01	.05
5. Approval	.10	.47	.16	.05	.21	.03	.00	.01	.07
6. Disapproval	.02	.40	.23	.08	.13	.04	.04	.02	.08
7. Task Orient	.02	.19[b]	.19	.13	.25	.02	.04	.08[a]	.10
8. Distancing	.16	.47	.15	.04	.15	.06	.02	.02	.10[a]
Response Prob.	1.00	.44	.17	.06	.19	.04	.02	.02	.06

B: Insecure Attachment Relations: (Total Frequency = 2116)

Activity	Prob. of Initiation	Prob. of Child Response Given Maternal Action							
		1	2	3	4	5	6	7	8
1. Subgoals	.26	.49[a]	.14	.06	.19	.05	.02	.01	.04
2. Labeling	.17	.26[b]	.34[a]	.06	.22	.04	.01	.02	.06
3. Perceptual	.10	.37	.11	.16[a]	.22	.05	.03	.02	.05
4. Functional	.19	.35	.12	.04	.36[a]	.05	.02	.02	.04
5. Approval	.09	.48	.11	.05	.19	.04	.02	.04	.07
6. Disapproval	.03	.30	.10	.07	.29	.01	.11[a]	.01	.11
7. Task Orient	.03	.35	.14	.02	.11	.06	.18[a]	.08[a]	.08
8. Distancing	.12	.32	.11	.07	.19	.12[a]	.05	.03	.11[a]
Response Prob.	1.00	.38	.16	.06	.23	.05	.03	.02	.06

[a]Indicates significantly above expected value (chi-square > 6.64, p < .01).
[b]Indicates significantly below expected value (chi-square > 6.64, p < .01).

when mother engaged in task orientation. The off-diagonal effects in Table 9.5A indicate that secure children also showed a greater level of response differentiation in reaction to maternal subgoals, labeling, perceptual, and functional cueing, as well as task orientation. In each of these cases, there was evidence that a particular form of child response was less likely to occur following each type of maternal initiation. In contrast, for insecure children, only maternal labeling was associated with a significant decrease in the use of a particular form of representational activity. Finally, among insecure children, maternal distancing was also associated with a significant increase in child approval, whereas in the secure group this tactic was significantly associated only with child distancing.

This series of analyses provides a preliminary understanding of how specific kinds of social experience constrain early representational development. Using traditional ANOVA techniques to examine the role of age, day-care experience, and attachment in explaining development of representational activity, we focused on variation in individual activity profiles. The transactional analysis allowed us to extend the study of developmental change to patterns of dyadic interaction that constitute the sharing of information between mothers and children. Together these research findings support the biosocial speculation that both the diversity and quality of children's early social relationships are associated with differential acquisition of specific patterns of representational activity. Analysis of age effects showed developmental change in both individual and interactive measures, which suggest zones of proximal development that may vary both in relation to maturational factors or experiential factors that may be invariant for all children in the sample. However, the emergence of early representational activity and variation in the way children coordinate subjective representations with mother appear related both to day-care experience and quality of primary attachment. Early experience with multiple social partners was associated with greater levels of overall activity, and more frequent use of distancing tactics during social interaction. In contrast, security of attachment was less related to measures of individual differences in activity, and more predictive of patterns in the dynamic of mother-child interaction.

Between 18 and 30 months, there was substantial increase in cognitive activity associated with the representation and communication of object attributes and relations between objects and problem-solving subgoals. In addition, there was evidence for the emergence of planning and monitoring skills necessary for more independent coordination of problem-solving activity. Mothers acted as co-participants in the construction of these abilities during this period because changes in their representational activity during play with their toddlers paralleled changes in the child's emerging abilities. In addition to these general age effects, children differed in both the rate and the quality of information exchanged with their mother—day-care children contributed more to the social episodes and used relatively more labelling, subgoal identification, functional cueing, and distancing. Effects of early social experience were also evident in the home-reared children's greater use of questions. These children appeared more dependent on maternal initiation of social episodes. Questioning tactics may be associated with these children's punctual adaptation to the asymmetrical demands that characterize the complementary roles in early adult-child social relations (Youniss, 1980). Such findings are consistent with results from recent studies investigating the effects of experience with peers and adults on children's discourse competence. Hay (1982) found that young children who had attended preschool used more sophisticated discourse skills than those who had remained at home. French (1985), in a detailed case study of language skills at 30 months, found more sophisticated conversational tactics during interaction with peers than with the more responsive and conversationally skilled mother. More sophisticated discourse skills apparently emerge only when they are necessary for maintaining ongoing communication and are most likely to be exercised during social contacts with conversationally unskilled partners rather than with adults.

Our second set of analyses attempted to better situate maternal and child constraint during joint play. Our log-linear analyses showed clearly the bidirectional influence of each partner in contributing to representational development. Although the supportive role of adults in facilitating emerging representational abilities has often been emphasized, the active contribution of the child to the exchange of information during mother-child interaction has received less empirical attention. Our exchange analyses that explored age-related changes in representational activity helped to clarify how communicative processes can facilitate early cognitive growth. Mutual imitation of forms of information was clearly evident in both mother- and child-initiated exchange. Dyadic imitation promotes synchrony during information exchange within particular interpersonal contexts and may facilitate the shared comparison of scripted or figurative knowledge. Although the impact of imitation of adult tactics on cognitive growth has been discussed in the context of maternal scaffolding (Bruner, Olver, & Greenfield, 1966), the complementary maternal matching of child activity suggests additional affective and communicative functions that may direct the course of subsequent development. The communicative function of matching levels of information exchange has been interpreted by Trevarthen (1986) as "ensuring an increasingly elaborate mental and behavioral engagement between the infant and other persons." The human tendency to imitate certain behaviors and not others is seen by Trevarthan as the result of innate biological mechanisms that predispose the infant to link its subjective evaluations of experience with those of others permitting the progressive co-construction of collective knowledge. A shared knowledge base is essential for the development of cooperation and facilitating social structures. An accumulating body of research suggests that co-adaptation of information exchange is intrinsically connected with interactive continuity in both adult-child and peer contexts. The affective function of imitation can be seen as the progressive association of values with action sequences involving particular persons and mutually interesting objects. Early imitation of affective components of behavior is essential to the child's construction of meaning and understanding of cultural values. We believe that the preschooler's increasing competence in reproducing functional units of behavior during the second and third years of life (Kuczynski, Zahn-Waxler, & Radke-Yarrow, 1987) results from progressive ability to coordinate affective and representational activity in the co-construction of culturally meaningful action units with significant social others.

Although our analyses of child differences in the use of representational activity failed to reveal substantial attachment effects, sequential analyses offered more precise information about how the quality of primary bonding and the diversity of early social relationships may influence emerging representational activity during episodes of structured play with mother. The exchange analyses at 30 months revealed that both mothers of secure and insecure children show a stable repertoire of representational tactics at the two age levels. However, secure children showed greater differentiation in responding to maternal initiatives. Security of attachment may influence social attention mechanisms that leads to greater sensitivity to social constraints within the co-constructive context and more optimal collaboration in goal-oriented problem-solving endeavors. In contrast, insecure children showed higher levels of maternal conduct management at 30 months suggesting possible deficits in these children's understanding of the functions of social coordination and of the possibility of joint committment to a common endeavour. Such interpersonal dynamics have already been associated with the cognitive style of insecure-resistant children in earlier studies (Frodi et al., 1985; Main, Kaplan, & Cassidy, 1985). Finally, security of attachment appears to have an impact on dyadic representation and execution of task-activities. Whereas both secure and insecure children strongly match the level of information provided by their mothers, insecure children show a less structured pattern of nonmatched dyadic response. The successful suppression of non-meaningful patterns of dyadic exchange may be essential for synchronizing social interaction, and prerequisite for the elaboration of intimate interpersonal relationships. Indirectly, such coordination would become a necessary condition for maximizing others' contributions to the child's developing representation of both the social and physical worlds.

CONCLUSIONS

The investigation of social interaction during early childhood strongly supports predictions from a biosocial model of early cognitive development that gives primacy to the social construction of intellectual activity. Both the quality and the diversity of interpersonal relationships influenced the transfer of information and shaped children's emerging representational activity. Past studies of social contraints on functioning have generally emphasized that parent-child communication establishes basic patterns of socioaffective adjustment that only indirectly shape the child's subsequent cognitive activity (Matas, Arend, & Sroufe, 1978; Shatz, 1984). Our results show more direct links between representational activity and early social experience. From a psychobiological perspective, these findings suggest that early social relations provide a species characteristic setting for the development of skill in the expression and representation of problem-solving tactics.

Both the diversity and the quality of social experience was associated with the more rapid emergence of complex problem-solving tactics. Day-care children were, in many instances, developmentally advanced in both communicative and representational competence. Our results support the view that diversified social experience may complement, or even compensate for, patterns of interpersonal communication that adversely modulate emerging intellectual functioning. In this regard, it is important to stress that in many instances, the problem-solving style of insecurely attached toddlers who had established stable social relationships in the day-care environment was equivalent to that of their securely attached peers socialized in the more familiar home setting. Such a finding is consistent with recent speculation that human ontogeny entails *experience-expectant* adaptation requiring the establishment of stable social bonds to assure normal maturation of both representational and communicative skills. Furthermore, in accordance with parental investment theory, these findings suggest that human infants may benefit from multiple parental resources, especially when they are caught in a potentially adverse primary attachment bond. To the extent that the social entourage facilitates or inhibits cognitive maturation, it is reassuring to note that supplementary parental care may help to recuperate early intellectual growth. The diversity, as well as the quality, of social relationships may constrain the acquisition of information and the development of representational activity. From this perspective, social constraints are intrinsic to all co-construction models of cognitive growth, and must be seen as prime movers for the development of both intellectual and social skills.

REFERENCES

Ainsworth, M. D., Blehar, M. C., Water, E., & Wall, S. *Patterns of attachment: A psychological study of the strange situation.* Hillsdale, NJ: Lawrence Erlbaum Associates, 1978.

Bakeman, R., & Brown, J. V. Early interaction: Consequences for social and mental development. *Child Development,* 1980, *51,* 437–447.

Beckwith, S. E., Kopp, C., Parmelee, A., & Marcy, T. Caregiver interaction and early cognitive development in preterm infants. *Child Development,* 1976, *47,* 579–587.

Belsky, J., Goode, M. K., & Most, R. K. Maternal stimulation and infant exploratory competence; Cross-sectional, correlational and experimental analyses. *Child Development,* 1980, *51* (1), 1168–1179.

Brazelton, T. B., Koslowski, B., & Main, M. The origins of reciprocity: The early mother-infant interaction. In M. Lewis & L. A. Rosenblum (Eds.), *The effect of the infant on its caregiver.* New York: Wiley, 1974.

Bretherton, I., & Waters, E. Growing points of attachment theory and research. *Monograph of the Society for Research in Child Development,* 1985, *50.*

Brown, A. L., Palincsar, A., & Armbruster, B. B. Instructing comprehension-fostering activities in interactive learning situations. In H. Mandl, N. Stein, & T. Trabasso (Eds.), *Learning and comprehension of texts.* Hillsdale, NJ: Lawrence Erlbaum Associates, 1986.

Brown, A. L., & DeLoache, J. S. Skills, plans and self-regulation. In R. Siegler (Ed.), *Children's thinking: What develops?* Hillsdale, NJ: Lawrence Erlbaum Associates, 1978.

Bruner, J. S., Olver, R. R., & Greenfield, P. M. (Eds.), *Studies in cognitive growth.* New York: Wiley, 1966.

Case, R. Intellectual development from birth to adulthood: A neopiagetian interpretation. In R. Siegler (Ed.), *Children's thinking: What develops?* Hillsdale, NJ: Lawrence Erlbaum Associates, 1978.

Cassidy, J. The ability to negotiate the environment: An aspect of infant competence as related to quality of attachment. *Child Development,* 1986, *57,* 331–338.

Charlesworth, W. R. Human intelligence as adaptation: An ethological approach. In L. Resnick (Ed.), *The nature of intelligence.* Hillsdale, NJ: Lawrence Erlbaum Associates, 1976.

Cohen, S., Beckwith, L., & Parmelee, A. Receptive language development in preterm children as related to caregiver-child interaction. Pediatrics, 1978, *61,* 16–20.

Colgan, P. W. *Quantitative ethology.* New York: Wiley, 1978.

Cunningham, C., Siegel, L., Spery, H., Clark, M., & Bow, S. The behavioral and linguistic interactions of specifically language-delayed and normal boys with their mothers. *Child Development,* 1985, *56,* 1389–1404.

Flavell, J. Metacognitive aspects of problem-solving. In L. B. Resnick (Ed.), *The nature of intelligence.* Hillsdale, NJ: Lawrence Erlbaum Associates, 1976.

Flavell, J. H., Speer, J. R., Green, F. L., & August, D. L. The development of comprehension monitoring and knowledge about communication. *Monographs of the Society for Research in Child Development,* 1981, *47* (5 Serial No. 192).

Frankel, M. T., & Rollins, H. A. Does mother know best? Mothers and fathers interacting with preschool sons and daughters. *Developmental Psychology,* 1983, *19* (3), 694–702.

French, L. *Effects of partner and setting on young children's discourse competence.* Paper presented at the meeting of the Society for Research in Child Development, Toronto, April 1985.

Frodi, A., Bridges, L., & Grolnick, W. Correlates of mastery-related behavior: A short-term longitudinal study of infants in their second year. *Child Development,* 1985, *56,* 1291–1299.

Greenough, W. T., Black, J. E., & Wallace, C. S. Experience and brain development. *Child Development,* 1987, *58,* 539–559.

Harmon, R., Suwalsky, J., & Klein, R. Infant's preferential response for mother versus an unfamiliar adult. *Journal of the American Academy of Child Psychiatry,* 1979, *18,* 437–449.

Hay, A. *The role of interactive experience in the development of discourse skills.* Unpublished Doctoral Dissertation, University of Illinois at Urbana-Champaign, 1982.

Hazen, N., & Durrett, M. Relationship of security of attachment to exploration and cognitive mapping ability in two-year-olds. *Developmental Psychology,* 1982, *18,* 751–759.

Hess, R. D., & Shipman, V. C. Early experience and socialization of cognitive modes in children. *Child Development,* 1965, *36,* 869–886.

Humphrey, N. K. The social function of intellect. In P. Bateson & R. Hinde (Eds.), *Growing points in ethology.* Cambridge: Cambridge University Press, 1976.

Hunt, J. The effect of variations in quality and type of early child care on development. In W. Fowler (Ed.), *Early experience and the development of competence.* New Directions for Child Development, 32. San Francisco: Jossey-Bass, 1986.

Klahr, D. Goal formation, planning and learning by preschool problem-solvers. In R. Siegler (Ed.), *Children's thinking: What develops?* Hillsdale, NJ: Lawrence Erlbaum Associates, 1978.

Kuczynski, L., Zahn-Waxler, C., & Radke-Yarrow, M. Development and content of imitations in the second and third years of life: A socialization perspective. *Developmental Psychology*, 1987, *23*(2), 276–282.

Macrae, J. W., & Herbert-Jackson, E. Are behavioral effects of infant day care programs specific? *Developmental Psychology*, 1975, *12*, 269–270.

Main, M. *Exploration, play and cognitive functioning as related to child-mother attachment.* Unpublished Doctoral Dissertation, Johns Hopkins University, Baltimore, 1973.

Main, M., Kaplan, N., & Cassidy, J. Security in infancy, childhood and adulthood: A move to the level of representation. In I. Bretherton & E. Waters (Eds.), Growing points of attachment theory and research. *Monograph of the Society for Research in Child Development*, 1985, *50*, 41–65.

Mash, E., & Johnson, C. A comparison of the mother-child interactions of younger and older hyperactive children. *Child Development*, 1982, *53*, 1371–1381.

Matas, L., Arend, R., & Sroufe, L. A. Continuity of adaptation in the second year: The relationship between quality of attachment and later competence. *Child Development*, 1978, *49*, 547–556.

Moss, E., & Blicharski, T. The observation of teaching and learning strategies in parent-child and teacher-child interaction. *Canadian Journal of Early Childhood Education*, 1986, *1*, 203–209.

Musatti, T. Early peer relations: The perspectives of Piaget and Vygotsky. In E. Mueller & C. Cooper (Eds.), *Process and outcome in peer relationships*. New York: Academic Press, 1986.

Nadel, J. *Imitation et communication entre jeunes enfants.* Paris: Presses Universitaires de France, 1986.

Ninio, A., & Bruner, J. S. The achievement and antecedents of labeling. *Journal of Child Language*, 1978, *5*, 1–15.

Pipp, S., & Harmon, R. Attachment as regulation: A commentary. *Child Development*, 1987, *58*, 633–647.

Price, G. G., Hess, R. D., & Dickson, W. F. Processes by which verbal-educational abilities are affected when mothers encourage preschool children to verbalize. *Developmental Psychology*, 1981, *17*(5), 554–564.

Rogoff, B. Adult assistance of children's learning. In T. Raphael & R. Reynolds (Eds.), *Contexts of literacy*. New York: Longman, 1984.

Shatz, M. Contributions of mother and mind to development of communicative competence: A status report. In M. Perlmutter (Ed.), *Parent-child interaction and parent-child relations in child development*. Hillsdale, NJ: Lawrence Erlbaum Associates, 1984.

Sigel, I. The relationship between distancing strategies and the child's cognitive behavior. In L. Laosa & I. Sigel (Eds.), *Families as learning environments for young children*. New York: Plenum, 1982.

Slade, A. Quality of attachment and early symbolic play. *Developmental Psychology*, 1987, *23* (1), 78–85.

Stern, D. *The first relationship.* Open Books/Fontana, London, 1977.

Strayer, F. F. Social ecology of the preschool peer group. In A. Collins (Ed), *Cognition, affect and social relations*. Hillsdale, NJ: Lawrence Erlbaum Associates, 1980.

Strayer, F. F. Biological approaches to the study of the family. In R. Parke, R. Emde, H. McAdoo, & G. Sackett (Eds.), *Review of child development research, 7*. Chicago: University of Chicago Press, 1984.

Strayer, F. F., Jacques, M., & Gauthier, R. L'évolution du conflit social et les rapports de force chez les jeunes enfants. *Recherches de Psychologie Sociale*, 1984, *5*, 57–73.

Strayer, F. F., & Trudel, M. Developmental changes in the nature and function of social dominance among young children. *Ethology and Sociobiology*, 1984, *5*, 279–295.

Strayer, F. F., & Trudel, M. L'éthologie sociale de l'enfant: Choix des comportements, modes de relevé et démarches analytiques. *Comportements*, 1985, *10*, 183–198.

Strayer, F. F., Moss, E., & Blicharski, T. Bio-social bases of representational activity during early childhood. In T. Winegar (Ed.), *Social interaction and the development of children's understanding*. Norwood, NJ: Ablex, 1988.

Strayer, F. F., & Trudel, M. Developmental changes in the nature and function of social dominance among young children. *Ethology and Sociobiology*, 1984, *5*, 279–295.

Strayer, F. F., & Trudel, M. L'éthologie sociale de l'enfant: Choix des comportements, modes de relevé et démarches analytiques. *Comportements*, 1985, *10*, 183–198.

Strayer, F. F., Trudel, M., Noël, J.-M., & Legault, F. La coordination des structures sociales chez les jeunes enfants: Perspectives transversales. *Revue Internationale de Psychologie Sociale*, sous presse.

Trevarthen, C. Communication and cooperation in early infancy: A description of primary intersubjectivity. In M. Bullowa (Ed.), *Before speech: The beginning of interpersonal communication*. New York: Cambridge University Press, 1979.

Trevarthen, C. Development of intersubjective motor control in infants. In M. G. Wade & H. T. A. Whiting (Eds.), *Motor development: Aspects of coordination and control*. Dordrecht: Martinus Nijhof, 1986.

Trevarthen, C. *First steps in a child's social understanding: Motives and purposes of intersubjectivity*. Paper presented at the biennial meeting of the Society for Research in Child Development, Baltimore, April 1987.

Trivers, R. Parental investment and sexual selection. In B. Campbell (Ed.), *Sexual selection and the descent of man, 1871–1971*. Chicago: Aldine, 1972.

Vliestra, A. G. The effect of strategy training and stimulus saliency on attention and recognition in preschoolers. *Journal of Experimental Child Psychology*, 1978, *25*, 17–32.

Wachs, T. D., & Gruen, G. E. *Early experience and human development*. New York: Plenum, 1982.

Waters, E., & Deane, K. E. Infant-mother attachment: Theories, models, recent data and some tasks for comparative developmental analysis. In L. Hoffman & R. Gandelman (Eds.), *Parenting: Its causes and consequences*. Hillsdale, NJ: Lawrence Erlbaum Associates, 1982.

Waters, E., & Deane, K. E. Defining and assessing individual differences in attachment relationship: Q-methodology and the organization of behavior in infancy and early childhood. In I. Bretherton & E. Waters (Eds.), Growing points of attachment theory and research. *Monograph of the Society for Research in Child Development*, 1985, *50*, 41–65.

Wertsch, J. V., McNamee, G., McLane, J. B., & Budwig, N. A. The adult-child dyad as a problem-solving system. *Child Development*, 1980, *51*, 1215–1221.

White, B. L., & Watts, J. C. *Experience and environment: Major influences on the development of the young child*. NJ: Prentice-Hall, 1973.

Youniss, J. *Parents and peers in social development: A Sullivan-Piaget perspective*. London: University of Chicago Press, 1980.

10

Between Caretakers and Their Young: Two Modes of Interaction and Their Consequences for Cognitive Growth

Marc H. Bornstein
National Institute of Child Health and Human Development
and *New York University*

INTRODUCTION

Myriad nuances texture everyday interactions between caretakers and babies. This chapter is concerned with two significant questions that attend these interactions: First, does the rich mélange of caretaking activities that are part of these interactions lend itself to systematization? And second, how do the most prominent modes of caretaker-infant interaction affect the young child's developing mind?

What kinds of people children are, and what kinds of adults children become when they grow up, reflect children's native capacities in complex continuing interplay with the diversity of early interactions they provoke and those that are provided for them. Research suggests that specific interaction experiences at specific points in the life cycle affect specific aspects of human growth in specific ways. From this perspective, caretaking plays a formative role in development. Thus, whether the child instigates different modes of interaction or, in the child's phenomenology, interactions arrive deus ex machina, the significance of the nature and timing of interactions the child experiences early in development cannot be underestimated. Even if some human characteristics are inborn and persist or modulate through time as a reflection of biological endowment, others originate and develop on account of experience, and development proceeds on the interplay of endowed attributes in the context of interactions experienced.

Two major perspectives within developmental study, those of Piaget (e.g., 1926) and of Vygotsky (e.g., 1962, 1978), hold that mental advance in childhood develops principally out of interpersonal exchanges, normally experiences that take place in natural interactions with caretaker (Kuhn, 1988; Tudge & Rogoff, 1989). However, patterns of caretaker interaction that influence children's development, especially their mental growth, are only presently undergoing taxonomic classification (e.g., Bornstein, 1988; The Consortium for Longitudinal Study, 1983; Gottfried, 1984; Wachs & Gruen, 1982): That is, an important movement in developmental psychology has the goals of identification, specification, and operationalization of categories of caretaking.

In practice, caretaker-infant interaction is intricate and multidimensional, and mothers and fathers regularly engage in combinations of caretaking. Many categories of caretaking interactions may be identified, including prominently nurturant, material, social, and didactic (Bornstein, 1988). This chapter features two, the *social* and *didactic*. I first define and then illustrate each with respect to mental development from infancy. Next, I review psychometric considerations associated with categorizing modes of interaction, including internal consistency, orthogonality, reliability, and stability. Then, I examine conditional relations that exist among these two modes of caretaking interaction, their developmentally changing effectiveness, and the specificity of antecedent-consequent relations in caretaking. Finally, I address briefly latent issues of causality between these caretaker interactions and cognitive growth in young children.

TWO MODES OF CARETAKING INTERACTION:
DEFINITIONS AND ILLUSTRATIONS

Amidst the activities caretakers ordinarily engage in with their infants, several categories of interaction can be distinguished. To qualify as a category, the mode of interaction must meet several criteria. First, the category must encompass a variety of distinguishable activities that normally can be expected to cohere in some degree. That is, individual categories of caretaking are not unitary, but subsume many diverse activities that aggregate into a conceptual set. Second, a category must be distinct from other categories. Categories of interaction of different types are naturally confounded in the everyday lives of caretakers and children. Yet, different modes of caretaking may be theoretically and operationally separable; modes of engagement are different, but they can be expected to overlap. To meet this criterion, categories must be distinguishable from one another, even if they are not necessarily or wholly mutually exclusive. Last, caretakers must engage in the category of interactive activities reliably. In other words, a category will have little psychological validity if it is not stable at least over short periods of time.

Two categories of caretaking that meet these several criteria are social and didactic interactions. In the pages to follow, I elaborate on these categories further, and I provide illustrations of how each of these two categories of caretaking in infancy affect mental growth in the child. Afterward, I detail results that support the psychometric adequacy of these categories. As a consequence of their psychological characteristics, these categories are emerging as invested with considerable practicable importance for child-rearing and may have significant heuristic value for developmental study.

Social Interactions

The social mode of interaction is comprised of the physical and verbal strategies parents use to express their feelings and to engage their young in primarily interpersonal exchanges. Rocking, kissing, physical comforting, smiling, nonverbal vocalizing, and maintaining playful face-to-face contact illustrate commonly observed types of social interactions. Parents regularly engage their young in various forms of social caretaking.

Purely social caretaking gambits appear to influence growth in diverse ways—even as Harlow (Harlow & Harlow, 1966) observed long ago; some effects specifically relate to mental development. Longitudinal research beginning in the 1970s suggested that generally warm, sensitive, affectionate, nonrestrictive parental care was positively associated with cognitive growth in children (e.g., Ramey, Farran, & Campbell, 1979; Solkoff & Matusak, 1975; Solkoff, Sumner, Weintraub, & Blase, 1969; Yarrow, Rubenstein, & Pedersen, 1975), and critical review of the literature indicated that the absence of social caretaking from early life could be deleterious to mental development (Rutter, 1979). Two more recent studies illustrate that affectively positive social caretaking predicts mental growth in the child. Bee, Barnard, Eyres, Gray, Hammond, Spietz, Snyder, and Clark (1982) found that maternal attentiveness during feeding when infants were 4 and 12 months of age significantly predicted children's 3-year language performance and 4-year IQ. Olson, Bates, and Bayles (1984) found that mothers' affectionately touching, rocking, holding, and smiling at their 6-month-olds significantly predicted a composite measure of cognitive/language competence in the same children at 2 years.

Didactic Interactions

Clearly, social overtures constitute a common and important class of caretaker-child interactions; the focus of social interactions is on the dyad. A second significant mode of caretaking locates its focus outside caretaker and infant per se, in extradyadic loci. Such interactions include caretakers' strategies in stimulating and arousing their offspring to the world outside the pair, in encouraging attention to properties, objects, or events in the environment, in introducing, mediating, and interpreting the external world, and in provoking or providing opportunities to observe, imitate, speak, and learn. Didactics may be physical (pointing, placing, guiding, or demonstrating) or verbal (describing, questioning, instructing, or labeling); they may elaborate on something already under the child's purview, or they may introduce something new.

On the basis of observation and research strategies adopted to establish causal links between caretaking interactions and developmental achievement, clear evidence has emerged that didactic interactions may promote mental development beginning in infancy (e.g., Carew, 1980; Clarke-Stewart, 1973). The idea of parental "scaffolding" (Bruner, 1983; Wood, 1989) aptly illustrates one kind of didactics: Scaffolding describes facets and functions of the teaching process (e.g., task induction, highlighting, analysis) that are requisite to children's learning because they support and augment the child's limited cognitive capacities and unassisted abilities. Bruner (1983), for example, registers numerous illustrations of the ways mothers in natural interactions with their young children help to foster the preverbal foundations of language essentially through such (informal and sometimes unconscious) didactic practices. Although children certainly instigate many encounters with their parents, adults are acknowledged to initiate, structure, and regulate how young children learn. Others, too, have documented propitious effects of caretaking didactics. For example, Belsky, Goode, and Most (1980) observed that didactic interactions of mothers were consistently associated with infants' exploratory competence at each of several ages across the first 2 years of life. Bornstein and his co-workers (1985; Bornstein, Miyake, & Tamis-LeMonda, 1985–1986; Tamis-LeMonda & Bornstein, 1989) found that both American and Japanese mothers who more often encouraged their young infants to attend to properties, objects, or events in the environment later had toddlers and older children who possessed greater verbal abilities and who scored higher on standardized tests of intelligence.

Social and didactic interactions occupy a substantial proportion of parenting—perhaps their popularity reflects their inherent ease and happy aspect. Empirical study shows that in the first 6 months, for example, caretakers readily engage in play and in instruction with their infants and young children (Bornstein & Tamis-LeMonda, 1988; Stern, 1977). Although research has documented that adults of many species engage their young in many ways, it seems that social and didactic overtures of the kinds described here are highly characteristic of human beings. Importantly, each has demonstrated validity for the growth of cognition, a central adaptation in humans.

TWO MODES OF CARETAKING INTERACTION: PSYCHOMETRIC ADEQUACY

Psychometric considerations dictate that, to possess construct validity, phenomena such as categories of interaction need to be internally consistent, reasonably independent of one another, and reliable at least over the short term.

Satisfaction of these criteria is prerequisite to evaluating their stability through time as well as their concurrent and predictive validity for other aspects of psychological development.

Internal Consistency and Orthogonality of Categories of Interaction

The two psychometric issues of internal consistency and orthogonality complement one another. The criterion of internal consistency applies where a construct (here a category of interaction) is composed of different items; to meet the criterion of internal consistency items in the construct must covary. Specifically, internal consistency requires that different activities composing the category will share a pattern of performance. It could be that different activities are performed with similar frequency, or that one (or more) of several activities simply covary in a patterned way. Thus, mothers who are more social should not only rock their infants more but may comfort them more, smile at them more, and so forth. Mothers who are less social should not only rock their infants less but may comfort them less, smile at them less, and so forth. Of course, more social mothers may express sociability in a chosen manner, but that manner ought to be accompanied by other social activities.

Relatedly, the principle of orthogonality requires that, if modes of interaction, for example, are to be considered separate, different modes must assess relatively independent (noncovarying) characteristics of the caretaker. To meet this criterion, activities in one construct must not strictly associate with activities in a different construct. Thus, if mothers who frequently rock, comfort, or smile at their infants also regularly focus their infants' attention, consistently scaffold, or persistently provide opportunities to imitate, social and didactic forms of caretaking may not be distinguishable as separate constructs. Of course, independence of categories of interaction need not be absolute; a moderate degree of overlap is acceptable if anticipated by theory. However, a high degree of overlap indicates that categories are redundant, and not only undermines their independence (Nunnally, 1978), but subverts their predictive power as well (Cohen & Cohen, 1983).

Heretofore, insufficient attention has been paid to the companion issues of internal consistency and orthogonality in classifying caretaking interactions and in evaluating their effects in development. This may be true because it has been widely assumed that parents behave in consistent ways across domains of interaction with their infants, and because caretaking has often been defined with respect to one (or a small number of) pervasive bipolar dimensions, described in the aggregate as good, sensitive, appropriate, or warm (see Hunt, 1979; Lamb & Easterbrooks, 1980; Schaefer, 1959; Wachs & Gruen, 1982; Wohlwill, 1973). The consequences of neglecting distinctions of internal consistency and orthogonality across categories of interaction may be considerable, however. For example, if caretaking activities categorized together do not covary or associate in some discernable pattern, those that are mutually related and influential in development may be mixed with others that are unrelated and not influential thereby masking specific effects or attenuating potential effects of those that are related and influential. Additionally, under such circumstances it would not be possible to identify which underlying category may be influential in specific spheres of development.

In several studies with mothers of babies in the first year of life, I have attempted to document the internal consistency and orthogonality of social and diadactic categories of interaction (e.g., Bornstein, 1985; Bornstein & Tamis-LeMonda, 1988; Vibbert & Bornstein, 1989). Dependably, individual, independently-coded activities within the social and within the didactic modes of interacting significantly intercorrelate (e.g., physical with verbal didactic encouragement), whereas activities in the separate modes, as well as composites of social and didactic caretaking, do not covary (e.g., didactic encouragement versus face-to-face social play). For example, Vibbert and Bornstein (1989) assessed several individual social activities in mothers interacting with their 13-month-olds, including mothers' affectively laden comments, smiling, mutual regard, and social play. These individual activities aggregate to represent social caretaking based on their a priori conceptual similarity; but the four activities also show an empirical pattern of positive covariation, and their internal consistency justifies their use in a composite. Furthermore, Bornstein and Tamis-LeMonda (1988) and Vibbert and Bornstein (1989) conducted studies at 2, 5, and 13 months intended to assess the relation between social and didactic caretaking, as previously defined. Results showed that the two categories consistently constitute independent modes of infant care. On these bases, social and didactic modes of interaction reflect two dimensions of caretaking that begin to meet two reasonably stringent criteria of psychometric adequacy, namely, internal consistency and orthogonality. Thus, these two forms of interaction may be distinguished as coherent, but mutually distinct entities.

Reliability and Stability
of Modes of Interaction

Beyond internal consistency and orthogonality, evidence of short-term reliability is basic to validating modes of caretaker interaction. A psychological phenomenon may possess momentary psychometric integrity, but its utility as a meaningful construct rests fundamentally on its replicability across retests spaced reasonably close together in time. Of course, maternal activities can be expected to change over long periods of time, and in response to children's development. But, if mothers varied wildly in their activities from day to day, it would not be possible to use these caretaking constructs to characterize infants' experiences meaningfully. Individual caretakers vary considerably in terms of the range of activities within each mode of caretaking, and the caretaker-child relationship is dynamic and transactional in nature; nonetheless, a growing literature gives evidence that caretakers are consistent in many aspects of their interactions, at least over short temporal periods necessary to establish psychometric reliability. Several studies have assessed maternal social and didactic activities repeatedly in the first year of life: Short-term day-to-day and week-to-week assessments reveal generally significant intraindividual reliability among caretakers in these modes of interaction, although some estimates fall short of significance (see Bornstein, 1985; Ruddy & Bornstein, 1982; Olsen-Fulero, 1982). For example, Bornstein and Tamis-LeMonda (1988) twice assessed social and didactic interactions among mothers of 2-month-olds and mothers of 5-month-olds, each time within a 1-week period: Most didactic activities (e.g., encouraging attention to the environment and speech) proved reliable, as did many social activities (e.g., responsiveness and social play), although some social interactions were less so (e.g., establishing face-to-face contact).

Over longer periods—months or years—caregiving requirements dramatically change of course; thus, some activities may not remain stable, whereas others may. Some may also transmute. Different modes of expression are more or less apt at different ages. Establishing the stability or instability of caretaking activities is essential because, as elaborated later, it is possible that some activities exert a profound influence on the development of the child on account of their cumulative nature. The long-term stability or instability of caretaking cannot be determined, however, until measurement reliability is distinguished from behavioral stability; for this reason, the psychometric criteria of internal consistency, orthogonality, and reliability are doubly important. Nonetheless, several studies document stability of maternal behavior over longer periods (e.g., Belsky, Gilstrap, & Rovine, 1984; Bradley, Caldwell, & Elardo, 1979; Clarke-Stewart & Hevey, 1981; Olson et al., 1984). In a follow-up of their study of short-term reliability of caretaking at 2 months, Bornstein and Tamis-LeMonda (1988) assessed the stability of mothers' social and didactic interactions between 2 and 5 months: Again, maternal speech and most didactic interactions (e.g., encouraging attention to the environment) were stable as were social interactions (e.g., aspects of responsiveness), but other social interactions were not stable (e.g., social play). Bornstein and Ruddy (1984) had earlier found 8-month stability in maternal didactic style between 4 and 12 months.

Stability of caretaking interactions can be expected to vary with many factors, substantively because of the age and temperament of the child and psychometrically because of the duration of the interval between assessments. That is, independent of how fixed in their ways caretakers may be, a baby's changing or a given baby's particular traits might differentially influence caretaking, just as extending the temporal duration between evaluations can normally be expected to attenuate stability coefficients. These several factors may interact with one another as well: For example, Belsky et al. (1984) found that mothers and fathers alike are generally more consistent over the 6-month period of their infants' growth from 3 to 9 months than they are over the 2-month period of their infants' growth from 1 to 3 months.

TWO MODES OF CARETAKING INTERACTION: MECHANISMS OF ACTION

Social and didactic modes of interaction not only meet several criteria of psychometric adequacy, but they are at least moderately predictive of later developmental status, as the foregoing findings document. In considering the consequences of modes of caretaking for child development, however, it is imperative to evaluate how these categories function in practice. The most prominent issues raised by an interaction orientation to caretaking concern, first, the statistically conditional character of interactions, second, their developmentally changing significance, and, third, the specificity of antecedent-consequent relations that best describe their function.

Statistical Conditionality Among Modes of Interaction

Many studies of interaction in development are designed on the assumption that modes of caretaking exert independent and linear effects on development; indeed, most investigators are happy to report univariate longitudinal outcomes. However, the assumption that interactions contribute to development only linearly and monistically precludes a consideration of potentially significant conditional influences; in other words, categories of interaction doubtlessly exert effects in concert with one another. For example, social and didactic interactions nearly always take place in a material setting (Parke, 1978; Wohlwill, 1983), but the independent or conditional contributions of material aspects of the interaction often go unanalyzed (if not unrecorded) in evaluating the influences of other interactions (cf. Wachs & Chan, 1986).

Statistical procedures can be applied to deepen our understanding of the unique as well as the joint contributions to development made by different categories of caretaking. These techniques illuminate direct as well as indirect influences of interaction experiences in development. Consider the following examples. As noted previously, Olson et al. (1984) found that mothers' social interactions with their 6-month-olds predicted a composite measure of children's cognitive competence at 24 months. However, path analysis of the investigators' longitudinal study revealed that mothers' social caretaking at 6 months actually influenced child outcome at 24 months indirectly through the mediation of maternal didactics at 13 months that directly predicted children's cognitive competences.

Two other studies report similarly influential social X didactic interactions. In one, Kuchuk, Vibbert, and Bornstein (1986) examined the joint influences of maternal social and didactic caretaking interactions on 3-month-olds' perceptual sensitivity to facial expressions. They studied the same infants in the laboratory and at home. In the home, naturally occurring didactic and social exchanges between mothers and infants were observed; in the laboratory, infants' abilities to detect variations of smiling in a single face were independently assessed. Analysis of conditional effects showed that strong relations existed between maternal didactics and infants' sensitivity, when infants were exposed to low or to middle levels of maternal social smiling, but, as infants experienced increasing amounts of social smiling, the association between maternal didactic directiveness and infants' sensitivity in the laboratory decreased. Put another way, maternal didactic directiveness at 3 months was most beneficial for infants' perceptual skill when directiveness occurred in the context of social exposure that was tempered.

In a second study, Vibbert and Bornstein (1989) examined the association between maternal social and didactic interactions and 13-month-olds' language competence. Here, mothers and infants participated in two home visits, one designed to assess interaction, and the other independently to assess infant language and play. When relations between mother and toddler were evaluated, it turned out that maternal object-centered didactics and social activities in the home were associated with toddler language and play skills. However, understanding of these relations was greatly enhanced when hierarchical regression techniques were used to examine simultaneous and conditional effects of different maternal activities on different toddler skills. For example, the influence of maternal didactic activities appeared to be conditionally related to maternal social activities. Infants whose mothers more often encouraged their attention to the environment scored higher on a standardized measure of language comprehension, whereas maternal social interactions did not contribute to this child competence. Moreover, toddlers whose mothers prompted them out of a context of low to medium levels of social interaction were the most verbally proficient, whereas the beneficial effects of maternal didactics were attenuated at high levels of social interaction.

These several studies give evidence that different modes of caretaking may statistically interact in guiding the course of development. In Olson's observation, it appears that modes of interaction transmute during development to maintain their efficacy; in Bornstein's studies, it appears that to take advantage of input the infant must be able to distinguish the signal of one category of activity embedded in the noise of another. Infants experience an intricate network of caretaking interactions in their everyday life. Beyond whatever documentable univariate effects each may induce, statistical conditionality among modes of caretaking interactions demonstrates that individual categories may influence one another in affecting development.

Developmental Change in Modes of interaction and its Significance

Caretaker interactions may exert unidimensional or conditional influences on the child's development. Whichever effect obtains, interactions can also vary over the course of development in their prevalence as well as in their concurrent or predictive validity for developmental outcome. Caretakers do not engage in all modes of interaction (or even individual activities) at all times in the life course equivalently often; moreover, modes of interaction themselves wax and wane in effectiveness, modulated in part at least by the developmental status of the child. Development is too complex and dynamic to concede that the general availability, or even the simple aggregation, of social or didactic sorts of interaction may be determinative.

Although caretakers will engage in all forms of interaction with their offspring over the course of childhood, normally they can be expected to stress one or another at different points in time. For example, Belsky et al. (1984) and Bornstein and Tamis-LeMonda (1988) found that parents' social overtures towards their infants tend to decrease in frequency over the first year, whereas parents' didactic interactions tend to increase in the same period, perhaps as the child shows greater responsiveness to didactics. Even within the category of didactic caretaking, verbal interactions quickly come to dominate physical ones in the mothers's repertoire. Such developmentally changing tendencies characterize parent speech and play as well (e.g., Crawley & Sherrod, 1984; Papoušek, Papoušek, & Bornstein, 1985).

Caretakers thus interact with their children in a different balance of patterns at different periods. Developmental changes in modes of caretaking in turn portend their own implications in development. Just as some modes of caretaking may never influence cognitive growth, or do so only moderately, and others always will, one category of interaction may have telling consequences at an early period but not at a later one; whereas a second category may have less consequential impact at the first time period, but make a considerable impression at the second. For example, Bee et al. (1982) found that mothers' instructional techniques predicted their children's IQ at 4 years with increasing power between 4 months and 4 years, whereas the efficacy of maternal attentiveness, mood, and the like during feeding tended reciprocally to lose predictive force over the same time period.

Similarly, physical strategies as opposed to verbal ones seem to possess more immediacy, meaningfulness, and efficacy for the very young, motorically inept nonverbal infant. Presumably, the changing nature of the active and increasingly independent child underlies the changing significance of these predictors (see too Carew, 1980). In the extreme case, an interaction may benefit or adversely affect growth depending on the developmental status of the child. For example, Goldberg (1977) found that maternal kinesthetic stimulation of infants in the first 6 months positively predicted their concurrent and future infant test performance over the first year, whereas the same kinesthetic stimulation in the second 6 months related negatively to infants' test performance. In the newborn period, proximal contact could constitute primary stimulation or most effectively engage and organize newborn attention and thereby promote performance, whereas later in infancy proximal contact might circumscribe experience by inhibiting the growth of exploratory skills.

Developmental study defines a kind of dynamic that integrates the changing nature of caretaker-child interactions with the changing effectiveness of different modes of interaction for different developmental outcomes. This dynamic reflects prior experiences as well as maturational forces intrinsic to the child. The two combine to render child and experience at any given time optimally to nonoptimally matched.

Specificity of Antecedent-Consequent Relations in Caretaking

Given the multivariate nature of interaction effects—consisting of different categories of interaction acting alone or in concert with one another and with the developmental status of the child—research confirms that caretaking effects do not generalize widely. More often, specific modes of interaction tend to yield specific developmental outcomes.

Consider the following models of antecedent—consequent relations, consisting of two independent interaction categories—say, Social and Didactic—and two independent developmental outcomes—say, Emotional and Cognitive. In the simplest case of predictive specificity, different antecedent categories of interaction (S and D) affect different consequent outcomes (E and C, respectively) without cross-over; that is, interaction mode S influences consequent E but not C, and interaction mode D influences consequent C but not E. A recent study conducted by Bornstein and Tamis-MeMonda (1988) provided a concrete example. They observed mothers and their infants at home in natural interactions twice, once when the babies were 2 months of age and once when 5 months of age. Mothers who more often engaged their 2- to 5-month-olds in face-to-face interactions (S) influenced the 5-month-olds to engage them more often (E) but not to explore the environment (C), whereas mothers who more often encouraged their 2- to 5-month-olds to attend to properties, objects, and events in the environment (D) had 5-months-olds who explored the environment visually and tactually (C) in preference to engaging their mothers (E). Thus, at both 2 and 5 months the attentional foci of mothers and infants are mutually keyed to one another. It is important to note that, at the two ages in this study, the two maternal activities were uncorrelated with one another as were the two infant activities.

Thus, specific caretaker interactions appear to link to specific competencies in the child. In the cognitive domain, the most frequently examined outcome is psychometrically measured intelligence, but it may be that Piagetian cognitive abilities, language skills, play sophistication, symbolic competence, exploration, creativity, or other differentiated manifestations of mental life represent outcome measures more appropriately matched to specific categories of interaction. Other possible models of association between cause and effect may also obtain, because, as we know, there are several modes of interaction and many possible developmental outcomes.

In overview, modes of caretaker interaction might affect development monistically, but they certainly often combine with one another in conditional ways. Modes of caretaker interaction also fluctuate in prevalence and vary in effectiveness with developmental status and other attributes of the child. Finally, it can be seen that specific modes of caretaker interaction influence specific aspects of growth and development.

TWO MODES OF CARETAKING INTERACTION: PLAUSIBLE CAUSE

Over short or long periods, caretakers' interactions influence the development of their young; many such experiences turn out to be intellectually beneficial. Thus, a set of plausible causes must be explicated. The exact means by which different modes of interaction function remain elusive, however. *How* do social caretaker-infant exchanges regulate children's cognitive performance? *How* do didactic caretaker-infant experiences govern children's intellectual accomplishments? No single mechanism accounts for ontogenetic change satisfactorily or comprehensively. Several relevant dimensions of causal relation may be proposed, however; it remains to future research to specify possible mechanisms of action.

One relevant dimension appears to be whether the influence is direct. As distinguished by Parke (1978), direct influences encompass processes by which social agents or physical events act on the child without additional mediation, whereas indirect influences encompass processes by which social agents or physical events act on the child through the mediation of some other agent(s) or event(s). It could be that didactic interactions accumulate to shape and texture children's mental life directly (Bornstein, 1988). Using lag-sequential analysis, I recently found that mothers' prompting to the environment regularly anticipates their 4-month-olds' attention to the environment. Alternatively, it could be that interactions of one type influence development through interactions with another. Material aspects of the environment may effect change alone or in the context of social or didactic interactions (Clarke-Stewart & Apfel, 1979).

In addition, modes of interaction could share the same mechanism of regulation. For example, maternal responsiveness could shape children's competencies or inculcate feelings of self-efficacy and control, whether instantiated as responsive social interactions (e.g., Bell & Ainsworth, 1972; Bradley, Caldwell, & Elardo, 1979; Coates & Lewis, 1984; Lewis & Goldberg, 1969) or as responsive didactic interactions (e.g., Bornstein & Tamis-LeMonda, 1989; Riksen-Walraven, 1978). Similarly, social and didactic interactions alike could stimulate brain growth that in turn underpins higher mental functioning.

Another consideration relevant to causal interpretation is the time intervening between antecedent interaction and developmental outcome. Consider the following two models of the time course of interaction effects. Possibly, a given interaction experienced at a particular time effects change in the child at that time and that change thereafter endures. This model is consonant with a sensitive period interpretation of experience effects (e.g., Bornstein 1989; Colombo, 1982). For example, Bornstein (1985) found that didactic interactions at 4 months contribute more to child intelligence test performance at 4 years than the same didactic interactions at 12 months, even though mothers remain stable in these didactic activities between 4 and 12 months. Similarly, other studies show that some early interaction effects persist even when the contributions of the same interactions at a later time are partialled (e.g., Tamis-LeMonda & Bornstein, 1989).

Or, possibly interactions aggregate in time to exert an influence over development through their consistency. That is, an interaction experienced at any one time does not necessarily surpass an effectance threshold; rather, longitudinal relations are structured by analogous interactions continually repeating over shorter time periods. Temporal stability in social or didactic caretaking could underwrite the cumulation of experiences that eventually exceed a threshold of change (Bornstein, 1988; Bornstein & Sigman, 1986; Stern, 1985). Olson et al. (1984), for example, found that consistency in maternal social and didactic interactions over the first 2 years of life predicted children's cognitive competence, above the unique contribution of early or later maternal interactions. Similarly, a number of studies have confirmed an attenuation of some early interaction effects when the contributions of later ones are partialled (e.g., Bradley & Caldwell, 1980; Gottfried & Gottfried, 1984). Thus, both sensitive period and cumulative impact interpretations find suggestive empirical support in the existing developmental literature. Of course, there is nothing to prevent each from operating in separate spheres.

In overview, modes of caretaking interactions may affect development over short or over long periods. Effects may be immediate, or they may cumulate; some may be direct, others indirect. Future study should further elucidate precise means by which specific interaction experiences influence development.

CONCLUSIONS AND IMPLICATIONS

Evaluating how categories of caretaker interactions influence human development points to the need to recognize a multivariate model of growth that (minimally) specifies the nature of the interactions themselves, their developmental timing and statistical conditionality, as well as their specific outcomes. The research literature clearly demonstrates that different interaction strategies deployed at different periods in different combinations reverberate on different child competencies. Thus, the mutivariate perspective requires researchers to operationalize and to identify clearly at least these chief factors.

Whether or not one or another mode of interaction bears on development can be seen therefore to depend on a host of factors, and no theoretically meaningful or potentially relevant interaction experience can be ruled ineffective on the basis of a single-instance failure to demonstrate predictive validity. In this domain of developmental research, highly specific associations as well as experimental phenomena like "sleeper effects" can be expected. In singlemindedly assaying one aspect of mental life while failing to evaluate alternatives, the developmental investigator risks overlooking potentially significant antecedent-consequent relations in cognitive growth or, more unhappily, being carried to the incorrect conclusion that an interaction category does not influence development when, in reality, it does, only the influence is circumscribed or specific. Thus, researchers and theoreticians alike need to exercise extreme circumspection about the developmental effectiveness of interactions based on any given test of any particular longitudinal association.

In this chapter I have identified two prominent modes of caretaker interaction with young children and discussed their role in the cognitive growth of the child. The two-fold taxonomy I have outlined leaves many questions unaddressed. At which point and for how long in development do these modes of interaction remain most effective? With what frequency and with what regularity are these categories or interaction optimally experienced? What are the determinants of these different categories of interaction? How do they vary within and among different caretakers?

The fact that these modes of interaction affect the course of development from early life by no means implies that one or another mode monistically predestines or fixes a child's developmental stature. Many factors contribute to human growth—although certain interactions may heavily influence growth in certain areas—and experiences of later life are widely acknowledged to account for large proportions of variance in every domain of mature human competence (e.g., Honzik, 1986). Inevitably, too, the sociological and economic status of caretakers, as well as personological and trait characteristics of caretaker and infant, will have to be considered (Bornstein, Gaughran, & Homel, 1986; Gottfried & Gottfried, 1984; McCall, 1979, 1981).

Although specifying the cause of an effect is always difficult, to expect effects without causes is less than reasonable. In everyday life, adults surely initiate and organize experiences for their young children, but just as surely children provoke adults to act in different ways at different times, and children select among the variety of experiences adults offer, somehow advantaging themselves of those experiences that are most appropriate, promising, or supportive. Thus, the accurate and most comprehensive view of interaction effects will always be a bi–directional one. Children actively participate in interactions that have consequences for their own development, and even as infants they may be far from passive recipients of experience. Nonetheless, the child experiences, and is differentially affected by, different modes of caretaking interaction. At base, these interactions mediate between cultural and social forces on adults and individual differences in growth and development in children. That is why the shifting focus to interaction is so satisfying.

ACKNOWLEDGMENTS

Supported by research grants (HD20559 and HD20807) and by a Research Career Development Award (HD00521) from the National Institute of Child Health and Human Development. I thank H. Bornstein and B. Wright.

REFERENCES

Bee, H. L., Barnard, K. E., Eyres, S. J., Gray, C. A., Hammond, M. A., Spietz, A. L., Snyder, C., & Clark, B. Prediction of IQ and language skill from perinatal status, child performance, family characteristics, and mother-infant interaction. *Child Development*, 1982, *53*, 1134–1156.

Bell, S. M., & Ainsworth, M. D. S. Infant crying and maternal responsiveness. *Child Development*, 1972, *43*, 1171–1190.

Belsky, J., Gilstrap, B., & Rovine, M. The Pennsylvania infant and family development project, I: Stability and change in mother-infant and father-infant interaction in a family setting—1-to 3-to 9-months. *Child Development*, 1984, *55*, 692–705.

Belsky, J., Goode, M. K., & Most, R. K. Maternal stimulation and infant exploratory competence: Cross-sectional, correlational, and experimental analyses. *Child Development*, 1980, *51*, 1168–1178.

Bornstein, M. H. How infant and mother jointly contribute to developing cognitive competence in the child. *Proceedings of the National Academy of Science*, 1985, *82*, 7470–7473.

Bornstein, M. H. Mothers, infants, and the development of cognitive competence. In H. E. Fitzgerald, B. M. Lester, & M. W. Yogman (Eds.), *Theory and research in behavioral pediatrics* (Vol. 4). New York: Plenum, 1988.

Bornstein, M. H. Sensitive periods in development: Structural characteristics and causal interpretations. *Psychological Bulletin*, 1989.

Bornstein, M. H., Gaughran, J., & Homel, P. Infant temperament: Theory, tradition, critique, and new assessments. In C. E. Izard & P. B. Read (Eds.), *Measuring emotions in infants and children* (Vol. 2). New York: Cambridge University Press, 1988.

Bornstein, M. H., Miyake, K., & Tamis-LeMonda, C. S. A cross-national study of mother and infant activities and interactions: Some preliminary comparisons between Japan and the United

States. *Annual Report of the Research and Clinical Center for Child Development*, 1985–1986, 1–12.

Bornstein, M. H., & Ruddy, M. G. Infant attention and maternal stimulation: Prediction of cognitive and linguistic development in singletons and twins. In H. Bouma & D. G. Bouwhuis (Eds.), *Attention and performance X: Control of language processes* London; Lawrence Erlbaum Associates, 1984.

Bornstein, M. H., & Sigman, M. D. Continuity in mental development from infancy. *Child Development*, 1986, *57*, 251–274.

Bornstein, M. H., & Tamis-LeMonda, C. S. *Activities and interactions of mothers and their first-born infants in the first six months of life: Stability, continuity, covariation, correspondence, and prediction*. Unpublished manuscript, National Institute of Child Health and Human Development, 1988.

Bornstein, M. H., & Tamis-LeMonda, C. S. Maternal responsiveness and cognitive development in children. In M. H. Bornstein (Ed.), *Maternal responsiveness: Characteristics and consequences*. San Francisco: Jossey-Bass, 1989.

Bradley, R. H., & Caldwell, B. M. Competence and IQ among males and females. *Child Development*, 1980, *51*, 1140–1148.

Bradley, R. H., Caldwell, B. M., & Elardo, R. Home environment and cognitive development in the first 2 years: A cross-lagged panel analysis. *Developmental Psychology*, 1979, *15*, 246–250.

Bruner, J. S. *Child's talk: Learning to use language*. Oxford: Oxford University Press, 1983.

Carew, J. V. Experience and the development of intelligence in young children at home and in day care. *Monographs of the Society for Research in Child Development*, 1980, *45* (6–7, Serial No. 187).

Clarke-Stewart, K. A. Interactions between mothers and their young children: Characteristics and consequences. *Monographs of the Society for Research in Child Development*, 1973, *38* (6–7, Serial No. 153).

Clarke-Stewart, K. A., & Apfel, N. Evaluating parental effects on child development. In L. S. Shulman (Ed.), *Review of research in education* (Vol. 6). Itasca, IL: Peacock, 1979.

Clarke-Stewart, K. A., & Hevey, C. M. Longitudinal relations in repeated observations of mother-child interaction from 1 to 1½ years. *Developmental Psychology*, 1981, *17*, 127–145.

Coates, D. L., & Lewis, M. Early mother-infant interaction and infant cognitive status as predictors of school performance and cognitive behavior in six-year-olds. *Child Development*, 1984, *55*, 1219–1230.

Cohen, J., & Cohen, P. *Applied multiple regression/correlation analysis for the behavioral sciences*. Hillsdale, NJ: Lawrence Erlbaum Associates, 1983.

Colombo, J. The critical period hypothesis: Research, methodology, and theoretical issues. *Psychological Bulletin*, 1982, *92*, 260–275.

The Consortium for Longitudinal Studies. *As the twig is bent: Lasting effects of preschool programs*. Hillsdale, NJ: Lawrence Erlbaum Associates, 1983.

Crawley, S. B., & Sherrod, K. B. Parent-infant play during the first year of life. *Infant Behavior and Development*, 1984, *7*, 65–75.

Goldberg, S. Social competence in infancy: A model of parent-infant interaction. *Merrill-Palmer Quarterly*, 1977, *23*, 163–177.

Gottfried, A. W. (Ed.). *Home environment and early cognitive development*. Orlando, FL: Academic, 1984.

Gottfried, A. W., & Gottfried, A. E. Home environment and cognitive development in young children of middle-socioeconomic-status families. In A. W. Gottfried (Ed.), *Home environment and early cognitive development*. Orlando, FL: Academic, 1984.

Harlow, H. F., & Harlow, M. K. Learning to love. *American Scientist*, 1966, *54*, 244–272.

Honzik, M. P. The role of the family in the development of mental abilities: A 50-year study. In N. Datan, A. L. Greene, & H. W. Reese (Eds.), *Life-span developmental psychology: Intergenerational relations*. Hillsdale, NJ: Lawrence Erlbaum Associates, 1986.

Hunt, J. McV. Psychological development: Early experience. *Annual Review of Psychology,* 1979, *30,* 103–143.

Kuchuk, A. Vibbert, M., & Bornstein, M. H. The perception of smiling and its experiential correlates in 3-month-old infants. *Child Development,* 1986, *57,* 1054–1061.

Kuhn, D. Cognitive development. In M. E. Lamb & M. H. Bornstein (Eds.), *Developmental psychology: An advanced textbook* (2d ed.). Hillsdale, NJ: Lawrence Erlbaum Associates, 1988.

Lamb, M. E., & Easterbrooks, M. A. Individual differences in parental sensitivity: Some thoughts about origins, components, and consequences. In M. E. Lamb & L. R. Sherrod (Eds.), *Infant social cognition: Empirical and theoretical foundations.* Hillsdale, NJ: Lawrence Erlbaum Associates, 1980.

Lewis, M., & Goldberg, S. The acquisition and violation of expectancy: An experimental paradigm. *Journal of Experimental Child Psychology,* 1969, *7,* 70–80.

McCall, R. B. Qualitative transitions in behavioral development in the first two years of life. In M. H. Bornstein & W. Kessen (Eds.), *Psychological development from infancy: Image to intention.* Hillsdale, NJ: Lawrence Erlbaum Associates, 1979.

McCall, R. B. Early predictors of later IQ: The search continues. *Intelligence,* 1981, *5,* 141–147.

Nunnally, J. *Psychometric theory.* New York: McGraw-Hill, 1978.

Olsen-Fulero, L. Style and stability in mother conversational behaviour: A study of individual difference. *Journal of Child Language,* 1982, *9,* 543–564.

Olson, S. L., Bates, J. E., & Bayles, K. Mother-infant interaction and the development of individual differences in children's cognitive competence. *Developmental Psychology,* 1984, *20,* 166–179.

Papoušek, M., Papoušek, H., & Bornstein, M. H. The naturalistic vocal environment of young infants: On the significance of homogeneity and variability in parental speech. In T. M. Field & N. Fox (Eds.), *Social perception in infants.* Norwood, NJ: Ablex, 1985.

Parke, R. D. Children's home environments: Social and cognitive effects. In I. Altman & J. F. Wohlwill (Eds.), *Human behavior and environment* (Vol. 3). New York: Plenum, 1978.

Piaget, J. *The language and thought of the child* (M. Gabain, trans.). London: Routledge & Kegan Paul, 1926.

Ramey, C. T., Farran, D. C., & Campbell, F. A. Predicting IQ from mother-infant interactions. *Child Development,* 1979, *50,* 804–814.

Riksen-Walraven, J. Effects of caregiver behavior on habituation rate and self-efficacy in infancy. *International Journal of Behavioral Development,* 1978, *1,* 105–130.

Ruddy, M., & Bornstein, M. H. Cognitive correlates of infant attention and maternal stimulation over the first year of life. *Child Development,* 1982, *53,* 183–188.

Rutter, M. Maternal deprivation, 1972–1978: New findings, new concepts, new approaches. *Child Development,* 1979, *50,* 283–305.

Schaefer, E. S. A circumplex model for maternal behavior. *Journal of Abnormal and Social Psychology,* 1959, *59,* 226–235.

Solkoff, N., & Matuzsak, D. Tactile stimulation and behavioral development among low birthweight infants. *Child Psychiatry and Human Development,* 1975, *6,* 33–37.

Solkoff, N., Sumner, Y., Weintraub, D., & Blase, B. Effects of handling on the subsequent development of premature infants. *Developmental Psychology,* 1969, *1,* 765–768.

Stern, D. *The first relationship.* London: Fontana, 1977.

Stern, D. *The interpersonal world of the infant.* New York: Basic Books, 1985.

Tamis-LeMonda, C. S., & Bornstein, M. H. Habituation and maternal encouragement of attention in infancy as predictors of toddler language, play, and representational competence. *Child Development,* 1989.

Tudge, J., & Rogoff, B. Peer influences on cognitive development: Piagetian and Vygotskian perspectives. In M. H. Bornstein & J. S. Bruner (Eds.), *Interaction in human development.* Hillsdale, NJ: Lawrence Erlbaum Associates, 1989.

Vibbert, M., & Bornstein, M. H. Specific associations between domains of mother-child interaction and toddler referential language and pretense play. *Infant Behavior and Development,* 1989.

Vygotsky, L. S. *Thought and language* (E. Hanfmann & G. Vakar, trans.). Cambridge, MA: MIT Press, 1962.

Vygotsky, L. S. *Mind in society* (M. Cole, V. John-Steiner, S. Scribner, & E. Souberman, Eds.). Cambridge, MA: Harvard University Press, 1978.

Wachs, T. D., & Chan, A. Specificity of environmental action, as seen in environmental correlates of infants' communication performance. *Child Development,* 1986, *57,* 1464–1474.

Wachs, T. D., & Gruen, G. *Early experience and human development.* New York: Plenum, 1982.

Wohlwill, J. *The study of behavioral development.* New York: Academic Press, 1973.

Wohlwill, J. Physical and social environment as factors in development. In D. Magnusen & V. Allen, (Eds.), *Human development: An interactional perspective.* New York: Academic Press, 1983.

Wood, D. J. Social interaction as tutoring. In M. H. Bornstein & J. S. Bruner (Eds.), *Interaction in human development.* Hillsdale, NJ: Lawrence Erlbaum Associates, 1989.

Yarrow, L., Rubenstein, J. L., & Pedersen, F. A. *Infant and environment: Early cognitive and motivational development.* New York: Wiley, 1975.

IV HOW TO FORMULATE THE INTERACTION PROBLEM?

11 Developmental Contextualism and the Life-Span View of Person-Context Interaction

Richard M. Lerner
The Pennsylvania State University

INTRODUCTION

Two concepts have permeated metatheoretical and theoretical discussions of the nature of development: nature and nurture. Today, use of these terms is somewhat unfashionable, suggesting to some an anachronistic conceptual distinction and/or a theoretically atavistic resurrection of a false, empirically useless division. Often, then, discussion of the nature-nurture issue is eschewed in favor of presentations of ideas about organism-environment interactions or, with even more popular currency, models of individual-context transactions.

In these discussions many psychologists act as if their discipline's history began at most 5 years prior to the time they received their Ph.D. (Sarason, 1973). Forgetting the warning of the historian George Santayana, they ignore their history and will be condemned to repeat it. Thus, except for some isolated exceptions (e.g., Baltes, 1979, 1987; Gottlieb, 1976a, 1976b; Turkewitz, 1987), in many current discussions of the nature of developmental change writers often use words that, although perhaps distinct from those employed in the literature of 20 to 50 years ago, refer to the same concepts and issues. Consequently, many of the conceptual advances found in this previous literature—advances that were arduously arrived at only after extended theoretical debates and empirical tests (e.g., Lehrman, 1953; Maier & Schneirla, 1935; Moltz, 1960; Schneirla, 1956, 1957; Tobach & Schneirla, 1968)—have been ignored.

For instance, this previous literature has demonstrated the logical traps, theoretical dead-ends, and empirical vacuity of attempting to treat organism and context as independent, nontransactive entities; that is, as parallel vectors or as main effects in a world of additive, linear combinations (Lerner, 1976, 1978,

1986). Indeed, this previous literature has stressed (see Tobach, Gianutsos, Topoff, & Gross, 1974) that one consequence of treating organisms, or in particular their genes, as independent of influence by, and as not dynamically interactive with, a complex and changing context, is the promulgation of pseudoscientific theories that promote racism (e.g., Lorenz, 1940), sexism (e.g., Freedman, 1979), social Darwinism (e.g., Wilson, 1975), and even militarism (e.g., Lorenz, 1966).

However, more recently, as a result of this lack of attention to past literature, the mistakes of the past are *in fact* being repeated—in areas such as the measurement of human intelligence and mental abilities (e.g., Eysenck & Kamin, 1981; Jensen, 1980); the study of animal and human social behavior, or sociobiology (e.g., Lorenz, 1965; Wilson, 1975); and the analysis of the biological (Lorenz, 1966) or environmental (Skinner, 1971) influences on either human nature, in general, or people's orientations concerning aggression, freedom, self-control, and self-esteem.

Ironically, perhaps no where in the literature of contemporary developmental psychology is there seemingly less acknowledgement of this past literature than in recent discussions of the role of the context in human functioning and change. In rediscovering the context (e.g., see Bandura, 1978; Bronfenbrenner, 1977, 1979; Jenkins, 1974; Mischel, 1977; Riegel, 1975, 1976a, 1976b; Sarbin, 1977), there has been quite limited acknowledgement that the dynamic qualities of organisms, contexts, and transactions between them, are topics that not only have extensive literatures in comparative and developmental psychology associated with them (e.g., Baldwin, 1895, 1909; Maier & Schneirla, 1935; Novikoff, 1945a, 1945b; von Bertalanffy, 1933), but also are topics whose literatures demonstrate valuable lessons elucidating issues of contemporary relevance.

Recently, however, Turkewitz (1987) reminded developmentalists of the contributions made to this past literature by the comparative psychologist T. C. Schneirla. Although lamenting the fact that many of Schneirla's ideas continue to go unacknowledged, Turkewitz noted that Schneirla's views of the character of the relation between organisms and contexts have been of central theoretical importance in at least one area of developmental psychology: the life-span perspective.

There is considerable merit in Turkewitz's observation. Indeed, as the life-span perspective has evolved over the last decade or so (e.g., Baltes, 1979, 1987; Brim & Kagan, 1980; Featherman, 1983, 1985; Lerner, 1976, 1978, 1986; Lerner & Kauffman, 1985), it has become increasingly clear that the view of contextual influences advocated in this perspective is one found as well in what Gottlieb (1976a, 1976b, 1983) has termed the probabilistic epigenetic view of development. In other words, the version of contextualism that best capitalizes on the advances of the past comparative and developmental literatures pertinent to the nature-nurture controversy is the same version of contextualism that underlies the view of organism-context relations found in the life-span perspective; this view is the probabilistic epigenetic conception of development articulated by Schneirla, and by his colleagues (e.g., Gottlieb, 1976a, 1976b, 1983; Lehrman, 1953; Thomas & Chess, 1970; Thomas, Chess, Birch, Hertzig, & Korn, 1963; Tobach, 1981).

In the remainder of this chapter I explain the nature of the probabilistic epigenetic view of organism-context relations or, as I have labeled it within the life-span literature (Lerner, 1986; Lerner & Kauffman, 1985), the developmental contextual view of human development. The connections between contextualism and probabilistic epigenesis are drawn, and the relation of the latter conception to the life-span view of human development are explored. Finally, I present some examples of both broad and narrow representations, or models, of development that may be derived from developmental contextualism, and I illustrate briefly the empirical use of these models. Given the scope of this agenda, and the space available to accomplish it, a broad brush stroke will have to be used. However, more detailed explications of my points can be found in several previous papers (most centrally Lerner, 1976, 1978, 1979, 1980, 1981, 1984, 1985, 1986, 1987; Lerner & Kauffman, 1985; Lerner & Lerner, 1987, 1989). It is useful to discuss first the relations between contextualism and probabilistic epigenesis.

CONTEXTUALISM AND PROBABILISTIC EPIGENESIS

An interest in the context of human development has a long history in philosophy and social science (for reviews see Dixon & Nesselroade, 1983; Kaplan, 1983). Contextualism began to attract increasing interest from psychologists during the late 1960s (e.g., Bandura, 1978, 1980; Bronfenbrenner, 1977, 1979; Jenkins, 1974; Kuo, 1967; Mischel, 1977; Rosnow, 1983; Rosnow & Georgoudi, 1986; Rosnow & Rosenthal, 1984; Sarbin, 1977). One basis for this interest was the growing theoretical and empirical literature that suggests it is necessary to forego an exclusively psychological analysis of individual development, and instead seek explanations that emphasize the multilevel bases of human functioning and the connections among levels (e.g., Baltes, 1987; Bronfenbrenner, 1979; Elder, 1975; Kuo, 1967; J. Lerner, 1983; Lerner, 1984; Lerner & Busch-Rossnagel, 1981; Novikoff, 1945a, 1945b; Magnusson & Allen, 1983; Tobach, 1981; Tobach & Greenberg, 1984).

Levels, in this literature, are conceived of as integrative organizations. That is,

> the concept of integrative levels recognizes as equally essential for the purpose of scientific analysis both the isolation of parts of a whole and their integration into the structure of the whole. It neither reduces phenomena of a higher level to those of a lower one, as in mechanism, or describes the higher level in vague nonmaterial terms which are but substitutes for understanding, as in vitalism. Unlike other

"holistic" theories, it never leaves the firm ground of material reality. . . . The concept points to the need to study the organizational interrelationships of parts and whole. (Novikoff, 1945a, p. 209)

Moreover, Tobach and Greenberg (1984, p. 2) stressed that

the interdependence among levels is of great significance. The dialectic nature of the relationship among levels is one in which lower levels are subsumed in higher levels so that any particular level is an integration of preceding levels. . . . In the process of integration, or fusion, *new* levels with their own characteristics result.

If the course of human development is the product of the processes involved in the "fusions" (or "dynamic interactions"; Lerner, 1978, 1979, 1984) among integrative levels, then the processes of development are more plastic than often previously believed (cf. Brim & Kagan, 1980).

To a great extent the developmental literature that suggests these ideas has been associated with the life-span view of human development (Lerner, Hultsch, & Dixon, 1983; Pepper, 1942). Within this perspective, the context for development is not seen merely as a simple stimulus environment, but rather as an "ecological environment . . . conceived topologically as a nested arrangement of concentric structures, each contained within the next" (Bronfenbrenner, 1979, p. 22) and including variables from biological, psychological, physical, and sociocultural levels, all changing interdependently across history (Riegel, 1975, 1976a, 1976b).

The life-span perspective is associated with a concern with issues of the relations between evolution and ontogeny, of life-course constancy and change, of human plasticity, and of the role the developing person plays in his or her own development (Baltes, 1987; Lerner, 1982; Lerner & Busch-Rossnagel, 1981; Scarr & McCartney, 1983; Tobach, 1981). These issues are linked by the idea that reciprocal relations (i.e., dynamic interactions; Lerner, 1978, 1979) between individuals and the multiple contexts within which they live characterize human development (Bronfenbrenner, 1979). Thus, all the issues raised by this perspective derive from a common appreciation of the basic role of the changing context in developmental change. It is the functional significance of this changing context that requires adoption of a probabilistic epigenetic view of an organism's development.

Features of Probabilistic Epigenetic Development

Since its inception as a specialization within the discipline, developmental psychology—or, as it was initially termed, genetic psychology (e.g., Hall, 1904)—has been dominated by a biological model of change. Indeed, the concept of development is biological in its scientific origin (Harris, 1957; von Bertalanffy, 1933). Although the particular version of biological change that has influenced developmental psychology has been and remains Darwinian in character (White, 1968), this common heritage has nevertheless led to the formulation of quite diverse models of development (Dixon & Lerner, 1988). For instance, mechanistic-behavioral conceptions of developmental change (e.g., Bijou, 1976; Bijou & Baer, 1961) and organismic-dynamic (e.g., Freud, 1949) and organismic-structural (e.g., Piaget, 1950) theories may be interpreted as derived from this Darwinian heritage (Dixon & Lerner, 1988).

However, despite this range of interpretations of the contribution of biology to psychological development, the organismic versions have been predominant in developmental psychology, and in fact have been termed strong developmental models (e.g., Reese & Overton, 1970). Thus, to the field of psychology in general, and perhaps to the scholarly community as a whole, the organismic theories of Freud (1949), Erikson (1959), and Piaget (1950) are typically held to be the classic, prototypic, or exemplary ones within developmental psychology (e.g., Emmerich, 1968; Lerner, 1976, 1986).

These instances of organismic theory, especially those of Freud and of Erikson, have been labeled *predetermined epigenetic* (Gottlieb, 1983). In this type of theory, biology is seen as the prime mover of development: Intrinsic (e.g., maturational) changes are seen to essentially unfold; although environmental or experiential variables may speed up or slow down these progressions they can do nothing to alter the sequence or quality (e.g., the structure) of these hereditarily predetermined changes (e.g., Gesell, 1946; Hamburger, 1957).

However, another view of biological functioning exists, one which sees biological and contextual factors as reciprocally interactive; as such, developmental changes are probabilistic in respect to normative outcomes, due to variation in the timing of the biological, psychological, and social factors that provide interactive bases of ontogenetic progressions (e.g., Schneirla, 1957; Tobach, 1981). It is this *probabilistic epigenetic* (Gottlieb, 1983) view of development that provides the theoretical underpinning of the life-span view of human development (Lerner & Kauffman, 1985).

In essence, a probabilistic epigenetic formulation does not emphasize the intrinsically predetermined or inevitable time tables and outcomes of development; instead, it stresses that the influence of the changing context on development is to make the trajectory of development less certain with respect to the applicability of norms to the individual (Gottlieb, 1970, 1983; Tobach, 1981). Thus, such a conception emphasizes the probabilistic character of development and in so doing admits of more plasticity in development than predeterministic conceptions. In other words, the contextual view of development stressed by the present writer (Lerner, 1976, 1978, 1979, 1980, 1981, 1984, 1985) and by other contributors to the life-span developmental psychology literature (e.g., Baltes,

1979, 1983, 1987; Brim & Kagan, 1980) is one labeled as "probabilistic epigenetic organismic" by Gottlieb (1970) and developed by him (Gottlieb, 1976a, 1976b) and earlier by Schneirla (1956, 1957) and Tobach and Schneirla (1968). The term *probabilistic epigenesis* was used by Gottlieb

> to designate the view that the behavioral development of individuals within a species does not follow an invariant or inevitable course, and, more specifically, that the sequence or outcome of individual behavioral development is probable (with respect to norms) rather than certain. (Gottlieb, 1970, p. 123)

Moreover, he explained that this probable, and not certain, character of individual development arises because

> probabilistic epigenesis necessitates a bidirectional structure-function hypothesis. The conventional version of the structure-function hypothesis is unidirectional in the sense that structure is supposed to determine function in an essentially nonreciprocal relationship. . . . The bidirectional version of the structure-function relationship is a logical consequence of the view that the course and outcome of behavioral epigenesis is probabilistic: it entails the assumption of reciprocal effects in the relationship between structure and function whereby function (exposure to stimulation and/or movement of musculoskeletal activity) can significantly modify the development of the peripheral and central structures that are involved in these events. (Gottlieb, 1970, p. 123)

But, are the changes depicted in the probabilistic epigenetic formulation of development completely dispersive? I think not. As explained by Gollin (1981), probabilistic, developmental change is not dispersive because the living system—the organism—has organization and internal coherence, and these features constrain the potentials of the *developmental context* to affect the system. He maintained that

> the determination of the successive qualities of living systems, given the web of relationships involved, is probabilistic. This is so because the number of factors operating conjointly in living systems is very great. Additionally, each factor and subsystem is capable of a greater or lesser degree of variability. Hence, the influence subsystems have upon each other, and upon the system as a whole, varies as a function of the varying states of the several concurrently operating subsystems. Thus, the very nature of living systems, both individual and collective, and of environments, assure the presumptive character of organic change. . . . The quality of the organization provides opportunities for change as well as constraints upon the extent and direction of change. Thus, while the determination of change is probabilistic, it is not chaotic. (Gollin, 1981, p. 232)

Gollin's position illustrates that one needs to understand that development occurs in a multilevel context, and that the nature of the changes in this context lead to the probabilistic character of development; but one needs to appreciate too that the organism shapes the context just as much as the context shapes the organism.

Essays by Scarr and her associates (Scarr, 1982; Scarr & McCartney, 1983) make similar points. For instance, Scarr (1982, pp. 852–853) noted that

> development does not merely emerge from the precoded information in the genes. Rather, development is a *probabilistic* result of indeterminant combinations of genes and environments. Development is genetically guided but variable and probabilistic because influential events in the life of every person can be neither predicted nor explained by general laws.

Wapner, Kaplan, and Cohen (1973) spoke similarly of the transactional character of people and their environments.

A final point about the probabilistic epigenetic view needs to be highlighted. Although both developmental contextual and mechanistic-behavioral perspectives make use of the context enveloping an organism in attempts to explain development, it is clear that they do so in distinctly different ways. Developmental contextual theorists do not adopt a reflexively reductionistic approach to conceptualizing the impact of the context. Instead, there is a focus on organism-context transactions, a commitment to using an interlevel, or relational, unit of analysis (Lerner, Skinner, & Sorell, 1980) and, as already emphasized, a concept of the context as composed of multiple, qualitatively different levels (e.g., Riegel, 1975, 1976a, 1976b). Moreover, although both the mechanistic and the developmental contextual perspectives hold that changes in the context become part of the organism's intraindividually changing constitution, the concept of organism found in the two perspectives is also quite distinct. The organism in developmental contextualism is not merely the host of the elements of a simplistic environment. Instead, the organism is itself a qualitatively distinct level within the multiple, dynamically interacting levels forming the context of life. As such, the organism has a distinct influence on that multilevel context that is influencing the organism. As a consequence the organism is, in short, not a passive host, but an active contributor to its own development (Lerner, 1982; Lerner & Busch-Rossnagel, 1981).

The Role of the Concept of "Interaction" in Developmental Contextualism

A developmental contextual perspective captures the complexity of a multilevel context (1) without ignoring the active role of the organism in shaping, as well as being shaped by, that context, and (2) without sacrificing commitment to useful prescriptive, universal principles of developmental change. These two foci are integrated within the contextual orientation at the level of the presumed *relation* between organismic and contextual processes. The contextual conceptualization of this relation differs substantially from those of the organismic and mechanistic perspectives (Lerner, 1985). That is, a *strong* concept of organism-environment interaction (Lerner & Spanier, 1978, 1980; Overton, 1973), transaction (Sameroff, 1975), or dynamic interaction (Lerner, 1978, 1979) is associated with probabilistic epigenesis. This version of interaction stresses that organism and context are always embedded each in the other (Lerner, Hultsch, & Dixon, 1983), that the context is composed of multiple levels changing interdependently across time (i.e., historically), and that because organisms influence the context that influences them, they are efficacious in playing an active role in their own development (Lerner & Busch-Rossnagel, 1981; Tobach, 1981).

Moreover, because of the mutual embeddedness of organism and context, a given organismic attribute will have different implications for developmental outcomes in the milieu of different contextual conditions; this is the case because the organism attribute is only given its functional meaning by virtue of its relation to a specific context. If the context changes, as it may over time, then the same organism attribute will have a different import for development. In turn, the same contextual condition will lead to alternative developments in that different organisms interact with it. To state this position in somewhat stronger terms, a given organismic attribute only has meaning for psychological development by virtue of its timing of interaction; that is, its relation to a particular set of time-bound, contextual conditions. In turn, the import of any set of contextual conditions for psychosocial behavior and development can only be understood by specifying the context's relations to the specific, developmental features of the organisms within it. This central role for the timing of organism-context interactions in the determination of the nature and outcomes of development is, of course, the probabilistic component of probabilistic epigenesis (Gottlieb, 1970; Kuo, 1967; Scarr, 1982; Scarr & McCartney, 1983; Tobach, 1981). But, what does such probabilism mean for the ways in which individuals can, through influencing their context, produce their own development? More important, for the ultimate worth of the developmental contextual view of development and of the life-span perspective embodied in it, we may ask what such probabilism means for the empirical study of human development.

To address these issues we should be clear that taking the probabilistic character of development seriously means focusing on the *relation* between organism and context and not on either element in the relation per se. The context enveloping a person is composed of, for example, a specific physical ecology and the other individually different and developing people with whom the person interacts (e.g., parents and peers). This context is as unique and changing as is the person lawfully individually distinct as a consequence of his/her particular genotype-environment interaction history. One cannot say completely in advance what particular features of the context will exist at a specific time in a given person's life. As a consequence, it is only possible to speak probabilistically of the effects that a given person may have on his or her context; of the feedback the person is likely to receive from the context; and of the nature of the person's development that will therefore ensue.

Thus, "person effects" on their own development are not so simple as they may seem at first. Indeed, the probabilism of development represents a formidable challenge for theory and research. To understand how people may influence their own development we need to do more than just have a conceptualization of the nature of the individual characteristics or processes involved in such effects. In addition, we need to conceptualize and operationalize the features of the context, or of the ecology, wherein significant interactions occur for the person. Next, we must devise some means, some model, by which person effects and contextual features may be integrated. Then, a last and by no means unidimensional task, is to translate all this conceptualization into methodologically sound research.

There is no laboratory within which all the preceding tasks have been fully accomplished. However, progress has been made in developing models with which such effects may be empirically studied. Data pertinent to the models derive from work in several laboratories, and, in now presenting the general features of some of these models, some of this research is noted.

MODELS OF PERSON-CONTEXT INTERACTION WITHIN DEVELOPMENTAL CONTEXTUALISM

Both life-span developmental and ecological developmental psychologists have described several intraindividual, interindividual, familial, social network, sociocultural, and historical variables presumed to be involved in the dynamic interactional processes described within developmental contextualism (e.g., Baltes, 1987; Bronfenbrenner, 1979; Featherman & Lerner, 1985; Lerner, 1984; Riegel, 1976a, 1976b; Schneirla, 1957). The resulting view of the range of the variables involved in development and of complexity of interrelations among them, is—to say the least—formidable. One depiction of this complexity, shown in Figure 11.1, represents well in my view the integrated and interdependent or dynamically interactive, levels of organization first spoken of by Novikoff (1945a, 1945b), developed further by Schneirla and his collaborators (e.g., Lehrman, 1970; Tobach, 1981; Tobach & Schneirla, 1968; Schneirla, 1956, 1957), and elaborated within developmental psychology by proponents of the life-span perspective (e.g., Baltes, 1987; Featherman, 1983, 1985; Lerner, 1976, 1984, 1986; Lerner & Kauffman, 1985).

To illustrate the empirical use in the extant developmental literature of the conception of integrative, dynamically interactive levels depicted in Figure 11.1, let me draw on two examples of pertinence to developmentalists; one involves characteristics of behavioral individuality, in regard to behavioral style or temperament, and the other involves characteristics of physical individuality, in

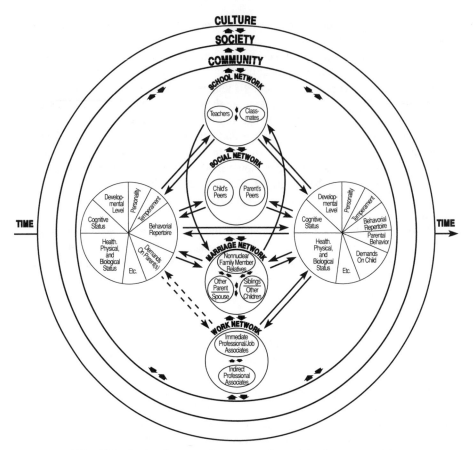

FIG. 11.1 A developmental contextual model of person-context interaction.

regard to physical maturation and physical attractiveness. In regard to temperament, the child development literature contains studies examining the relation, within-the-child, of temperament and other characteristics of individuality, such as personality (Buss & Plomin, 1975) or cognitive status variables (such as "social referencing"; Campos, 1980–81; Feinman & Lewis, 1983). In turn, other studies examine how the child's temperamental individuality influences the parent- (typically the mother-) child relationship (Crockenberg, 1981) and/or the mother's emotional adjustment (Brazelton, Koslowski, & Main, 1974). Such studies provide data constituting "child effects" on their significant others—others which, to developmental psychologists (Belsky, Lerner, & Spanier, 1984), represent a component of the child's context, here an interpersonal one. These studies comprise one portion of the bidirectional effects (here of child → parent) discussed in the child development literature (e.g., Bell, 1974; Belsky,

1984; Belsky et al., 1984; Lerner & Spanier, 1978; Lewis & Rosenblum, 1974; Scarr & McCartney, 1983).

These child–parent studies stand in contrast to those that examine how parental characteristics—such as temperament (Thomas, Chess, & Birch, 1970), demands on the child regarding the child's temperament (Thomas, Chess, Sillen, & Mendez, 1974), or cognitive status (e.g., stage of cognitive development; Sameroff, 1975)—influence the child; such studies are parent → child ones, and provide the other direction of effect to complement child → parent studies. Other studies in the temperament literature examine the influence of the parent's social network on the child's temperament, on the mother's characteristics, or on the parent-child relationship (e.g., Crockenberg, 1981); in turn, some studies examine how children with different temperaments produce different responses in their social (e.g., school) network (East, Lerner, & Lerner, 1988). Still other studies examine how child-temperament⇄parent-demand relations vary in relation to their embeddedness in different social classes or communities (Thomas et al., 1974) or in different cultural settings (Super & Harkness, 1981).

In regard to characteristics of physical individuality, let me focus on a variable—menarche—which is a central one in the study of biological-psychosocial interrelations in early adolescence (Brooks-Gunn & Petersen, 1983; Hamburg, 1974; Petersen, 1983; Ruble, 1977; Ruble & Brooks-Gunn, 1982). The adolescent developmental literature contains studies examining the relation, within-the-person, of menarche (e.g., whether it occurs early, on time, or late) and other characteristics of individuality, as for example, perceptions of self (Tobin-Richards, Boxer, & Petersen, 1983), cognition (Hamburg, 1974; Petersen, 1983), or the experience of menstrual discomfort (Brooks-Gunn & Ruble, 1983). In turns, other studies examine how the occurrence of menarche influences a girl's relations with the significant others in her context (e.g., Brooks-Gunn & Matthews, 1979; Lynch, 1981; Simmons, Blyth, & McKinney, 1983; Westney, Jenkins, & Benjamin, 1983). Such studies provide data constituting "adolescent effects" on that portion of their social context composed of significant others, and as such comprise one portion of the bidirectional effects (here an adolescent → social context one) discussed in this literature (e.g., Belsky et al., 1984; Lerner & Spanier, 1978; Petersen & Taylor, 1980).

These adolescent → social context studies stand in contrast to those that examine how contextual features—like parental demands regarding desired behavior in their adolescent children (e.g., Anthony, 1969; Windle & Lerner, 1986), continuities or discontinuities in school structure (Blyth, Simmons, & Bush, 1978; Hamburg, 1974; Simmons, Blyth, Van Cleave, & Bush, 1979), or cultural beliefs regarding menstruation (Brooks-Gunn & Ruble, 1980; Ruble & Brooks-Gunn, 1979)—influence the adolescent undergoing the biopsychosocial transition of menarche; such studies are social context → adolescent ones, and provide the other direction of effect to complement the adolescent → social context one.

Still other studies in the adolescent development literature examine how adolescent menarche⇄social context relations (e.g., in regard to adolescents and their peers) vary in relation to their embeddedness in more molar levels of the context, such as different social classes (e. g., Hamburg, 1974; Simmons, Brown, Bush, & Blyth, 1978), cultures (Hamburg, 1974; Lerner, Iwawaki, Chihara, & Sorell, 1980; Mussen & Bouterline-Young, 1964; Paige, 1983), or historical eras (Elder, 1974).

In summary, several of the interrelations illustrated in the model in Figure 11.1 are found in the extant literature on behavioral and physical individuality. Although relatively few of the studies in this literature assess both directions of relation between one component (or level) of the model and another (cf. Bell, 1974; Lewis & Lee-Painter, 1974), the bidirectionality of relations discussed in this literature (e.g., Bell, 1974; Belsky, Lerner, & Spanier, 1984; Lerner & Spanier, 1978; Lewis & Rosenblum, 1974) emerges when studies are integrated within a representation like the one presented in Figure 11.1. Furthermore, by helping to integrate extant studies, the model also points to individual–social context relations that are uninvestigated but that may be of potential importance.

This use of the model for furthering research points out other features of the model that should be stressed. It probably would not be useful or even possible to do research testing the model as a whole. Instead, this or similar representations (e.g., Baltes, 1987) of person-context relations can guide the selection of individual and ecological variables in one's research, and provide parameters about the generalizability of one's findings. This representation should serve as a reminder that we need to consider whether the results of a given study may be generalized beyond the particular individual and ecological variables studied therein and applied to other community, societal, cultural, and historical contexts.

To illustrate how the model of Figure 11.1 may be used as a guide for the selection of variables from the individual and contextual levels depicted (i.e., the interpersonal and physical features of the settings within which one lives), I show how my own research is based on selected components of the model. In Figure 11.2, the restricted or reduced model used in my research on individual⇄context relations is shown.

The studies we have conducted have focused on how the demands regarding characteristics of behavioral or physical individuality (e.g., temperament or physical attractiveness, respectively) held by a child's or an adolescent's parents, teachers, or peers are associated with different levels of adaptation, or adjustment, among children with various repertoires of temperamental individuality or with distinct characteristics of physical attractiveness (e.g., East, Lerner, & Lerner, 1988; J. Lerner, 1983; J. Lerner, Lerner, & Zabski, 1985; Lerner, Jovanovic, & Delaney, 1987; Lerner, Jovanovic, Delaney, & Hess, 1987; Nitz, Lerner, Lerner, & Talwar 1988; Windle et al., 1986). The rationale for this focus arises from our interest in testing a notion derived from the conception of inte-

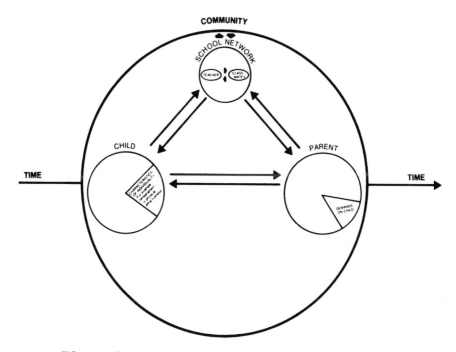

FIG. 11.2   The variables and levels of analysis studied in the individual-social context research of R. Lerner and J. Lerner.

grated, dynamically interactive levels represented in Figure 11.1; this derived notion is termed the "goodness of fit" model.

The Goodness of Fit Model

To explain this model, let me note that the person and the context described in Figures 11.1 and 11.2 will be individually distinct as a consequence of the unique combination of genotypic and phenotypic features of the person and of the specific attributes of his or her context. The presence of such individuality is central to understanding the goodness-of-fit model. As a consequence of characteristics of physical individuality (for example, in regard to body type or facial attractiveness; Sorell & Nowak, 1981) and/or of psychological individuality (for instance, in regard to conceptual tempo or temperament; Kagan, 1966; Thomas & Chess, 1977), children promote differential reactions in their socializing others; these reactions may feed back to children, increase the individuality of their developmental milieu, and provide a basis for their further development. Schneirla (1957) termed these relations *circular functions*. It is through the establishment of such functions in ontogeny that people may be conceived of as producers of their own development (Lerner & Busch-Rossnagel, 1981). However, this circular functions idea needs to be extended. In and of itself the notion is mute regarding the specific characteristics of the feedback (for example, its positive or negative valence) a child will receive as a consequence of his or her individuality. What may provide a basis of the feedback?

Just as a child brings his or her singular characteristics to a particular social setting, there are demands placed on the child by virtue of the physical and/or social components (i.e., the significant others) in the setting (J. Lerner & R. Lerner, 1983). According to Super and Harkness (1981), the developing person's context is structured by three kinds of influences: The physical and social setting; culturally regulated customs involved in socialization; and the psychology of the caregivers or the other significant people with whom the developing person interacts. This psychology is termed an *ethnotheory* (Super & Harkness, 1980, 1981, in preparation); in other words, significant others' beliefs, attitudes, expectations, or values regarding the meaning or significance of particular behaviors. Together, the three types of influence comprise the *developmental niche* of a person, or the set (or sets) of structured demands on the developing person (Super & Harkness, 1981). It is these demands that provide the functional significance for a given characteristic of individuality; if congruent with the demands of a significant other (e.g., a parent), this characteristic should produce a positive adjustment (adaptation). If that same attribute is incongruent with such demands, a negative adjustment would be expected.

To illustrate, consider the case of the child in a family context and of the psychosocial and physical climate promoted by the parents. Parents can vary in their cognitive and behavioral attributes (e.g., in regard to their child-rearing attitudes and parenting styles; Baumrind, 1971); parents can vary, too, in the physical features of the home they provide. These parent-based psychosocial and physical characteristics constitute presses for, or demands on, the child for adaptation. Simply, parent characteristics are translated or transduced into demands on the child.

The child's individuality in differentially meeting these demands provides a basis for the feedback he or she receives from the socializing environment. For example, considering the demand domain of attitudes, values, or expectations, teachers and parents may have relatively individual and distinct expectations about behaviors desired of their students and children, respectively. Teachers may want students who show little distractibility, because they would not want attention diverted from a lesson by the activity of children in the classroom. Parents, however, might desire their children to be moderately distractible—for example, when they require their children to move from television watching to the dinner table or to bed. Children whose behavioral individuality was either generally distractible or generally not distractible would thus differentially meet the demands of these two contexts. Similarly, Parke (1978) argued that the attitudes, values, and expectations for behavior held by a child's significant others represent a highly important basis for interaction. According to Parke

(1978), the same behavior from a child may have a very different meaning in various settings, and this difference may reflect the demand structure of the context, a structure composed in part of attitudes, values, and expectations. Thus, attitudes, values, or expectations about particular child behaviors—or, in the terms of Super and Harkness (1981), the ethnotheory about particular behaviors—represent one set of contextual demands to which children must adjust if they are to successfully meet the challenges present in their world. In other words, problems of adjustment to school demands or to home demands might thus develop as a consequence of a child's lack of match, or ''goodness of fit,'' in either or both settings.

Tests in my laboratory of this goodness of fit model have been quite extensive (e.g., J. Lerner, 1984; J. Lerner & R. Lerner, 1983; Lerner & Lerner, 1987, 1989; Lerner et al., 1986; Windle & Lerner, 1986; Windle et al., 1986). Here, then, it is necessary only to present briefly some recently obtained findings, ones derived from our Pennsylvania Early Adolescent Transitions Study (PEATS), a short-term longitudinal study of approximately 150 northwestern Pennsylvania early adolescents, from the beginning of sixth grade across the transition to junior high school and to the end of the seventh grade.

In one study derived from the PEATS, East, Lerner, and Lerner (1988) determined the overall fit between adolescents' temperament and the demands of their peers regarding desired levels of temperament. Based on the circular functions notion involved in the goodness of fit model, they predicted that although no significant direct paths would exist between adjustment and either temperament, measured alone, or temperament-demands fit, fit would influence adolescent-peer social relations that, in turn, would influence adjustment; in short, significant mediated paths, but insignificant direct paths, were expected. These expectations were supported. For nine of the twelve measures of adjustment employed (involving parents' ratings of behavior problems; teachers' ratings of scholastic competence, social acceptance, athletic competence, conduct adequacy, and physical appearance; and students' self-ratings of scholastic competence, social acceptance, athletic competence, conduct adequacy, physical appearance, and self-worth), both of the two mediated paths (between adolescent-peer group fit and peer relations, and then between peer relations and adjustment) were significant; in no case, however, was a significant direct path found.

Nitz, Lerner, Lerner, and Talwar (1988) found similar results regarding temperamental fit with parental demands and adolescent adjustment. Although at the beginning of sixth grade the number of significant relations between the adjustment measures and temperament-demands fit did not exceed the number of significant relations between temperament alone and adjustment, at both the middle and the end of sixth grade the percentage of significant relations between fit and adjustment scores was significantly greater than the corresponding percentages involving temperament alone. Moreover, and underscoring the interconnections among the child-family relation and the other key contexts comprising the ecology of human development, Nitz, Lerner, Lerner, and Talwar found virtually interchangeable results when fit scores with the peer demands were considered.

Finally, in regard to physical attractiveness, Lerner et al. (1987) found that the circular functions component of the goodness of fit model was supported in regard to academic achievement. Based on the presence of a "what is beautiful is good" stereotype (Langlois, 1986), teachers were expected to differentially evaluate adolescents who differed on physical attractiveness (PA). These different evaluations should influence the achievements of adolescents and, as well, their self-evaluations of their academic competence; these self-perceptions should then, in turn, influence achievement. In both cases, however, it was expected that these indirect paths between PA and achievement would be significant whereas direct paths between PA and achievement would not. The results of Lerner et al. (1987) confirm these expectations in respect to two indices of achievement—grade point average and scores on a standardized achievement test, the California Achievement Test/Form C at the beginning, middle, and end of sixth grade.

Given the previously described support for the developmental contextually derived goodness of fit model, as well as the support found in other studies from our laboratory (e.g., J. Lerner, 1984; J. Lerner & R. Lerner, 1983; Lerner & Lerner, 1987, 1989), it is useful to make some final statements regarding the developmental contextual view of human development.

CONCLUSIONS

The concepts of organism, of context, and of the relations between the two found in a probabilistic epigenetic, developmental contextual perspective are, as a set, quite complex ones, ones that impose formidable challenges on those who seek to generate feasible research. As I have argued, such a developmental contextual perspective leads to an integrated, multilevel concept of development, one in which the focus of inquiry is the organism-environment dynamic interaction. Furthermore, such a contextual orientation places an emphasis on the potential for intraindividual change in structure and function—for plasticity—across the life span.

The major challenge of this perspective is, as I have noted, the derivation and empirical testing of models reflecting the nature of dynamic, interlevel interactions across time. As I have indicated, one reasonably successful path we have taken involves the testing of the goodness of fit model of person-context relations. Of course, the goodness of fit model is not the only conception of person-context relations that may be derived from a contextual orientation. Indeed, there are perhaps an infinity of possible interlevel relations that may occur and potentially a similarly large array of ways to model them. At this writing, we simply have not devoted enough thought and empirical energies to their investigation.

In overview, I have pointed to some key conceptual and methodological issues that remain to be resolved if a developmental-contextual perspective is to be successfully applied to study individual-context relations. Pessimism because of the presence of these unresolved issues is not warranted, however. Every approach to human development has limitations. That there are problems to be resolved in regard to developmental contextualism does not single it out from other developmental paradigms. Indeed, given that it was only in the 1970s that the developmental contextual view came to the fore, the clearness with which the problems have been articulated, the methodological advances that have already been made (e.g., Nesselroade & Baltes, 1979), and the several data sets that speak to the empirical use of this perspective (Baltes, 1987; Brim & Kagan, 1980; Lerner, 1984) constitute reasons for great optimism for the future.

ACKNOWLEDGMENTS

A previous version of this chapter was presented as an Invited Address to the Eighth German Conference on Developmental Psychology, Bern, Switzerland, September 13–16, 1987. The author's work on the present chapter was supported in part by a grant from the William T. Grant Foundation and by NIMH Grant MH 39957. The author thanks Lisa Crockett, Jacqueline V. Lerner, Jonathan Tubman, and Fred W. Vondracek for their comments about previous drafts of this chapter.

REFERENCES

Anthony, J. The reaction of adults to adolescents and their behavior. In G. Caplan & S. Lebovici (Eds.), *Adolescence*. New York: Basic Books, 1969.

Baldwin, J. M. *Mental development in the child and the race*. New York: Macmillan, 1895.

Baldwin, J. M. *Darwin and the humanities*. Baltimore: Review Publishing, 1909.

Baltes, P. B. Life-span developmental psychology: Some converging observations on history and theory. In P. B. Baltes & O. G. Brim, Jr. (Eds.), *Life-span development and behavior* (Vol. 2). New York: Academic Press, 1979.

Baltes, P. B. Life-span developmental psychology: Observations on history and theory revisited. In R. M. Lerner (Ed.), *Developmental psychology: Historical and philosophical perspectives*. Hillsdale, NJ: Lawrence Erlbaum Associates, 1983.

Baltes, P. B. Theoretical propositions of life-span developmental psychology: On the dynamics between growth and decline. *Developmental Psychology*, 1987, *23*, 611–626.

Bandura, A. The self system in reciprocal determinism. *American Psychologist*, 1978, *33*, 344–358.

Bandura, A. Self-referent thought: A developmental analysis of self-efficacy. In J. H. Flavell & L. D. Ross (Eds.), *Cognitive social development: Frontiers and possible futures*. New York: Cambridge University Press, 1980.

Baumrind, D. Current patterns of parental authority. *Developmental Psychology Monographs*, 1971, *4*(No. 1, Part 2).

Bell, R. Q. Contributions of human infants to caregiving and social interaction. In M. Lewis & L. A. Rosenblum (Eds.), *The effect of the infant on its caregiver*. New York: Wiley, 1974.

Belsky, J. The determinants of parenting: A process model. *Child Development,* 1984, *55,* 83–96.

Belsky, J., Lerner, R., & Spanier, G. *The child in the family.* Reading, MA: Addison-Wesley, 1984.

Bijou, S. W. *Child development: The basic stage of early childhood.* Englewood Cliffs, NJ: Prentice-Hall, 1976.

Bijou, S. W., & Baer, D. M. *Child development: A systematic and empirical theory* (Vol. 1). New York: Appleton-Century-Crofts, 1961.

Blyth, D. A., Simmons, R. G., & Bush, D. The transition into early adolescence: A longitudinal comparison of youth in two educational contexts. *Sociology of Education,* 1978, *51,* 149–162.

Brazelton, T. B., Koslowski, B., & Main, M. The origins of reciprocity: The early mother-infant interaction. In M. Lewis & L. A. Rosenblum (Eds.), *The effect of the infant on its caregivers.* New York: Wiley, 1974.

Brim, O. G., Jr., & Kagan, J. (Eds.). *Constancy and change in human development.* Cambridge: Harvard University Press, 1980.

Bronfenbrenner, U. Toward an experimental ecology of human development. *American Psychologist,* 1977, *32,* 513–531.

Bronfenbrenner, U. *The ecology of human development.* Cambridge, MA: Harvard University Press, 1979.

Brooks-Gunn, J., & Matthews, W S. *He and she: How children develop their sex role identity.* Englewood Cliffs, NJ: Prentice-Hall, 1979.

Brooks-Gunn, J., & Petersen, A. C. (Eds.). *Girls at puberty: Biological and psychosocial perspectives.* New York: Plenum, 1983.

Brooks-Gunn, J., & Ruble, D. N. Menarche: The interaction of physiology, cultural, and social factors. In A. J. Dan, E. A. Graham, & C. P. Beecher (Eds.), *The menstrual cycle: A synthesis of interdisciplinary research.* New York: Springer, 1980.

Brooks-Gunn, J., & Ruble, D. N. The experience of menarche from a developmental perspective. In J. Brooks-Gunn & A. C. Petersen (Eds.), *Girls at puberty.* New York: Plenum, 1983.

Buss, A. H., & Plomin, R. *A temperament theory of personality development.* New York: Wiley, 1975.

Campos, J. J. *Human emotions: Their new importance and their role in social referencing.* Annual Report for the Research and Clinical Center for Child Development, Sapporo, Japan: Hokkaido University, Faculty of Education, 1980–81.

Crockenberg, S. B. Infant irritability, mother responsiveness, and social support influences on the security of infant-mother attachment. *Child Development,* 1981, *52,* 857–865.

Dixon, R. A., & Lerner, R. M. A history of systems in developmental psychology. In M. H. Bornstein & M. E. Lamb (Eds.), *Developmental psychology* (2d ed.). Hillsdale, NJ: Lawrence Erlbaum Associates, 1988.

Dixon, R. A., & Nesselroade, J. R. Pluralism and correlational analysis in developmental psychology: Historical commonalities. In R. M. Lerner (Ed.), *Developmental psychology: Historical and philosophical perspectives.* Hillsdale, NJ: Lawrence Erlbaum Associates, 1983.

East, P. L., Lerner, R. M., & Lerner, J. V. *Early adolescent-peer group fit, peer relations, and adjustment.* Manuscript submitted for publication, 1988.

Elder, G. H., Jr. *Children of the great depression.* Chicago: University of Chicago Press, 1974.

Elder, G. H., Jr. Age differentiation and the life course. In A. Inkeles, J. Coleman, & N. Smelser (Eds.), *Annual review of sociology* (Vol. 1). Palo Alto, CA: Annual Reviews, 1975.

Emmerich, W. Personality development and concepts of structure. *Child Development,* 1968, *39,* 671–690.

Erikson, E. H. Identity and the life-cycle. *Psychological Issues,* 1959, *1,* 18–164.

Eysenck, H. J., & Kamin, L. *The intelligence controversy.* New York: Wiley, 1981.

Featherman, D. L. Life-span perspectives in social science research. In P. B. Baltes & O. G. Brim, Jr. (Eds.), *Life-span development and behavior* (Vol. 5). New York: Academic Press, 1983.

Featherman, D. L. Individual development and aging as a population process. In J. R. Nesselroade &

A. von Eye (Eds.), *Individual development and social change: Explanatory analysis.* New York: Academic Press, 1985.

Featherman, D. L., & Lerner, R. M. Ontogenesis and sociogenesis: Problematics for theory about development across the lifespan. *American Sociological Review,* 1985, *50,* 659–676.

Feinman, S., & Lewis, M. Social referencing at ten months: A second-order effect on infants' responses to strangers. *Child Development,* 1983, *54,* 878–887.

Freedman, D. G. *Human sociobiology: A holistic approach.* New York: Free Press, 1979.

Freud, S. *Outline of psychoanalysis.* New York: Norton, 1949.

Gesell, A. L. The ontogenesis of infant behavior. In L. Carmichael (Ed.), *Manual of child psychology.* New York: Wiley, 1946.

Gollin, E. S. Development and plasticity. In E. S. Gollin (Ed.), *Developmental plasticity: Behavioral and biological aspects of variations in development.* New York: Academic Press, 1981.

Gottlieb, G. Conceptions of prenatal behavior. In R. Aronson, E. Tobach, D. S. Lehrman, & J. S. Rosenblatt (Eds.), *Development and evolution of behavior: Essays in memory of T. C. Schneirla.* San Francisco: N. H. Freeman, 1970.

Gottlieb, G. Conceptions of prenatal development: Behavioral embryology. *Psychological Review,* 1976a, *83,* 215–234.

Gottlieb, G. The roles of experience in the development of behavior and the nervous system. In G. Gottlieb (Ed.), *Neural and behavioral specificity: Studies on the development of behavior and the nervous system* (Vol. 3). New York: Academic Press, 1976b.

Gottlieb, G. The psychobiological approach to developmental issues. In M. M. Haith & J. J. Campos (Eds.), *Handbook of child psychology: Infancy and biological bases* (4th ed., Vol. 2). New York: Wiley, 1983.

Hall, G. S. *Adolescence: Its psychology and its relations to physiology, anthropology, sociology, sex, crime, religion, and education* (Vols. 1 and 2). New York: Appleton, 1904.

Hamburg, B. Early adolescence: A specific and stressful stage of the life cycle. In G. Coelho, D. A. Hamburg, & J. E. Adams (Eds.), *Coping and adaptation.* New York: Basic Books, 1974.

Hamburger, V. The concept of development in biology. In D. B. Harris (Ed.), *The concept of development.* Minneapolis: University of Minnesota Press, 1957.

Harris, D. B. (Ed.). *The concept of development.* Minneapolis: University of Minnesota Press, 1957.

Jenkins, J. J. Remember that old theory of memory: Well forget it. *American Psychologist,* 1974, *29,* 785–795.

Jensen, A. R. *Bias in mental testing.* New York: Free Press, 1980.

Kagan, J. Reflection-impulsivity: The generality and dynamics of conceptual tempo. *Journal of Abnormal Psychology,* 1966, *71,* 17–24.

Kaplan, B. A trio of trials. In R. M. Lerner (Ed.), *Developmental psychology: Historical and philosophical perspectives.* Hillsdale, NJ: Lawrence Erlbaum Associates, 1983.

Kuo, Z. Y. *The dynamics of behavior development.* New York: Random House, 1967.

Langlois, J. H. From the eye of the beholder to behavioral reality: The development of social behaviors and social relations as a function of physical attractiveness. In C. P. Herman (Ed.), *Physical appearance, stigma, and social behavior: The Ontario Symposium on Personality and Social Psychology.* Hillsdale, NJ: Lawrence Erlbaum Associates, 1986.

Lehrman, D. S. A critique of Konrad Lorenz's theory of instinctive behavior. *Quarterly Review of Biology,* 1953, *28,* 337–363.

Lehrman, D. S. Semantic and conceptual issues in the nature-nurture problem. In L. R. Aronson, E. Tobach, & J. S. Rosenblatt (Eds.), *Development and evolution of behavior: Essays in memory of T. C. Schneirla.* San Francisco: Freeman, 1970.

Lerner, J. V. A "goodness of fit" model of the role of temperament in psychosocial adaptation in early adolescents. *Journal of Genetic Psychology,* 1983, *143,* 149–157.

Lerner, J. V. The import of temperament for psychosocial functioning: Tests of a "goodness of fit" model. *Merrill-Palmer Quarterly,* 1984, *30,* 177–188.

Lerner, J. V., & Lerner, R. M. Temperament and adaptation across life: Theoretical and empirical issues. In P. B. Baltes & O. G. Brim, Jr. (Eds.), *Life-span development and behavior* (Vol. 5). New York: Academic Press, 1983.

Lerner, J. V., Lerner, R. M., & Zabski, S. Temperament and elementary school children's actual and rated academic performance: A test of a "goodness of fit" model. *The Journal of Child Psychology and Psychiatry*, 1985, *26*, 125–136.

Lerner, R. M. *Concepts and theories of human development*. Reading, MA: Addison-Wesley, 1976.

Lerner, R. M. Nature, nurture, and dynamic interactionism. *Human Development*, 1978, *21*, 1–20.

Lerner, R. M. A dynamic interactional concept of individual and social relationship development. In R. Burgess & T. Huston (Eds.), *Social exchange in developing relationships*. New York: Academic Press, 1979.

Lerner, R. M. The uses and abuses of sociobiology. *Contemporary Psychology*, 1980, *25*, 470–472.

Lerner, R. M. Adolescent development: Scientific study in the 1980s. *Youth and Society*, 1981, *12*, 251–275.

Lerner, R. M. Children and adolescents as producers of their own development. *Developmental Review*, 1982, *2*, 342–370.

Lerner, R. M. *On the nature of human plasticity*. New York: Cambridge University Press, 1984.

Lerner, R. M. Adolescent maturational change and psychosocial development: A dynamic interactional perspective. In J. Brooks-Gunn, A. C. Petersen, & D. Eichorn (Eds.), Timing of maturation and psychological adjustment. *Journal of Youth and Adolescence*, 1985, *14*, 355–372.

Lerner, R. M. *Concepts and theories of human development* (2d ed.). New York: Random House, 1986.

Lerner, R. M. A life-span perspective for early adolescence. In R. M. Lerner & T. T. Foch (Eds.), *Biological-psychosocial interactions in early adolescence: A life-span perspective*. Hillsdale, NJ: Lawrence Erlbaum Associates, 1987.

Lerner, R. M., & Busch-Rossnagel, N. A. *Individuals as producers of their development: A life-span perspective*. New York: Academic Press, 1981.

Lerner, R. M., Hultsch, D. F., & Dixon, R. A. Contextualism and the character of developmental psychology in the 1970s. *Annals of the New York Academy of Sciences*, 1983, *412*, 101–128.

Lerner, R. M., Iwawaki, S., Chihara, T., & Sorell, G. J. Self-concept, self-esteem, and body attitudes among Japanese male and female adolescents. *Child Development*, 1980, *51*, 847–855.

Lerner, R. M., Jovanovic, J., & Delaney, M. *Pubertal maturation, intellectual aptitude, and achievement in males and females: Findings from the Pennsylvania Early Adolescent Transitions Study (PEATS)*. Paper presented at the 1987 biennial meeting of the Society for Research in Child Development, Baltimore, April 1987.

Lerner, R. M., Jovanovic, J., Delaney, M., & Hess, L. E. *Early adolescent physical attractiveness and academic competence*. Paper presented at the Fifty-Eighth annual meeting of the American Psychological Association, Arlington, VA, April 1987.

Lerner, R. M., & Kauffman, M. D. The concept of development in contextualism. *Developmental Review*, 1985, *5*, 309–333.

Lerner, R. M., & Lerner, J. V. Children in their contexts: A goodness of fit model. In J. B. Lancaster, J. Altmann, A. S. Rossi, & L. R. Sherrod (Eds.), *Parenting across the life span: Biosocial dimensions*. Chicago: Aldine, 1987.

Lerner, R. M., & Lerner, J. V. Organismic and social contextual bases of development: The sample case of early adolescence. In W. Damon (Ed.), *Child development today and tomorrow*. San Francisco: Jossey-Bass, 1989.

Lerner, R. M., Lerner, J. V., Windle, M., Hooker, K., Lenerz, K., & East, P. L. Children and adolescents in their contexts: Tests of a goodness of fit model. In R. Plomin & J. Dunn (Eds.), *The study of temperament: Changes, continuities, and challenges*. Hillsdale, NJ: Lawrence Erlbaum Associates, 1986.

Lerner, R. M., Skinner, E. A., & Sorell, G. T. Methodological implications of contextual/dialectic theories of development. *Human Development*, 1980, *23*, 225–235.

Lerner, R. M., & Spanier, G. B. A dynamic interactional view of child and family development. In R. M. Lerner & G. B. Spanier (Eds.), *Child influences on marital and family interaction: A life-span perspective.* New York: Academic Press, 1978.

Lerner, R. M., & Spanier, G. B. *Adolescent development: A life-span perspective.* New York: McGraw-Hill, 1980.

Lewis, M., & Lee-Painter, S. An interactional approach to the mother-infant dyad. In M. Lewis & L. A. Rosenblum (Eds.), *The effect of the infant on its caregiver.* New York: Wiley, 1974.

Lewis, M., & Rosenblum, L. A. (Eds.). *The effect of the infant on its caregiver.* New York: Wiley, 1974.

Lorenz, K. Durch Domestikation verursachte Storungen arteigenen Verhaltens. *Zeitschrift fur angewandte Psychologie und Charakterkunde*, 1940, *59*, 2–81.

Lorenz, K. *Evolution and modification of behavior.* Chicago: University of Chicago Press, 1965.

Lorenz, K. *On aggression.* New York: Harcourt, Brace & World, 1966.

Lynch, M. E. *Paternal androgeny, daughters' physical maturity level, and achievement socialization in early adolescence.* Unpublished Doctoral Dissertation, Cornell University, 1981.

Magnusson, D., & Allen, V. L. (Eds.). *Human development: An interactional perspective.* New York: Academic Press, 1983.

Maier, N. R. F., & Schneirla, T. C. *Principles of animal behavior.* New York: McGraw-Hill, 1935.

Mischel, W. On the future of personality measurement. *American Psychologist*, 1977, *32*, 246–254.

Moltz, H. Imprinting: Empirical basis and theoretical significance. *Psychological Bulletin*, 1960, *57*, 291–314.

Mussen, P. H., & Bouterline-Young, H. Relationships between rate of physical maturing and personality among boys of Italian descent. *Vita Humana*, 1964, *7*, 186–200.

Nesselroade, J. R., & Baltes, P. B. *Longitudinal research in the study of behavior and development.* New York: Academic Press, 1979.

Nitz, K. A., Lerner, R. M., Lerner, J. V., & Talwar, R. Parental and peer demands, temperament, and early adolescent adjustment. *Journal of Early Adolescence*, 1988, *8*, 243–263.

Novikoff, A. B. The concept of integrative levels of biology. *Science*, 1945a, *62*, 209–215.

Novikoff, A. B. Continuity and discontinuity in evolution. *Science*, 1945b, *101*, 405–406.

Overton, W. F. On the assumptive base of the nature-nurture controversy: Additive versus interactive conceptions. *Human Development*, 1973, *16*, 74–89.

Paige, K. E. A bargaining theory of menarcheal responses in preindustrial cultures. In J. Brooks-Gunn & A. C. Petersen (Eds.), *Girls at puberty.* New York: Plenum Press, 1983.

Parke, R. Parent-infant interaction: Progress, paradigms, and problems. In G. D. Sackett (Ed.), *Observing behavior. Vol. 1: Theory and implications in mental retardation.* Baltimore: University Park Press, 1978.

Pepper, S. C. *World hypotheses.* Berkeley: University of California Press, 1942.

Petersen, A. C. Pubertal change and cognition. In J. Brooks-Gunn & A. C. Petersen (Eds.), *Girls at puberty.* New York: Plenum, 1983.

Petersen, A. C., & Taylor, B. The biological approach to adolescence: Biological change and psychological adaptation. In J. Adelson (Ed.), *Handbook of adolescent psychology.* New York: Wiley, 1980.

Piaget, J. *The psychology of intelligence.* New York: Harcourt Brace, 1950.

Reese, H. W., & Overton, W. F. Models of development and theories of development. In L. R. Goulet & P. B. Baltes (Eds.), *Life-span developmental psychology: Research and theory.* New York: Academic Press, 1970.

Riegel, K. F. Toward a dialectical theory of development. *Human Development*, 1975, *18*, 50–64.

Riegel, K. F. The dialectics of human development. *American Psychologist*, 1976a, *31*, 689–700.

Riegel, K. F. From traits and equilibrium toward developmental dialectics. In W. J. Arnold & J. K. Cole (Eds.), *Nebraska symposium on motivation*. Lincoln: University of Nebraska Press, 1976b.

Rosnow, R. L. Von Osten's horse, Hamlet's question, and the mechanistic view of causality: Implications for a post-crisis social psychology. *The Journal of Mind and Behavior*, 1983, *4*, 319–338.

Rosnow, R. L., & Georgoudi, M. (Eds.). *Contextualism and understanding in behavioral research*. New York: Praeger, 1986.

Rosnow, R. L., & Rosenthal, R. *Understanding behavioral science: Research methods for research consumers*. New York: McGraw-Hill, 1984.

Ruble, D. N. Premenstrual symptoms: A reinterpretation. *Science*, 1977, *197*, 291–292.

Ruble, D. N., & Brooks-Gunn, J. Menstrual symptoms: A social cognition analysis. *Journal of Behavioral Medicine*, 1979, *2*, 171–194.

Ruble, D. N., & Brooks-Gunn, J. The experience of menarche. *Child Development*, 1982, *53*, 1557–1566.

Sameroff, A. Transactional models in early social relations. *Human Development*, 1975, *18*, 65–79.

Sarason, S. B. Jewishness, Blackishness, and the nature-nurture controversy. *American Psychologist*, 1973, *28*, 962–971.

Sarbin, T. R. Contextualism: A world view for modern psychology. In J. K. Cole (Ed.), *Nebraska symposium on motivation, 1976*. Lincoln: University of Nebraska Press, 1977.

Scarr, S. Development is internally guided, not determined. *Contemporary Psychology*, 1982, *27*, 852–853.

Scarr, S., & McCartney, K. How people make their own environments: A theory of genotype-environment effects. *Child Development*, 1983, *54*, 424–435.

Schneirla, T. C. Interrelationships of the innate and the acquired in instinctive behavior. In P. P. Grassé (Ed.), *L'instinct dans le comportement des animaux et de l'homme*. Paris: Mason et Cie, 1956.

Schneirla, T. C. The concept of development in comparative psychology. In D. B. Harris (Ed.), *The concept of development*. Minneapolis: University of Minnesota Press, 1957.

Simmons, R. G., Blyth, D. A., & McKinney, K. L. The social and psychological effects of puberty on white females. In J. Brooks-Gunn & A. C. Petersen (Eds.), *Girls at puberty*. New York: Plenum, 1983.

Simmons, R. G., Blyth, D. A., Van Cleave, E. F., & Bush, D. M. Entry into early adolescence: The impact of school structure, puberty, and early dating on self-esteem. *American Sociological Review*, 1979, *44*, 948–967.

Simmons, R. G., Brown, L., Bush, D. M., & Blyth, D. A. Self-esteem and achievement of black and white early adolescents. *Social Problems*, 1978, *26*, 86–96.

Skinner, B. F. *Beyond freedom and dignity*. New York: Knopf, 1971.

Sorell, G. T., & Nowak, C. A. The role of physical attractiveness as a contributor to individual development. In R. M. Lerner & N. A. Busch-Rossnagel (Eds.), *Individuals as producers of their development: A life-span perspective*. New York: Academic Press, 1981.

Super, C. M., & Harkness, S. Anthropological perspectives on child development. *New Directions for Child Development* (No. 8). San Francisco: Jossey-Bass, 1980.

Super, C. M., & Harkness, S. Figure, ground, and gestalt: The cultural context of the active individual. In R. M. Lerner & N. A. Busch-Rossnagel (Eds.), *Individuals as producers of their development: A life-span perspective*. New York: Academic Press, 1981.

Super, C. M., & Harkness, S. *The development niche: Culture and the expressions of human growth*, in preparation.

Thomas, A., & Chess, S. Behavioral individuality in childhood. In L. R. Aronson, E. Tobach, D. Lehrman, & J. Rosenblatt (Eds.), *Development and evolution of behaviors: Essays in memory of T. C. Schneirla*. San Francisco: W. H. Freeman, 1970.

Thomas, A., & Chess, S. *Temperament and development*. New York: Brunner/Mazel, 1977.

Thomas, A., Chess, S., & Birch, H. G. The origin of personality. *Scientific American,* 1970, *223,* 102–109.

Thomas, A., Chess, S., Birch, H. G., Hertzig, M. E., & Korn, S. *Behavioral individuality in early childhood.* New York: New York University Press, 1963.

Thomas, A., Chess, S., Sillan, J., & Mendez, O. Cross-cultural study of behavior in children with special vulnerabilities to stress. In D. F. Ricks, A. Thomas, & M. Roff (Eds.), *Life history research in psychopathology.* Minneapolis: University of Minnesota Press, 1974.

Tobach, E. Evolutionary aspects of the activity of the organism and its development. In R. M. Lerner & N. A. Busch-Rossnagel (Eds.), *Individuals as producers of their development: A life-span perspective.* New York: Academic Press, 1981.

Tobach, E., Gianutsos, J., Topoff, H. R., & Gross, C. G. *The four horses: Racism, sexism, militarism, and social Darwinism.* New York: Behavioral Publications, 1981.

Tobach, E., & Greenberg, G. The significance of T. C. Schneirla's contribution to the concept of levels of integration. In G. Greenberg & E. Tobach (Eds.), *Behavioral evolution and integrative levels.* Hillsdale, NJ: Lawrence Erlbaum Associates, 1984.

Tobach, E., & Schneirla, T. C. The biopsychology of social behavior or animals. In R. E. Cooke & S. Levin (Eds.), *Biologic basis of pediatric practice.* New York: McGraw-Hill, 1968.

Tobin-Richards, M. H., Boxer, A. M., & Petersen, A. C. The psychological significance of pubertal change: Sex differences in perceptions of self during early adolescence. In J. Brooks-Gunn & A. C. Petersen (Eds.), *Girls at puberty.* New York: Plenum, 1983.

Turkewitz, G. Psychobiology and developmental psychology: The influence of T. C. Schneirla on human developmental psychology. *Developmental Psychobiology,* 1987, *20,* 369–375.

von Bertalanffy, L. *Modern theories of development.* London: Oxford University Press, 1933.

Wapner, S., Kaplan, B., & Cohen, S. B. An organismic-developmental perspective for understanding transactions of men and environments. *Environment and Behavior,* 1973, *5,* 255–289.

Westney, O. E., Jenkins, R. R., & Benjamin, C. A. Sociosexual development of preadolescents. In J. Brooks-Gunn & A. C. Petersen (Eds.), *Girls at puberty.* New York: Plenum Press, 1983.

White, S. H. The learning-maturation controversy: Hall to Hull. *Merrill-Palmer Quarterly,* 1968, *14,* 187–196.

Wilson, E. O. *Sociobiology: The new synthesis.* Cambridge, MA: Harvard University Press, 1975.

Windle, M., Hooker, K., Lenerz, K., East, P. L., Lerner, J. V., & Lerner, R. M. Temperament, perceived competence, and depression in early- and late-adolescents. *Developmental Psychology,* 1986, *22,* 384–392.

Windle, M., & Lerner, R. M. The goodness of fit model of temperament-context relations: Interaction or correlation? In J. V. Lerner & R. M. Lerner (Eds.), *Temperament and social interaction during infancy and childhood. New Directions for Child Development* (Vol. 31). San Francisco: Jossey-Bass, 1986.

12 Lags and Logs: Statistical Approaches to Interaction

Roger Bakeman
Lauren B. Adamson
Peter Strisik
Georgia State University

INTRODUCTION

Much has been written recently about how sequential analysis may help researchers preserve and manipulate the events in a stream of observed behavior (e.g., Bakeman & Gottman, 1986, 1987; Sackett, 1987). These works celebrate the elegant match between recent ideas about the process of social interaction and quantitative methods for documenting such patterns. Yet for many, these festivities may seem marred by impenetrable technical discussions. Our intent in writing this chapter is to present sequential statistical approaches to interaction in a way that is relatively free of complex terminology and intimidating notation.

One insight greatly facilitates this endeavor. When sequential problems are cast in log-linear terms, their analysis becomes almost straightforward. Moreover, the basic approach should seem familiar to researchers previously schooled in traditional approaches to data analysis and hypothesis testing. First, we attempt to demonstrate this happy state of affairs. Then, we present specific examples of log-linear solutions to common sequential analytic problems.

BASIC CONCEPTS

In this first section we discuss how sequential data should be structured for sequential analysis, distinguishing between dimensions (or variables) of interest and their mutually exclusive and exhaustive levels (or codes). We also note the difference between event and time sequences and between sequences that permit and do not permit codes to repeat (i.e., follow themselves). Then we discuss how sequential data can be arranged in contingency tables, make some introductory comments about log-linear analysis, and show how the familiar chi-square is simply a special case of a log-linear analysis.

Event and Time Sequences

One way to capture interactive phenomena is to code successive events. What constitutes an event can vary, as we discuss later on, but at the very least it is a bounded unit that can be segregated from the passing stream of behavior. Following definitions and rules specified by the investigator, trained observers then categorize the event. It seems reasonable to call data that result from this process of coding sequential events event sequences or *event sequential data.*

Often events are coded on just one dimension. (A *dimension* is a categorical variable; the codes associated with it represent the permissible *levels* that the dimension can assume.) For example, Bakeman and Adamson (1984) defined five mutually exclusive and exhaustive codes that they used to characterize the dimension of infants' engagement:

Engagement state (five levels):
(1) Unengaged
(2) Onlooking
(3) Person engagement
(4) Object engagement
(5) Joint engagement

In this case, the events coded were engagement states and the coding allowed Bakeman and Adamson to represent mother-infant interaction as sequences of such states.

Events can also be coded on more than one dimension. For example, simplifying the Marital Interaction Coding System (Hops, Willis, Patterson, & Weiss, 1971) somewhat, we could code turns of talk on two dimensions:

Function of successive turns (five levels):
(1) Complains
(2) Emotes
(3) Approves
(4) Empathizes
(5) Negates
Speaker for each turn (two levels):
(1) Husband
(2) Wife

In this particular example, turns of talk were coded on two dimensions: function, which had five permissible codes, and speaker, which had two. Because the codes that can be assigned to a dimension are sometimes confused with the dimension itself, we use letters to identify dimensions and numbers for codes, as already shown; or else we simply separate permissible codes with slashes—e.g., Yes/No—and assume that the name of the dimension is understood from context.

A second way to represent data dealing with interactive phenomena is as a series of coded time intervals. In this case, the events coded are time intervals, and so it seems reasonable to call such data time sequences or *time sequential data*. The intervals used are often short, for instance, a 5- or 10-second interval is common, but both shorter and longer intervals are also used. As with events, time intervals can be coded on more than one dimension.

For example, influenced by Parten (1932), Bakeman and Brownlee (1980) trained observers to code a toddler's predominant play state (one dimension) for successive 15-second intervals of videotaped observations made during a free-play period:

Play state (five levels):
(1) Unoccupied
(2) Solitary
(3) Together
(4) Parallel
(5) Group

A more complex example is provided by Vietze, Abernathy, Ashe, and Faulstich (1978). Their observers coded successive 1-second intervals on two dimensions:

Infants' behavior (five levels):
(1) Vocalize
(2) Look
(3) Smile
(4) Cry
(5) None

Mothers' behavior (four levels):
(1) Vocalize
(2) Look
(3) Touch/Play
(4) None

A still more complex example is suggested by the work of Konner (1977). He coded each successive 5-second interval of !Kung mother-infant interaction for the (1) presence, or (2) absence, of a number of different behaviors. In this case, each behavior served as a dimension. Examples of some of the dimensions he used are: (a) Infant vocalization, (b) Caretaker vocalization, (c) Adult response to fret, (d) Infant and mother face-to-face, and (e) Infant smile.

As these examples demonstrate, event sequences and time sequences are really the same. Only the coding unit—events versus time intervals—distinguishes between them. Both event and time sequential data consist of strings of numbers (or other symbols) representing the codes assigned to successive events or intervals, for one or more dimensions. Thus it should be no surprise that the analyses described subsequently apply equally to either kind of sequence.

We have distinguished between event and time sequences here because the terms appear frequently in the literature and because organizing the examples this way makes it easier, we think, for readers to recognize in them something that applies to their own work. The important point is to note the essential similarity between event and time sequences (actually time sequences can be regarded as a particular kind of event sequence) and to realize that any collection of coding schemes can be, and for sequential analysis should be, structured as sets of mutually exclusive and exhaustive codes, each set representing a dimension of interest.

Repeatable and Nonrepeatable Codes

A second distinction, one that has important implications for subsequent analyses, is between sequences that allow codes to repeat (i.e., to follow themselves) and those that do not. The requirement that adjacent codes be different applies to so many coding schemes in actual use that some writers (e.g., Sackett, 1987) suggest that all event sequences are so restricted. But in fact only some are. For example, successive turns of talk could be, and often are, assigned the same code (see Dorval & Eckerman, 1984).

The distinctions between event and time sequences and between sequences that allow codes to repeat and those that do not, yield the four possibilities presented in Table 12.1. If the unit coded is a time interval, there seems to be no reason to prohibit an interval from being assigned the same code as the immediately previous one, and so we regard the time-interval/nonrepeatable-code possibility as a null or empty category. Time sequences, then, always allow codes to repeat. Event sequences are a different matter. If the unit coded is a state, then by definition codes cannot repeat—any repeated code would just be a continuation of the same state, not a new code. For other kinds of events, however, like turns of talk, codes may be, and often are, allowed to repeat.

This distinction is important because analytic procedures are somewhat differ-

TABLE 12.1
Examples of Different Types of Sequences

Unit Coded	Adjacent Codes	
	Repeatable	Nonrepeatable
Event	Hops' marital turns of talk	Bakeman & Adamson's engagement states
Time Interval	Vietze's mother and infant codes	No example, null category

ent for sequences that do and do not allow codes to repeat. In fact, applying procedures appropriate for sequences of repeatable codes to sequences of nonrepeatable codes can yield incorrect results. Moreover, and very much to the point given the general thrust of this chapter, procedures for dealing with nonrepeatable code sequences are easily handled in a log-linear context.

Lags

A common question asked by researchers who study interaction is "What follows what?" When an infant smiles, does the mother vocalize? When one spouse complains, does the other spouse offer sympathy or respond with a complaint? Do spouses in general, or perhaps just certain groups of spouses, respond to negative behavior with reciprocal negative behavior? The general question is, "Is there any systematic relation between adjacent (or near-adjacent, or even concurrent) behaviors?"

A useful word to indicate displacement in time is *lag*. In common usage, lag indicates that something (like a laggard) has fallen behind, but more specifically a lag may be defined as any interval between events. Sometimes this can be confusing: One convention is to identify the consequent event with an index of zero and antecedent events with negative indices; another convention—and the one we follow—is to identify the first antecedent event of interest with an index of zero and subsequent events with positive indices. Thus, if we think of later events (or intervals) as lagging earlier events and if we say that the earlier event (often called the criterion, or given, or antecedent event) occupies lag position 0 and later events (often called target or consequent events) occupy lag positions 1, 2, and so forth, then the general question becomes, "Does behavior at lag position 0 affect behavior at lag 1? at lag 2? at lag 8? and so forth?"

We might ask, for example, "If a baby is coded Cry at lag 0, is he or she likely to be coded Cry at lag 1? at lag 2? at lag 8? and so forth?"; that is, "Does Cry occur in runs and/or does it recur cyclicly?" Or, concerned with reciprocal relations, we might ask, "If a toddler is coded Unoccupied at lag 0 is he or she likely to be coded Solitary at lag 1?" And similarly, "If coded Solitary at lag 0, is he or she likely to be coded Unoccupied at lag 1?'' Finally, given a concern with concurrent relations, we might ask, ''Is a mother more likely to vocalize at lag 0 if her baby is also vocalizing at lag 0?''

Contingency Tables

The first step in answering questions such as those just posed usually involves organizing the sequential data into frequency or contingency tables (Castellan, 1979). If just two dimensions are of interest, then the resulting table is easy to visualize. For example, if an investigator were interested in adjacent (lag 0-lag 1) relations and if successive turns of talk had been coded using the simplified Marital Interaction Coding System (MICS) defined earlier, then first a two-dimensional 5 × 5 table would be defined. The rows could represent lag 0 and the columns lag 1 behavior; the five rows and columns would represent the five permissible MICS codes (see Table 12.2).

Next, each successive pair of adjacent codes would be categorized and a tally added to the appropriate cell. For example, imagine the following coded sequence:

(1 = Complains, 2 = Emotes, 3 = Approves, 4 = Empathizes, 5 = Negates):

3 4 1 4 1 1 5 2 4 4 3 5 5 5 1 2 4

and imagine further a ''moving window'' that operates as follows:

(3 4) 1 4 1 1 5 2 4 4 3 5 5 5 1 2 4

3 (4 1) 4 1 1 5 2 4 4 3 5 5 5 1 2 4

3 4 (1 4) 1 1 5 2 4 4 3 5 5 5 1 2 4

etc.

The first window would result in a tally being added to the cell in the third row and fourth column (the Approves-Empathizes cell), the second a tally to the cell in the fourth row and first column (the Empathizes-Complains cell), and so forth. The total N would indicate the number of adjacent code pairs (which would be 16 in this case because there were 17 codes total) and each cell would indicate how often each transition occurred—e.g., how often Empathizes was followed by Complains. The final tallies resulting from this small segment of data are given in Table 12.2.

It is important to stress how general such tables can be. Rows might represent codes for an infant's lag 0 behavior and columns codes for the mother's lag 0 (or lag 1, etc.) behavior. Or rows might represent an infant's lag 0 behavior and columns the infant's lag 1 (or lag 2, lag 3, etc.) behavior. Moreover, such tables are not confined to the two dimensions of rows and columns. Triplets of codes instead of pairs of codes could be tallied, and in such cases dimensions 1, 2, and

TABLE 12.2
Example Tallies for the Marital Interaction Coding System

Lag 0	Lag 1					Totals
	Compln	Emote	Approv	Empthz	Negate	
Complain	/	/		/	/	4
Emote				//		2
Approve				/	/	2
Empathize	//		/	/		4
Negate	/	/			//	4
TOTALS	4	2	1	5	4	16

3 might correspond to lag 0 (rows), lag 1 (columns), and lag 2 behavior respectively (this third dimension could be visualized as slices of a cube). In this case, the first or "(3 4 1)" window from the data segment given in the previous paragraph would cause us to add one tally to the cell in the third row, the fourth column, and the first slice of a 5 × 5 × 5 cube.

In addition, not all dimensions need refer to lag positions. For example, dimension 1 could be the spouse (Husband/Wife); dimension 2, lag 0 codes for that spouse; and dimension 3, the other spouse's lag 1 response. For the MICS code, this would result in a 2 × 5 × 5 table: one 5 × 5 slice would indicate the husband's responses to his wife, whereas the other 5 × 5 slice would indicate the wife's responses to her husband. This table would allow us to test whether husbands and wives respond to each other in a similar way. In sum, because dimensions can encode any categorical research factor (male/female, old/young, preterm/fullterm, partner1/partner 2, clinic/normal, mother/father/adolescent, 3-month/6-month/9-month, etc.), subsequent analyses of such tables can investigate not just sequential effects, but effects of other research factors as well as any interactions between them.

Logs and Logits

Given appropriately constructed contingency tables, log-linear methods allow researchers to answer questions like "What interactive patterns characterize these individuals/dyads/families?" and "Are interactive patterns different for different kinds of individuals/dyads/families?" Yet, in spite of their considerable advantages (see Kennedy, 1983), log-linear methods, with just a few notable exceptions (e.g., Cohn & Tronick, 1987; Green, 1988; Stevenson, Ver Hoeve, Roach, & Leavitt, 1986), are seldom used by behavioral researchers.

True, the theoretical work is relatively new (e.g., Bishop, Fienberg, & Holland, 1975; Goodman & Kruskal, 1954) and too often couched in intimidating notation. Easy to use and widely available computer programs (like SPSS' LOG-LINEAR: Norusis, 1985; SPSS, 1986) and texts intended specifically for social scientists (e.g., Haberman, 1978, 1979; Kennedy, 1983; Upton, 1978) and non-statisticians (e.g., Fienberg, 1980) have appeared only recently. Even the name can be intimidating. However, just as a skillful driver need not know how to fix an engine, and just as a conceptually correct user of multiple regression need not know how to invert a matrix, so too proper use of log-linear methods does not require that a user even know exactly what a logarithm, logit, or odds ratio is.

The log-linear approach may seem more foreign to psychologists and other social science researchers than it actually is. As several writers have noted (e.g., Kennedy, 1983), the conceptual overlap with traditional analysis of variance and multiple regression is considerable. This is especially true for logit models, which form an important and useful subclass of log-linear models. Moreover, for simple problems, familiar chi-square and log-linear analyses are almost identical. In the next section we compare chi-square, log-linear, and logit approaches, stressing their common features.

Chi-Square: Taking the Log View

A chi-square analysis

Imagine that we had recorded conversations between spouses and had subsequently coded the content for each turn of talk using the simplified MICS described previously. Imagine further that we are interested in negative reciprocity—defined as the tendency to respond to a negative statement with another one (this example is inspired by Cousins & Power, 1986)—and that classifying pairs of adjacent turns of talk for the Negate code (lag 0 Negate/Other, lag 1 Negate/Other) resulted in the tallies given in Table 12.3. To test whether there is a relation between lag 0 and lag 1 Negate codes, we could simply compute a chi-square, using the data in Table 12.3 and the standard chi-square formula:

$$\chi^2 = \sum \frac{(\text{obs-exp})^2}{\text{exp}}$$

Because the chi-square for Table 12.3 is 35.7, $p < .001$, and because the expected frequency for the lag 0 = Negate/lag 1 = Negate cell is 31.9 whereas the observed frequency is 62, we would conclude that Negate followed Negate more often than one would expect, given the base rate for Negate. Thus, these data apparently reflect a pattern of negative reciprocity.

A log-linear model

The chi-square analysis just presented can easily be recast in log-linear terms. When we compute expected cell frequencies from the row and column totals, we are in effect guided by a model. The model assumes that cell frequencies reflect

TABLE 12.3
Counts for Negative Reciprocity

	Lag 1		
Lag 0	Negate	Other	Totals
Negate	62	235	297
Other	236	2243	2479
TOTALS	298	2478	2776

the overall (or marginal) distributions of lag 0 and lag 1 responses and nothing more. If this model, which assumes that row and column variables are independent, generates cell frequencies fairly similar to those actually observed, then chi-square will be small and we can accept the relatively parsimonious model that includes just a lag 0 (row) and a lag 1 (column) effect.

If chi-square is large, however, then we would reject the simple two-term [LAG0] [LAG1] model just presented. In order to generate tallies that fit the observed data, a three-term [LAG0] [LAG1] [LAG0 LAG1] model is required, in which the third term represents the association (or interaction) between lag 0 and lag 1 codes. (Terms are enclosed in brackets; here all terms are listed, even lower-order terms implied by higher-order ones.)

In the case of a two-dimensional table, adding this third term results in a saturated model (a model that contains all possible effects). By definition, a saturated model generates tallies identical to those observed, and so it always fits the data perfectly. In substantive terms, if only the three-term model generates expected scores that fit the observed data, then categories for adjacent turns are associated and not independent. The chi-square analysis yielded the same result; the advantage of a log-linear approach, although not demonstrated by this simple example, is that the effects of more than just two variables (or dimensions) can be considered concurrently.

A logit model

For our purposes, logit models have two major advantages. First, unlike the more general log-linear models, logit models require that response (or criterion or dependent) variables be segregated from explanatory (or predictor or independent) variables. Asking "How is this (dependent) variable affected by these (independent) variables?" is faithful to the way we typically conceptualize questions and is a familiar way of summarizing multiple regression and analysis of variance (ANOVA) results as well. Second, at a more practical level, a logit model is specified with fewer terms than a corresponding log-linear model, and those terms correspond to ANOVA-like main effects and interactions.

For the current example, a logit analysis would identify lag 1 as the response and lag 0 as the explanatory variable. The no-effect model (which corresponds to the log-linear independence model) would consist of a single term, [LAG 1], whereas the main-effect model (corresponding to the log-linear interaction model) would consist of two terms, [LAG1] [LAG1 LAG0]. The first term is analogous to the grand mean in an ANOVA design whereas the second term indicates that the distribution of scores at lag 1 is affected by events at lag 0. If the first model generated scores that did not fit the data whereas the second did, a main effect for lag 0 would be indicated.

The ease of a logit compared to a log-linear model is more evident as the number of dimensions increases. For example, a saturated loglinear model for a three-dimensional table would involve the following terms:

[A] [B] [C] [A B] [A C] [B C] [A B C]

whereas the corresponding saturated logit model, with dimension C as the dependent variable, would require just:

[C] [A C] [B C] [A B C]

In this case, the first term, [C], is analogous to the grand mean whereas the [A C] term represents a main effect for A, the [B C] term, a main effect for B, and the [A B C] term, the A × B interaction.

Let us now consider what the output for a logit analysis of the data in Table 12.3 would look like. First consider the output for the [LAG1] [LAG1 LAG0] model. Because it is saturated, the expected counts generated by the model for each of the four cells of Table 12.3 are identical with the observed. As a result, the chi-square goodness-of-fit statistics are zero, as are the *residuals* (the differences between observed and expected counts for each cell). More interesting are the estimated parameter *coefficients*. The coefficient associated with the [LAG1 LAG0] term is .23, its standard error is .040, and its z value is 5.8. This significant z value ($p < .001$) suggests that the main effect of LAG0 on LAG1 is significant and that a model without the [LAG1 LAG0] term would generate expected counts quite discrepant from those observed; in other words, eliminating the [LAG1 LAG0] term from the saturated model would result in an ill-fitting model.

As a general rule, instead of adding terms until a fitting model is found, it often makes sense to begin interpretation of a logit analysis with an examination of the parameter coefficients computed for the saturated model precisely because these coefficients indicate which terms are important and which terms can be eliminated. Moreover, these coefficients can be interpreted in a manner analogous to regression coefficients (see SPSS, 1986, pp. 576–579).

Next consider the output associated with the [LAG 1] or no-effect model. As expected, given the coefficients for the saturated model, the chi-square goodness-of-fit statistics are large and significant, indicating poor fit. (Likelihood ratio chi-square $= 29.7$, Pearson chi-square $= 35.7$, $df = 1$ and $p < .001$ for both; because these statistics only approximate chi-square, values for the two may be different; if there is a conflict, usually the likelihood ratio chi-square is favored.) These significant chi-squares, coupled with large residuals, convinces us to regard the no-effect model as inadequate. (If most residuals were small, e.g. < 2, we might accept a model even if its associated chi-squares were significant). Thus, the traditional chi-square, the log-linear, and the logit analysis all lead us to conclude that whether or not the antecedent turn is negative significantly affects whether or not the consequent turn will be negative. As noted earlier, these data appear to reflect a pattern of negative reciprocity.

Residuals and Z-Scores

For other than saturated models, expected counts will usually be different from observed. The question then is, "How should the differences between observed and expected values (the residuals) be evaluated?" In other words, "When is it appropriate to claim that the observed count for a particular cell is significantly greater (or significantly less) than the count generated by a particular model?"

There are at least three reasons why such information is valuable. First, as noted earlier, if all or most residuals are insignificant, it often makes sense to accept the model in question even if the goodness-of-fit statistics are significant, especially if that model is more parsimonious than the next likely candidate. Second, a single large residual can indicate an error in the data or an outlier, which at the very least should occasion discussion. Third, and perhaps most important for devotees of sequential analysis, the analysis of residuals indicates which patterns or sequences occur with greater than chance frequency. This becomes a more interesting question when tables larger than the current 2×2 are considered.

A number of statistics, most distributed approximately as z, have been proposed for the analysis of residuals. One early suggestion, applied to sequential analysis (Bakeman, 1978; Sackett, 1979), used the computation appropriate for a binomial test, but as Allison and Liker (1982) pointed out, this assumes that probability estimates used in the computation represent true values when in fact they are observed values subject to sampling error. Another suggestion is the *standardized residual,* which is simply the residual divided by the square root of its expected value (Bishop, Fienberg, & Holland, 1975, pp. 136–137; Haberman, 1973). This has the merit of being easy to compute, but it tends to underestimate the true value. Another suggestion is the *adjusted residual,* which, according to Haberman, is a better approximation to z (1978, pp. 77–79). It is also equivalent to the computation suggested by Allison and Liker (1982). In addition, for 2×2 tables, all four adjusted residuals are equivalent, which makes intuitive sense, whereas the standardized residuals are not. (See Table 12.4; as a general rule, the approximation to z for standardized residuals is less

TABLE 12.4
Residuals for No-Effect Logit Model (Negative Reciprocity)

LAG0 Code	LAG1 Code	Obs. Count	Exp. Count	Residual	Std. Residual	Adj. Residual
Negate	Negate	62	31.9	30.1	5.33	5.97
Other	Negate	236	266.1	−30.1	−1.85	−5.97
Negate	Other	235	265.1	−30.1	−1.85	−5.97
Other	Other	2243	2212.9	30.1	0.64	5.97

adequate when the number of levels for variables is small.) For all these reasons, we recommend the adjusted residual as the best index of how much observed cell values deviate from their expected values.

COMMON PROBLEMS

In the previous section we analyzed data from the 2×2 contingency table given in Table 12.3. Our intent was to demonstrate, in the context of an admittedly simple example, how easily a log-linear or logit approach to sequential analysis might proceed. In this section we demonstrate further how a number of common problems in sequential analysis can be solved by applying logit models to the appropriate contingency tables. In addition, we show how sequential effects and effects of other research factors can be investigated concurrently. First, however, we address the fundamental question of whether there is enough relatedness in the data even to justify further exploration.

Omnibus Tests of Sequential Constraint

Unless one plans a priori to examine only a few specified patterns, so many different patterns can be tested during an exploratory sequential analysis that the risk of finding some significant by chance alone (type I error) is high. For example, with only five codes on one dimension, 25 different two-event sequences (lag 0-lag 1 pairings) could be tested for significance, given repeatable codes, and 20, given nonrepeatable ones. Before individual two-event sequences are tested, however, the investigator should first determine whether adjacent codes are related in general. Only if they are does it make sense to proceed with an examination of particular pairs.

Such an omnibus test is easily accomplished with an appropriate logit model. Consider, for example, a 5×5 table like the one portrayed in Table 12.2 (repeatable code) or Table 12.5 (nonrepeatable codes). If the counts generated by the no-effect model failed to fit the observed tallies (as indicated by goodness-of-

TABLE 12.5
Counts for Infants' Engagement State

| Lag 0 | Lag 1 | | | | | Totals |
	Uneg	Onlook	Object	Person	Joint	
Unengaged	—	36	38	10	11	95
Onlooking	25	—	107	8	95	235
Object	39	120	—	20	147	326
Person	8	15	14	—	12	49
Joint	25	61	170	11	—	267
TOTALS	97	232	329	49	265	972

fit statistics significantly different from zero), we would infer that lag 1 events are indeed affected by lag 0 ones. Only then would we proceed to individual tests of two-event sequences—just as analysis of variance users would proceed to post hoc tests of differences between pairs of group means only in the presence of a significant group main effect.

One technical matter cannot be ignored. Given nonrepeatable codes, the number of transitions from a particular code at lag 0 to the same code at lag 1 will be zero, not because the transition did not occur (an empirical matter), but because by definition it could not occur (a structural matter). Log-linear programs usually let the user specify which cells, if any, contain such a priori or *structural zeros;* the programs then adjust degrees of freedom and expected counts accordingly.

Testing for Particular Patterns

Usually investigators want to know more than just whether adjacent codes are related in general. They want to know about particular patterns, such as: "Do married couples demonstrate negative reciprocity?"; "Is parallel play a bridge to group play for toddlers?"; "Do mothers respond to their infants' cries by picking them up?"; "How are infants engaged just prior to becoming jointly engaged with their mothers?"

The information needed to answer these questions is produced by the omnibus tests just described. Given the no-effect model, adjusted residuals greater than 1.96 (or less than -1.96) pinpoint which cells differ significantly ($p < .05$) from expected. Of course, the larger the total number of tallies and the larger the expected count for a particular pattern, the better the approximation to z will be; but in general, large residuals indicate sequences that occur significantly more (or less) often than the base rates for their individual components would suggest.

As an example, consider the Bakeman and Adamson (1984) study mentioned earlier. Their counts for pairs of adjacent engagement states observed for 15-month-old infants with their mothers are given in Table 12.5 and results from the no-effect model are given in Table 12.6. This analysis suggests that infants rarely proceeded directly from an Unengaged to a Joint engagement state (the adjusted residual is -3.96), instead infants moved first from Unengaged to Onlooking ($z = 3.48$) and then from Onlooking to Joint engagement ($z = 2.73$). After Joint engagement, Object play was likely ($z = 4.07$), Onlooking unlikely ($z = -3.27$). There was also some suggestion of reciprocal movement between Unengaged and Person engagement (z's = 3.34 and 2.20), but the small expected counts cause us to regard this result with caution.

TABLE 12.6
Residuals for Logit No-Effect Model (Infants' Engagement State)

LAG0 Code	LAG1 Code	Obs. Count	Exp. Count	Residual	Std. Residual	Adj. Residual
Unengaged	Unengaged	0	0	0	0	0
Onlook	Unengaged	25	23.1	1.86	.39	.47
Object	Unengaged	39	42.0	−2.98	−.46	−.67
Person	Unengaged	8	3.9	4.08	2.06[a]	2.20[a]
Joint	Unengaged	25	28.0	−2.96	−.56	−.71
Unengaged	Onlook	36	22.5	13.53	2.85[a]	3.48[a]
Onlook	Onlook	0	0	0	0	0
Object	Onlook	120	119.1	.90	.08	.16
Person	Onlook	15	11.1	3.89	1.17	1.37
Joint	Onlook	61	79.3	−18.32	−2.06[a]	−3.27[a]
Unengaged	Object	38	41.4	−3.41	−.53	−.77
Onlook	Object	107	121.0	−13.96	−1.27	−2.42[a]
Object	Object	0	0	0	0	0
Person	Object	14	20.5	−6.48	−1.43	−1.95
Joint	Object	170	146.2	23.8	1.97[a]	4.07[a]
Unengaged	Person	10	3.8	6.16	3.14[a]	3.34[a]
Onlook	Person	8	11.2	−3.23	−.96	−1.13
Object	Person	20	20.4	−.37	−.08	−.11
Person	Person	0	0	0	0	0
Joint	Person	11	13.6	−2.56	−.70	−.85
Unengaged	Joint	11	27.3	−16.28	−3.12[a]	−3.96[a]
Onlook	Joint	95	79.7	15.32	1.72	2.73[a]
Object	Joint	147	144.6	2.44	.20	.42
Person	Joint	12	13.5	−1.49	−.41	−.49
Joint	Joint	0	0	0	0	0

[a]$p < .05$

Testing for Group Differences

As Castellan (1979), Allison and Liker (1982), and others noted, the contingency table or log-linear approach is advantageous because it can easily be generalized to more complicated situations. For example, a follow-up question for the analysis just presented might be, ''Does the Onlooking-to-Joint engagement pattern characterize older infants as well?'' Indeed, often investigators want to know not only which interactive patterns occur in their data, but whether different groups of infants, dyads, couples, and so forth, manifest different patterns.

As an illustration of the log-linear approach to such questions, we use an example based on a study by Gottman (1980) and reanalyzed by Allison and Liker (1982; see Table 12.7). Two questions posed by Gottman were: ''Is a wife's acting or not dependent on whether her husband has just acted?'' And, ''Is the degree of this dependency different for distressed and nondistressed couples?''

In order to determine the strength of different effects, first we computed the coefficients for the no-effect or saturated logit model (see Table 12.8). The significant [WIFE1] term merely tells us that the probabilities for the wife's two responses at lag 1 (Act/No-Act) were not equal. The significant [WIFE1 HUSB0] term signals a husband main effect: Wives acted 49% of the time when their husbands had just acted but only 34% of the time when their husbands had not. Similarly, the significant [WIFE1 GROUP] term indicates a group main effect: distressed wives acted 34%, and nondistressed wives 55%, of the time. However, the degree of dependency was not significantly different for distressed

TABLE 12.7
Counts for Wife's Acts

Husband Lag 0	Wife Lag 1		Totals
	Act	No-Act	
A. Distressed Couples			
Act	76	100	176
No-Act	79	200	279
TOTALS	155	300	455
B. Nondistressed Couples			
Act	80	63	143
No-Act	43	39	82
TOTALS	123	102	225

Note. Based on Gottman (1980); counts from Allison and Liker (1982).

TABLE 12.8
Coefficients for Saturated Logit Model (Wife's Acts)

Term	Coefficient	Z-Value
[WIFE1]	−.108	−2.52
[WIFE1 HUSB0]	.099	2.32
[WIFE1 GROUP]	−.192	−4.48
[WIFE1 HUSB0 GROUP]	.064	1.49

and nondistressed groups. If it were, then the husband by group interaction (indicated by the [WIFE1 HUSB0 GROUP] term) would be significant. Indeed, a model with this term eliminated generated expected counts not significantly different from those observed (likelihood ratio chi-square = 2.23, Pearson chi-square = 2.24, $df = 1$, $p = .135$ for both), verifying that the effect of the husband on the wife did *not* interact with type of couple. This is the same conclusion Allison and Liker reached.

For a second example of the ease with which log-linear analyses combine sequential and other variables, let us return to the notion of negative reciprocity discussed by Cousins and Power (1986). Recall that turns of talk were recorded as Negate or Other; Table 12.3 gives tallies for all two-event sequences so coded. However, some sequences began with the wife, others with the husband speaking, and in addition, some couples were categorized as moderately adjusted and others as very highly adjusted. Thus the data in Table 12.3 could be reclassified into four separate 2 × 2 tables: One table for each type of couple would tally sequences that began with the wife, the other sequences that began with the husband. Combining these four tables results in a four-dimensional 2 × 2 × 2 × 2 table. This table is not easy to visualize, but its four dimensions are:

(a) Lag 0 (Negate/Other)
(b) Lag 1 (Negate/Other)
(c) Initiator (Husband/Wife)
(d) Adjustment (Moderate/High)

The saturated model for this table would include eight terms:

[LAG1] [LAG1 LAG0] [LAG1 INI] [LAG1 ADJ]
[LAG1 LAG0 INI] [LAG1 LAG0 ADJ] [LAG1 INI ADJ]
[LAG1 LAG0 INI ADJ].

As before, a significant coefficient associated with the first term indicates only that the two LAG1 response categories are not equally probable. The next three terms indicate main effects and answer the questions: is the probability of Negate at lag 1 affected by whether the lag 0 code is Negate or not, by whether the initiator is the husband or wife, and by whether the couples are moderately or highly adjusted? The following three terms indicate two-way interactions and address an interesting series of questions: Is one spouse more likely than the other to elicit negative reciprocity, is one adjustment group more likely than the other to manifest negative reciprocity, and is the likelihood that one spouse more than the other will elicit a negative response different for the two adjustment groups? The final term indicates a three-way interaction; if a fitting model required it, interpretation would depend on the data. The point of this example, however, is to show how easily other variables can be incorporated with sequential ones in a single log-linear design so that the analysis of appropriate logit models can answer substantive questions concerned both with sequential patterns and with group differences in the manifestation of those patterns.

Additional Applications of Logit Models

Space does not permit extended explication here, but we should point out that a number of common problems in sequential analysis—e.g., analyzing important but rare events, testing for stationarity, and controlling for autocorrelation—afford simple and elegant log-linear solutions.[1] Investigators may suspect, for example, that certain events profoundly affect the events that follow. Yet, if these influential events occur only rarely, two few tallies may be accumulated for a reliable sequential analysis. A solution is to treat the rare event as a point of demarcation, a point in time when the rules may change. Then, in addition to whatever dimensions were coded at first, the other events can also be coded Before/After, depending on their position relative to the rare event. If the sequencing of these other events is affected by the rare event, then no fitting model can ignore the Before/After dimension.

Testing for stationarity can be viewed in a similar way. When conducting a sequential analysis, we assume that the data collected were generated by an underlying process. Thus pooling data generated by more than one process together is a serious matter. Such data lack ''stationarity,'' which means that the process or rule responsible for generating the data has changed midstream. If we regard a point at which the rules might change as a rare event, then the test procedure for stationarity is the same as that for rare events—a test for the importance of a Before/After dimension in our analysis.

Logit models can also be used to examine autocorrelative effects. Because a persons's present behavior is often best predicted from that person's past, not from someone else's past, before concluding that one individual influences an-

---

[1]An extended version of this chapter is available from the first author. It details these topics and, in addition, gives SPSS statements for all models discussed.

other (e.g., a mother, her child; a husband, his wife), it is often important first to control for the person's own past (Allison & Liker, 1982; Gottman & Ringland, 1981). This is easily accomplished with a log-linear approach. For example, one dimension of a contingency table could code wife's present behavior; another, husband's antecedent behavior; and a third, the wife's antecedent. Then, given the logit model:

$$[W1] \; [W1 \; W0] \; [W1 \; H0],$$

the [W1 W0] term would represent the wife's autocorrelative effect, and the [W1 H0] term, the effect of the husband's past on his wife's present, controlling for the wife's past behavior.

CONCLUSIONS

In the course of writing this chapter, we have become passionately committed to the log-linear approach. First, it provides a simple, single, unified way of treating most common sequential analysis problems. Investigators need only construct contingency tables, labeled and lagged in ways that reflect their substantive concerns. Nothing more, except for some clear thinking (and a computer program like SPSS' LOGLINEAR), is needed. Second, other variables (e.g., clinic/non-clinic, parent/child, 3-month/6-month/9-month) can easily be combined with sequential variables in a single design. This results in straightforward analyses than can reflect an investigator's substantive concerns with considerable fidelity. In addition, log-linear analyses have a number of technical advantages. For example, they are statistically efficient and make few assumptions about the data.

Throughout this chapter, we have stressed the simplicity of the log-linear approach as well as its conceptual overlap with topics more familiar to behavioral investigators, such as analysis of variance. We should further stress, however, that—as simple as we think log-linear analyses may be—our discussion has left a number of useful and technical topics untouched. We encourage interested readers to consult both local experts and the references cited here (e.g., Kennedy, 1983; Norusis, 1985) for further advice and information. Still, the information provided here should allow readers to begin with relatively simple log-linear sequential analyses almost immediately.

ACKNOWLEDGMENTS

We thank Jeffrey Cohn, Daryl Nenstiel, Bruce Dorval, Josephine Brown, David Baldwin, Marguerite Stevenson, and William Griffin for comments on an earlier draft. Portions of this work were supported by grant HD23206 from the National Institute of Child Health and Human Development.

REFERENCES

Allison, P. D., & Liker, J. K. Analyzing sequential categorical data on dyadic interaction: A comment on Gottman. *Psychological Bulletin, 1982, 91,* 393–403.

Bakeman, R. Untangling streams of behavior: Sequential analyses of observation data. In G. P. Sackett (Ed.), *Observing behavior* (Vol. *2, Data collection and analysis methods,* pp. 63–78). Baltimore: University Park Press, 1978.

Bakeman, R., & Adamson, L. B. Coordinating attention to people and objects in mother-infant and peer-infant interaction. *Child Development, 1984, 55,* 1278–1289.

Bakeman, R., & Brownlee, J. R. The strategic use of parallel play: A sequential analysis. *Child Development, 1980, 51,* 873–878.

Bakeman, R., & Gottman, J. M. *Observing interaction: An introduction to sequential analysis.* New York: Cambridge University Press, 1986.

Bakeman, R., & Gottman, J. M. Applying observational methods: A systematic view. In J. Osofsky (Ed.), *Handbook of infant development* (2d ed., pp. 818–854). New York: Wiley, 1987.

Bishop, Y. M. M., Fienberg, S. R., & Holland, P. W. *Discrete multivariate analysis: Theory and practice.* Cambridge, MA: MIT Press, 1975.

Castellan, N. J., Jr. The analysis of behavior sequences. In R. B. Cairns (Ed.), *The analysis of social interactions: Methods, issues, and illustrations* (pp. 81–116). Hillsdale, NJ: Lawrence Erlbaum Associates, 1979.

Cohn, J. F., & Tronick, E. Z. Mother-infant face-to-face interaction: The sequence of dyadic states at 3, 6, and 9 months. *Developmental Psychology, 1987, 23,* 68–77.

Cousins, P. C., & Power, T. G. Quantifying family process: Issues in the analysis of interaction sequences. *Family Process, 1986, 25,* 89–105.

Dorval, B., & Eckerman, C. O. The development of conversation. *Monographs of the Society for Research in Child Development, 1984, 49* (No. 2).

Fienberg, S. E. *The analysis of cross-classified categorical data* (2d ed.). Cambridge, MA: MIT Press, 1980.

Goodman, L. A., & Kruskal, W. H. Measures of association for cross-classifications. *Journal of the American Statistical Association, 1954, 49,* 732–764.

Gottman, J. M. *Marital interaction: Experimental investigations.* New York: Academic Press, 1980.

Gottman, J. M., & Ringland, J. T. The analysis of dominance and bidirectionality in social development. *Child Development, 1981, 52,* 393–412.

Green, J. A. Loglinear analysis of cross-classified ordinal data: Applications in developmental research. *Child Development, 1988, 59,* 1–25.

Haberman, S. J. The analysis of residuals in cross-classified tables. *Biometrics, 1973, 29,* 205–220.

Haberman, S. J. *Analysis of qualitative data* (Vol. 1). New York: Academic Press, 1978.

Haberman, S. J. *Analysis of qualitative data* (Vol. 2). New York: Academic Press, 1979.

Hops, H., Willis, T. A., Patterson, G. R., & Weiss, R. L. Marital Interaction Coding System, Eugene, OR: University of Oregon and Oregon Research Institute, 1971. (order from ASIS/ NAPS, Microfiche Publications, 305 E. 46th St., New York, NY 10017).

Kennedy, J. J. *Analyzing qualitative data: Introductory log-linear analysis for behavioral research.* New York: Praeger, 1983.

Konner, M. Infancy among the Kalahari Desert San. In P. H. Leiderman, S. R. Tulkin, & A. Rosenfeld (Eds.), *Culture and infancy: Variations in the human experience* (pp. 287–327). New York: Academic Press, 1977.

Parten, M. B. Social participation among preschool children. *Journal of Abnormal and Social Psychology, 1932, 27,* 243–269.

Norusis, M. J. *SPSSX advanced statistics guide.* New York: McGraw-Hill, 1985.

Sackett, G. P. The lag sequential analysis of contingency and cyclicity in behavioral interaction research. In J. Osofsky (Ed.), *Handbook of infant development,* (pp. 623–649). New York: Wiley, 1979.

Sackett, G. P. Analysis of sequential social interaction data: Some issues, recent developments, and a causal inference model. In J. Osofsky (Eds.), *Handbook of infant development,* (2d ed., pp. 855–878). New York: Wiley, 1987.

SPSS *SPSSX user's guide* (2d ed.). New York: McGraw-Hill, 1986.

Stevenson, M. B., Ver Hoeve, J. N., Roach, M. A., & Leavitt, L. A. The beginning of conversation: Early patterns of mother-infant vocal responsiveness. *Infant Behavior and Development,* 1986, *9,* 423–440.

Upton, G. J. G. *The analysis of cross-tabulated data.* New York: Wiley, 1978.

Vietze, P. M., Abernathy, S. R., Ashe, M. L., & Faulstich, G. Contingent interaction between mothers and their developmentally delayed infants. In G. P. Sackett (Ed.), *Observing behavior* (Vol. 1, *Theory and application in mental retardation,* pp. 115–132). Baltimore: University Park Press, 1978.

13 The Gene-Culture Connection: Interactions Across Levels of Analysis

Charles J. Lumsden
Department of Medicine
University of Toronto

INTRODUCTION

Whether engaged in thought or action, human beings are biological organisms exploiting a largely cultural environment. Their psychological development joins three great levels of organization—the genetic, the cognitive, and the social—into a single pattern of causal interaction. For any aspect of human development, it is appropriate to ask the degree to which a behavior reflects an intrinsic biological nature, a mediating cognitive process, a shaping cultural factor. All researchers agree for instance that at a rather trivial level we are constrained by our biological make-up. Few dispute that a lack of wings effectively bars us from aerial competition with hummingbirds and dragonflies. But controversy arises when we dig deeper and ask what role, if any, biological factors play in specifying the particulars of thought and in the differences observed among individuals and among societies with respect to social behavior. A number of investigators have asserted that biology is irrelevant to such enterprises (e.g., Bock, 1980; Harris, 1979; Sahlins, 1976; Trigg, 1982). Though biological constraints may exist, they are more or less constant across all individuals and cultures, producing a uniform potential for cognitive development overlain by the effects of social learning. The interaction of biology with mind is nil.

This strictly environmentalist view of human psychology, socialization, and cultural evolution is of course subject to empirical scrutiny. The results have been disquieting. Particularly relevant are investigations indicating innate biases in many aspects of human cognitive development, including proportionate representation of vision versus other perceptual modalities in vocabularies, color classification, forms of mother-infant bonding and communication, the timing of the fear-of-stranger responses, predication during logic, and phoneme formation in the development of linguistic structures (see Lumsden & Wilson, 1981, 1985; Lumsden & Gushurt, 1985; Findlay & Lumsden, 1988, for extensive reviews). These data provide strong evidence that for many facets of human socialization, the strictly environmental view is unwarranted. Instead we must think of biological and environmental information acting together, and combining with individual cognitive activity to determine patterns of mental development. The resulting system of interactions in development is termed *gene-culture transmission* (Lumsden & Wilson, 1981, 1983, 1985).

The concept of gene-culture transmission is more than a reminder that both genetic and cultural factors ultimately influence development. Rather, it suggests the existence of a specific developmental strategy within human beings, in which innately prescribed mechanisms in the growing mind determine that some, rather than other, aspects of the cultural environment will affect mental development. Thus, for example, spatial proximity of peers during early years of development is overwhelmingly likely to constitute the cultural basis for individual sibling incest avoidance, even when alternative plausible influences such as general social trends or strong training pressures are present (Shepher, 1971; Wolf, 1968; Wolf & Huang, 1980). A developmental strategy of this nature contrasts markedly with that of the pure cultural transmission inherent in an environmentalist perspective. In the latter, genetic constraints within the developing organism allow cultural effects wide latitude in what can be learned and how. In gene-culture transmission, on the other hand, the individual is born with information determining likely developmental pathways. These respond only to certain kinds of cultural input, and then only in certain directions.

At the heart of gene-culture transmission are the *epigenetic rules,* genetically encoded algorithms that modulate the developmental responses to ambient conditions. The existence of epigenetic rules in no way implies that cognition and behavior are genetically hardwired (i.e., that knowledge of the composition of an individual's genome allows us to predict behavior or cognition): In *Homo sapiens,* only a tiny fraction of stereotypical autonomous behaviors are innately determined. Rather, the epigenetic rules organize the logic of an organism's developmental response to experience. In his seminal monograph *The Strategy of the Genes,* C. H. Waddington (1957) likened organic development to a ball rolling on a hilly surface. In the case of complete environmental determinism, the surface is flat; the ball wanders erratically at the whim of every environmental stimulus. But more generally the situation is epigenetic: information in the genome has the potential to prescribe a sharply ridged surface. For all but the most highly determined behaviors (corresponding to pathways through very deep valleys), development is to a greater or lesser degree sensitive to environmental perturbation; the ball can, for example, be diverted from one valley to another. But it cannot perch upon a peak. To the psychologist, peaks in the epigenetic landscape represent forbidden designs for the human mind, fenced off by the genetic constitution of the individual.

The empirical evidence supporting the notion of epigenetic rules has been reviewed elsewhere (Lumsden, 1983; Lumsden & Gushurst, 1985; Lumsden & Wilson, 1981, 1983, 1985; and see below). Suffice it to say here that, consistent with the instances already cited, most aspects of human cognitive development and socialization for which there are appropriate data are apparently sustained by gene-culture transmission, rather than by pure cultural transmission or its converse, genetic determinism. Thus cognition, learning, and enculturation appear to reflect the activity of a tightly integrated, hierarchical system of interactions. At the center is the developing organism, with causal influences upon it reaching upward from biology and stretching downward from the overlying social structure. This interactive system is called a heterarchy, in which all the various levels of organization are highly interdependent.

Very recently it has become possible to represent formally, and thus map with quantitative precision, this interacting system of genes, mind, and culture. The basic step has been to create a strengthened alliance between evolutionary theory and the human sciences. The alliance takes the form of mathematical models built to specify the mechanics of gene-culture transmission, including its effects on individual thought and action. Reciprocally, the consequences for social history of the individual's capacity for learning, discovery, and choice can be deduced with some exactitude (at least for simple models!) and incorporated into methods of historical explanation.

The role of evolutionary thinking is crucial to this enterprise. Most of science is concerned with *how*-questions: how the understanding of number develops, how action potentials are generated, how genes prescribe information. Evolutionary theory concentrates on *why*-questions: why the pattern of human creative potential develops in a certain way or why parents behave altruistically toward their offspring. All psychological phenomena call for both why- and how-questions (Lumsden & Wilson, 1983). The scientific query *"why?"* can be answered only by the study of history, and the history of psychobiological processes is by definition evolution. In this manner, through the why-questions, psychological phenomena can be embedded deductively in historical process—both cultural and biological—and vice versa.

People, however, do not duplicate themselves during the process of biological reproduction. They replicate their genes. From the viewpoint of evolutionary theory, all of the traits of individuals are potential enabling devices for the expansive replication of hereditary material. Color vision, linguistic competence, nerve cell circuits, aesthetic sensibility, and tenderness toward children are potentially means by which genes spread through future generations. Thus with the same stroke that sets mind within history, an evolutionary approach creates both the rationale and methodology for inferring the contributions of underlying biological factors to individual and social development.

This prospect of a mathematically based theoretical psychology, setting mind in the context of biological and cultural process, is I believe an important one. Not only does psychological explanation then take account of the evolutionary background to human behavior across the lifespan, but reciprocally, evolutionary thinking is enriched by psychological concepts. Evolutionary attempts at explaining our behaviors and mental characteristics traditionally have employed a folk-theoretic psychology bordering on the utterly simplistic, if not profoundly embarrassing (see reviews in Lumsden & Wilson, 1981, 1983). The rapprochement of behavioral and evolutionary disciplines is therefore one of great potential and timeliness. My intent here is to sketch the mechanism linking genes, mind, and culture as clarified by evolutionary studies in recent years, and to describe how a formal approach to psychological variables mediating learning, development, and choice can be developed on the basis of this new knowledge.

TRANSITIONS FROM MIND TO CULTURE

A key interaction that can be very usefully examined, once the existence of epigenetic rules has been delineated and their role in sustaining human mental development described, is the translation from cognition to cultural pattern. Progress here means that properties of culture—that is, properties of the socially shared and transmitted systems of information by which people understand the world and act within it—can be deduced from information about the core properties of human nature and their epigenesis. One would also then be in a position to estimate both the effects that alterations in the core properties exert on culture and society and the way in which at least some epigenetic rules appear to use information about large-scale properties of culture (such as the existence of certain religions, or the net frequency of usage of a particular belief or behavior) in guiding mental development and individual decision making.

Decision Making

In carrying out this step from mind to culture, one must account not only for the correlated activity of many individuals' developmental histories in the presence of diverse learnable information, but also for the overall cultural properties and the influence these patterns have on cognition. In evolutionary time, multiple genotypes with different epigenetic rules and cognitive properties are exposed to the culture. To calculate Darwinian fitness, a life-history reproduction function must be evaluated for each genotype in the interacting assembly of organisms. The procedure we have followed is to recognize the inherently probabilistic nature of human choice and decision together with the inevitable uncertainties about environment and social structure. One can then formulate the approach in a manner that predicts the likelihood of observing given cultural patterns of behavior. (For example, in .8 of societies, .3 of the members express culture trait c_1 and .7 express c_2, where c_1 and c_2 are learnable belief systems stored as schemas in long-term memory; in .1 of the societies, .5 of the members express c_1 and .5

express c_2; and so on through all possible patterns of c_1 and c_2 expression or usage.) Thus, in deriving such likelihood distributions or *ethnographic curves* (Lumsden & Wilson, 1981, 1985), we are in fact dealing with the basic patterns of cultural diversity of the kind traditionally inferred by cultural anthropologists and other social scientists. An ethnographic curve represents the set of probabilities that a given society will possess particular cultural patterns.

Our chain of reasoning can be illustrated by means of a brief formal sketch. Detailed discussion can be found in Lumsden and Wilson (1981). For ease of illustration, consider a society that contains N members at time t, of whom n_1 base their actions on trait c_1 and n_2 on c_2 during a given time interval. From the standpoint of choice, an individual life history contains a succession of decision points at which outcomes must be determined and their consequences evaluated. A relevant product of the epigenetic rules for this type of activity is the function $u_{ij}(n_1)$ representing the likelihood that that at a decision point an individual using c_i in behavior will decide to use c_j when the other n_1 members are using c_i. (By "usage" I meant that an individual's activity is significantly influenced by the particular learnable belief or knowledge system.)

The mean lifetime between sequential decision points at which epigenetic rules take effect, is τ_1 for a c_1 user and τ_2 for a c_2 user. The quantities τ_1 and τ_2 are the means of the probability distributions for holding times in states c_1 and c_2. The probability densities are assumed exponential, so that the underlying cognitive system obeys the dynamics of the Markovian learning and decision process. In other words, the psychology of choice and decision is influenced by the presence of memory, but these memories extend only a fixed interval into the past (in the case of the Markovian approximation, one time-step into the past). Despite its simplicity, this approximation has proven useful in many applications to individual decision and group dynamics (e.g., Atkinson, Bower & Crothers, 1965; Bartholomew, 1973; Coleman, 1964, 1973; Greeno, 1974; Kemeny & Snell, 1962).

How are the properties of the epigenetic rules translated into a social pattern? The heart of the procedure is a balance equation written to specify the rate at which the entire culture changes from one state to another. In essence, we are searching for the rate and direction of change of ethnographic curves of various kinds of cultures, and the steady-state ethnographic curves toward which many societies as a whole tend to converge. The transition rates for decision making are given by the function $v_{ij}(n_1)$ for each individual where

$$v_{12}(n_1) = \tau_1^{-1}u_{12}(n_1) \text{ and } v_{21}(n_1) = \tau_2^{-1}u_{21}(n_1). \qquad [1]$$

The transition rates express the probabilities per unit time that, given a specific preference of choice, a particular choice will be made. Activity in the society as a whole can then be characterized at time t by the vector $\mathbf{n} = (n_1, n_2)$, the number of individuals using the two culture traits. The quantity of interest is the probability $P(\mathbf{n},t)$, the likelihood at time t that n_1 members are using c_1 and n_2

are using c_2 in planning their behavior. The set of probabilities $\{P(\mathbf{n},t)\}$ for all possible usage patterns subject to the constraint $n_1 + n_2 = N$ is the ethnographic curve of the society.

To link the properties of the ethnographic curve $P(\mathbf{n},t)$ to individual psychology, we note that in any differential interval of time dt the probability of two or more simultaneous decisions is of the order $(dt)^2$ and is negligible. Then if the society moves from state (n_1', n_2') at time t to a different state (n_1,n_2) at time $t + dt$, it can only be that

$$(n_1', n_2') = (n_1 + 1, n_2 - 1) \text{ or } (n_1', n_2') = (n_1 - 1, n_2 + 1). \qquad [2]$$

It follows that the whole-society transition rate to or from a state $\mathbf{n} = (n_1, n_2)$ is equal to the transition rate $v_{ij}(n_1)$ for an individual multiplied by the number of individuals in the c_i group from which the transition took place. It can then be shown that the rate of change in any cultural state $\mathbf{n}$ is related to the possible alternative patterns of cultural organization and to the transition rate functions for individual choice by the formula:

$$\begin{aligned}
\frac{dP(n_1,n_2,t)}{dt} = & (n_1 + 1)v_{12}(n_1 + 1,n_2 - 1)P(n_1 + 1,n_2 - 1,t) \\
& + (n_2 + 1)v_{21}(n_1 - 1,n_2 + 1)P(n_1 - 1,n_2 + 1,t) \\
& - [n_1 v_{12}(n_1,n_2) + n_2 v_{21}(n_1,n_2)]P(n_1,n_2,t)
\end{aligned} \qquad [3]$$

for $0 < n_1 < N$, with similar forms when $n_1 = 0$, or $n_1 = N$. Thus, for example, the coefficient multiplying the ethnographic likelihood P in the first term of Equation [3] reflects a process in which, as the number n_1 of individuals in the c_1 group increases, the rate of change in the ethnographic curve $P(\mathbf{n},t)$ rises in direct proportion. This direct proportional relationship linking the product of group size together with the psychology of preference and the ethnographic curve is expressed in each of the terms contributing additively to Equation [3].

If an individual lifetime contains sufficiently many points of choice and decision then, except for a relatively brief interval of initial decay, the ethnographic curve for this process is well approximated by the steady state

$$P(n_1,n_2) = P(0,N) \binom{N}{n_1} \exp \sum_{i=1}^{n_1} \ln \frac{v_{21}(i - 1)}{v_{12}(i)} \qquad [4]$$

where

$$P(0,N) = \left[1 + \sum_{n_1=1}^{N} P(n_1,N - n_1) \right]^{-1} \qquad [5]$$

is the normalization factor guaranteeing that the sum of $P(\mathbf{n},t)$ over all possible cultural states $\mathbf{n}$ adds to unity. Thus, the basic structure of an ethnographic curve is that of a product of ratios in which the individual ratios express the relative likelihoods of transition across the range of possible cultural patterns. The steady-state model is best suited to $P(n_1,n_2)$ that are relatively sharp (low variance) and unimodal. Unimodal $P(n_1,n_2)$, which can arise easily with nonlinear rules for choice $v_{ij}(n_1)$, can trap the society in long-lived metastable states far from the steady-state condition (Lumsden, 1988).

When the group size N is large, these relations for the ethnographic curve can be cast into a more convenient form by using continuous variables. For two-schema systems a convenient measure for the cultural pattern is the variable

$$\xi \equiv 1 - 2n_1/N. \qquad [6]$$

Evidently the variable ξ takes on values between -1 and 1 depending on the number of c_1 individuals in the society. When no member has chosen c_2, the value of ξ is -1. A social revolution that sweeps a society's traits entirely from c_1 to c_2 changes the value of ξ from -1 to $+1$. The variable ξ changes by progressively smaller increments $\Delta\xi = N^{-1}$ as N increases. In the limit $\Delta\xi \rightarrow 0$ of large group sizes the equation of motion for the ethnographic curve is accurately modeled by a continuous-variable expression

$$\frac{\partial}{\partial t} P(\xi,t) = \frac{-\partial}{\partial\xi} [X(\xi)P(\xi,t)] + \frac{1}{2} \frac{\partial^2}{\partial\xi^2} [Q(\xi)P(\xi,t)] \qquad [7]$$

easier to solve than the formulation [3] in terms of discrete variables n_1. The functions $X(\xi)$, $Q(\xi)$ express the effects on cultural pattern of the transition rates for individual choice. The structure of $X(\xi)$, $Q(\xi)$ is once more that of additive functions whose individual terms are proportional to the abundance of usage and the transition rate function for making individual choices:

$$X(\xi) = (1 - \xi)v_{12}(\xi) - (1 + \xi)v_{21}(\xi) \qquad [8]$$

$$Q(\xi) = \frac{2}{N} [(1 - \xi)v_{12}(\xi) + (1 + \xi)v_{21}(\xi)] \qquad [9]$$

The associated steady-state of the ethnographic distribution is then simply

$$P(\xi) = \frac{C}{Q(\xi)} \left[\exp\ 2 \int_{-1}^{\xi} \frac{X(\xi')}{Q(\xi')}\ d\xi' \right], \qquad [10]$$

where C is a normalization constant determined by the requirement that the total area under $P(\xi)$ be equal to unity, and the integral plays the role in Equation [10] of the summation of discrete variates in equation [4].

The Structure of Ethnographic Curves

A steady-state ethnographic curve does not mean that the society itself is static or unchanging in time. A society is a system in flux, in which the numbers of its members using different traits c_i to organize their behavior. As individuals encounter decision situations and some switch their active c_i, the cultural pattern moves back and forth on the usage scale $n_1 = 0, 1, 2,. . .,N$. The ethnographic curve expresses the proportion of its history that the society spends in a particular cultural pattern $\mathbf{n} = (n_1,n_2)$. Equivalently, for this class of models it also expresses the proportion of an ensemble of very similar societies expected to be characterized at any time by a particular pattern of cultural usage or expression $\mathbf{n}$.

It is possible to quantify the response of the ethnographic curves to changes in the likelihood $u_{ij}(n_1)$ and transition rates $v_{ij}(n_1)$, which, we recall, are themselves developmental products of the epigenetic rules. For a wide range of u_{ij} and v_{ij} behaviors, the ethnographic curves shift from a unimodal to a sharply multi-modal form when the characteristic parameters of the usage bias curves cross a short interval (Lumsden & Wilson, 1981, 1985). Moreover, the ethnographic curve is sensitive to small changes in the epigenetic rules of its members. Because of the location of the quantities $\ln v_{ij}(n_1)$ in the exponent of $P(n_1,n_2)$, only a small amount of innate bias in the epigenetic rules, favoring one or the other of the learnable culture traits c_i, can be amplified to cause relatively large changes at the cultural level.

Are the epigenetic rules of human cognitive development in fact strong enough to create this type of amplification effect? It seems that the answer is yes. When quantitative estimates are made from data concerning the development of c_i choice or activation, this ratio deviates substantially from unity—in other words, from the unbiased state. For example, in early sugar preference (Maller & Desor, 1974), the usage likelihood ratio c_1, c_2 is between .4/.6 and .25/.75, a bias that extends at least into childhood and affects the behavioral practices surrounding adult cuisine. In the case of greater attention to the schematic design of the human face (Freedman, 1974), the ratio has been between $\geq .51/.49$ and $\geq .6/.4$, depending on the competing designs employed. The bias leads to long-term focusing on the face, especially the eyes; the facilitation of parent-offspring bonding, and possibly the facilitation of later forms of interpersonal bonding. During the first 5–7 years of life, children reared in close domestic proximity avoid full sexual relationships with a bias approaching 100%. In the adult years this aversion shapes marriage patterns and cultural taboos against sibling incest. Other epigenetic rules show comparable deviations from the tabula rasa state, all of which are sufficently large to create large-scale changes in the structure of the ethnographic curves.

FEEDBACK: FROM CULTURE
AND COGNITION TO THE GENES

Under the influence of the biologically grounded epigenetic rules, the members of a society create a substantial portion of their own environment in the form of culture, within which each mind develops. But the society is also a biological population in which the form of the epigenetic rules can vary genetically. The relative survival and reproductive success of different genotypes depend both on the culture schemas c_i (plans, belief systems, knowledge structures, etc.) the society's members employ in organizing their behavior, and on the surrounding culture that sets the context of each specific decision. The interaction of these two levels—person as embodied mind, and culture—constitutes a heterarchical structure. In hierarchies or multilevel structures of classical conception, whole-system properties are created by interactions among the component subsystems. In contrast, cultures are heterarchies—mixed-level systems where subsystems (the individual person)—perceive and respond to whole-culture features, including institutions, social norms, and usage patterns. At the same time, individual actions come together to determine these whole-culture features (for detailed discussion, see Findlay & Lumsden, 1988). Thus, genetic and cultural evolution are coupled together in a manner that constitutes a single coevolutionary system (Figure 13.1). Much discussion has focussed on whether, and under what circumstances, this coupling is strong or weak (review in Findlay & Lumsden, 1988; Lumsden, 1988; Lumsden & Wilson, 1981, 1985).

We have found that it is possible to formulate the structure of this heterarchial interaction and the resulting coevolutionary system in mathematical terms, allowing a quantitative analysis of its import for developmental psychology. In the mathematical theory of population genetics, evolution is defined as a change from generation to generation in the relative abundance of different genes (i.e., changes in the gene frequencies). Similarly, an evolutionary approach of relevance to psychology and the interaction across multiple levels must track changes in both the gene frequencies and the relative abundance of culturally transmitted traits c_i. The culture traits c_i, prior to their encoding as schemas in the individual person, are the raw material of culture used by the epigenetic rules in assembling the mind. Thus, in place of the more familiar population-genetic equations of the form:

$$p_k(t) = \text{function of the other gene frequencies and environmental parameters}$$

for the change over time of frequency p_k of a gene G_k, one wants to formulate equations that reveal explicitly the behavior-dependent interactions of genetic change with alterations in cultural form:

$$p_k(t) = \text{function of the gene frequencies,}$$
$$c_i \text{ frequencies, and environmental properties;} \qquad [14a]$$

$$c_k(t) = \text{function of the gene frequencies,}$$
$$c_i \text{ frequencies, and environmental properties} \qquad [14b]$$

for genes G_k and culture traits c_k. (For convenience I have used the same symbol, c_k, to refer both to the culturally manifested schema itself and to its relative

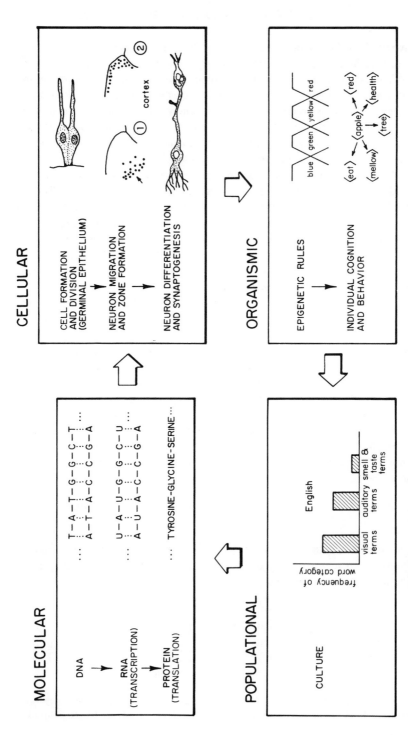

FIG. 13.1. The circuit of gene-culture coevolution showing the principal levels of interaction. From Lumsden and Wilson (1981). Reprinted by permission.

abundance in the class of schemas of similar type. In general, the intended meaning will be clear from the context.)

Analysis of systems with equations of the form [14a &b] present a challenge not only because of the complexity of the dependent phenomena, but also because of the multiple levels of interaction represented in the coevolutionary circuit (recall Figure 13.1). The epigenetic rules, their operation during mental development, and the vagaries of individual decision and behavior all intervene. Until recently, it has not been possible to formulate this linkage conceptually in a manner that takes account of its effects while placing genes and culture in correct juxtaposition, as in Equation [14].

To see what can now be done, let us for brevity use the symbol G represent the level of genetic organization, M the level of mental and behavioral organization, and C the level of cultural organization. We have seen that a description of the operation of the epigenetic rules provides a means of transition between G and M. Let us denote this action of transition between the two levels G and M by Ep, so that $Ep: G \rightarrow M$. The translation between individual decisions (represented by the decision functions u_{ij}, v_{ij}) and cultural patterns represented by the ethnographic curve $P(\mathbf{n},t)$ provides a mapping B between mind M and culture C: $B : M \rightarrow C$. Thus under the combined action of Ep and B, the levels G, M, and C are linked

$$
\begin{array}{c}
\overset{Ep}{G \rightarrow M} \\
\downarrow {\scriptstyle B} \\
C
\end{array}
\qquad [15]
$$

Coevolutionary systems with the form of Equation [14] will follow if it is possible to find the transition mapping T of gene-culture translation between G and C such that T is equivalent in its action to the combined operations $B \cdot Ep$:

$$
\begin{array}{c}
\overset{Ep}{G \rightarrow M} \\
{\scriptstyle T}\searrow \; \downarrow {\scriptstyle B} \\
C
\end{array}
\qquad [16]
$$

Because T is produced by the system of interactions $B \cdot Ep$ and the dynamics φ of gene-culture coevolution predict the future state of the system from its current state and the rules [14] of evolutionary change, we have the relations

$$
\begin{array}{ccc}
G(t_0) & \overset{T}{\rightarrow} & C(t_0) \\
{\scriptstyle \varphi}\downarrow & & \downarrow {\scriptstyle \varphi} \\
G(t_1 > t_0) & \underset{T}{\rightarrow} & C(t_1 > t_0)
\end{array}
\qquad [17]
$$

expressing how the inter-level transitions T and the process φ of coevolution work together to shape the patterns of genetic (G) and cultural (C) order for the times t_0, t_1 and so on relevant to the history of society.

In the interactive structure [17] as presented above, the gene-culture connection looks like a fancy exercise in genetic determinism, with all the causal effects feeding forward from genes through the mind to culture. That this is manifestly *not* the case is seen by noting that processes Ep and B are both highly culture-dependent (culture C providing learnable information and judgemental context to Ep and B respectively), so $Ep = Ep(C)$, $B = B(C)$, whence

$$
\begin{array}{ccc}
& Ep(C) & \\
G & \rightarrow & M \\
{\scriptstyle T=T(C)} \searrow & & \downarrow {\scriptstyle B(C)} \\
& C &
\end{array}
\qquad [18]
$$

and the dynamic picture is in actuality

$$
\begin{array}{ccc}
G(t_0) & \overset{T(G,C)}{\rightarrow} & C(t_0) \\
{\scriptstyle \varphi(G,C)} \downarrow & & \downarrow {\scriptstyle \varphi(G,C)} \\
G(t_1 > t_0) & \underset{T(G,C)}{\rightarrow} & C(t_1 > t_0)
\end{array}
\qquad [19]
$$

So culture is active in sustaining its own creation, a relationship of high-level self-dependency utterly typical of multilevel systems in which there is feedback from a higher level of organization (culture C in this case) to lower levels (such as G and M).

We have been especially interested in mathematical methods that solve the highly interactive heterarchical structure of Equations [18] - [19] in specific cases. In order to summarize the approach, consider again the simplest relevant case, that of a single epigenetic rule processing two schemas c_1 and c_2. The epigenetic rule is influenced by a single genetic locus on a chromosome, at which the gene can take two forms A and a. (Changes in single genes can have selective and highly specific effects on brain organization and development, on mental epigenesis, and on higher psychological functions such as choice and decision; see Findlay & Lumsden, 1988, and Lumsden & Wilson, 1981, 1983 for reviews.) Thus relative to the genetic locus of interest, the society is a biological population containing the three genotypes AA, Aa, and aa. Correspondingly there are three classes of choice function, represented by the transition probabilities

$$
u_{ij}^{AA}(n_1), \ u_{ij}^{Aa}(n_1), \ u_{ij}^{aa}(n_1)
$$

and the transition rates

$$
v_{ij}^{AA}(n_1), \ v_{ij}^{Aa}(n_1), \ v_{ij}^{aa}(n_1)
$$

All of these quantities are influenced by the pattern n_1 of overall usage within the society. The ethnographic curve for the genotypic classes also has a more complex form than previously:

$$g(n_I^{AA},\ n_I^{Aa},\ n_I^{aa},t) = \text{the probability that, at time } t,\ n_I^{AA} \text{ of the}$$
$$\text{genotypes } AA \text{ are using } c_1 \text{ and so on} \qquad [20]$$

This ethnographic curve obeys an equation of motion that involves the epigenetic rules and usage patterns of all the genotypes (e.g., Lumsden & Wilson, 1981, p. 275). It can be shown that the distribution $g(t)$ approaches a steady-state, and if the social group is not too small (≥ 50 individuals) and is not too close to transition thresholds that shift the ethnographic curve from unimodality to multi-modality, then $g(t)$ will in general be unimodal and sharply peaked. As a result, the pattern n_1 of overall c_i usage will tend to lie close to its modal value, as will the distribution mean. The steady-state ethnographic curve again models $g(t)$ accurately if an individual life cycle is long enough to contain many decision points for each member (Lumsden, 1988); then $g(t)$ is for most of each generation in a form close to the steady-state solution. In turn, an analytical expression that approximates the exact steady-state curve follows from the observation that the usage pattern n_1 can with little loss in accuracy then be replaced by its mean value $\bar{n}_I$. The society is thereby treated as a group of individuals rearranged from interacting with one another to interacting with a mean field of schema usage or cultural expression. After working out the probable patterns of individual decision and behavior in the presence of such a field, one finds an equation relating the expected frequency of c_1 usage, $\bar{v} = \bar{n}_I/N$, directly to the frequencies p of gene A and q of gene a. The epigenetic rules appear via the usage biases, but in a manner that transforms them into an inter-level map between the frequencies of the genes and the frequencies of the traits c_i. Similarly, equations directly relating the frequency of genes to the c_i frequencies by way of the choice functions, the patterns of individual decision making, and the specifics of the maturational timetables follow the same principle.

Analysis of these representations, Equations [18] and [19], involving the entire circuit of coevolutionary interactions, has brought to light several noteworthy psychological consequences of the coupling across levels. First, the tabula rasa state of pure cultural transmission is predicted to be unstable in general. Under a wide array of conditions that we have investigated, in which differential fitness benefits accrue from competing c_i choices, genotypes prescribing a perfect lack of bias toward the c_i are replaced by genotypes prescribing epigenetic rules that assemble decision functions favoring the adaptive c_i. The result is consistent with the general if not universal occurrences of biasing in the epigenetic rules of human behavior, as documented earlier in this chapter.

When individuals become sensitive to the decisions and actions of other members of the society, the evolutionary replacement of epigenetic rules closer to the tabula rasa state can be accelerated. This catalytic relation can also be reciprocal. If sensitivity to cultural patterns is itself under genetic control, it can be enhanced by natural selection through its consistent association with the more successful c_i.

Although biased epigenetic rules and sensitivity to usage can increase the overall rate of gene-culture coevolution, cultural transmission itself tends to slow genetic evolution *within* the coevolutionary process. The reason is that any capacity to acquire less favorable cultural schema—a property implicit in both pure cultural and gene-culture transmission—will reduce the effectiveness of natural selection below that made possible by pure genetic transmission.

Nevertheless, genetic evolution of epigenetic rules can proceed quickly in biocultural systems. Even when the innate bias is weak in comparison with that generally observed in human developmental studies, the rate of change of gene frequency can be high enough even under mild natural selection to achieve the near replacement of one gene variant by another within as few as 50 generations, or about 1,000 years. This places the genetic changes possible via coevolutionary interaction within historical time scales.

Moreover, because of the sensitivity of both epigenetic rules and decision functions to the actions of others to the culture, natural selection of the genotypes is contingent on gene-frequency. Its direction and intensity are determined by the number of individuals using alternative schemas and consequently also by the frequencies of the competing gene variants that underlie the epigenetic rules. Under appropriate conditions the frequency dependence can lead to increased genetic diversity. For example if the genetic fitness or contribution generated by a particular schema usage begins to decline or is suppressed beyond a certain threshold of material benefit, the genes favoring an associated epigenetic developmental bias may not become fixed. When the fitness suppression is moderate, the alleles will stabilize at an intermediate frequency. When it is sufficiently strong the gene frequencies enter a chaotic regime in which they fluctuate widely.

Fitness suppression may be a common phenomenon in human societies. Among the !Kung San hunter-gatherers of the Kalahari desert, excessive attempts to accumulate goods and enhance personal status are met with ridicule merging in the more extreme cases to hostility. The result is the maintenance of modestly egalitarian societies (Lee, 1969). In economically more complex societies, role specialization and division of labor introduce another kind of suppression effect. Rising production of goods and services leads to intensifying competition, unstable markets, and ultimately a reduction in absolute benefits to the specialized producers. Higher costs in transport, storage, and processing can also play an inhibitory role. The feedback has produced a spreading out of economic and social roles, as conceived by traditional economic theory. But it might also have created a diversification of the genotypes underscoring role epigenesis and an enhanced degree of human genetic individuality, augmenting the remarkable cognitive and cultural diversity that are hallmarks of our species.

CONCLUSION: TRANS-LEVEL INTERACTION
AND COEVOLUTIONARY CIRCUITS

It is evident that the heterarchical organization of interactions among genes, mind and culture forms a circuitlike arrangement of causal influences. Principal steps around the circuit have been inferred by using information from a range of data including population genetics, neurobiology, cognitive and developmental psychology, sociobiology, and the social sciences. We envisage a sequence in which competing learnable schemas are introduced in a society through innovation and cross-cultural exchange. Individual members of the society are predisposed through the epigenetic rules to use certain of them rather than others during cognitive development and subsequent behavior. The epigenetic rules affect the likelihood that a particular cognitive design will be achieved at a given time t. The behavioral effects of the design can be explained by shifting the analysis from purely developmental effects to subsequent activity in individual decision making, for example, the probabilities of individual transition to alternative activities in specified environments.

In the circuit of coevolution, the genetic fitness of individuals is determined by their choices of behaviors and the resultant impact these behaviors have on survival and reproduction, as well as by the concurrent choice and usage by other members of the society—in other words, by the surrounding culture. The relation between individual genetic fitness and schema choice is a general observation and has been explicitly documented in a wide variety of behavioral categories, including diet (Gajdusek, 1970), body marking (Blumberg & Hesser, 1975), sexual practice (Daly & Wilson, 1978), marital customs (Daly & Wilson, 1978), economic practice (Irons, 1979), and others.

In human beings genes and fitness do not dictate behavior; rather, they generate the organic processes of mental development, which we have termed epigenetic rules, that draw information from culture to assemble the mind and channel its operation. Behavior is only one product of mind as it deals with the events of daily life. Thus, whereas traditional evolutionary theory has attempted to treat the transition from genes to culture as a black box and largely neglected psychology, there are in fact three major interactive steps across levels of organization: from genes to the regularities of mental development, from mental development to decision and individual behavior, and from individual behavior to culture. The structures of mind are most effectively understood in terms of developmental processes, which are underwritten by genes whose frequencies are the result of protracted interaction of behavior and selection forces working within the gene-culture heterarchy. Thus to understand mind and its development is not just to perceive the rich detail of its composition, but to codify and follow it through each interaction in the coevolutionary circuit; from physiological time and historical change to evolutionary time and genetic change, and back again.

ACKNOWLEDGEMENTS

The work reviewed here was supported by Population Biology Grant number A0393 from the Natural Sciences and Engineering Research Council of Canada and MRC Scholar and Scientist career development awards from the Medical Research Council of Canada.

REFERENCES

Atkinson, R. C., G. H. Bower, & E. J. Crothers. *An introduction to mathematical learning theory.* New York: Wiley, 1965.

Bartholomew, D. J. *Stochastic models for social processes.* (2d ed.). New York: Wiley, 1973.

Blumberg, B. S., & J. E. Hesser. Anthropology and infectious diseases. In A. Dawson (Ed.), *Psychological anthropology* (pp. 260–294). New York: Oxford University Press, 1975.

Bock, K. *Human nature and history: A response to sociobiology.* New York: Columbia University Press, 1980.

Coleman, J. S. *Introduction to mathematical sociology.* New York: Free Press, 1964.

Coleman, J. S. *The mathematics of collective action.* Chicago: Aldine, 1973.

Daly, M., & M. Wilson. *Sex, evolution and behavior.* North Scituate, MA: Duxbury, 1978.

Findlay, C. S., & C. J. Lumsden. *The creative mind: Toward an evolutionary theory of discovery and innovation.* London: Academic Press, 1988.

Freedman, D. G. *Human infancy: An evolutionary perspective.* Hillsdale, NJ: Lawrence Erlbaum Associates, 1974.

Gajdusek, D. C. Physiological and psychological characteristics of stone age man. *Science and Technology,* 1970, *33,* 26–33, 56–62.

Greeno, J. G. Representation of learning as discrete transition in a finite state space: In D. H. Krantz, R. C. Atkinson, R. D. Luce, P. Suppes (Eds.), *Contemporary developments in mathematical psychology* (Vol. 1, *Learning, memory and thinking,* pp. 1–43). San Francisco: W. H. Freeman, 1974.

Harris, A. Recent findings on infant socialization from North American research. *International Social Sciences Journal,* 1979, *31,* 415–428.

Irons, W. Cultural and biological success. In N. A. Chagnon & W. Irons (Eds.), *Evolutionary biology and human social behavior: An anthropological perspective* (pp. 257–272). North Scituate, MA: Duxbury, 1979.

Kemeny, J. G., & J. L. Snell. *Mathematical models in the social sciences.* Waltham, MA: Blaisdell Publishing Co., 1962.

Lee, R. B. Eating Christmas in the Kalahari. *Natural History,* 1969, *78,* 14, 16, 18, 21, 22, 60–63.

Lumsden, C. J. Cultural evolution and the devolution of *tabula rasa. Journal of Social & Biological Structures,* 1983, *6,* 101–114.

Lumsden, C. J. Gene-culture coevolution: A test of the steady-state hypothesis for gene-culture translation. *Journal of Theoretical Biology,* 1988, *130,* 391–406.

Lumsden, C. J., & A. C. Gushurst. In J. H. Fetzer (Ed.), *Sociobiology and epistemology* (pp. 3–28). Dordrecht: D. Reidel, 1985.

Lumsden, C. J., & E. O. Wilson. *Genes, mind and culture: the coevolutionary process.* Cambridge, MA: Harvard University Press, 1981.

Lumsden, C. J., & E. O. Wilson. *Promethean fire: Reflections on the origin of mind.* Cambridge, MA: Harvard University Press, 1983.

Lumsden, C. J., & E. O. Wilson. The relation between biological and cultural evolution. *Journal of Social & Biological Structures,* 1985, *8,* 343–359.

Maller, O., & J. A. Desor. Effect of taste on ingestion by human newborns. In J. Bosma (Ed.), *Fourth symposium on oral sensation and perception* (pp. 297–311). Washington DC: Government Printing Office, 1974.

Sahlins, M. *The use and abuse of biology: An anthropological critique of sociobiology.* Ann Arbor, MI: University of Michigan Press, 1976.

Shepher, J. Mate selection among second-generation kibbutz adolescents and adults: incest avoidance and negative imprinting. *Archives of Sexual Behavior,* 1971, *1,* 293–307.

Trigg, R. *The shaping of man: Philosophical aspects of sociobiology.* Oxford: Blackwell, 1982.

Waddington, C. H. *The strategy of the genes.* London: Allen & Unwin, 1957.

Wolf, A. P. Adopt a daughter-in-law, marry a sister: A Chinese solution to the problem of the incest taboo. *American Anthropologist,* 1968, *70,* 864–874.

Wolf, A. P. & C. S. Huang. *Marriage and adoption in China.* Stanford: Stanford University Press, 1980.

About the Authors

LAUREN B. ADAMSON is an associate professor of psychology at Georgia State University. She received her BA from Swarthmore College and her PhD from the University of California, Berkeley. Her research interests include early communication development and the emergence of gender differences in social behavior.

ROGER BAKEMAN is professor of psychology at Georgia State University. He received his BA from Antioch College and his PhD from the University of Texas at Austin. Bakeman is currently on the editorial boards of *Child Development and Infant Behavior and Development* and has served as a member of review panels for the National Science Foundation and the National Institutes of Health. He has both applied and written about observational methods in research and is co-author with John M. Gottman of *Observing Interaction: An Introduction to Sequential Analysis*.

CINDY S. BERGEMAN is a doctoral student in the College of Health and Human Development at the Pennsylvania State University at University Park. She received her BS from the University of Idaho and completed her first year of graduate training at the Institute for Behavioral Genetics at the University of Colorado at Boulder. The focus of her current research is quantitative genetic analyses of individual differences in the aging process, utilizing data from the Swedish Adoption/Twin Study of Aging.

MARC H. BORNSTEIN is senior research scientist and head, Section on Child and Family Research, at the National Institute of Child Health and Human Development. He holds a BA from Columbia College and MS and PhD degrees from Yale University. Bornstein has received the C. S. Ford Cross-Cultural Research Award, the B. R. McCandless Young Scientist Award, and a J. S. Guggenheim Foundation Fellowship. He coauthored *Development in Infancy* and *Perceiving Similarity and Comprehending Metaphor*, and is general editor of *The Crosscurrents in Contemporary Psychology Series,* including *Psychological Development from Infancy, Comparative Methods in Psychology, Psychology and Its Allied Disciplines,* and *Sensitive Periods in Development.* He has also coedited *Developmental Psychology: An Advanced Textbook* and *Stability and Continuity in Mental Development*. Bornstein has contributed more than 100 papers in the areas of human experimental, methodological, comparative, developmental, cross-cultural, and aesthetic psychology.

MAGALI C. BOVET is director of studies in developmental psychology at the University of Geneva. She received her PhD from the same university. She spent 1 year at the Center for Cognitive Studies of Harvard University. Her fields of interest are cross-cultural comparison of cognitive development, the development of causality, and learning. She is the co-author with B. Inhelder and H. Sinclair of *Learning and the Development of Cognition.*

JEROME BRUNER is research fellow at the Russell Sage Foundation and research professor at New York University. A past President of the American Psychological Association, he has previously held Professorships at Harvard, Oxford, and the New School for Social Research. His most recent books are *Actual Minds, Possible Worlds* (1986), *In Search of Mind* (1983), and *Child's Talk* (1983). He has been honored by the Distinguished Scientific Award of the APA (1964), the Gold Medal of the CIBA Foundation (1973), and the Balzan Prize for 1987. He received his AB from Duke University and a PhD in Psychology from Harvard University. He is currently at work on a book on the narrative structures of autobiography.

SUSAN CURTISS is an associate professor in the Department of Linguistics at the University of California at Los Angeles. She received her BA from the University of California at Berkeley and her PhD from the University of California at Los Angeles. Curtiss has been an associate editor of the *Journal of Speech and Hearing Disorders* and the editor of *UCLA's Working Papers in Cognitive Linguistics.* She is the author of *GENIE: A Psycholinguistic Study of a Modern-Day "Wild Child"* and numerous articles on a variety of topics related to abnormal language and language acquisition, including dementia, mental retardation, linguistic isolation, and developmental language disorders.

RICHARD M. LERNER is professor of child and adolescent development and director of the Center for the Study of Child and Adolescent Development at the Pennsylvania State University. He received his PhD from the City University of New York. Lerner has been a Fellow at the Center for Advanced Study in the Behavioral Sciences and is a Fellow of the American Association for the Advancement of Science and of Divisions 2, 7, and 9 of the American Psychological Association. He is co-editor of the annual advances series, *Life-Span Development and Behavior,* and associate editor of the *International Journal of Behavioral Development.* He is the author or editor of 19 books, including *On the Nature of Human Plasticity, Concepts and Theories of Human Development,* and *Career Development: A Life-span Developmental Approach.* His research focuses on personality and social development in childhood and adolescence.

CHARLES J. LUMSDEN is professor of medicine at the University of Toronto. His undergraduate and graduate degrees, all in theoretical physics, are from Toronto. Lumsden is interested in evolution of mind and the relations between biological and cultural history. He is coauthor of *Genes, Mind, and Culture: The Coevolutionary Process, Promethean Fire: Reflections on the Origins of Mind,* and *The Creative Mind.* He has published extensively on mathematical theories of gene-culture coevolution.

ELLEN MOSS is professor of developmental psychology at the University of Quebec at Montreal and currently holds a Career Development Fellowship awarded by the Social Sciences and Humanities Research Council of Canada. Her research is primarily concerned with the influence of early social experience on cognitive development.

SILVIA A. PARRAT-DAYAN is scientific advisor at the Jean Piaget Archives, University of Geneva. She received her MA in psychology from the University of Buenos Aires, Argentina. She was awarded a federal fellowship by the Swiss government to study under Professor Piaget at the University of Geneva. She received her PhD from the University of Geneva and now continues to do research there in cognitive development. Her main fields of interest are the development of number concept and causality as well as the history of child care and development in French-speaking countries.

ROBERT PLOMIN is professor of human development in the College of Health and Human Development at the Pennsylvania State University at University Park. He received his PhD at the University of Texas at Austin. Plomin joined the faculty of the Institute for Behavioral Genetics at the University of Colorado at Boulder, and spent a year at the Center for Advanced Study in the Behavioral Sciences at Stanford. He has written recent books on behavioral genetics, *Behavioral Genetics,* developmental behavioral genetics, *Development, Genetics, and Psychology,* and on the longitudinal Colorado Adoption Project, *Nature and Nurture during Infancy and Early Childhood.*

BARBARA ROGOFF is professor of psychology at the University of Utah. She received her BA from Pomona College, studied at the University of Geneva, and received her PhD from Harvard University. Rogoff is editor of the *Newsletter of the Society for Research in Child Development,* serves on a variety of editorial boards, and coordinates efforts on ''Psychological and Pedagogical Problems of Teaching and the Development of Preschool and School-Age Children'' for the American Council of Learned Societies—Soviet Ministries of Education. Her research focuses on the social context of cognitive development, particularly children's planning and remembering in the context of collaboration with adults and peers, as well as in cultural context. She is co-editor of *Everyday Cognition: Its Development in Social Context* and *Children's Learning in the "Zone of Proximal Development."* She has been a Kellogg Fellow and is a fellow at the Center for Advanced Study in the Behavioral Sciences at Stanford.

EMANUEL A. SCHEGLOFF is professor of sociology at the University of California at Los Angeles. He received his BA from Harvard College and his MA and PhD from the University of California at Berkeley. He has been a fellow of the Netherlands Institute for Advanced Study in the Social Sciences and Humanities, and has served on a variety of editorial boards in several disciplines. His publications have been addressed to a range of topics in the analysis of conversation and other forms of talk in interaction, including turn-taking, repair, the structure of interactional occasions, action and topic sequences, and gesture and body behavior among others.

CATHERINE E. SNOW is professor of human development and psychology at the Harvard Graduate School of Education. She received her BA from Oberlin College and her PhD in psychology from McGill University. She taught in the Institute for General Linguistics, University of Amsterdam, before moving to Harvard. She is editor of *Applied Psycholinguistics,* former president of the International Association for the Study of Child Language, and co-director of the Child Language Data Exchange System (CHILDES). She has done research in the areas of language development, social interaction with infants and young children, cultural differences in child-rearing, literacy development both at home and in school, and second language acquisition.

FLOYD FRANCIS STRAYER is professor of psychology and director of the Human Ethology Laboratory and the Department of Psychology at the University of Quebec at Montreal. He received his BS degree from Columbia University in New York, and his PhD from Simon Fraser University in Vancouver, B.C. Dr. Strayer has been an Invited Research Scientist at the Washington Regional Primate Center in Seattle, and at the Laboratoire de Psychobiologie de l'Enfant in Paris. His was also a Philips Visiting Scholar at Haverford College. His research interests focus on human and primate social ethology, social development in natural settings, and ontogenetic constraints imposed by the social ecology of small stable groups.

PETER STRISIK is interested in the sequential analysis of psychotherapy transcripts. He received his BA from the University of South Florida and currently is a graduate student in clinical psychology at Georgia State University.

JONATHAN TUDGE is assistant professor of child development at the University of North Carolina at Greensboro. He received his BA and M.Phil. from British Universities (Lancaster and Oxford), and his PhD from Cornell. He spent 2 years working as a postdoctoral researcher with Barbara Rogoff at the University of Utah. His primary area of interest is in social influences (peer and adult-child) on cognitive development. He has undertaken research on this topic in the Soviet Union, under the auspices of the American Council of Learned Societies, and is also engaged in US and Soviet collaborative research into adolescent perceptions of US-Soviet relations.

J. -JACQUES VONÈCHE is professor of developmental psychology at the University of Geneva. He received his PhD from the University of Louvain, Belgium. He was tenured at Clark University and was a visiting professor at Rutgers, Harvard, Toronto, and Columbia. He is the co-editor with H. E. Gruber of *The Essential Piaget* and with B. Inhelder and R. Garcia of *Epistemologie Génétique et Equilibration*. He is on the editorial board of *New Ideas in Psychology* and co-editor of *Les Archives de Psychologie*. His interests are in development and perception and in theoretical and critical psychology.

DAVID JAMES WOOD is professor of psychology at the University of Nottingham, England. After gaining both BA and PhD degrees at Nottingham, he spent 2 years as postdoctoral fellow at Harvard. Subsequently, he spent a year at Oxford University as a member of Bruner's Oxford Preschool Research Group. Wood is currently on the editorial board of the British Journal of Developmental Psychology and the International Journal of Behavioral Development. He is interested in the role of instruction in intellectual and linguistic development with special reference to deaf children. He is co-author of *Working with Under-Fives* and *Teaching and Talking with Deaf Children,* and author of *How Children Think and Learn.*

AUTHOR INDEX

SUBJECT INDEX